Sharing Power, Securing Peace?

Does power sharing bring peace? Policymakers around the world seem to think so. Yet, while there are many successful examples of power sharing in multi-ethnic states, such as Switzerland, South Africa and Indonesia, other instances show that such arrangements offer no guarantee against violent conflict, including Rwanda, Yugoslavia, Zimbabwe and South Sudan. Given this mixed record, it is not surprising that scholars disagree as to whether power sharing actually reduces conflict. Based on systematic data and innovative methods, this book comes to a mostly positive conclusion by focusing on practices rather than merely formal institutions, studying power sharing's preventive effect, analyzing how power sharing is invoked in anticipation of conflict, and by showing that territorial power sharing can be effective if combined with inclusion at the center. The authors' findings demonstrate that power sharing is usually the best option to reduce and prevent civil conflict in divided states.

LARS-ERIK CEDERMAN is Professor of International Conflict Research, ETH Zürich. He is the author of *Emergent Actors in World Politics: How States and Nations Develop and Dissolve* (1997), co-author of *Inequality, Grievances and Civil War* (Cambridge, 2013, with Kristian Skrede Gleditsch and Halvard Buhaug), as well as numerous articles in scientific journals.

SIMON HUG is Professor in the Department of Political Science and International Relations, University of Geneva. His research has been published in leading outlets, including the *American Political Science Review*, *American Journal of Political Science*, *Legislative Studies Quarterly*, and the *Journal of Conflict Resolution*.

JULIAN WUCHERPFENNIG is Professor of International Affairs and Security at the Centre for International Security, Hertie School, Berlin. His research has been published in leading outlets, including the *American Political Science Review*, *American Journal of Political Science*, *Journal of Politics*, *International Organization* and *World Politics*.

Sharing Power, Securing Peace?

Ethnic Inclusion and Civil War

Lars-Erik Cederman
ETH Zürich

Simon Hug
University of Geneva

Julian Wucherpfennig
Hertie School, Berlin

CAMBRIDGE
UNIVERSITY PRESS

CAMBRIDGE
UNIVERSITY PRESS

University Printing House, Cambridge CB2 8BS, United Kingdom

One Liberty Plaza, 20th Floor, New York, NY 10006, USA

477 Williamstown Road, Port Melbourne, VIC 3207, Australia

314–321, 3rd Floor, Plot 3, Splendor Forum, Jasola District Centre, New Delhi – 110025, India

103 Penang Road, #05–06/07, Visioncrest Commercial, Singapore 238467

Cambridge University Press is part of the University of Cambridge.

It furthers the University's mission by disseminating knowledge in the pursuit of education, learning, and research at the highest international levels of excellence.

www.cambridge.org
Information on this title: www.cambridge.org/9781108418140
DOI: 10.1017/9781108284639

First published 2022

A catalogue record for this publication is available from the British Library.

ISBN 978-1-108-41814-0 Hardback
ISBN 978-1-108-40655-0 Paperback

Contents

Figures

Tables

Preface

In the course of this project, we have received a lot of help and support from a number of generous colleagues. Two book workshops were held; one at Peace Research Institute Oslo on November 29, 2018, and the other at the University of Essex on December 4, 2018. We would like to thank the participants at those events for their invaluable comments, including Scott Gates, Halvard Buhaug, Håvard Strand, Helga Malmin Binningsbø, Kristian Gleditsch and Brian Philipps. Lars-Erik Cederman gave a brief presentation of the book project at the University of Konstanz on October 10, 2019, while Simon Hug presented parts of the manuscript at the University of Oxford on November 30, 2018. We also presented the book at the Annual Meeting of the American Political Science Association on September 9, 2020, together with Cyrus Samii and Elisabeth King, who introduced their own new book on group rights. Dawn Brancati and Scott Gates served as engaged and constructive discussants. In addition, Andreas Juon offered excellent comments on several of the book's chapters.

The project would not have been possible without the support of the members of the International Conflict Research group at ETH. Nils-Christian Bormann, Luc Girardin, Seraina Rüegger, Andreas Schädel, Francisco Villamil, among others, contributed analytical ideas and help with data collection, especially as regards the Ethnic Power Relations dataset and the GROWup data portal. Valuable intellectual input from students was gathered when materials from the book were used in teaching, including sessions on power sharing in ETH's MAS program on Mediation in Peace Processes. The book has also profited greatly from inspiring exchanges with Brendan O'Leary and Nicholas Sambanis, who both have contributed crucial insights on power sharing. Finally, we would like to thank the anonymous reviewers of the manuscript and the editors at Cambridge University Press, Lew Bateman and John Haslam, for their unflinching support.

We are also indebted to coauthors and publishers of several articles that preceded this book. Chapter 5 draws on research that was first published in Bormann et al. (2019). We thank Nils-Christian Bormann, Scott Gates, Benjamin Graham, and Kaare Strøm, for excellent collaboration, and the latter three for their permission to use their IDC dataset. Chapter 6 first appeared as Wucherpfennig, Hunziker and Cederman (2016). Philipp Hunziker's theoretical and methodological contribution was instrumental for the success of that project. Chapter 7 is based on Wucherpfennig (2021). Chapter 8 relies heavily on research that appeared in Cederman et al. (2015). We are grateful to Andreas Schädel for his important contributions to that research effort. We also want to acknowledge crucial contributions by Kristian Gleditsch, who coauthored Cederman, Gleditsch and Wucherpfennig (2017) and Cederman, Gleditsch and Wucherpfennig (2018). These two articles constitute the basis of Chapters 10 and 11, respectively. We would like to express our gratitude to our coauthors and the publishers of these articles for their generous permission to use material from these publications in the current book.

Finally we would like to acknowledge financial support from the Swiss National Science Foundation for the original research project on "Ethnic Inclusion and Power-Sharing Institutions" out of which this book emerged (Grant No. 143213).

1 Introduction

Does power sharing bring peace? Policy makers around the world certainly appear to agree. Whether instituted as shared governmental power at the central level or territorially through autonomy arrangements, power sharing is becoming an increasingly common way of governing multiethnic states. Since the end of the Cold War, such provisions have become an important ingredient of an emerging global accommodative regime that helps prevent and resolve ethnic conflict (Gurr, 2000*a*). International actors, including the United Nations and regional organizations such as the European Union, routinely rely on power sharing in order to implement a peaceful political order during and after interventions (McCulloch and McEnvoy, 2018). Such efforts have triggered a veritable surge of inclusive governance in sub-Saharan Africa, where virtually all post-conflict agreements after the end of the Cold War feature provisions of this type (Mehler, 2009; Spears, 2013).

Various success stories around the world have bolstered the trend toward increased reliance on power sharing. South Africa is often mentioned as a particularly striking case of successful stabilization of a deeply divided society (Wantchekon, 2000; Cheeseman, 2011; Gloppen, Forthcoming). It is difficult to imagine how the entrenched discrimination imposed by the apartheid system could otherwise have been overcome. Already in the 1980s, political scientists proposed power sharing as a constitutional pathway to peace (Lijphart, 1985*b*), and the South African case has subsequently been held up as a model for conflict resolution in Africa (e.g., Wantchekon, 2000). The conflict between the Republicans and the Unionists in Northern Ireland constitutes another case that seemed nearly insoluble even to proponents of power-sharing arrangements (McGarry and O'Leary, 2004). The Good Friday Agreement of 1998 showed, however, a way toward reconciliation (Taylor, 2011; McEvoy, 2014, 61ff).[1] Aceh offers yet another highly

---

[1] Unfortunately, Britain's leaving the European Union threatens to undermine the compromise, which in the worst case could cause violent conflict to recur.

visible example of a seemingly endless conflict that was brought to an end through an inclusive compromise. In this case, shared power at the regional level helped keep the peace (Wennmann and Krause, 2009; Stepan, 2013). In addition, other countries, such as Switzerland and Belgium, have made preventive use of governmental and territorial power-sharing arrangements,[2] thus avoiding damaging political violence even before it got the chance to break out.

Yet, other cases provide evidence that power sharing offers no guarantee against recurrent violent conflict. Indeed, the list of failed experiments of shared rule between ethnic groups that did experience the onset of civil war is long. For example, power sharing was attempted in Cyprus from independence in 1960 but collapsed in December 1963 and has thereafter never been reimplemented despite repeated attempts (McGarry, 2017). The Arusha Accords tried to stabilize Rwanda by bringing all parties to one table, but this experiment failed spectacularly with the eruption of the genocide in the spring of 1994 (Prunier, 1995; Falch, Rudolfsen and Becker, Forthcoming). More recently, South Sudan's brief experience of shared power came to an abrupt end shortly after the country became independent in 2011, when the interethnic governing coalition fell apart and civil war broke out (Roessler, 2016). The disintegration of communist states after the end of the Cold War, most notably those of the Soviet Union and Yugoslavia, also illustrates that territorial power sharing can produce intense violent conflict and human suffering. In the eyes of many observers, this experience has given ethnic federalism a bad name more generally (Bunce, 1999; Snyder, 2000; Roeder, 2009). There are also instances where shared executive power served to bring peace to conflict-torn places after previous false starts, although the current state of peace remains quite fragile, as illustrated by Bosnia and Herzegovina, Burundi and Lebanon (Butenschøn, Stiansen and Vollan, 2015).

Given this mixed record, it is perhaps not surprising that scholars disagree about whether power sharing actually reduces conflict despite strong support among policy makers. Inspired by Arend Lijphart's (1969, 1977) pioneering theoretical work on "consociationalism," some scholars argue that power-sharing institutions, both within the central government and through autonomy arrangements, reduce conflict by lowering the stakes and reducing grievances (see, e.g., Gurr, 2000b;

---

[2] The territorial power-sharing arrangement in Switzerland was a concession of the victors in the short civil war of 1847, while the governmental power-sharing arrangements took decades to be put in place (Steiner, 1974).

Lijphart, 2002; Norris, 2008; McGarry and O'Leary, 2009). Other researchers are much more critical of Lijphart's initial theoretical vision and its concrete implementations (see, e.g., Horowitz, 1985; Rothchild and Roeder, 2005*b*). Their criticism is based on the idea that shared power, whether centrally or regionally implemented, tends to deepen ethnic cleavages and render the task of governing even more difficult than in the absence of such accommodative institutions.

This book revisits the central debate about the effect of power sharing on conflict by directly drawing on conflict research. While very rich and nuanced in terms of institutional detail , the existing literature on power sharing tends to be much weaker in its assessment of conflict processes. This limitation applies even to studies of peace agreements and conflict resolution more generally. As argued by Wolff and Cordell (2010, 307),

> most existing theories of conflict resolution are consequences focused, i.e., they seek to explain why certain institutional designs offer the prospect of sustainable peace and stability, while others do not. They do this by offering normative and pragmatic accounts of the desirability and feasibility of particular institutions in divided societies, but these are not always, let alone successfully, grounded in theories of conflict, nor are the assumptions made about the drivers of conflict always fully spelt out. Yet, it is essential to understand the causes of conflict before viable prescriptions for its resolution can be offered.

In other words, in order to understand how to reduce conflict, we need to know its causes. Following in the footsteps of Ted Gurr and other conflict researchers, we adopt this principle explicitly. Our previous work on inequality and conflict has shown that political inequality and exclusion of ethnic groups can cause grievances, which, in turn, increase the risk of civil war (see, e.g., Cederman, Gleditsch and Buhaug, 2013). Inclusion, therefore, should bring peace. Specifically, conflict research of this type tells us that the path to durable peace goes through the reduction of inequality, in particular among ethnic groups.

Obviously, power sharing can also be introduced in order to regulate relations among nonethnic actors, such as ideological movements and political parties that define themselves in ideological terms, rather than in terms of ethnicity. Such cases include institutional efforts to end conflict in Cambodia (Binningsbø, 2013) and Colombia (Zukerman Daly, 2014). In fact, much of the literature addresses more general conditions, such as "plural societies" (Lijphart, 1977) or "deeply divided places" (O'Leary, 2012). Whether explicitly or implicitly, however, most cases referred to revolve around ethnic, rather than nonethnic, divisions. This is hardly surprising because since the end of World War II (WWII), most internal conflicts have been fought along ethnic lines. Furthermore, the fear of division and violence in multiethnic societies serves as by far the most important motivation for power sharing (see, e.g. Butenschøn, Stiansen and Vollan, 2015).

It needs to be stressed that the type of conflict research that we have used as a starting point is far from uncontroversial (Cederman and Vogt, 2017), and even if its findings hold, there is no guarantee that inclusion can be successfully implemented. As experienced by peacemakers in South Africa and Northern Ireland, reversing decades of exclusion is notoriously difficult, especially if it has been accompanied by widespread and persistent violence. Such circumstances tend to become increasingly irreversible as the corrosive impact of unequal norms and institutions continue to produce resentment and hatred. Equally importantly, it is far from obvious that the incumbent leaders are willing to take the risk of opening up the ruling coalition to potential opponents and former rebels, because there are no ironclad guarantees that such experiments would prevent the incumbents from losing power in the future, and possibly even being exposed to discrimination and violence themselves.

For these reasons, it would be foolish to simply extrapolate from previous work on inequality and conflict. All the same, we believe that the simple formula linking inclusion to peace is, in essence, correct. Before reaching any firmer conclusions about the actual impact of power-sharing arrangements on large-scale political violence, however, we need to address a number of issues that have hindered a balanced assessment of this effect in previous research. We do so by considering four difficulties that we believe may stack the deck against our core hypothesis:

- *Practices rather than institutions*: Going beyond recent studies, we analyze the effect of power-sharing practices, rather than that of formal institutions. Instead of seeking an answer in constitutional texts, our approach focuses squarely on actual behavior, whether prescribed by formal institutions or prescribed by informal norms. This is crucial, because there is no guarantee that what has been agreed *sur papier* will be reflected in a country's actual power distribution. Peace agreements may or may not be implemented as promised (Walter, 2002; Quinn and Joshi, 2016). In addition, focusing merely on formal institutions misses the important fact that shared power often hinges on informal agreements, as illustrated by consociationalism as practiced in Switzerland and by a number of recent African cases of post-conflict power sharing (Spears, 2013). While taking formal institutions seriously, this book, therefore, relies mostly on behavioral data that capture de facto power access (see Pospieszna and Schneider, 2013). This move is based on our finding that formal power-sharing institutions induce peace by operating through power-sharing practices (see also Bormann et al., 2019). Thus, once the focus shifts from formal institutions to practices, we find that inclusive governance appears to be much more effective as a conflict-reduction method.

- *Full rather than partial samples*: Another limitation afflicting current research relates to the common tendency to restrict the analytical scope to post-war settings and, in some cases, to specific parts of the world. Of course, there is nothing wrong with focusing on such research questions, but the use of post-conflict samples comes at the cost of possibly obscuring the preventive role of power sharing. Clearly, there are many stable countries that have not experienced conflict for a very long time, and this is at least partly thanks to such inclusive institutions. This is one of the main reasons why our empirical analysis covers the entire world, including pre- and post-conflict settings, because otherwise it would be impossible to capture the full impact of power sharing on peace and war. Furthermore, there is an additional reason to trace decision-making even before the first violent conflict breaks out. To see this, we turn to the third weakness of the conventional literature.

- *Considering the endogenous nature of power sharing*: Most existing studies treat power sharing as an exogenous independent variable, whether of the governmental or of the territorial type. Yet, this assumption is clearly misleading, because governments' decisions to include some groups but not others may reflect anticipated, future conflict. The problem is that institutional choices or accommodating practices by governments cannot be considered as a random treatment. In fact, it stands to reason that governments may be more inclined to include groups that could cause trouble otherwise. But if this is true, then the correlation between power sharing and conflict is affected by governmental decisions made in the shadow of potential conflict rather than by an inherent tendency of power sharing to generate conflict outcomes. By the same naïve logic, we would have to close all hospitals, because, after all, death is a much more likely outcome for hospital patients compared to people who are not hospitalized. Yet, again, the link between hospitals and mortality derives from the fact that those who are seriously ill tend to seek hospitalization, while those who are in good health do not. Needless to say, hospitals are nevertheless important and should not be abolished. By the same token, it could well be that power-sharing arrangements are doing a lot of good even though they often cannot fully prevent violence, since in their absence, conflict may have been even more likely. One of the most important goals of this book is to introduce conceptual reasoning along these lines to the study of power sharing, as well as a set of tools that address such concerns head-on and help us grapple with this difficulty. Indeed, with such corrections, power sharing looks considerably more attractive as a possible solution to ethnic conflict.

- *Interactions between governmental and territorial power sharing*: The power-sharing literature tends to treat shared power within the state's center and between the center and its periphery in separate studies, or to consider them simply as additive elements. We argue that both dimensions should be studied together since territorial power sharing often needs to be supplemented with its governmental counterpart to be truly pacifying. Indeed, in the absence of the latter, decentralization may easily become a slippery slope. While this danger has been a major focus in studies of federalism (Riker, 1964; Filippov, Ordeshook and Shvetsova, 2004; Bednar, 2008), it has rarely been acknowledged in the literature on power sharing (for a notable exception, see McGarry and O'Leary, 2009). Doing so is, however, crucial since focusing on autonomy in isolation from power relations at the center of the state obscures the full conflict-reducing potential of decentralized institutions.

All things considered, when it comes to securing peace, power sharing is considerably better than its (scientific) reputation. While there are clearly situations where it does little to dampen conflict, or may even worsen the situation, *on average* its pacifying effect is relatively robust. Thus, it is all the more important to identify the conditions under which inclusive practices help stabilize deeply divided societies, and where this is not the case. In this book, we furthermore devote considerable attention to figuring out the types and combinations of power-sharing arrangements that promise to be the most effective. In the end, we reach the conclusion that policy makers have so far been right to prioritize inclusive governance. Yet, ironically, the recent surge in xenophobia and ethnic nationalism indicates that this consensus may be weakening together with the liberal world order as a whole.

Part I

Theories and Concepts

2 Power Sharing and Conflict in the Literature

This chapter surveys the existing literature on power sharing, with a special focus on how it relates to conflict. In a first section, we offer an historical overview of how the literature has developed, followed by a discussion of the arguments and evidence for and against power sharing, emphasizing in particular its consequences for peace and conflict. We then turn to a critique of previous writings to prepare the ground for the derivation of this book's main theoretical arguments in the next chapter.

2.1 The Evolution of the Literature on Power Sharing and Conflict

Power sharing through inclusion and elite cooperation has emerged as the dominant approach to governance in contexts characterized by deeply divided societies (Lijphart, 2002). However, it is far from the only architecture that can be envisaged for this purpose. Other important ways of managing existing ethnic divisions include hegemonic control (Lustick, 1979) and "outsourced" governance through intervention (Sobotka, 2016). Alternatively, the problem can be "solved" by eliminating differences coercively through genocide and ethnic cleansing, or more benignly through self-determination or assimilatory integration (McGarry and O'Leary, 1993).

Obviously, adherents of liberal democracy view many of these alternatives as morally repugnant and squarely incompatible with democratic governance. In fact, the challenge of multi-ethnic governance is so tricky that classical liberals were generally skeptical about the prospects of democracy in ethnically diverse states. In his classical statement, John Stewart Mill (1962 [1961], 82–91) claimed that such polities are inherently unstable and would ultimately call for "a constitutionally unlimited, or at least a practically preponderant, authority in the chief ruler." To the extent that the Anglo-Saxon liberals believe that ethnically diverse states could be brought together under a unified democratic roof, they rely on democratic representation of individuals with a penchant for integration through voluntary assimilation.

Pluralist theory of democracy expects that checks and balances combined with the separation of powers will produce multiple and shifting majorities that minimize the risks of lasting majority dominance (e.g., Almond, 1956). In such a system, individuals of all ethnic extractions will also enjoy sufficient protection thanks to strong civil liberties and a vibrant civil society that work as counter-balances to potential state oppression (Roeder, 2005). It is also hoped that such a pluralistic arena of politics will create sufficient room for inter-ethnic and multi-dimensional identification as a way of breaking down ethnic boundaries. In his classical statement, Lipset (1960) argued that cross-cutting cleavages, which contribute to bridging deep ethnic or social divides, will help sustain democracy and stability.

2.1.1   The first generation of power-sharing studies

The intellectual history of power sharing can be seen as a direct reaction to the pluralist theory of democracy that dominated political science in the United States and the United Kingdom after World War II. More than anyone else, it was the Dutch political scientist Arend Lijphart who laid the foundations of what would become the main alternative to the Anglo-Saxon approach. Inspired by selected democracies in Western Europe, Lijphart (1969) argued that democracy was possible, contrary to the stance of pluralist scholars, in deeply divided polities. In his view, the Netherlands, Belgium, Switzerland and Austria had been able to overcome deep social and ethnic divides by relying on elite cooperation rather than on electoral competition within majority systems (see also Lehmbruch, 1967; Steiner, 1974). Labeling the alternative approach *consociationalism*, his classical definition identifies four main components: (1) an executive ruled through a grand coalition of group representatives, (2) segmental autonomy, especially in cultural affairs, (3) proportionality in civil service appointments, and (4) veto rights for each group.

Lijphart's original formulation of consociationalism is not limited to ethnic divides, but also applies to other ideological differences, as illustrated by the inclusion of the Netherlands and Austria as prototypical cases. However defined, the cleavages are to be managed rather than transcended. In this sense, consociational systems explicitly recognize groups as foundational building blocks instead of relying exclusively on individuals as the beneficiaries of democratic rights and freedoms. Furthermore, Lijphart's concept presupposes that the groups are led by enlightened elites who represent their group members and effectively defend their collective rights.

It should also be noted that consociationalism requires constant inclusion of virtually all groups rather than operating through shifting majorities. Instead of trying to outmaneuver their opponents, the groups' representatives are expected to seek compromise solutions that are acceptable to all groups. The stress, then, is on elite-level accommodation and pragmatic "deal making" as opposed to electoral competition and confrontation. Crucially, group elites are assumed to fear armed conflict so much that they will support a "self-denying prophecy" (Lijphart, 1975, 215) of accommodation in the name of national peace as opposed to risky hostility. In this sense, Lijphart's classical concept hinges much more on behavior and practices supported by a political culture and a sense of mutual trust than on formal institutions (Lijphart, 1968, 24).

Unsurprisingly, Lijphart's original formulation of consociationalism attracted immediate criticism from the defenders of the pluralist position. In an early critique, Barry (1975b) questioned the extent to which the model applied to the four cases that inspired the theory in the first place. In particular, he took issue with the use of the Netherlands and Switzerland in this context (for the latter case, see also van Schendelen, 1984).

Furthermore, Barry (1975b) argued that because of the emphasis that Lijphart placed on political stability in the definition of consociatialism, the concept became tautological and thus obsolete as a causal explanation of peace. Even worse, according to Barry (1975a), consociational devices risk making conflict more protracted and violent. Thus, he did not see any chance that Lijphart's consociational recipe would improve the prospects of peace in war-torn societies: "What worries me at present is that attempts to apply the 'consociational model' outside its original area (especially in divided societies such as Northern Ireland and Canada) may make things worse" (Barry, 1975a, 395).

Other scholars came to similarly pessimistic conclusions. In a seminal book, Rabushka and Shepsle (1972) contended that ethnic mobilization inevitably undermines inter-ethnic trust in "plural societies," that is polities that are deeply divided along ethnic lines. For this reason, there is little hope for stable democracy in such settings, not least because moderate politicians tend to be electorally outflanked by ethnic extremists. Likewise, Nordlinger (1972, 31) argued against territorial power sharing, specifically in the form of ethnic federalism, as a tool for conflict resolution because it "may actually contribute to a conflict's exacerbation and the failure of conflict regulation." Anticipating more recent criticisms of territorial power sharing, Nordlinger conceived of consociational pacts as fragile Nash equilibria that are likely to break down because of a lack of cooperative incentives (see Lustick, 1997, 99).

2.1.2   The second generation of power-sharing studies

Despite the critics' misgivings about exporting consociationalism to cases of ethnic conflict beyond Western Europe, this is precisely where the debate moved next. Led by Lijphart, this wave of scholarship gave rise to a second generation of writings on power sharing, which, compared to the first generation, can be characterized through three gradual shifts: (1) a general expansion of the application beyond Western Europe, (2) a shift of the main attention from the consequences of power sharing for democracy to its impact on conflict, and finally (3) an increased stress on formal institutions rather than on elite behavior.

We first consider the shift toward a broader application of consociationalism. Lijphart's (1977) analysis of Czechoslovakia, Lebanon, and Cyprus as consociational cases marked the push beyond Western Europe (see also, e.g., Lehmbruch, 1974). As described in Andeweg's (2000) comprehensive review, the consociational universe was also expanded to include Malaysia and Colombia (from 1958 to 1974). Thanks to Lijphart's (1996) high-profile article in the *American Political Science Review*, India became one the most important intellectual "battle grounds" in this debate. Arguing that this country embraced consociationalism from independence through the 1960s, Lijphart credited this particular form of power sharing with the relative stability of the country during that period. Unsurprisingly, this interpretation has turned out to be quite controversial. In a careful study, Wilkinson (2000) questions Lijphart's reading of Indian history by asserting that Nehru's India described a "ranked society" rather than a consociational system. In contrast, after Nehru's death, the country became increasingly inclusive by offering some representation to previously excluded groups, such as the Muslims and the Backward Castes.

The second shift pertains to the scholarly tendency away from a focus on democracy to analyze stability and peace (see Bogaards, 2014, 4f). To a large extent, this reorientation of the consociational literature followed naturally from the enlargement of its geographic scope from Western Europe to include also developing countries where the soil was perceived much more fertile for conflict than for democracy. Lijphart took the lead in this development as well. Most importantly, Lijphart's (1985b) influential book *Power-Sharing in South Africa* paved the way for a more normative application of consociationalism as a peace strategy. While the

apartheid regime had tried to justify its racist rule by characterizing the
1983 Constitution as "consociational," Lijphart promoted the concept as
the key to serious reforms with the goal of overcoming decades of racist
discrimination and domination. To a large extent, the subsequent efforts
at ending conflict in South Africa confirmed the pivotal role played by
power sharing in the peace process (see, e.g., Andeweg, 2000, 517). Yet,
many scholars remain quite critical as regards Lijphart's self-described
"impressionistic" approach to measurement, and more generally, his
penchant for highly prescriptive theorizing (see especially Laitin, 1987;
Lustick, 1997).

Finally, the second generation of consociational theorizing has tended
to drift away from the initial focus on elite behavior toward a commitment to formal institutions. Again, Lijphart himself has played a
formative role in steering the literature in this particular direction.
Most importantly, Lijphart (1984) broadened his theoretical perspective
by proposing the notion of "consensus democracy," which features a
series of institutional devices (see also Lijphart, 1999). Explicitly pitted
against majoritarian democracy, consensual systems are characterized
by oversized cabinets, the separation of powers, multi-party systems,
proportional representation, corporatist interest groups, bicameralism,
federalism and decentralization, an entrenched constitution, judicial
review, and an independent central bank (see Andeweg, 2000, 512–513).
According to its inventor, consensus democracy makes for a "kinder
and gentler" type of politics that provides better democratic solutions,
especially, but not only, in deeply divided polities (Lijphart, 1999,
302). In contrast, Lijphart's initial definitional criteria were "largely
behavioral and broadly defined; they may find expression in the rather
specific institutional arrangements of consensus democracy, but they
are not confined to these mechanisms" (Andeweg, 2000, 513). Indeed,
following the general trend toward institutionalism in political science
(Shepsle, 1979; March and Olsen, 1984; Hall and Taylor, 1996), much
of the recent literature on power sharing stresses formal institutions at
the expense of behavior (see, e.g., Norris, 2008), a bias that, as argued
below, has continued to dominate also the next generation of studies
(see, e.g., Bogaards, 2019).

2.1.3   The third generation of power-sharing studies

The three shifts of the second generation have become even more
accentuated in the recent, more specialized conflict-research literature
that concentrates on power sharing and conflict. Much of this scholarly
activity centers on post-conflict situations, focusing particularly on the

role of power sharing in conflict management and resolution (for a comprehensive review, see Binningsbø, 2013, Forthcoming). Recurrent conflict typically serves as the main outcome of interest, although democracy and democratization have by no means disappeared from the scientific agenda (see, e.g., Jarstad and Sisk, 2008; Hartzell and Hoddie, 2015; Hartzell and Mehler, 2019). They focus predominantly on underdeveloped countries since that is where most internal conflicts take place, thus rendering the geographic scope even broader compared to the first two generations of power-sharing studies. Finally, the institutionalist bent is if anything even more pronounced in this literature, not least because many studies trace the effect of institutional provisions of peace agreements.

Whereas the general literature on consociationalism mostly employs qualitative research designs that compare entire countries, conflict researchers have been more prone to using quantitative approaches. This has at least partly helped to mitigate some of the conceptual and measurement issues that haunted the first and second generation of power-sharing studies (cf. Lustick, 1997). Furthermore, the conflict literature on power sharing tends to steer clear of the highly normative perspective that dominated the general debates about consociationalism.

Rather than using Lijphart's four consociational components, conflict researchers have come to employ a typology that explores power sharing agreements along their political, military, territorial and economic dimensions (see Binningsbø, 2013, 96). In a pioneering series of studies, Hartzell and Hoddie conclude that post-conflict peace becomes more likely the more dimensions peace agreements feature (Hartzell and Hoddie, 2003; Hoddie and Hartzell, 2005; Hartzell and Hoddie, 2007). In other words, their results suggest that, in order to minimize the risk of recurrent conflict, peace makers should try to craft agreements that comprise all four dimensions of power sharing (see also Walter, 2002).

To a large extent, the identified political, military, territorial and economic dimensions of power sharing overlap with the original definition of consociationalism. Indeed, the somewhat sweeping label "political" is usually understood to denote any representation of groups' representatives within the state's central decision making organs, without necessarily limiting this to grand coalitions or the state's executive. Moreover, the territorial dimension of power sharing partly coincides with Lijphart's segmental autonomy, although it excludes non-territorial cases. Lijphart (2002) himself has proposed that these two dimensions, that is governmental power sharing and autonomy, constitute the most important of the initial four contained in his classical definition of consociationalism. The two remaining dimensions in Hartzell and Hoddie's (2003) conceptualization, that is military and economic power sharing, are more directly related to post-conflict situations and do not feature as clearly in Lijphart's original formula.[1]

In this book, we will mostly restrict the attention to the political and territorial aspects of power sharing, although we prefer to replace the former label with governmental power sharing, since it is difficult to argue that military, territorial, or for that matter, economic, power sharing could be viewed as non-political. In the following chapter, we will offer our own definitions of governmental and territorial power sharing institutions and practices, and with the latter return to Lijphart's (1968) initial conception.

2.2 Arguments and Evidence for and against Power Sharing

Having presented the literature in roughly chronological order, we now turn to a brief survey of what previous studies have found with regard to the effects of the various dimensions of power sharing on conflict. Despite reliance on systematic data, the literature has come to contradictory conclusions. Partly, the crux is that researchers use several, partly incompatible definitions and datasets (see, e.g., Binningsbø, 2013, Forthcoming). Thus, both for governmental and territorial power sharing, there are studies that find either peace-inducing or conflict-enhancing effects. Generally, these studies account for executive power sharing as a means of offering mutual security for previous combatants as well as reducing grievances by including previously excluded conflict parties. These two classes of mechanisms correspond closely to distinctive, yet partly complementary, theories of civil war that stress opportunities and grievances, respectively (see Cederman and Vogt, 2017).

The opportunity-driven account explains how the government and the rebels are in the grips of a commitment problem (Fearon, 1995, 1998). Compared to interstate conflict, this problem is especially acute in the context of civil wars because the rebels are expected to disarm (Walter, 2002). However, as pointed out by Fearon (1998), there is no guarantee that the government will not renege on its concessions, which similarly applies to the rebels, who may start fighting again unless they are forced to disarm. In such situations, power sharing can make it harder for either side to stab the other in the back. More specifically, power sharing lessens the risk of conflict recurrence through provisions that reduce the fear of falling victim to opportunism, while raising the costs of renewed violence

---

[1] Lijphart's (1968) conception of proportionality in civil service appointments might also comprise the military as discussed and studied by Barak (2012) and Wilkinson (2015).

(Mattes and Savun, 2009). Others also believe in the stabilizing influence of power sharing, but are more skeptical that former combatants will be able to keep the peace without the help of third parties (e.g., Walter, 2002).

The grievance-reducing effect of power sharing follows Lijphart's (1975, 210) original logic of "self-denying prophecies." Instead of viewing the conflict parties as hopelessly trapped in a collective action dilemma, the idea is that they will realize the danger and potential cost of (possibly renewed) fighting, and therefore seek a collaborative solution based on compromise and accommodation (Du Toit, 1989; Bogaards, 1998). This underlying assumption undergirds most studies that link inequality and grievances to civil war. For example, Gurr (1994) argues that governments can achieve peaceful outcomes by offering inclusive arrangements to previously excluded and discriminated ethnic groups. In fact, Gurr (2000*a*) conjectures that the decline of ethnic conflict since the 1990s is to a large extent attributable to an accommodative regime based on power sharing, group rights, regional autonomy, and international intervention. Arguing along the same lines, Cederman, Gleditsch and Buhaug (2013) view inclusion as a major pathway to peace.

However, whether offered as a way of overcoming opportunism or as an inclusive strategy toward grievance reduction, power sharing may also cause various problems. As regards the grievance-driven account that is the closest to Lijphart's classical approach, it is far from obvious that ethnic elites will be inclined to cooperate and show tolerance. Arguing that consociationalism is "motivationally inadequate," Horowitz (2002, 20) questions why leaders of powerful groups would have an incentive to seek compromise if they think they can get away with domination. In this sense, owing to elitist recalcitrance and ideological stubbornness, Lijphart's "self-denying prophecy" may never be realized. Moreover, there may also be strong incentives in favor of ethnic outbidding that risks marginalizing moderate leaders (Rabushka and Shepsle, 1972; Horowitz, 1985).

The opportunity-driven arguments in favor of power sharing are more resistant to such a fundamental criticism because they address commitment problems more directly. Nevertheless, there is no guarantee that coopting potential rebels will produce stable peace. Bringing past combatants into the governing coalition increases the probability of infighting, for example, through military coups (see Bormann et al., 2019). Focusing specifically on sub-Saharan Africa, Roessler (2011) suggests that some governmental elites prefer to rule based on a narrow ethnic base, while excluding potential rebels, even if this triggers civil wars in the periphery of the state. Such coup-proofing may be safer for the members of the ruling elite as long as the external threat can be managed as a low-intensity civil war (see also Roessler, 2016; Bormann et al., 2019).

Along similar lines, Tull and Mehler (2005a) warn that the inclusion of potential or past rebels could create a moral hazard problem that encourages such actors to resort to violence in order to secure a seat at the negotiation table (see also Jarstad, 2008; Mehler, 2009). While inclusive strategies tend to reduce the risk of renewed fighting in the immediate aftermath of civil war, the stabilizing prospects could be much more problematic from a longer temporal perspective.

Likewise stressing its pernicious long-term consequences, more fundamental critiques of power sharing as a pacification method argue that the goal should be the creation of incentives that help transcend, rather than manage, ethnic cleavages. In his direct attack on Lijphart's consociationalism, Horowitz (1985) offers the most prominent example of such an integrationist perspective, which is sometimes labeled "centripetalism" (see Reilly, 2016). This approach to conflict resolution builds directly on Anglo-Saxon majoritarianism in that it tries to overcome ethnic divisions by offering institutional incentives in favor of shifting majorities, such as vote pooling and the separation of powers. Drawing on the same constitutional principles, Rothchild and Roeder (2005a) also argue against power sharing since, in their minds, it risks freezing ethnic identities, while undermining democratic quality and political stability by empowering the challengers of the regime. In its lieu, they propose an alternative under the heading of "power dividing" that guarantees individual civil rights while minimizing the risks of minority exclusion through institutional provisions that encourage flexible identification and dynamic coalitions (see also Strøm et al., 2017).

In addition to the general discourse on power sharing as a strategy of pacification, a more specialized debate has emerged that concerns territorial power sharing and conflict in particular. Unsurprisingly, the arguments advanced in this context partly overlap with those proposed in connection with power sharing more generally. At the same time, this literature also proposes mechanisms that apply specifically to territorial power sharing in the form of devolution, autonomy and full-fledged federalism.

This more specialized scholarship highlights how territorial autonomy promises to overcome commitment problems by offering former rebels a measure of security based on the resource base that regional, autonomous institutions offer (see, e.g., Hartzell, Hoddie and Rothchild, 2001; Hoddie and Hartzell, 2005; Mattes and Savun, 2009). In addition, governmental concessions send a costly signal that the government is willing to compromise, even after a military victory (see especially Lake and Rothchild, 2005; Jarstad and Nilsson, 2008). In terms of grievances, powerful theoretical arguments in favor of territorial power sharing can be found in the political economy literature. In a seminal article, Tiebout (1957) argued that decentralization that divides a polity into partially independent jurisdictions offers an effective way of accommodating heterogeneous preferences in key policy areas. If the government is ready to concede autonomy, such arrangements could go a long way toward reducing the grievances of previously excluded groups (see also Dower and Weber, 2015). For example, Bermeo (2002, 99) claims that territorial power sharing will encourage "minorities in federal states to engage in fewer acts of armed rebellion, to experience lower levels of economic and political discrimination, and to harbor lower levels of grievances concerning political, economic, and cultural policy." Furthermore, it is hoped that territorial power sharing constitutes an attractive compromise that contributes to moderating the agenda of secessionists (Hechter, 2000).

The other side of this debate stresses what it views as the inherent dangers of devolving power. As we have seen, the fear of a "slippery slope" goes back to pioneering contributions by Nordlinger (1972) and others. The experiences in Nigeria (Ikporukpo, 1996; Suberu, 2004; Rustad, Forthcoming) and Sudan (Green, 2011) constitute early illustrations, while the collapse of the former Soviet Union and Yugoslavia further accentuated the fears of the critics of territorial power sharing, especially when this is in the form of ethnic federalism (see, e.g., Brubaker, 1996; Bunce, 1999; Roeder, 1991; Snyder, 2000).

Again, the critics have targeted the arguments in favor of territorial power sharing both from an opportunity and a grievance perspective. They contend that, far from stabilizing the political system, offering autonomy to ethnic groups is likely to equip them with resources that they can use to strengthen their bids to secede from the state (Elkins and Sides, 2007, 693). Thus, instead of stabilizing the polity, concessions of this type provide radical separatists with even more powerful weapons with which they can dismantle the system as a whole. The fears of a slippery slope apply to the rebels' motivations, because moderate reforms may whet their appetite for more radical ones (Chapman and Roeder, 2007; Roeder, 2009). Indeed, it is far from certain that separatists will find co-habitation under one roof sufficient to satisfy their nationalist aspirations, especially if governmental concessions are interpreted as a sign of weakness. Furthermore, in large multi-ethnic states, autonomy reforms offered to one group may create dangerous precedents that could accelerate the centrifugal tendencies of the polity by empowering other minorities to seek far-reaching concessions, including secession (Walter, 2006*a*). Based on his experience with Canada, Kymlicka (1998) highlights the tensions inherent in such asymmetric arrangements.

2.3   General Weaknesses of the Power-Sharing Literature

Our reading of the vast literature on power sharing and conflict has been necessarily selective. All the same, it does indicate that research in this area suffers from several general weaknesses that make it very difficult to assess the effectiveness of governmental and territorial power sharing. More specifically, to follow up the critique advanced at the end of the previous chapter, we contend that there are four main problems that frustrate research on this topic, namely (1) a tendency to focus exclusively on formal institutions, (2) selective empirical coverage, (3) the implicit but common assumption that such institutions are exogenously given, and finally, (4) a failure to study interactions between specific types of power sharing.

2.3.1   Focus on formal power-sharing institutions

Based on our overview of the literature, we now see more clearly that researchers of power sharing have shifted their agendas gradually toward formal institutions. Especially in comparative politics, research on power sharing and its consequences has moved from a focus on practices, as in Lijphart's early work, to formal institutions that are *assumed* to induce the practices that he originally conceptualized as consociational (Lijphart, 1975, 1977). More recently, scholars studying the impact of power sharing on conflict have come to equate power sharing with institutions that in some cases are only remotely or indirectly linked to the original conception, such as proportional representation (Cohen, 1997; Norris, 2008; Mukherjee, 2006; Pospieszna and Schneider, 2013) and federalism (Cohen, 1997; Saideman et al., 2002; Norris, 2008; Schneider and Wiesenhomeier, 2008). However, such formal institutions do not necessarily imply power-sharing practices (Jarstad and Nilsson, 2008; Pospieszna and Schneider, 2013). In this context, Rothchild and Roeder (2005*b*) usefully distinguish between formal institutions that create opportunities for power sharing (e.g., proportional representations) and those that create mandates (e.g., reserved seats in the executive), or "soft" and "hard" power-sharing arrangements in Gates and Strøm's (Forthcoming-*a*) terminology. With few exceptions, such as Pospieszna and Schneider (2013), this tendency to focus on formal institutions has been reinforced by the use of datasets that offer measures of formal provisions rather than practices. In Chapter 4, we will rely on one of the most prominent, recent examples of such a dataset, namely the Inclusion, Dispersion and Constraints (IDC) Dataset (see Strøm et al., 2017).

2.3.2   Selective empirical coverage

We have also found that, despite sustained attempts to reach broader conclusions, the rich literature on power sharing remains quite fragmented. Most of the previous research has covered select cases, making it difficult, if not impossible, to set up objective comparisons. As indicated by our literature review, early writings on consociationalism suffered from acute problems of this kind, although Lijphart and others did make an effort to expand the consociational universe. The third generation of studies of power sharing is similarly prone to this problem. Many researchers highlight cases that have already experienced conflict, while ignoring the ones that have remained peaceful. As argued by McGarry and O'Leary (2009), the collapse of the communist states may have exerted too much of an influence on attempts to reach general conclusions about the viability of ethnic federalism (see also Grigoryan, 2012; Anderson, 2013). More generally, the focus on conflict cases has led to a characterization of power sharing as a part of formal peace agreements (see, e.g., Hartzell and Hoddie, 2007). To be sure, such a partial perspective on power sharing offers important insights on managing violent conflict once it breaks out. At the same time, however, it obscures the potentially useful conflict-preventive role that such arrangements can play before political violence transforms relations. For this reason, it seems risky to assume that governmental and territorial power-sharing practices are equally effective before and after the first outbreak of armed conflict. As convincingly argued by Gates et al. (2016), we therefore need more comprehensive datasets that cover larger samples of power sharing regardless of conflict occurrence.

2.3.3   Exogenous institutions assumption

Scholars studying power sharing have often failed to pay attention to the problem of endogeneity and reverse causation. However, Przeworski (2004) warns that institutions are almost always endogenously chosen, thus making causal inferences about their effectiveness difficult. For example, if governments offer power-sharing concessions to ethnic groups as a way of reducing or preventing anticipated violence, the previous literature may have underestimated their pacifying effect. Conversely, if governments tend to exclude potential "troublemakers," power sharing may have a more limited pacifying effect than suggested by naïve empirical analyses. While several scholars are aware of the problem (e.g., McGarry and O'Leary, 2005; Anderson, 2013; Sambanis and Milanovic, 2014; Grigoryan, 2012), there are still relatively few attempts to guard against endogeneity, and those that do so leave room for improvement. In an attempt to study the unifying influence of federalism and proportional representation in multi-ethnic states, Elkins and Sides (2007) propose instrumental variables for institutions by relying on arguably exogenous factors that predict these institutions, but say less about whether these instruments satisfy the exclusion restriction (see, e.g., Sovey and Green, 2011). Likewise, Cammett and Malesky (2012) introduce as instrument for power sharing a measure that uses values of this variable in neighboring countries while excluding the country in question. Again, however, it is unlikely that this strategy fulfills the exclusion restriction since there are many ways, for example, linked to conflict diffusion, by which inclusive institutions – or their absence – may affect the likelihood of conflict in contiguous states through pathways unrelated to the institutions in the state itself (for a critique, see Betz, Cook and Hollenbach, 2018).[2]

2.3.4   *Failure to analyze links between governmental and territorial power sharing*

Our account of the literature also shows that whether power is shared within the central government or territorially through autonomy arrangements is a crucial question that has often been swept under the rug in past studies on the topic. For example, Lijphart (1985*a*) attempted to extend his notion of consociationalism to federalism by assuming the latter to be a functional equivalent of elements of consociational democracy. However, this analytical shift makes the analysis of interactions between governmental and territorial power sharing difficult. Yet, Wolff (2011, 45) reminds us that "[t]hose critical of consociationalism as a whole often focus on its power-sharing dimension, while critics of territorial approaches to conflict management in divided societies normally ignore it altogether. Until recently, supporters of consociationalism, too,

---

[2] While they explore endogeneity with respect to democracy rather than power sharing, Elbadawi and Sambanis (2002) propose a two-stage model, but including the political institutions of previous periods as an instrument is unlikely to entirely solve the problem.

were oblivious to the significance of the (necessary) complementarity of power sharing and [territorial self-government]." Similarly, as we have seen, conflict researchers have tended to treat these two types of power sharing (and others) as equivalent components of compound indices implying that "more is better" (e.g., Hartzell and Hoddie, 2007), while other studies discuss one but not the other (e.g., Bakke and Wibbels, 2006; Christin and Hug, 2012). Furthermore, there is little agreement on whether either dimension of power sharing mitigates conflict. Some authors endorse power sharing as a conflict resolution approach while remaining more skeptical about the effect of autonomy (Walter, 2002; Mattes and Savun, 2009; Walter, 2009). In contrast, Jarstad (2008) argues that autonomy curbs conflict more effectively than governmental power sharing (for contrasting evidence, see also Martin, 2013; Pospieszna and Schneider, 2013). With few exceptions, such as McGarry and O'Leary (2009) to which we will return in the next chapter, the literature on autonomy and conflict does not make an attempt to analyze how territorial and governmental power sharing interact.

As argued in Chapter 1, once these problems have been properly addressed, we suspect that the assessment will tilt more decisively in favor of inclusive practices. Indeed, our four main arguments, already introduced above, flow directly from our diagnosis of the main difficulties afflicting the mainstream literature.

3 Key Concepts and Arguments of Our Approach

The previous chapter outlines a number of weaknesses that afflict the literature on power sharing and conflict. Addressing these difficulties directly, the present chapter proposes a theoretical framework that seeks to offer a more balanced assessment of the inclusion-peace argument. The framework will inform our empirical investigations in the remainder of the book. The task of the present chapter is to give an account of our theoretical thinking, and to derive our master hypotheses, which will inform the empirical analysis to follow after this chapter.

3.1 Theoretical Concepts and Core Arguments

As stated already in Chapter 1, our approach uses as its theoretical starting point our previous research on the opposite phenomena, namely exclusion and conflict. Inspired by earlier work on grievances and ethnic conflict by (Gurr, 1993, 2000*b*), this argument is laid out in a series of publications, including most comprehensively in the book *Inequality, Grievances and Civil War* (Cederman, Gleditsch and Buhaug, 2013). In the the current greed-versus-grievance debate, this research program attempts to resurrect grievance-based accounts in the civil-war literature that have been eclipsed by explanations driven by "greed" (Collier and Hoeffler, 2004) and "opportunities" (Fearon and Laitin, 2003). In brief, Cederman, Gleditsch and Buhaug claim that the individualist bias in these critiques of grievance-based approaches to civil war has obscured processes that generate grievances and conflict due to "horizontal inequalities" between ethnic groups (Stewart, 2008).[1]

Clearly, horizontal inequalities can manifest themselves along several dimensions. Stewart (2008) argues that such inequalities can be political, economic, social and cultural. While all these dimensions are potentially

---

[1] This individualist bias is inherent in conventional measures of ethnic fractionalization (Cederman and Girardin, 2007) and the Gini coefficient (Cederman, Weidmann and Gleditsch, 2011).

relevant to power sharing, we will focus our current theory-building effort on the ethno-political dimension. In multi-ethnic states, power sharing primarily represents an attempt to reduce ethnic inequality by fostering inclusive arrangements that give the relevant ethnic groups access to political power, whether at the center or regionally or both.

As suggested in Chapter 1, the focus on ethnic inclusion makes sense for several reasons.[2] First, since World War II, a clear majority of civil conflicts have been fought along ethnic lines. In fact, since 1946, almost 70 percent of all years of civil conflict have been of ethnic nature.[3] Second, both governmental and territorial power sharing are usually proposed primarily as ways to prevent conflict in multi-ethnic states (see, e.g., Butenschøn, Stiansen and Vollan, 2015), although it is not hard to find past and present cases of non-ethnic power sharing, as illustrated by Cambodian and Colombian history (see, e.g., Jarstad, 2008; Binningsbø, 2013). We will return to this issue in Chapter 12. Third, for pragmatic reasons, the limitation to ethno-political inclusion facilitates the identification of actors thanks to preexisting datasets on ethnic groups and their access to political power.

To justify their main theoretical claim, Cederman, Gleditsch and Buhaug (2013, Ch. 3) sketch a causal pathway that starts with horizontal inequalities and then continues via grievances all the way to the outbreak of civil conflict. Far from being deterministic, this extended chain requires that a series of conditions be fulfilled and can therefore be easily broken at several points. First, in order to generate grievances, horizontal inequalities typically build on existing ethnic identities that allow the group members to compare themselves to other groups. Furthermore, such comparisons have to be perceived as unjust and framed as such to generate mass appeal. Second, should widely held grievances emerge, there is still no guarantee that civil conflict will break out, because the mobilization efforts require both resources and organization (Tilly, 1978). Thus even though strongly felt anger with the government often helps to accelerate the mobilization effort, it may not be enough to trigger civil conflict, especially if the government is able to ruthlessly suppress unorganized resistance (Kalyvas, 2006). Should the opposition be able to

---

[2] Following Weber (1978, 385–398) we define ethnicity as any subjectively experienced sense of commonality based on the belief in common ancestry and shared culture (Weber 1978, 385–398). The sense of cultural commonality can be expressed along linguistic, religious, somatic or other lines. An ethnic group, then, is as a cultural community based on a common belief in putative descent (see also Cederman, 2013).

[3] According to the ACD2EPR dataset, there have been 2086 conflict years from 1946 through 2017, and 1448 of these were ethnic (Vogt et al., 2015). Yet after 2015, the number of non-ethnic civil conflicts appears to have overtaken the ethnic ones. We will come back to this issue in Chapter 11.

mobilize armed resistance against the ethnic group(s) in power, however, governmental repression would likely increase the risk of conflict even further (Goodwin, 1997).

To sum up, the main argument of the grievance paradigm, then, is that horizontal inequality in the form of political exclusion of ethnic groups increases the risk of civil conflict compared to cases where groups are included in the political system. This is so because the marginalized groups are likely to harbor grievances relating to inequality and disempowerment that increase the risk of rebellion. The conclusion is that, on average, exclusion causes civil conflict. The flip side of the same argument tells us that low levels of ethno-political inequality should lead to lower levels of conflict. Since power sharing stands for a reduction of this type of inequality, it follows that inclusion should in most cases produce peace.

To render this sweeping formula more precise, we need to define more clearly what is meant by inclusion through power sharing. Instead of relying on Lijphart's (1969) four or more dimensions of power sharing, we propose a definition that reduces the number of dimensions to a bare minimum, namely the sharing of executive power and group autonomy. This conceptualization corresponds closely to what Lijphart (2002, 39) highlights as the "primary characteristics" among the original four components that his classical, four-dimensional definition included.[4] Thus, we define power sharing as inclusive practices affecting ethnic groups, either by giving them influence of the state's executive or over regional decision making:

Definition. *Governmental power-sharing practices* stand for the inclusion of representatives from more than one ethnic group in the country's central executive decision-making, offering meaningful possibilities to influence policies in line with the groups' interests.

Definition. *Territorial power-sharing practices* stand for the delegation of partial executive power to at least one regional body through which representatives of ethnic groups are able to control decision-making in line with their groups' interests.

These definitions call for further clarification:

- "Practice" denotes actual behavior in accordance with formal or informal rules. Therefore, it could be misleading to use informal

---

[4] Moreover, these two categories also resemble Strøm et al.'s (2015) "inclusive" and "dispersive" types of power sharing, to which we will return in the next chapter.

power sharing as a synonym for power-sharing practices. Neither is it appropriate to equate this definition with Lijphart's (1969) notion of "grand coalitions," although the current conceptualization comes close. The most important distinction pertains to the notion of inclusion, which in our case goes well beyond grand coalitions in terms of empirical scope. Specifically, the only thing that governmental power-sharing practices presuppose is that executive power be shared by at least two ethnic groups. This definition offers an intuitive way of capturing governmental power-sharing behavior at the group level. Yet, it is still possible to study variation of inclusiveness all the way up to comprehensive governments of national unity. Indeed, such demanding conceptualizations are often used in the field of comparative politics with regard to democratic states.

- As a rule, governmental power-sharing practices are most obviously compatible with Lijphart's original notion of consociationalism, although they are not necessarily incompatible with integrationist systems, such as the United States, which can offer meaningful group representation for minorities through the presidency or cabinet positions. What matters is that ethnic elites enjoy *de facto*, regular access to executive decision-making.

- It should also be noted that inclusiveness refers to representation in the state's executive, rather than in other branches of government. In democratic regimes, this amounts to the presidency and/or the cabinet. In contrast, executive power in authoritarian regimes may be vested in the party leadership or in military juntas.

- The definition of territorial power-sharing practices does require that at least one group enjoys decision-making autonomy at the regional level in a territorially delimited part of the polity. By definition, this presupposes a formal anchoring of the practices in constitutional or common laws, whether through federalism, autonomy or devolution (McGarry and O'Leary, 2010). However, such arrangements may exist merely formally without enabling the groups to exercise actual power (see especially the description of the Ethnic Power Relations Dataset in Chapter 4). Moreover, there is no expectation that there is a strict one-to-one correspondence between the ethnic group's settlement area and the boundaries of the regional unit(s). In some cases, such as the cantons of Switzerland, group autonomy can be enjoyed within several administrative units. However, completely non-ethnic cases of "national" federalism are not included in the definition unless the federal subunits allow for *de facto* representation of ethnic groups.

- Finally, the definition of territorial power-sharing practices also comprises behavior that stems from explicit governmental concessions rather than from unilateral cases of "self-exclusion" by *de facto* seceding from the state, as illustrated by the Abkhazians in Georgia from the early 1990s (although the secession attempts are typically only recognized by a few, if any, sovereign states). In these cases, there is no agreed basis for power sharing outside the realm of self-determination, which is why we do not count such cases as examples of territorial power sharing.

Having pinpointed what we mean by power-sharing practices, we are now ready to state our first master hypothesis, which also is the main claim of this book:

Master Hypothesis 1. Power-sharing practices reduce the risk of civil conflict.

Based on our definitions of governmental and territorial power-sharing practices, this central claim can be broken up into two sub-hypotheses:

Master Hypothesis 1a. Governmental power-sharing practices reduce the risk of civil conflict.

Master Hypothesis 1b. Territorial power-sharing practices reduce the risk of civil conflict.

These hypotheses can be derived directly from Cederman, Gleditsch and Buhaug (2013) in what will henceforth refer to as the *grievance-reducing logic*: if a group is included in the government, it is going to be much harder, though perhaps not impossible, for potential rebels to make the case for rebellion than in cases of marginalization.[5] Furthermore, with possibilities to wield influence from within the political system thanks to shared power, group representatives can be expected to have much less of an incentive to undermine the system itself through violent means. In such inclusive settings, there is less room for grievances that blame the government for unfavorable conditions. Consequently, this also implies that the potential rebels' mobilization effort becomes harder to orchestrate, because there are fewer potential leaders ready to challenge the rules of the game. Moreover, inclusion also reduces the number of aggrieved potential rebels who are willing to join the

---

[5] Some radical ethno-nationalist activists may not find cohabitation and compromise attractive for ideological or self-interested reasons, and may therefore rebel against the government to entirely oust the incumbents or by fighting for full independence rather than territorial power sharing (see especially Chapter 9). Cederman, Gleditsch and Buhaug (2013, Ch. 4) provide examples of included groups that have fought against other members of the governing coalition.

resistance movement in the first place. Faced with more cooperative ethnic elites, the incumbent regime is likely to feel less threatened and will thus be more inclined to attempt to co-opt potential challengers rather than excluding them or using repressive measures against them.

Viewed from this perspective, power sharing primarily reduces civil conflict through "anger reduction," by placating and co-opting potential rebels. By addressing the sources of injustice, the grievance-reducing logic builds peace by offering concessions that serve to diminish, or possibly even fully reverse, perceived inequality and unfairness. The government's willingness to negotiate in order to find a viable compromise can be expected to weaken the position of hardliners on both sides.[6] Arguably, governance based on inclusive rule also increases the governmental responsiveness to the ethnic groups' needs and preferences in a way that ethnically dominant rulers do not. Inclusion of those affected by the policies, in turn, allows these actors to encourage increased provision of public goods and other benefits that could in turn further reduce grievances relating to underdevelopment and ethno-economic inequality. In particular, territorial power sharing has the potential of bringing governance closer to the people such that their preferences can be satisfied in a decentralized manner (Tiebout, 1957).

Of course, beyond this stylized grievance-driven scenario, power sharing may be linked to peace – and possibly even conflict – through alternative links. It should be noted that the contributions to this literature by Gurr (2000*b*), Cederman, Gleditsch and Buhaug (2013) and others stress that inequality and grievances represent an important, but far from the only, conflict-inducing mechanism. These authors specifically keep the door open to explanations that highlight opportunistic mobilization and material motivations that may operate in tandem with, and sometimes even in close interaction with, grievance-related mechanisms.

Unfortunately, however, a narrow, mutually exclusive perspective, which insists on the irrelevance of grievances, is still alive and well in the literature, and has made it difficult to overcome the original "greed-versus-grievance" dichotomy. Yet, rather than pitting one explanatory paradigm against the other in sweeping "tests," it makes more sense to consider these classes of explanations as overlapping in theoretically important ways (Cederman and Vogt, 2017). More recently, attempts have been made to bridge the divide by extending the grievance

---

[6] Yet, radical activists, so-called "spoilers," may still manage to undermine the spirit of compromise by refusing to accept governmental power-sharing concessions (Stedman, 1997).

arguments to encompass theoretical ideas drawn from bargaining theory, stressing an opportunity-based logic (see, e.g., Roessler, 2016).

Along these lines, we widen the theoretical scope by explicitly considering how inclusive practices can contribute to building inter-ethnic trust. This *confidence-building logic* complements the grievance-reducing logic by considering power sharing's ability to overcome mistrust, especially in post-conflict situations. Previous work highlighting grievances has generally tended to stress frustration and resentment rather than fear, but there is no reason to believe that only one type of emotion applies to conflict processes (Petersen, 2002). Given the asymmetric situation in most civil conflicts, rebels have good reasons to fear the government, and so mobilization efforts tend to build on both resentment and fear. By claiming to provide protection from governmental attacks, rebels seek support from their own constituencies. In their campaigns, governments also exploit emotions by painting a threatening picture of the rebels, both with respect to vulnerable populations' exposure to rebel violence and more broadly, threats of escalating violence and political chaos, including territorial disintegration of the state.

While inclusive governance likely pacifies by removing or diminishing resentment, as outlined above, shared power may also reduce uncertainty and alleviate commitment problems that bargaining approaches view as prime drivers of civil war (Fearon, 1998; Walter, 2009; Blattman and Miguel, 2010). The most important aspect pertains to the fear of either side reneging on promises encapsulated in a peace agreement (Fearon, 1998; Fearon, 2004). Simply put, any offer by the government to include representatives of opposing groups in governmental decision-making could be reversed at some later point if the power balance shifts. However, knowing this, the rebels are likely to be reluctant to give up arms and may resort to arms again.

Clearly, commitment problems of this type may undermine power sharing and trigger conflict. For this reason, some authors believe that power sharing requires external security guarantees to be successful (Walter, 2002). Still, it may be that well-designed inclusive rules and practices introduce safeguards that are able to lock the process in a peaceful equilibrium, for instance through calls for the withdrawal of foreign troops, border seals and the installation of buffer zones (Mattes and Savun, 2009). Even short of full-fledged, peace-enforcing intervention, international transparency and observers may increase the cost of violation so much that the parties refrain from reneging on previous agreements.

The extent to which these measures will work without external enforcement is an open question. Roessler and Ohls (2018) argue that most cases of successful power sharing in Sub-Saharan Africa have been informal arrangements agreed by the parties without foreign intervention (see also Roessler, 2016). In this sense, power sharing has to be "self-enforcing" through actual behavior that reflects the interest of the relevant parties rather than imposed through external intervention and externally guaranteed formal peace agreements.

This reasoning has a number of implications that invite us to overcome the four weaknesses of the literature that the previous chapter identified:

• The first implication of this reasoning is that, because formal institutions may not be properly implemented and could constitute little more than "cheap talk," we will have to study actual behavior rather than *de jure* provisions. The centrality of power-sharing practices flows naturally out of the exclusion-theoretic framework that we have adopted as our starting point and it also supports further scrutiny of the commitment problem and self-enforcing power sharing in states with weak institutions.

• The second immediate consequence of our theoretical extension stressing the problems of committing to power sharing requires us to consider the specific conditions under which power sharing is introduced. The issue is whether there is enough trust to sustain power sharing or whether key actors are so fearful of the other side's possible reneging that inclusive arrangements are likely to collapse. In particular, we anticipate that post-war situations pose formidable challenges in terms of mistrust, and for this reason, it may be misleading to generalize from cases of conflict resolution to cases that have not yet seen violence.

• Third, the need to investigate the conditions of successful power sharing also raises the important question of what motivates such arrangements in the first place. In particular, as has been the case with the general literature on power sharing (see Chapter 2), the exclusion-conflict research program has mostly treated exclusion as if it were given (Fearon, 2010; Roessler, 2016). In response to these critiques, our current attempt to extend and adapt grievance-based conflict theories urgently calls for endogenization of governments' decisions to include or exclude potential rebels. Again, attention to the actors' strategic reasoning requires a broader perspective that includes inter-group relations prior to the outbreak of the first armed conflict.

• A final aspect of the theoretical extension to confidence-building issues concerns the motivations of potential or actual secessionists when offered territorial power sharing as a concessions. Again, the extent to which trust will be allowed to develop depends crucially on how well embedded such actors are in the overall political system. For this reason, we need to study how a combination of both territorial and governmental power sharing may be necessary to provide a more stable basis for decentralized decision-making through autonomy and federalism.

In the following four sections, we extend the theoretical reasoning along these analytical dimensions with the goal of deriving our remaining master hypotheses.

3.2   From Formal Institutions to Ethnic Elites' Practices

Rather than limiting our analysis to practices, we extend the analytical scope to *de jure* aspects of power sharing. As we have argued, it is misleading to focus all analytical fire power on formal institutions if, in fact, actual behavior matters more directly for peaceful outcomes. This, however, is no more than a theoretical claim. In order to evaluate whether practices are indeed central, we need to get our concepts right. This section sets the stage for the introduction of the relevant data in Chapter 4 and an explicit empirical comparison of formal institutions and practices in Chapter 5.

In close correspondence to our definitions of governmental and territorial power-sharing practices, we propose the following master concepts that capture the formal dimension of shared power:

Definition. *Formal governmental power-sharing institutions* are formal provisions for mandated collective inclusiveness in the central executive organs of the state.

Definition. *Formal territorial power-sharing institutions* are formal provisions that delegate some decision-making powers to a governmental authority in charge of a subnational territory.

These paired definitions call for further comments:

• Less abstractly, governmental power-sharing institutions feature inclusive rules, such as mandated coalition requirements, mutual veto, and any form of reserved executive positions for specific political actors irrespective of electoral results or power struggles within the government. Territorial power-sharing institutions correspond to a set of institutional arrangements that offer subnational populations a measure of self-rule, be it through federalism, autonomy or devolution (see McGarry and O'Leary, 2010; Wolff, 2013).

- The proposed conceptualization of governmental power-sharing institutions by no means limits these to Lijphart's (1969) "grand coalitions" that feature virtually all groups in a society. While our empirical analysis will consider the size of coalitions, we agree with McGarry and O'Leary (2004, 15) that "what makes consociations feasible and work is joint consent across the significant communities, with the emphasis on jointness." In fact, our definition is even more permissive than this. The only thing that is required for governmental power-sharing institutions to apply is that there is any type of provision that offers formal guarantees of representation to specific, named groups, parties or other collective entities as opposed to individuals. In this sense, our notion of formal power-sharing institutions are more general than the definitions of practices. The latter are explicitly defined in relation to ethnic groups.
- It should also be noted that these definitions do not require the polity in question to be democratic. Although most cases of governmental power sharing in authoritarian regimes amount to informal arrangements of spoils sharing (see, e.g., Svolik, 2012), formal institutions within parties and dictatorial regimes can prescribe power sharing in these kinds of contexts (see, e.g., Gandhi, 2008; Magaloni, 2008). Furthermore, peace agreements may also offer formal provisions in systems that are not entirely democratic (see, e.g., Vandeginste, 2013; Lewis, Heathershaw and Megoran, 2018). Likewise, ethnofederal institutions in the former USSR and Yugoslavia illustrate that territorial power sharing does not have to be democratic. Yet, some authors question whether non-democratic systems can be considered consociational on the grounds that group elites may fail to represent their members' interests (see, e.g., McGarry and O'Leary, 2009).
- Unlike Lijphart's (1969) original definition, territorial power-sharing institutions are, as the label suggests, restricted to territorial arrangements. We will thus not consider non-territorial arrangements that offer cultural autonomy to specific groups, such as the schemes proposed by the "Austro-Marxists" (Bauer, 1907; Renner, 1918), or the institutions of linguistic self-determination within Brussels (Bodson and Loizides, 2017).
- We explicitly refer to autonomy and other territorial arrangements as cases of power sharing although there is a "dividing" logic involved. After all, these schemes presuppose that the authority in the polity be "vertically" shared between the center and subnational entities as an alternative to their division through secession. In her cogent analysis of this aspect, Bednar (2011) argues that in federal systems there is a "geopolitical division," but that governments at the two levels share responsibilities.

Having defined the key concepts pertaining to formal power sharing, we are now ready to derive another set of master hypotheses. Given our critique of literature, and the implications of the exclusion-theoretic framework, it can be asserted that the effect of formal institutions is likely to operate through actual behavior rather than through other channels (see Bormann, 2014). In this sense, power-sharing practices are more proximate causes of peace and conflict than formal provisions:

> It cannot be stressed enough that ... behavior within the institution – not just the institution in isolation – determines whether institutions are outcome-consequential, or, as is more often uttered, whether institutions matter. (Diermeier and Krehbiel, 2003, 127)

Moreover, as we have argued, some cases of informal power sharing exert an influence on conflict independently of, or even in contradiction to, formal institutions.[7] More generally speaking, Helmke and Levitsky (2004, 725) define informal institutions as "created, communicated, and enforced outside of officially sanctioned channels." While we reserve the institutional label for formal provisions, this conceptualization closely resembles our understanding of the term "power-sharing practices." In this sense, informal power sharing does not need to reinforce formal structures, but may in fact modify and compete with them. Furthermore, in weakly institutionalized states, informal practices become even more important (Grzymala-Busse, 2010). Because these environments are the ones that see the most conflict, researchers who are interested in such outcomes cannot limit themselves to the analysis of formal rules, but need to consider informal practices as well. This observation is particularly relevant in the case of Sub-Saharan Africa. Thus, whereas much of the existing conflict research on Africa traces the operation of formal rules enshrined in constitutions and peace agreements, Roessler and Ohls (2018, 427) argue in favor of an approach to power sharing and conflict that considers informal rules and understands such arrangements as self-enforced equilibria that emerge endogenously from political deal making.

Based on this reasoning, we postulate the following:

Master Hypothesis 2. Practices channel the main conflict-reducing effect of formal power-sharing institutions and also reduce conflict even in the absence of formal institutions.

Of course, there is no guarantee that the net pacifying effect of power-sharing practices as opposed to formal arrangements is in favor of

---

[7] Thus, it is problematic to argue that "informal arrangements are merely a supplement to already established formal rules" (Schneckener, 2002, 219).

practices. Some authors argue that informal power sharing increases, rather than decreases, the risk of conflict. For example, Spears (2013) views African leaders' wide-ranging reliance on informal power-sharing deals as a destabilizing, short-term practice rather than as a source of long-term stability. Others claim that formal power sharing is more likely to be invoked in particularly difficult, conflictual cases, such as Lebanon, in lieu of measures that do not require formal institutionalization (Strøm et al., 2017). For these reasons, our main claim will require empirical validation that compares the effect on conflict of governmental and territorial power-sharing practices with those of their formal counterparts.

In any case, we believe that the focus on practices helps pave the way for analysis of the role of confidence building in power sharing. While this constitutes a first helpful step, we need to take additional steps. In particular, the extent to which the commitment problem will reduce the effectiveness of power sharing depends critically on the particular decision-making context.

3.3   Analyzing Both Pre- and Post-conflict Situations

As shown in Chapter 2, much of the literature on power sharing and conflict focuses on whether such arrangements can reduce the risk of recurrent conflict. For this reason, most studies limit their samples to post-conflict situations, that is states and regions that have already experienced armed conflict. In the previous chapter, we argued that such a limitation may introduce bias and risks losing sight of the preventive effect of power sharing in situations where no political violence has so far occurred. The empirical chapters in this book therefore rely on full samples that go beyond post-conflict situations. This approach resonates with that of Gates et al. (2016), who, for similar reasons, rely on a complete set of cases that includes both pre-conflict and post-conflict observations.

Indeed, there are good reasons to believe that governmental or territorial power sharing would have a conflict-preventing effect prior to the first onset of conflict. In fact, such a general focus harmonizes with a recent shift toward preventive measures against conflict instead of an exclusive focus on conflict resolution in war-torn societies (see, e.g., Carment et al., 2016). This reorientation of international support efforts toward preventive measures is particularly visible in the recent report on *Pathways for Peace* (United Nations and World Bank, 2018) and in the United Nations' Sustainable Development Goals.[8]

---

[8] See www.un.org/sustainabledevelopment/peace-justice/).

From an analytical standpoint, the widening of the empirical sample to pre-conflict settings opens up new possibilities to evaluate the impact of prior conflict compared to situations where such preconditions do not exist. Especially in cases where rebels are not definitively defeated on the battle field and continue to enjoy a measure of protection from their own territory, territorial power-sharing concessions may be particularly risky. This is so for several reasons.

Once an armed conflict erupts it drastically changes the relationship between the group and the incumbent government (Brubaker and Laitin, 1998).[9] Recent research along these lines controls for previous conflict, but does not go as far as analyzing how this modifies the impact of ethnic groups' power access (see, e.g., Cederman, Wimmer and Min, 2010; Cederman, Gleditsch and Buhaug, 2013). Indeed, the effectiveness of governments' concessions to ethnic groups may well depend on whether the relationship has thus far been peaceful or not. In other words, what works as a preventive measure before the outbreak of violence may be less successful in a post-conflict setting.

In principle, protracted violence could make both sides of a conflict less likely to resort to arms again.[10] However, the empirical record suggests that recurrent conflict is much more likely than first onsets, leading Collier et al. (2003, 5) to label this a "conflict trap" (see also Walter, 2004). With respect to ethnic conflict, the results point in the same direction. For example, Cederman, Wimmer and Min (2010) find that ethnic groups' likelihood of experiencing recurrent conflict increases with the number of past onsets (see also Cederman, Gleditsch and Buhaug, 2013). Building on these arguments, we identify three sets of mechanisms that connect such a conflict history with recurrent outbreaks of fighting:

First, as regards attitudes to violence, armed conflict ceases to be unthinkable and becomes part of the repertoire of protest actions that the opposition can resort to. Such a breach of trust can be very hard to recover from, especially after long and bitter fighting. Social psychologists offer convincing explanations of the mechanisms that lead to intractable conflicts, including collective memory of past fighting, an "ethos" of conflict, and collective emotional orientations (Bar-Tal, 2013). Clearly, without an active will to organize reconciliation and confidence building, memories of such events can live on for decades (Rydgren, 2007). Failure to break the cycle of resentment

---

[9] The reasoning in this section draws heavily on Cederman et al. (2015).

[10] War wariness can lead ex-combatants to "forgive and forget," as Samii (2013) shows for the case of Burundi. Yet, in Burundi, learning occurred after two relapses of fighting.

risks transforming group-government relations into hatred that could flare up quite easily (Petersen, 2002; Bar-Tal, 2013). In fact, previous conflict may heighten human suffering that engenders violence-related grievances that deepen already existing inequality-related resentment.

Second, with respect to the internal organization of the conflict parties, past conflict also tends to radicalize both sides. Radicalization typically leads to a splintering of the fronts, with hardliners insisting on fighting instead of accepting compromises (see, e.g., Asal, Brown and Dalton, 2012). Such a pattern includes attempts to outbid more moderate politicians with uncompromising and extremist positions (Rabushka and Shepsle, 1972; Horowitz, 1985). Fragmentation will lead to a lack of control on both sides, giving spoilers more room to block the implementation of peace initiatives, as Cunningham (2011) convincingly shows for the case of self-determination movements (see also Cunningham, 2014; Cunningham, Bakke and Seymour, 2011).

Third, in terms of fighting capacity, armed combat leaves behind not only mental scars but also typically an infrastructural legacy conducive to renewed conflict. In particular, failed or partial disarmament leaves both former rebels and governmental militias with recruitment networks, weapons, bases and resources, on the basis of which new campaigns can be launched (Wood, 2008; Walter, 2009).

All in all, as already mentioned above, the experience of previous conflict changes the relationship between groups and governments fundamentally. It is therefore all the more important to *prevent* conflict from happening in the first place. For reasons outlined above, especially grievance and fear reduction, we expect power-sharing practices to have such a preventive effect. At the same time, an exclusive focus on post conflict situations (as practiced by much of the literature) is likely to induce selection bias that is likely to underestimate the effect of seeking compromise through power sharing, precisely because post-conflict situations are particularly prone to (renewed) violence to begin with (Strøm et al., 2017). Taken together, it would therefore be a mistake to study the effect of power sharing on the basis of partial samples with incorrect baselines.

Moreover, in line with much of the recent literature (see Chapter 2), we also expect power-sharing practices to be effective as a reactive measure of dampening renewed conflict. While a reversal to violence is a constant background risk in post-conflict situations, this also opens up room to reduce fear and grievances through provisions to previously excluded or discriminated groups.

We summarize these arguments with another master hypothesis:

Master Hypothesis 3. Power-sharing practices have a pacifying effect both before and after the first conflict but the risk of conflict onset is generally higher in the latter case.

Thanks to our reliance on comprehensive datasets that cover both types of situations, we will be able to evaluate this argument in greater detail, especially in Chapter 8. This research design stands a better chance of doing justice to power-sharing practices than those relying on more restrictive samples. More specifically, and related to our next argument, such a comprehensive dataset also allows us to evaluate in more detail under what conditions power-sharing institutions and practices are put into place.

3.4   Endogenizing Power-Sharing Practices

In the last section of the literature review in Chapter 2, we introduced the problem of endogeneity with respect to future conflict. Clearly, neither governmental nor territorial power sharing can be assumed to occur as if in a random experiment. Quite on the contrary, we have to assume that their occurrence is related to the risk of conflict in one way or another. In fact, the evaluation of the pacifying effects of these practices hinges critically on whether they are typically invoked in situations that are particularly conflictual, or whether governments are more likely to exclude potentially threatening groups in the shadow of future conflict (Fearon, 2010).[11] The problem is that both possibilities are entirely plausible depending on the case in question.

The former option, which could be described as *co-optation*, entails "inclusion of potential trouble makers." This scenario corresponds closely to Lijphart's "self-denying prophecy," which was referred to in the previous chapter. Beyond the European cases that Lijphart (1969) used as his source of inspiration, over-sized coalitions comprising all important ethnic groups have also been common in Sub-Saharan Africa, at least in part because of their anticipated stabilizing effect (Francois, Rainer and Trebbi, 2015). The latter option, which is tantamount to "exclusion of potential trouble makers," can be referred to as *risk*

---

[11] Warning against the assumption that inclusion and exclusion can be treated as independent variables, Fearon (2010) suggests that treating them in this way is tantamount to what Rodrik (2012) calls "policy regressions."

diversion. It is also a distinct possibility, especially in cases where the government fears that governmental power sharing will give rebels an opportunity to topple the government through a military coup. In such scenarios, Roessler (2011) explains, incumbent elites may calculate that fighting a low-intensity war far away from the capital is preferable to opening the doors to insurrection in the capital, or possibly even within the presidential palace.

While these considerations are certainly to be taken seriously their generality is far from guaranteed even in Sub-Saharan Africa. As we have seen, Roessler (2016) offers an important extension of his earlier analysis by considering the conditions under which power sharing is "self-enforcing," focusing on the power relationship between the government and its potential challengers (see also Roessler and Ohls, 2018). Conceiving of the decision-making situation as a security dilemma in weakly institutionalized states, this interpretation anticipates that governmental power sharing will be more likely to hold as long as the power balance between the two sides is reasonably even, which allows each side to threaten the other side credibly. Despite its theoretical importance, however, Roessler's approach is yet to be backed up by an empirical research design that takes endogeneity into account explicitly.

Thus, we are more inclined to follow Lijphart's original co-optation logic by postulating the following:

Master Hypothesis 4. Governments are more likely to introduce governmental and territorial power sharing in order to co-opt potential rebels than less threatening groups, which means that power sharing cannot be considered exogenous in studies of conflict onset.

Whether co-optation or risk diversion applies is not merely of academic interest, but crucially affects our ability to assess the effectiveness of governmental and territorial power sharing. Indeed, naïve analysis that fails to take endogeneity into account is likely to underestimate such effects if governments tend to include ethnic groups that are likely to take up arms. Conversely, the opposite situation featuring exclusion of potential trouble makers would lead us to overestimate the pacifying influence of power sharing arrangements.

To set the empirical record straight, this book uses two strategies that are designed to handle endogeneity in general, and reverse causation in particular. First, one effective way of overcoming the problem of endogeneity is *instrumental variable estimation* (for an overview, see Sovey and Green, 2011). The basic idea behind this approach is to find a variable, referred to as the instrument, that correlates with the potentially endogenous regressor but is otherwise unrelated to the dependent variable (for applications to civil conflict, see, e.g., Miguel, Satyanath and Sergenti, 2004; Savun and Tirone, 2011). Put differently, in order to assess the validity of the exclusion-conflict nexus, we need to articulate a causal pathway that directly affects inclusion but is otherwise unrelated to conflict (for more details, see Chapters 6 and 8).

Second, we will also rely on *strategic models*, which offer a more intuitive and direct way of capturing endogeneity. Pioneered by McKelvey and Palfrey (1998) and Signorino (1999) for sequential move games, this approach allows us to capture strategic interaction by formulating a statistical model that mirrors the theoretically assumed strategic interaction. By assuming that actors make errors when they make their choices at respective decision nodes, it is possible to generate probability distributions associated with each action, and thus also over all possible outcomes of the strategic interaction. The method enables us to estimate the effect of covariates by assigning them to the utilities that the actors in the game obtain from each of the possible outcomes. In our particular case, we use statistical strategic models to analyze how the government's use of power sharing depends on how it expects the (potential) rebels to react. We will return to these issues in Chapters 7 and 9.

3.5   Analyzing Links between Governmental and Territorial Power Sharing

Without blurring the concepts of governmental and territorial power-sharing practices, this book explicitly studies the links between these types of inclusive governance. More specifically, our analysis highlights the extent to which these two forms of power sharing complement and reinforce each other, bearing in mind that a failure to do so risks losing sight of the full potential of territorial power sharing (see McGarry and O'Leary, 2004).

Yet, it is important to take the critics' concerns seriously. Chapter 2 refers to several scholars, including Nordlinger (1972) and Roeder (2005), who have warned against the centrifugal tendencies of ethnic federalism and other types of autonomy granted to ethnic groups (see also Roeder, 2007). In brief, their main concern refers to the risk that territorial power sharing will empower and encourage separatism. Such fears of a "slippery slope" are also widespread among political leaders in multi-ethnic states. The ultimate risk faced by constitutional engineers is that federal and autonomous arrangements turn out to be unstable equilibria that tip over into either recentralization or the collapse of the polity (see, e.g., Roeder, 2009; Griffiths, 2016). Ultimately, the most acute challenge lies in enforcing constitutional deals in the face of uncertainty and weak institutions, especially in postwar settings characterized by mistrust and even hatred.

We posit that governmental power sharing can play a crucial role as a complement to shared territorial power. This combined confidence-building effect is likely to be particularly pronounced in relationships that have already seen violence. To see this, we return to the three specific mechanisms that we used to motivate Master Hypothesis 3. First, in terms of attitudes to violence, it can be expected that granting excluded groups regional autonomy may be helpful because it allows group leaders to argue for peaceful change within the system. In a post-conflict situation such concessions may also send a costly signal of governmental moderation (Lake and Rothchild, 2005, 123). Yet, territorial power sharing is less effective than governmental power sharing as a pacifying tool in a climate of suspicion. Executive-level power sharing among the conflict parties creates a bargaining framework that gives them a stake in the cohesion of the state: "By this means, ethnonationalist leaders will be transformed from peripheral magnates anxious to drain power from the state into stakeholders committed to upholding it" (Hechter, 2004, 288). Moreover, such a consociational setup makes it easier to restore inter-ethnic trust and to reduce uncertainty for all parties: "By promoting an iterated exchange process, power-sharing institutions can prove reassuring, laying the basis for an ongoing relationship" (Rothchild, 2008, 150).

Second, we have argued that fragmentation of the separatist movement increases the risk of secessionist war. Under such circumstances, inclusive practices at the level of the state's central executive may help prevent further splintering by showing that the government is ready to offer more far-reaching concessions than mere regional autonomy. Governmental power sharing could thus serve to reduce grievances more effectively, through more significant and costly concessions, while at the same time prompt more frequent interactions between the parties that will increase transparency and restore confidence. If inclusively implemented, the governmental component of power sharing gives moderate group representatives an incentive to invest in the country's future (Mattes and Savun, 2009). In other words, the combination of territorial and governmental power-sharing practices are likely to have both a grievance-reducing and a confidence-building impact.

Finally, adding governmental power-sharing practices to an autonomy deal has the potential of curbing separatists' mobilizational capacity. This mechanism operates primarily through fear-reduction and increased transparency, by improving the government's ability to monitor potential separatists' mobilization efforts while steering them away from creating institutions that can be used as a nascent government (see, e.g., Hartzell and Hoddie, 2003). Yet, safeguards relying on governmental power sharing can also be expected to reduce mobilization through grievance reduction, because recruitment of radicalized rebels is generally harder the more accommodative the government's approach becomes (Cederman, Gleditsch and Buhaug, 2013, Ch. 3).

For all these reasons, it seems reasonable to conclude that territorial power sharing will be stabilizing provided that appropriate safeguards are in place. We can now sum up the relevant logic in our final master hypothesis:

Master Hypothesis 5. The peace-inducing effect of territorial power-sharing practices is reinforced if they operate in tandem with governmental power-sharing practices.

In Chapter 8, we will offer a more thorough derivation of this claim, while disaggregating it into operational hypotheses. In fact, this master hypothesis can be seen as a special case of a more general point that has received support in the literature on peace agreements. For example, Hartzell and Hoddie (2007) argue that the more dimensions peace keeping encompasses, the more likely its pacifying impact (see also Hoddie and Hartzell, 2003). Moreover, there are other ways to provide incentives that provide ethnic elites with incentives to invest in the overall political system of a state, including electoral requirements in favor of trans-ethnic party affiliation (Horowitz, 1985). Yet, we believe that despite its pacifying potential, the synergy between governmental and territorial power sharing remains understudied. Failure to consider this connection is likely to obscure the full potential of territorial power-sharing practices as tools of conflict reduction and may lead analysts to reject such instruments prematurely.

3.6   Conclusion

In this chapter, we have laid out our main theoretical ideas that we will rely on and further develop in the empirical chapters that follow in the next part of the book. Rather than analyzing the institutional details of power sharing merely as parts of peace agreements, our approach builds on an integrated theory of conflict. As proper medical treatment requires a proper diagnosis, this research strategy assumes that ways to end and prevent conflict depend on its proper diagnosis.

However, this means that successful conflict reduction hinges on the appropriateness of the chosen theory of conflict. Because our previous work in the area has focused on the link between exclusion and conflict, it suggests that inclusive governance is both intuitive, appealing and empirically promising. Yet, as we have argued, it would be a mistake to treat the grievance-reducing logic as a straightforward extrapolation from the original exclusion argument. Indeed, this is the reason why we consider the confidence-building impact of power sharing as well. Such an extended theoretical scope turns the attention to opportunity-related aspects, including the problems relating to uncertainty and mistrust. At this point, we thus bring the extended theory to bear on empirical data in the second part of the book.

Part II

Analyzing the Effect of Power Sharing on Civil War

4   Power Sharing and Civil War: Data and Baseline Models

This chapter sets the stage for the empirical analyses that will be presented in the following chapters. We first introduce data on power-sharing practices before turning to formal institutions. The chapter closes with an overview of how these data are used to address the four main arguments in the subsequent empirical chapters.

4.1   Power-Sharing Practice and Its Effect on Conflict

Since we argue that power-sharing practices, rather than formal institutions, exert a direct effect on conflict, it is imperative to find a suitable dataset on ethnic groups and their access to political power. Until recently, the most established data resource of this kind was the Minorities at Risk dataset (Gurr, 1993), which, as the name suggests, catalogues information on minorities that are targeted by their respective states, including their grievances, level of political mobilization and rebellious activities (see also Gurr, 2000b). The Minorities at Risk (MAR) dataset broke new ground as regards the political relevance of ethnic groups and soon became the standard source for studies of ethnic mobilization, protest, and ethnic group rebellion (see, e.g., Birnir et al., 2015; Gurr and Moore, 1997; Olzak, 2006; Walter, 2006b).

However, the MAR dataset's focus on minorities "at risk" makes it less suitable for our purposes. Although featuring some "advantaged minorities," the dataset remains incomplete since it does not include majority groups, some of which may be at risk of being challenged by disadvantaged minorities or are indeed discriminated against themselves in regimes of ethnic minority rule. For inferential analyses, this particular sample composition is unproblematic as long as the outcome of interest is unrelated to the mechanism of group selection applied in MAR, but it may lead to biased results otherwise (Hug, 2013).[1] Since our

---

[1] In response to these concerns, the MAR research team recently presented a new dataset of ethnic groups, labeled A-MAR, that introduces a comprehensive list of

analysis cannot assume away this problem, we need to rely on a more comprehensive group list.

4.1.1 Operationalizing power-sharing practices with the Ethnic Power Relations Dataset

Fortunately enough, there is such an alternative. Inspired by the pioneering approach of the MAR dataset, the *Ethnic Power Relations* (EPR) data provide a more comprehensive selection of politically relevant ethnic groups, including minorities *and* majorities, and discriminated as well as state-controlling groups (Vogt et al., 2015). Wherever possible, we will rely on a version that offers coverage from 1946 through 2017.[2] The EPR dataset defines ethnicity as a subjectively experienced sense of commonality based on a belief in common ancestry and shared culture (Weber, 1946). Different markers may be used to indicate such shared ancestry and culture, such as a common language, similar phenotypical features, or adherence to the same faith. An ethnic group is considered politically relevant if at least one political organization has claimed to represent its interests at the national level or if its members are subjected to state-led political discrimination.

The EPR dataset provides annually coded information on politically relevant ethnic groups, their relative sizes as a share of the total population, and their access to state power. In agreement with our definition of governmental power sharing, state power refers to executive power, that is the number of seats in the cabinet or control over the army in military regimes.[3] Power access is measured with an ordinal scale composed of three main categories, depending on whether a group (1) controls power alone, (2) shares power with other ethnic groups, or (3) is excluded from executive state power. Each of these three main categories is divided into several subcategories:

"socially relevant" ethnic identities by relying on a mainly "cultural" definition of (potentially) relevant ethnic groups (Birnir et al., 2015).

[2] EPR version 1.1 was introduced by scholars from ETH Zürich and the University of California in Los Angeles (UCLA) on the basis of an online expert survey (Cederman, Wimmer and Min, 2010). Recently, a version of EPR was published with coverage until 2021.

[3] It should be noted that influence is measured in terms of *de facto* influence rather than the mere number of cabinet posts. Specifically, the EPR dataset does not count "token representation" as real influence, although the data draw a distinction between the subcategories of monopoly and dominant groups (see below). For example, Iraq's foreign minister Tariq Aziz's in Saddam Hussein's cabinet is not coded as a representative of the Christian community in Iraq despite Aziz's own Christian identity since he in no effective way represented this group in the country's policy making. Obviously, whether token representation applies is a difficult judgment call, but still preferable to mechanical counts of cabinet positions.

1. *The group rules alone:* Monopoly or dominant groups. In contrast to monopoly power, the status of dominant indicates "token" representation of other ethnic groups in the executive.
2. *The group shares power:* Senior partners or junior partners, depending on the group's absolute influence in the executive (i.e., irrespective of group size).
3. *The group is excluded:* Powerless, discriminated, or self-excluded groups. While powerless means that the group is simply not represented (or does not have influence) in the executive, discrimination indicates an active, intentional, and targeted discrimination by the state against group members in the domain of public politics. The special category of self-exclusion applies to groups that have voluntarily excluded themselves from central state power, in the sense that they control a particular territory of the state, which they have declared independent from the central government (as, e.g., Northern Cyprus).

Groups falling into one of the first two main categories can be regarded as politically *included* in distinction to the *excluded* groups in the third main category.[4] For the purpose of this book, we operationalize governmental power-sharing practices as the second of the three categories, that is both senior and junior partners.

In addition to the national power variable, the dataset measures access to executive power at the regional level with a separate *regional autonomy* variable, which is used to operationalize territorial power-sharing practices.[5] For a group to be coded as regionally autonomous, two conditions must be jointly satisfied. First, there must be a meaningful[6] and active regional executive organ that operates below the state level (e.g., the departmental, provincial, or district level) but above the local administrative level, *and* group representatives must exert actual influence on the decisions of this entity, acting in line with the group's local interests.

---

[4] These categories can also be referred to as *ethnic groups in power* or EGIPs, and *marginalized ethnic groups* or MEGs (Cederman and Girardin, 2007).

[5] In previous versions of EPR, regional autonomy status was coded as a subcategory of exclusion at the national level. However, in the current version it is treated as an independent category. Note that the autonomy dimension is not coded for "monopoly" and "dominant" groups since their political interests are assumed to be sufficiently represented at the level of the central state.

[6] The term "meaningful" here refers to executive organs that carry out core competencies of the state, involving, for example, cultural rights (language and education) and/or significant economic autonomy (e.g., the right to levy taxes or very substantial spending autonomy).

Table 4.1. *EPR group years by power access category (1946–2017)*

	No terr. power sharing	Terr. power sharing	Total
One group rule	4,750 (11.7%)	0	4,750 (11.7%)
Gov. power sharing	9,265 (22.8%)	2,260 (5.6%)	11,525 (28.4%)
Exclusion	18,627 (45.9%)	5,651 (13.9%)	24,278 (59.9%)
Total	32,642 (80.5%)	7,911 (19.5%)	40,553 (100.0%)

The second condition also implies that a given regional entity must have *de facto* (as opposed to mere *de jure*) political power. Federal states, such as Switzerland or India, are the most typical (but not the only) such systems of regional autonomy. The Kurdistan Regional Government in northern Iraq is another example of meaningful political power at the substate level. In contrast, the regional administrative subdivisions in many Central and East European countries do not possess any political or fiscal powers and thus cannot be considered meaningful political decision-making bodies. Furthermore, nonterritorial forms of autonomy (such as the recently established minority councils in Serbia) do not fall under this definition of regional autonomy.

Table 4.1 provides an overview of all group years from 1946 through 2017 by the three main categories of central power access as well as regional autonomy. For the relevant sample period, 28.4 percent of the groups participated in governmental power-sharing arrangements, as opposed to 11.7 percent that ruled alone. As many as 59.9 percent of the groups had no access to central power. In terms of territorial power sharing, 19.5 percent of the groups were coded as enjoying some kind of *de facto* regional autonomy. The table also indicates that territorial power sharing is more likely for excluded groups (13.9 percent) than for included groups (5.6 percent).

Shifting the focus to the last year of the sample, 2017, we repeat this exercise in Table 4.2 in order to get a feeling for what the most recent cross-sectional sample looks like. Specifically, there were 244 ethnic groups that participated in governmental power-sharing arrangements of which 49 were also granted territorial power sharing. By contrast, 70 groups ruled alone and 408 groups were excluded. The latter category comprised 89 groups that enjoyed territorial power sharing. All in all, the number of territorial power-sharing groups was 138 out of a total sample of 724. A direct comparison with Table 4.1 tells us that whereas governmental power-sharing practices have become more common compared to the average frequencies since 1946 (an increase from 28.4 percent

Table 4.2. *EPR group years by power access category in 2017*

	No terr. power sharing	Terr. power sharing	Total
One group rule	70 (9.7%)	0	70 (9.7%)
Gov. power sharing	196 (27.1%)	49 (6.8%)	245 (33.9%)
Exclusion	319 (44.1%)	89 (12.3%)	408 (56.4%)
Total	585 (80.9%)	138 (19.1%)	723 (100.0%)

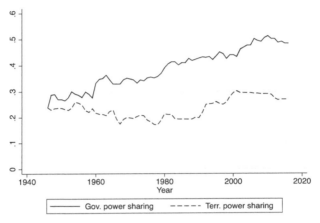

Figure 4.1 Trends in shares of countries with governmental and territorial power sharing

to 33.9 percent) the frequency of territorial power sharing has declined somewhat (a decrease from 19.5 percent to 19.1 percent).

4.1.2   Global and regional trends in power-sharing practices

Having introduced the group-based coding of EPR, we are now ready to trace the evolution of power-sharing practices thus measured at the macro level. Since the end of World War II, how much power sharing has there been around the world? Are there trends toward more or less governmental and territorial power-sharing practices? Aggregating the group-level coding to the country level, Figure 4.1 provides an overview of the main trends in governmental and territorial power sharing since 1946 through 2017. In this first graph, we display the share of countries that feature at least one group-level instance of either type of political inclusion. The graph tells us that the number of countries whose executives include shared power has gone up from a fourth to around half

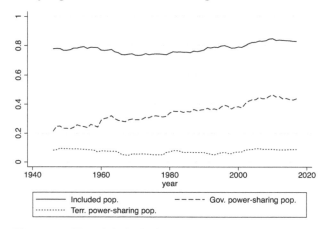

Figure 4.2 Trends in inclusion and governmental and territorial power sharing as countries' population share

by the end of the sample. In contrast, territorial power sharing has not seen any significant increase from the end of World War II, although the share of countries has grown somewhat from lows around 20 percent to around 30 percent.

However, these simple initial measures of power sharing at the country level may prove somewhat misleading, since they do not reflect changes that ensue when power sharing is applied to more rather than fewer groups. For this reason, Figure 4.2 traces the same two types of power sharing, together with overall inclusion in the government whether through one-group rule or governmental power sharing, as average share of each country's population from 1946 through 2017. Whereas the population shares of included groups declined slightly until the 1970s and increased after that, governmental power-sharing practices have recorded a steady increase since 1946 from about a fifth up to more than double that share. In contrast, the trend for territorial power sharing has not changed all that much over the past seventy years. Furthermore, the level did not exceed 10 percent of the states' population.

Yet, the global trends obscure major differences between the world regions. Before considering power sharing specifically, we study the regional distribution of the overall level of inclusion. Figure 4.3 reveals that whereas the West is characterized by very high levels of inclusion amounting to around and beyond 90 percent, the other extreme is represented by the Middle East and North Africa (MENA) states that reach an average of only 70 percent with a generally falling trend.

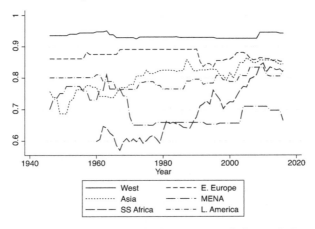

Figure 4.3 Trends in inclusion as countries' population share represented in executive

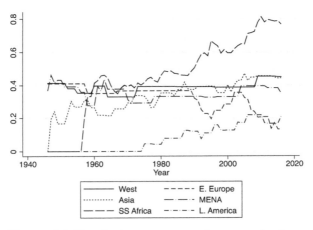

Figure 4.4 Trends in governmental power sharing as countries' population share

All other world regions appear to converge to shares around 80–85 percent, with Sub-Saharan Africa and to some extent also Asia, exhibiting increasing trends.

We now turn to explicit measures of power sharing. Figure 4.4 subtracts the share of the population that is represented through groups that rule alone from the total included population and shows the remaining average share of that is represented through governmental power sharing. Here the increasing trend of the Sub-Saharan cases that by far surpasses that of other world regions is striking. It turns out that almost all of the high level of inclusion in Africa, as recorded by the previous figure, can be attributed to a powerful surge in governmental power-sharing practices. In recent years, as many as 80 percent of the Sub-Saharan groups participated in some kind of governmental power-sharing arrangement. In contrast, the West, Asia and the MENA region experienced much more modest numbers, at about half of the African level and with much more stability in the trends. To some extent, Asia differs from this pattern because, there, governmental power sharing has gained in popularity, from around a fifth of the population. Interestingly, in Eastern Europe (here including the Former Soviet Union as well), the trend is pointing downward from shares of about 40 percent falling below half of that level in recent years. In contrast, Latin America has seen growing numbers from no governmental power sharing at all until well into the 1970s up to levels comparable to Eastern Europe.

Finally, we explore the trends in territorial power-sharing practices around the world (see Figure 4.5) . From this perspective, the decline of power sharing in Eastern Europe and the former Soviet Union becomes even more dramatic. In fact, this region was the bastion of territorial power sharing until the end of the Cold War, reaching as high a level as 40 percent during the final two decades under communism. Yet, recent years have seen a decrease down to less than 10 percent. In the West, by contrast, territorial power-sharing practices have been gaining in prominence from about 15 percent up to well above 20 percent. There has also been a more modest growth of territorial power sharing

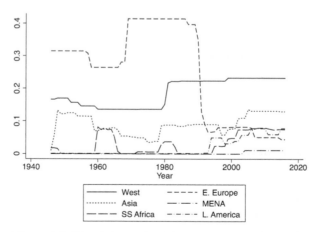

Figure 4.5 Trends in territorial power sharing as countries' population share

in Asia, following a fall until about 1980. However, the levels are only slightly more than half of those recorded for Western states. As with governmental power sharing, Latin America has experienced some new cases of territorial power sharing in more recent years, but the level remains well below 10 percent. Finally, the MENA region is positioned at the very bottom of this comparison with hardly any cases of territorial power sharing at all.

4.1.3   Power-sharing practices and conflict: Country-level evidence

It is now time to have a first look at the link between power-sharing practices and conflict. To establish this link, group-specific conflict data are needed. Again, the EPR dataset provides the necessary information (Vogt et al., 2015). The ACD2EPR component dataset contains this important building block. Originally introduced by Wucherpfennig et al. (2012), this dataset establishes a mapping between the EPR group and the Armed Conflict Dataset (ACD) of the Uppsala Conflict Data Program (Gleditsch et al., 2002). Thus, a group-level conflict is coded if there is at least one fighting rebel organization that has advanced a claim on behalf of the relevant EPR group and there is significant recruitment of fighters from that group.

In this section, we aggregate the power sharing and conflict variables to the country level. Thus, following our definition of governmental power-sharing practices, this coding indicates that a country features governmental power sharing as soon as there are at least two EPR groups that engage in power sharing. Likewise, we identify territorial power-sharing practices at the country level as soon as there is at least one EPR group that enjoys autonomy. Similarly, conflict onsets are aggregated to the country level for any country year that includes at least one group-level onset.

Based on these simple specifications, Table 4.3 depicts the correlation between governmental power-sharing practices and the outbreak of

Table 4.3. *Conflict frequency conditional on governmental power sharing at country level*

	No conflict onset	Conflict onset	Total
No gov. power sharing	4,652 (97.9%)	98 (2.1%)	4,750
Gov. power sharing	3,187 (97.2%)	91 (2.8%)	3,278
Total	7,839 (97.6%)	189 (2.3%)	8,028

$\chi^2 = 4.29$, $p = 0.038$

Table 4.4. *Conflict frequency conditional on territorial power sharing at country level*

	No conflict onset	Conflict onset	Total
No terr. power sharing	5,994 (98.2%)	109 (1.8%)	6,103
Terr. power sharing	1,845 (95.8%)	80 (4.2%)	1,925
Total	7,839 (97.8%)	189 (2.3%)	8,028

$\chi^2 = 39.75$, $p = 0.000$

ethnic civil conflict using all group years from 1946 through 2017 as the sample. This first simple test of Master Hypotheses 1a would lead us to believe that power sharing has a conflict-fueling, rather than a pacifying, effect. In fact, the probability of outbreak increases from 2.1 percent to 2.8 percent for country years with governmental power sharing. The correlation is significant at the level of $p = 0.038$. The positive link between power sharing and conflict is even stronger in the case of territorial power sharing, as shown by Table 4.4. Here the probability increases from 1.8 percent to 4.2 percent as soon as there is at least one EPR group that has been granted territorial autonomy. If this were the final word on Master Hypothesis 1b we would have to reject it.

Yet, it would be very much premature to use such correlational information to conclude that power sharing has a conflict-provoking impact. Naïve tests of this kind say nothing about confounding variables that may introduce biases. For this reason, we turn to a series of multiple regression models (see Table 4.5). These models regress the governmental and territorial power-sharing variables, together with various control variables, on the onset of ethnic civil conflict. The control variables include the ethnic fractionalization index based on the relevant EPR groups, logged and lagged Gross Domestic Product (GDP) and population of the state in question, as well as an indicator for ongoing conflict during the previous year.[7]

Using the simple dichotomous measures of power sharing as in Figure 4.1, Model 1 in Table 4.5 reports relatively weak effects on conflict that cannot be statistically separated from zero. Whereas countries with any power sharing at the center are less inclined to experience civil war, the opposite appears to hold for those with at least one

---

[7] It should be noted that the onset variable is coded as 0 for ongoing conflict. In addition, the models feature peaceyears counts as a cubic polynomial (not shown) (Carter and Signorino, 2010).

Table 4.5. *Country-level analysis of power sharing (PS) and conflict*

	(1) Conflict onset	(2) Conflict onset	(3) Conflict onset	(4) Conflict onset
Gov. PS at all	−0.273 (0.222)			
Terr. PS at all	0.272 (0.227)			
Incl. pop. share		−0.879** (0.339)		
Dominant pop. share			−1.103* (0.534)	
Gov. PS pop. share			−0.767* (0.336)	
Terr. PS pop. share			−0.528 (0.371)	
Gov. PS groups				−0.965** (0.368)
Terr. PS groups				0.150 (0.335)
Ethnic frac.	1.159** (0.443)	0.589 (0.385)	0.424 (0.565)	1.117** (0.419)
Log GDP, lag	−0.325** (0.101)	−0.284** (0.103)	−0.277** (0.105)	−0.329*** (0.094)
Log population, lag	0.204*** (0.056)	0.258*** (0.053)	0.288*** (0.061)	0.191** (0.059)
No. prev. conflicts	0.136*** (0.024)	0.144*** (0.026)	0.148*** (0.026)	0.138*** (0.024)
Ongoing conflict	−0.912** (0.325)	−0.905** (0.336)	−0.883** (0.334)	−0.913** (0.319)
Constant	−3.006** (1.126)	−2.974** (1.047)	−3.164** (1.191)	−2.521* (1.116)
Observations	7871	7871	7871	7871
Pseudo R^2	0.142	0.145	0.147	0.146

Standard errors in parentheses
$+ p < 0.1$, $* p < 0.05$, $** p < 0.01$, $*** p < 0.001$

autonomous group. Thus these results offer no support to Master Hypothesis 1a and 1b. To facilitate comparison with previous research, we continue by evaluating how the included population influences the outbreak of internal conflict. The literature has established a strong link between exclusion of ethnic groups and rebellion (see, e.g., Cederman, Gleditsch and Buhaug, 2013). Since this book studies power sharing, Model 2 evaluates the opposite relationship, namely whether the demographic size of the included groups reduces the risk of conflict. Indeed, this is exactly what we find. However, as we have seen above, the size of the included population also encompasses those groups that rule alone, which should not be confused with power sharing. For this reason, Model 3 divides the included population into dominant groups, that include the EPR categories monopoly and dominant, and those groups that share power, here labeled as "governmental power sharing population share." In addition, Model 3 also features the share of the population that enjoys territorial power sharing, which is independent of the first two population measures. The coefficient estimates indicate that the dominant population share is negatively, and weakly significantly, associated with conflict reduction. Moreover, there is indeed a negative and significant effect for governmental power sharing on political violence. The influence of territorial power sharing is also negative, but less pronounced and does not reach conventional levels of significance.

Finally, Model 4 replaces the population-based measures of governmental and territorial power sharing with indicators that are based on the relative count of groups. The "governmental power-sharing group share" captures the share of all politically relevant EPR groups that participate in governmental power sharing. Similarly, the group share of territorial power sharing measures the proportion of all groups that are autonomous. Again, we get a strong result for governmental power-sharing practices: The coefficient is both negative and strongly significant. However, the share of territorial power-sharing groups exhibits a positive effect, albeit far from significant.

To conclude our preliminary country-level analysis, we investigate the predicted effect of power sharing on the probability of conflict onset (see Figure 4.6). Based on the estimates of Model 3 above, the figure shows that the probability of conflict onset decreases steadily from over 0.03 per year for countries with no governmental power sharing at all down to below 0.02 where all groups are included in a grand coalition. These probability differences may not seem very large, but since they are annual, they amount to considerable differences over longer time periods. For example, countries that run an annual risk of conflict at 0.03 experience an increase in conflict probability amounting to 0.08 over a ten year period compared to those countries that remain at an annual probability of 0.02. The predicted effects for the group share of included groups is very similar to the population-based share (cf. Model 4).

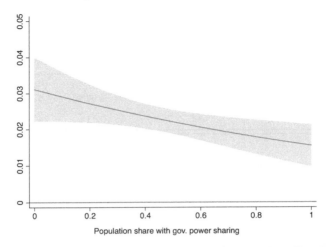

Figure 4.6 Predicted effect on the probability of conflict onset by the population share enjoying governmental power sharing

4.1.4 Power-sharing practices and conflict: Group-level evidence

The country-level analysis of the previous section offers some hints of a possible conflict-reducing effect of governmental power sharing on conflict (see Master Hypothesis 1a), but so far, we have found little evidence of any link between territorial power sharing and onset, thus casting doubt on Master Hypothesis 1b. Yet, this is hardly surprising because highly aggregated data tend to obscure relationships at the subnational level (Cederman and Gleditsch, 2009). This problem is especially serious for large countries, where national statistics say very little about the conditions in parts of the country. For example, it is unlikely that Russian indicators will tell us much about the risks of conflict in Chechnya since this region is very far from representative of the country as a whole. It is thus hardly surprising that we get stronger indications of an effect of governmental than of territorial power sharing. After all, territorial, and especially separatist, conflicts tend to occur in large countries and affect relatively limited and typically peripheral areas that may coexist with relative peace at the center of the country, as has mainly been the case in Russia and India.

For this reason, it makes sense to analyze both governmental and territorial power sharing with disaggregated, group-level data that are able to establish a more direct link between group-level properties and behavior. Fortunately, the EPR dataset provides information on both dimensions. Rather than treating power sharing as a property of the state,

Table 4.6. *Conflict per group-year and power-sharing category,*
1946–2017

	No terr. PS	Terr. PS	Total
No gov. power sharing	176 (1.00%)	18 (0.33%)	194 (0.85%)
Gov. power sharing	32 (0.35%)	21 (0.97%)	53 (0.47%)
Total	208 (0.79%)	39 (0.51%)	247 (0.73%)

then, this data resource views it as a property of specific groups. This is a major advantage in cases where the state treats the ethnic groups of the country differently. Far from being a dichotomous trait as implied by the Lijphartian notions of grand coalitions, we treat ethnic inclusion as an actor-specific feature that may vary from group to group depending on governmental policies. As we noted in the previous chapter, territorial power sharing does not have to be universally applied but can be highly asymmetric, as shown by cases such as Spain and the United Kingdom.

In this sense, group-level analysis is the most natural way to make use of information from the EPR dataset. As a first cut, we consider descriptive statics on the conflict propensity of groups benefiting from governmental and territorial power sharing. The margins of Table 4.6 tell us that both governmental and territorial power sharing appear to be associated with reductions in conflict propensity. Thus, in the absence of governmental power sharing, the average EPR group exhibits a conflict risk of 0.85 percent which is nearly cut by half down to 0.47 percent for those groups that benefit from governmental power sharing. Likewise, no territorial power sharing yields an onset probability of 0.79 percent, which is higher than 0.51 percent, the average conflict risk with territorial power sharing.[8] However, the internal cells of the table reflect a more complex relationship. In fact, both dimensions of power sharing are interdependent in that the effect of governmental power sharing depends on its territorial counterpart and vice versa. In other words, shared governmental power appears to pacify group behavior if the group in question is not autonomous. Likewise, territorial power sharing reduces conflict, but only in the absence of governmental power-sharing practices.

Again, it would be imprudent to draw far-reaching conclusions from such a simple correlational story. Clearly, the relationship between the

---

[8] T-tests reveal that both differences are significant at the $p = 0.0001$ and the $p = 0.0011$ levels respectively.

Table 4.7. *Group-level analysis of power sharing (PS) and conflict*

	(1) Conflict onset	(2) Conflict onset	(3) Gov. onset	(4) Terr. onset
Gov. PS	−0.858*** (0.206)	−0.828*** (0.202)	−0.735* (0.323)	−0.886** (0.292)
Terr. PS		−0.130 (0.295)	−0.178 (0.760)	−0.192 (0.339)
Gov. downgrade	1.270*** (0.207)	1.084*** (0.254)	1.657*** (0.325)	−0.442 (0.480)
Terr. downgrade		1.220* (0.577)	1.342 (1.255)	1.865*** (0.486)
Rel. group size	2.964* (1.298)	2.861* (1.331)	4.628* (1.861)	4.974* (2.177)
Rel. group size^2	−2.107 (1.699)	−2.023 (1.721)	−2.174 (2.007)	−10.347** (3.448)
No. prev. conflicts	0.727*** (0.094)	0.727*** (0.093)	0.796*** (0.090)	0.615*** (0.107)
Log country GDP, lag	−0.436*** (0.090)	−0.427*** (0.090)	−0.583*** (0.162)	−0.325* (0.152)
Log country population, lag	0.054 (0.072)	0.049 (0.080)	−0.154+ (0.088)	0.190+ (0.102)
Ongoing conflict	0.642** (0.224)	0.659** (0.224)	0.011 (0.339)	0.771* (0.318)
Constant	−1.471 (0.979)	−1.453 (1.034)	−0.760 (1.816)	−3.962* (1.618)
Observations	33,690	33,486	33,661	33,571
Pseudo R^2	0.143	0.145	0.157	0.164

Standard errors in parentheses
$+ \, p < 0.1$, $* \, p < 0.05$, $** \, p < 0.01$, $*** \, p < 0.001$

the independent and dependent variables may change dramatically once we consider other explanatory factors. As confirmed by current research and the country-level analysis presented above, multiple regression offers a better way of establishing whether power sharing affects the risk of rebellion. Table 4.7 presents a series of models pitched at the group level. In all cases, we rely on the aforementioned coding of group-level onset offered by the ACD2EPR dataset.

With disaggregated analysis, it is straightforward to code governmental and territorial power sharing based on the corresponding group-level properties. We rely on model specifications proposed by Cederman, Gleditsch and Buhaug (2013, Ch. 4). Following their approach, the models feature variables that indicate whether the group in question has experienced a status reversal during the previous two years, either with respect to governmental power sharing or also territorial power sharing (see "gov. downgrade" and "terr. downgrade" respectively).[9] Furthermore, the models also feature a variable that measures the groups' relative demographic size compared to the included population. We expect an inverse U-shaped relationship since smaller groups should be less likely to trigger territorial conflict due to their limited resources. Yet, very large groups are more inclined to try to topple the government in a governmental conflict. Thus, we enter relative group size as both linear and squared terms.[10]

In keeping with previous research, we also introduce a variable that counts the rebellion that the group experienced since the beginning of the sample or independence. As in the country-level analysis in the previous section, the models feature country-level controls for GDP per capita and population. There is also a dummy variable for ongoing conflict based on the ACD2EPR conflict data indicating if there was an ongoing conflict involving any other group in the country during the preceding year. Finally, as before, we use "peaceyears" (not shown) to capture the panel structure of the dataset (Beck, Katz, and Tucker, 1998).

As the country-level models of the previous section, the group-level analysis offers clear evidence of a pacifying effect exerted by governmental power sharing. However, territorial power sharing also exhibits some reduction in conflict propensity, but this effect does not reach statistical significance in any of the models. Model 1 in Table 4.7 offers a straight-forward replication of Cederman, Gleditsch and Buhaug's (2013, Ch. 4) analysis, according to which inclusion through governmental power sharing has a powerful conflict-dampening influence, and status reversals tend to trigger conflict. All the control variables behave as reported in previous research: Small and very large groups tend to rebel less than mid-sized ones and the number of previous conflicts boost the risk of civil war. Onsets are significantly rarer in highly developed countries but population size does not have a strong influence

---

[9] It should be noted that Cederman, Gleditsch and Buhaug (2013, Ch. 4) only analyzed downgrading with respect to governmental power sharing.

[10] The quadratic specification corresponds directly to (Cederman et al., 2015) rather than to (Cederman, Gleditsch and Buhaug, 2013). Relative group size $g \in [0, 1)$ comparing the population of the group G to the population of the incumbent I is defined as $\frac{G}{G+I}$ if the group is excluded and as G/I if the group is included (since the rebelling group left the incumbent coalition and would otherwise be counted twice).

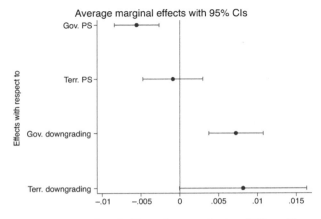

Figure 4.7 Predicted effect of power sharing (PS) and its revocation on probability of group-level onset

on the dependent variable. Shifting the attention to Model 2, we again fail to detect a strong conflict-reducing effect of territorial power sharing. Yet, status reversals through revoked autonomy are associated with a significantly higher risk of conflict that is of the same order of magnitude as downgrading with respect to governmental power sharing. These findings remain robust even when we divide the dependent variable into governmental and territorial onsets (see Models 3 and 4, respectively). Whereas governmental power sharing continues to reduce the risk of either type of rebellion, the pacifying influence of its territorial counterpart is much more modest and can never be statistically separated from zero.

Following the procedure of the previous section, we also provide predicted marginal conflict probabilities as a function of our main independent variables based on Model 2. Figure 4.7 confirms that power sharing exerts a clearly conflict-dampening effect in line with Master Hypothesis 1a. Yet, the same clear difference does not exist for territorial power sharing (see Master Hypothesis 1b). In this case, the effect cannot be distinguished from zero.

The effects of downgraded status are clearer than that of the static power-sharing variables. The two lower effect bars in Figure 4.7 reveal that groups that are rejected from included status are much more likely to rebel against the government. It should be noted that this effect is several times stronger than the difference between insiders and outsiders as shown in Figure 4.7 and the marginal positive effect on conflict probability is clearly separated from zero. There is a similar pattern for status reversals that concern territorial power sharing. In this case, however, the effect is less precisely estimated but still above zero.

All in all, our preliminary exploration of the EPR data has shown that governmental power-sharing practices may be associated with a decline in conflict probability, thus offering some tentative support for Master Hypothesis 1a. The evidence confirming that the same link for territorial governmental sharing is more mixed (see Master Hypothesis 1b). To get a firmer grip on whether these associations correspond to a causal effect, we will need to consider the remaining Master Hypotheses in the remaining empirical chapters. But we are still not done with our survey of the key data sources.

4.2   Formal Power Sharing and Its Effect on Conflict

Having explored the data on power-sharing practices, we now turn to corresponding data on formal power-sharing institutions. As shown in the two previous chapters, the move from Lijphart's (1968, 24) original conception of consociationalism as elite behavior to formal institutional features has led to a broadening of the institutional elements that are considered to constitute power sharing. This conceptual shift is, for instance, reflected in scholars tending to consider a proportional electoral system as evidence of "proportionality," which appears as one of the four main elements in the original conception of consociationalism.[11] The literature that assesses the effect of power-sharing provisions in peace agreements has introduced categories such as "political," "economic," and "military" power sharing, which considerably broadens the possible ways in which power can be shared.

Our conceptual discussion in the previous chapter emphasizes that this profusion of conceptions has contributed in no small way to the confusion that afflicts the literature on power sharing. Chapter 3 introduced definitions of both governmental and territorial power-sharing institutions that return to the key formal institutional elements that enable the sharing of power.

This endeavor resembles the research program on power sharing that was initiated by Kaare Strøm, Scott Gates, and their colleagues (Gates et al., 2016; Graham, Miller and Strøm, 2017; Strøm et al., 2017), whose impressive and comprehensive data collection effort returns to the

---

[11] In Lijphart's (1968) original conception, "proportionality" referred to the allocation of positions in the civil service. A much closer conceptualization appears in studies that consider the make-up of the armed forces (for instance Barak, 2012; Wilkinson, 2015).

original features highlighted in Lijphart's (1968) early writings.[12] In their conception, power can be shared in three different ways, namely through inclusion and dispersion or by constraining political power. Inclusiveness implies that there are institutional provisions that guarantee certain groups and actors participation in government affairs.

This type of power sharing is closely related to Lijphart's (1977) first two elements, namely the presence of a grand coalition and a mutual veto in governmental decision-making. Dispersive power sharing, on the other hand, comprises formal institutions that devolve power to sub-national entities. In the later interpretation of Lijphart's (1977) fourth element, namely segmental autonomy, by Lijphart (1985a) himself, federal arrangements and other measures of decentralization became an integral part of this dimension. Finally, constraining power sharing relies on formal institutions that limit the full exercise of power by the government and thus comes close to Rothchild and Roeder's (2005b) notion of "power dividing."

Thus, the two first dimensions of Strøm et al.'s (2015) Inclusion, Dispersion and Constraints (IDC) Dataset closely correspond to our notions of governmental and territorial power sharing. The data offers invaluable information on the formal institutions of power sharing gleaned from constitutions and peace agreements for the period 1975 to 2009. Hence, in what follows, we rely on their data collection to measure formal governmental and territorial power sharing.

Focusing exclusively on the executive, we use the following three variables drawn from the IDC dataset to capture governmental power sharing:[13]

- Mandated Grand Coalition
- Mutual Veto
- Reserved Executive Positions (Mandated)

---

[12] Their data collection covers a global sample of countries for the years 1975 to 2009. To code these formal institutional measures, they consulted constitutions and peace agreements. While their coding effort also comprises a partial assessment of whether an institutional provision was actually implemented, their dataset does not provide information about which groups or parties are targeted by specific inclusive and dispersive provisions. Thus, in this chapter we will only offer information on measures of power sharing coded at the national level. In a complementary coding effort, we identified which ethnic groups were targeted and/or could profit from the respective institutional provisions. We will present and discuss this data in more detail in the next chapter. There, we will treat this group-level information in the same way as we do the country-level data in this chapter.

[13] Strøm et al. (2017) also consider "Reserved Legislative Seats (Mandated)," but given our (and Lijphart's) focus on the executive, we exclude this variable from our conception of formal governmental power sharing.

Table 4.8. *Frequency of formal governmental power-sharing institutions*

	Grand coalition	Mutual veto	Reserved seats
No	4,835	4,741	4,737
Yes	48	173	159

Note: The entries correspond to the number of country-years between 1975 and 2009

While a mandated grand coalition and a mutual veto in a narrow sense correspond to Lijphart's (1977) first two dimensions of consociational elite behavior, the third dimension ensures that some seats in the executive are reserved for specific groups, parties, etc., which, if implemented, induces a more inclusive executive than in its absence.

Table 4.8 reports the distribution of country-years according to whether any of the three governmental power sharing institutions are present or not. It clearly transpires from this table that constitutions and peace agreements rarely include such provisions. In less than one per cent of all country-years there was a formal provision mandating a grand coalition. Slightly more frequent are provisions that assign a mutual veto to specific groups or that reserve seats in the executive for representatives of these groups.

To operationalize formal territorial power-sharing institutions, we use the following components from the IDC data (Strøm et al., 2015):[14]

- State/provincial governments locally elected
- Sub-national tax authority
- Sub-national education authority
- Sub-national police authority

These four elements reflect two dimensions. First, they indicate whether subnational units are governed by locally elected officials who are not appointed from the center. Second, they tell us if these authorities exert autonomous decision-making powers in specific central policy areas.

[14] To capture dispersive institutions, Gates et al. (2016) use a set of additional elements that we do not rely on. More specifically, we leave aside the indicator whether there are "State Constituencies in the Senate" and whether it holds that "Municipal governments are locally elected." Both of these indicators do not directly refer to the sharing of power at the regional level, which is the level we rely on in our definition (see Chapter 3).

Table 4.9. *Frequency of formal territorial power-sharing institutions*

	Local elections	Authority over:		
		tax	education	police
None	2,229	3,058	2,879	3,201
Only legislature/yes	1,392	1,540	1,503	1,585
Legislature and executive	1,034			

Note: The entries correspond to the number of country-years between 1975 and 2009

Table 4.9 reports the frequency of these territorial institutional provisions.[15] Compared to formal governmental power sharing institutions, formal provisions for territorial power sharing are much more prevalent in constitutions and peace agreements. Each of these elements exists in roughly one third of all country-years covered by the data collected by Strøm et al. (2017).

While we will offer a more detailed and case specific discussion of these institutional power-sharing measures in the next chapter, we now turn to the question of how these indicators can be combined into a single measure of formal governmental, respectively territorial, power sharing. Strøm et al. (2017) rely on factor analysis based on all twenty-one indicators covering inclusive, dispersive and constraining power-sharing provisions and extract three orthogonal factors. While proceeding in this way has the advantage of simplicity, the assumed underlying measurement model is problematic. For this reason, we rely on an item-response theory (IRT) model (see Martin, Quinn and Park., 2011) to estimate latent scores for each of our analytical dimensions, namely governmental and territorial power sharing.[16]

While we offer a more detailed discussion of the characteristics of formal governmental and territorial power-sharing institutions below, Figures 4.8 and 4.10 show how the averages of these measures have evolved in time and space. Regarding governmental power sharing,

[15] Note that the variable "Local elections" takes three values, namely 0 if neither legislature or executive is elected at the local level; 1 if the legislature is locally elected but the executive appointed by the central government; 2 if both the legislature and executive are locally elected" (Strøm et al., 2015).

[16] We offer a more detailed explanation of our derived measure of formal institutional power sharing in the online appendix to this chapter. There, we also compare our measures with those proposed by Strøm et al. (2017) and discuss why the indicators for constraining power sharing, in our view, are much closer to what Rothchild and Roeder (2005b) define as "power dividing" in opposition to "power sharing" (for a similar approach, see Bormann et al., 2019).

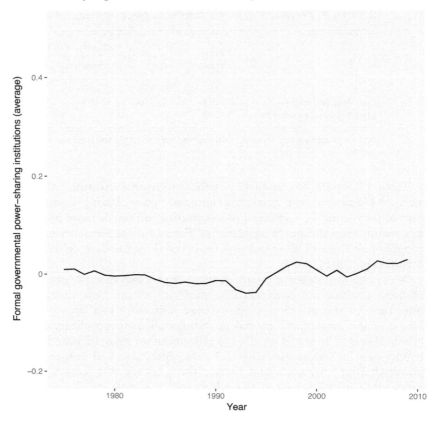

Figure 4.8 Formal governmental power-sharing institutions over time around the globe (average values)

Figure 4.8 reveals two trends at the global level: Throughout the 1970s and 1980s, formal institutions of governmental power sharing declined, and only started to increase again in the 1990s.

Figure 4.9 shows the divergent regional trends that underline the average trends. Most striking is the precipitous drop in the averages of formal institutions for governmental power sharing in Eastern Europe in the early 1990s. This, obviously, is linked to the collapse of the Soviet Union and the subsequent changes in the communist countries in this region. In the late 1990s, some of this drop was reversed, which, in turn, was followed by an additional decrease in formal governmental power sharing in Eastern Europe. Next to these dramatic changes the

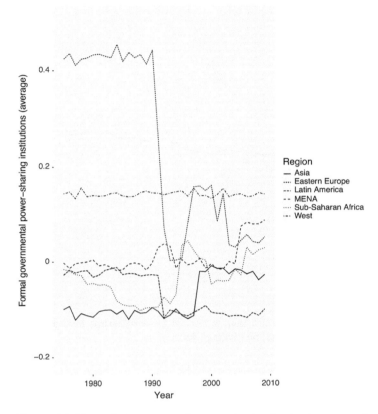

Figure 4.9 Formal governmental power-sharing institutions over time and regions (average values)

trends for the other regions depicted in Figure 4.9 are more modest. Thus, in the MENA region one observes a slight expansion in formal governmental power sharing. In Asia, a jump in the average level of our measure occurred in the late 1990s, while Latin America saw a decrease at around the same time. Finally, in Sub-Saharan Africa the last years of the Cold War period were characterized by a decline, followed by an increase, while for the Western world some variations across time around an almost identical average level shows some stability.

Regarding formal territorial power sharing, Figure 4.10 displays an overall trend towards more regional autonomy over the whole period covered by Strøm et al.'s (2017) data. This corresponds well with Gurr's (2000b) assessment that regional autonomy has become a more frequent

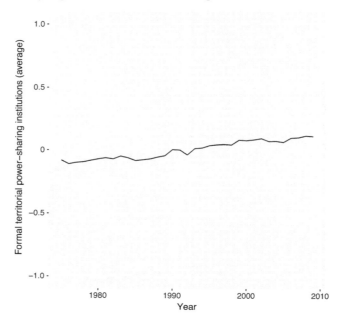

Figure 4.10 Formal territorial power-sharing institutions over time around the globe (average values)

means of addressing demands for self-determination until 2000. Again, Figure 4.11 shows that some important regional differences are hidden within this general trend. First of all, compared to Figure 4.9, we observe a slightly less dramatic drop in the presence of formal institutions for territorial power sharing in Eastern Europe. This drop again occurs at the beginning of the 1990s, but is followed by a rather steady recovery. Then, in the "West" and Asia, there is a slight, respectively a considerable, increase in the average values of our latent measure. Finally, while in the MENA region an upward trend is observable between 1975 and 2009, in Sub-Saharan Africa a slight decrease is followed by a slight increase in the averages.

Having presented how our measure for formal governmental and territorial power sharing evolved over time and space, we can now assess how these institutional provisions relate to ethnic conflicts. In Figures 4.12 and 4.13 we depict graphically the relationship between the extent of power sharing on the horizontal axis and whether in a particular country-year on ethnic conflict onset occurred (vertical axis). Given the dichotomous nature of the variables depicted on the vertical axes, we

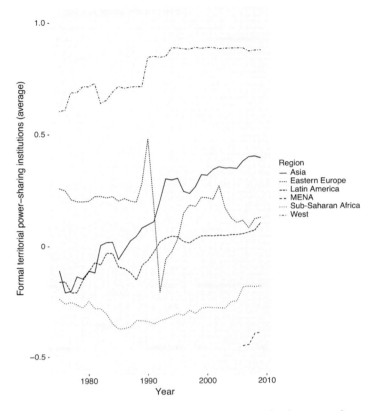

Figure 4.11 Formal territorial power-sharing institutions over time and regions (average values)

also depict a "naive" linear regression line which should simply be taken as a summary of the cloud of points depicted in the two panels.

In both figures there is barely any noticeable tendency, and if there is one it is a positive one. This implies that countries with more extensive formal power sharing institutions, both of the governmental and territorial kind, are slightly more likely to see ethnic conflict onsets. These results, however, have to be taken with a grain of salt. While this impressionistic analysis relies on a comprehensive dataset, and thus includes both pre- and post-conflict situations (see Master Hypothesis 3), it fails to evaluate our other arguments: We neither consider the issue of practices versus formal institutions (Master Hypothesis 2), nor do we consider interactions between governmental and territorial

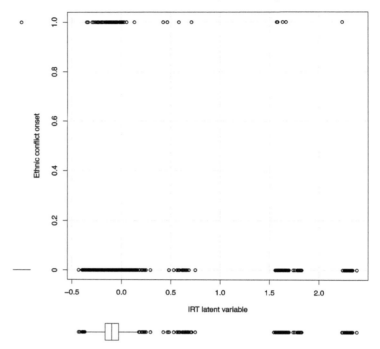

Figure 4.12 Formal governmental power-sharing institutions and ethnic conflict onset

power sharing (Master Hypothesis 5). And most importantly, we do not consider at all the reasons for which these formal power sharing institutions were adopted and thus face a considerable endogeneity problem (Master Hypothesis 4).

As a further (incomplete) step toward addressing these endogeneity concerns is to admit that there are certain characteristics that influence both ethnic conflict onsets and are related to the presence of formal power-sharing institutions. The introduction of additional explanatory variables as confounders more explicitly acknowledges that this is merely a preliminary observational study with no control over the treatment assignment, namely whether power-sharing institutions are adopted or not.

In Table 4.10 we report the results of a set of logit models where our main independent variables are our measures of formal governmental

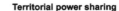

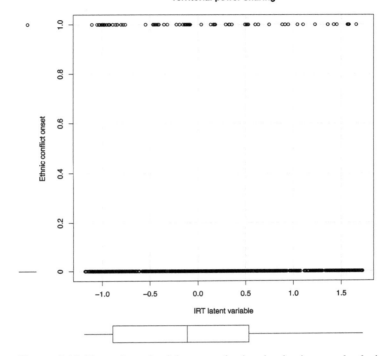

Figure 4.13 Formal territorial power-sharing institutions and ethnic conflict onset

and territorial power sharing. Our dependent variable corresponds to the onset of an ethnic conflict, respectively of an ethnic conflict related to territory. In addition to our main independent variables we add a set of control variables frequently used in conflict studies (Hegre and Sambanis, 2006).[17]

Despite adding controls for possible confounding factors our results regarding the effects of formal power-sharing institutions remain disappointing. In Table 4.10 we find a positive coefficient for our proposed measure of formal governmental power sharing, which is estimated, however, with a considerable amount of uncertainty (Model 1).

[17] The analyses reported here come close to those used by Bormann et al. (2019) as starting point for a causal mediation analysis. We will come back to this type of analysis in the next chapter, as it allows us to disentangle the effects of formal institutions from practices.

Table 4.10. *Governmental and territorial power-sharing institutions and ethnic conflict onset*

	(1)	(2)	(3)
	Conflict onset		Terr. onset
Gov. PS	0.256		
	(0.229)		
		0.095	0.067
		(0.166)	(0.219)
Log GDP per capita, lag	−0.561**	−0.560**	0.068
	(0.239)	(0.247)	(0.332)
Log Population, lag	0.498***	0.430**	0.912***
	(0.191)	(0.204)	(0.273)
ELF	0.704	0.769	0.868
	(0.478)	(0.478)	(0.681)
Prev. conflict	0.162***	0.167***	−0.004
	(0.052)	(0.054)	(0.051)
Constant	−5.133***	−4.678***	−11.021***
	(1.555)	(1.716)	(2.513)
Observations	4,506	4,506	5,017
Log likelihood	−359.577	−359.973	−218.066
Akaike inf. crit.	737.154	737.947	454.131

Note: * $p < 0.1$; ** $p < 0.05$; *** $p < 0.01$

The estimated coefficients for our control variables are in line with findings in the literature that richer countries are more likely to remain peaceful, while larger ones have a higher chance of seeing conflicts break out.

The overarching conclusion regarding the effect of formal power sharing is similar for territorial arrangements (see Table 4.10, Models 2 and 3). Our measure for formal territorial power sharing is positively associated with the likelihood of an ethnic conflict onset, whether generally (Model 2) or when limited to territorial conflicts (Model 3). In all cases, however, the uncertainty attached to the estimated coefficients reported in Table 4.10 is considerable, implying that we find no statistically significant effect of formal power-sharing institutions.

These results to some extent echo those reported in Gates et al. (2016) and Bormann et al. (2019). Formal power sharing institutions aiming at making a government more inclusive and at dispersing power appear not to affect ethnic conflict onsets.[18] However, these very preliminary analyses obviously are unable to handle any serious endogeneity concerns, nor do they consider the effect of power-sharing practices and the interplay between different types of power sharing

The empirical analyses in this chapter merely set the stage for the rest of the book. In fact, the country-level and the group-level analyses presented here fail to address the weaknesses of the literature as described in Chapter 3. We have not tried to compare the effects of informal power sharing to its formal, institutional counterpart (see Master Hypothesis 2). Nor have we attempted to tell apart situations before and after the first outbreak of conflict (Master Hypothesis 3). Furthermore, all models up to this point have treated power sharing as an exogenous factor (Master Hypothesis 4). Finally, we also have not made any effort to study interactions between governmental and territorial power sharing (Master Hypothesis 5). Instead, our goal has been much more modest: To take account of previous research and to provide an analytical baseline for the empirical analysis to follow in the remaining chapters of the book.

4.3   Plan of the Remaining Empirical Chapters

In the remaining chapters of Part II we evaluate our master hypotheses (MHs) that were introduced in Chapter 4 (see Table 4.11). All five chapters deal with the main challenge of assessing whether power sharing begets peace. Whereas Chapter 5 considers both governmental and territorial power sharing systematically (see MHs 1a and 1b), the remaining chapters specialize on either of these two respective hypotheses.

Adopting a comparative perspective, Chapter 5 evaluates the effect of formal institutions and practices on conflict onset (MH 2). Once having found that the effect mainly runs through practices, Chapters 6 and 7 proceed by considering the problem of endogeneity in the context of governmental power sharing (see MH 4) using instrumental-variable analysis and strategic estimation respectively. Without leaving

---

[18] To be precise, Gates et al. (2016) consider all conflict onsets and not only ethnic ones, and find evidence that their measure of "constraining" power sharing reduces the likelihood of conflict onset.

Table 4.11. *Plan of empirical chapter in Part II: Testing Master Hypotheses (MHs)*

		Chapter 5	Chapter 6	Chapter 7	Chapter 8	Chapter 9
MH 1a	Gov. power sharing	✓	✓	✓		
MH 1b	Terr. power sharing	✓			✓	✓
MH 2	Practice/inst.	✓				
MH 3	Pre/post-conflict			✓	✓	✓
MH 4	Endogeneity		✓	✓	✓	✓
MH 5	Gov./terr.				✓	✓

endogeneity aside, Chapter 8 shifts the main focus to territorial power sharing by analyzing the interactive effect of territorial and governmental power sharing (MH 5) as well as the contrast between pre- and post-conflict settings (MH 3). Finally, Chapter 9 follows up this analysis based on a strategic model.

5   Contrasting Formal Power-Sharing
Institutions and Practices*

As argued in Chapter 2, power sharing has over time become associated with particular formal political institutions. By focusing on the latter, scholars as a rule implicitly assume that formal institutions presumed to induce power sharing actually do so (for a notable exception see Pospieszna and Schneider, 2013). This is problematic for several reasons. First, from the literature on peace agreements, we know that many of the respective provisions fail to be implemented. Consequently, if we want to understand the effect of power sharing, only considering formal institutions will lead to biased conclusions as our main independent variable would be measured with error. Second, as Lijphart's (1969) focus on power-sharing practices highlights, these can also emerge without any formal institutions. Again, considering only power-sharing institutions will therefore miss the mark. In Chapter 3, we introduced Master Hypothesis 2 to capture this logic.

In order to test this master hypothesis, this chapter explores how formal power-sharing institutions relate to power-sharing practices and demonstrates the importance of the latter. Figure 5.1 summarizes our argument (cf. Bormann et al., 2019). The diagram shows three causal pathways that influence the outbreak of conflict. From left to right, the direct effect of formal power sharing triggers conflict without any involvement of practices. In the middle, formal institutions exert a mediated effect through practices (see the dashed arrow). Finally, it is also possible that power-sharing practices will have an independent, informal effect on onset that has nothing to do with formal institutions.

According to Master Hypothesis 2, we expect the direct effect to be dominated by the mediated effect. In order to test this effect, we will rely on mediation analysis (see Imai, Keele and Tingley, 2010). As argued

---

* In several parts of this chapter, we draw on the article by Bormann et al. (2019).

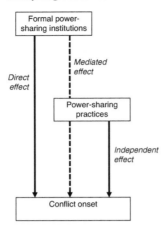

Figure 5.1 The effect of formal institutions and practices on conflict onset

above, however, we also believe that power-sharing practices can come about independently of formal institutions, and that their effects might be important as well. Thus, apart from assessing whether the effects of formal institutions are essentially mediated by practices we also wish to explore whether practices unrelated to formal institutions affect conflict onsets as well.

What does this conceptualization imply for our empirical analysis? First, we need to assess whether there is evidence supporting our view that not all formal power-sharing institutions are actually implemented. Next, it is necessary to assess whether formal rules (possibly devised without reference to ethnic groups) affect power-sharing practices among ethnic groups. Thanks to additional group-level data collection complementing Gates et al.'s (2016) dataset, we are able to assess this link both at the country and group levels. In both instances we find cases where formal power-sharing institutions have not been implemented, and thus remained without consequences for practices, as well as situations where power-sharing practices have been granted without formal power-sharing institutions. Thus, our theoretical approach depicted in Figure 5.1 seems justified.

As a next step, we therefore test the underlying propositions. Then we present empirical analyses showing that the effect of power-sharing practices induced by formal institutions on conflict is much smaller than the effect of these practices that is unrelated to institutional arrangements. Thus even from a substantive point of view, an exclusive focus on the effect of formal power-sharing institutions is misleading. The chapter ends with a discussion of whether our results are likely to be undermined by the endogeneity of both power-sharing institutions and practices.

5.1   The Implementation of Formal Power-Sharing Institutions

As noted in Chapter 2, the literature on peace-agreements finds that far from all provisions are actually implemented (Hoddie and Hartzell, 2003; Jarstad and Nilsson, 2008; Ottmann and Vüllers, 2015; Quinn and Joshi, 2016; Strøm et al., 2017). For instance, Jarstad and Nilsson (2008, 215) estimate that 75 percent of political pacts contained in peace agreements are implemented. For territorial and military pacts, however, this rate of implementation drops to 55 percent, respectively 34.5 percent (see also Quinn and Joshi, 2016).

As conceptualizations of power-sharing institutions in the literature on peace-agreements often lack clarity, it is a great advantage that the dataset produced by Gates et al. (2016) also provides information on the implementation of selected formal power-sharing arrangements. We depict this information in Table 5.1, which shows whether, according to Strøm et al. (2015), particular formal provisions for governmental power sharing have been implemented. These data are available for two of three power-sharing elements that we retain, as Strøm et al. (2015) do not offer this information on the implementation of the mutual veto or any of the indicators related to formal territorial power sharing.

For the two formal power-sharing provisions for which Table 5.1 provides information, we note that at most three quarters are implemented (Reserved executive positions), while for grand coalitions the record drops to two thirds.[1] Consequently, this simple table tells us that it is problematic to assume there to be a one-to-one relationship between formal power-sharing institutions and conflict without taking implementation into account.

The information depicted in Table 5.1 is, however, not without drawbacks. For instance, while it is true that there were reserved seats in the government of Bosnia and Herzegovina between 1996 and 2010 for different ethnic groups, it is far from obvious that this guaranteed a meaningful representation of all ethnic groups. Hence, even if a provision for reserved executive positions is formally implemented, such formal

---

[1] It is reassuring that these numbers fall very close to what Jarstad and Nilsson (2008, 215) find for the implementation of political pacts (namely 75 percent).

Table 5.1. *Power-sharing institutions and their implementation*

Power-sharing institution	Implemented	Not implemented
Grand coalition	Côte d'Ivoire 2007–2009 Zaire (DRC) 2004–2006 Rwanda 1993–2010 South Africa 1994–1996 Yemen 1991–1993 Fiji 1998–2010	Zaire (DRC) 1995–1997 Rwanda 1992 Nigeria 1975–1978
Reserved executive positions	Yugoslavia 1975–1991 Bosnia and Herzegovina 1996–2010 Guinea-Bissau 1999 Burundi 1995–2010 Angola 1995,1996, 1998 Sudan 2006–2010 Lebanon 1975–2010 Tajikistan 1999–2000 Fiji 1998–2010	Yugoslavia 1992 Tajikistan 1997–1998 Colombia 1975–1991 Cyprus 1975–2010

representation does not automatically generate power-sharing practices. While the lack of implementation of a formal power-sharing provision offers clear evidence that there is a lack in the sharing of power, it still might be the case that informal institutions induce accommodation (separate from constitutions and peace-agreements). In order to further assess both practices elicited by institutions and the practices unrelated to formal institutions, we shift our focus to practices. Equipped with information on power-sharing practices among ethnic groups, we can now assess the link between formal institution and practices depicted in Figure 5.1 in greater detail.

5.2   Formal Power-Sharing Institutions and Power-Sharing Practices

Our evaluation of how formal power-sharing institutions affect power-sharing practices relies on information coded in the EPR data (see Chapter 4). These data allow us to assess whether particular formal power-sharing institutions empower ethnic groups, and to detect the power-sharing practices that emerge in the absence of formal institutions. As suggested by Figure 5.1, both of these elements are necessary

Table 5.2. *Formal governmental power-sharing institutions and practices*

Coalition	Mandated grand coalition		Reserved seats in government		Mutual veto	
	no	yes	no	yes	no	yes
No	2,253	26	2,242	40	2,276	9
Yes	1,693	22	1,621	84	1,591	129

Table 5.3. *Formal territorial power-sharing institutions and practices*

| Groups with autonomy | Local elections | | | Authority over: | | | | | |
| | | | | taxes | | education | | police | |
	no	legislative.	legislative & executive	no	yes	no	yes	no	yes
No	1,683	967	611	2,319	888	2,228	894	2,414	998
Yes	187	282	348	271	513	286	464	328	409

to evaluate Master Hypothesis 2. As will be shown below, not all formal power-sharing institutions explicitly target ethnic groups. Thus, we are interested in the extent to which formal power-sharing institutions generate practices that allow ethnic groups to share power.

5.2.1   Country-level analysis

We start our assessment of the link between formal institutions and practices by considering aggregate information. Given the definition of power-sharing practices that we introduced in Chapter 3, it makes sense to consider situations where at least two ethnic groups have access to national executive positions as governmental power-sharing practice. Similarly, territorial power-sharing practices exist if at least one ethnic group enjoys regional autonomy. Tables 5.2 and 5.3 display the links between these indicators for practices and those on which our measures for formal power-sharing institutions are based (see Chapter 4).

While these tables show that there is a link between formal institutions and practices, the relationship is far from perfect. For instance, in Table 5.2 we find that in more than half the country-years in which formal institutions mandated a grand coalition, the government did not allow access to executive positions to two or more ethnic groups. Only in twenty-two out of forty-eight cases the corresponding mandate lead to the sharing of power among ethnic groups. For the two other indicators for formal institutions the link is much stronger. Thus, formal provisions for reserved seats in government and mutual vetoes are much more likely to lead to ethnically inclusive governments. This table also illustrates that in close to forty percent of all country-years, ethnic power-sharing practices are present even in the absence of formal institutional rules.

When we consider territorial power-sharing practices and formal institutions (Table 5.3) we find a much closer link. In the absence of elections at the subnational level or the absence of authority in any of the three policy domains, there are very few country-years during which at least one group had regional autonomy according to the EPR-data. In part, this relates to the fact that the coding of ethnic groups' "regional autonomy" depends on institutional provisions. Nevertheless, Table 5.3 also shows that not all institutional provision-granting authority to elected subnational organs necessarily empowers ethnic groups. While ethno-federal systems contain such a link, in other cases, the way in which a territory is divided up sometimes fails to empower ethnic groups at all, despite the formal institutional means available.

As we did in Chapter 4, we here rely on the share of the population affected by territorial power-sharing practices. In our analyses below, we use these measures as well that follow Bormann et al. (2019) quite closely. Consequently in Figures 5.2 and 5.3, we show how these population shares relate to the formal institutional provisions. Surprisingly, in neither of the two figures are there strong relationships. Thus, when it comes to governmental power-sharing institutions there is a considerable difference for provisions for a mutual veto. More specifically, if a mutual veto is prescribed then the share of the included population is on average considerably larger than in the absence of such a provision. It should be noted that the share of the excluded population in the former case is very small with few exceptions.

For the other two provisions we either find an opposite effect (grand coalition) or only small differences. Thus, generally, institutions guaranteeing a grand coalition or reserved seats in the executive hardly increase the share of the included population.

The picture is slightly different in the case of territorial power sharing. In Figure 5.3 it is clear that the share of the population that has been granted regional autonomy is small. Nevertheless, this figure shows that the presence of each of the institutional dimensions leads to a higher share of the population that profits from regional autonomy. Again, this finding is unsurprising given the partial reliance on formal institutional elements to determine if ethnic groups have regional autonomy.

The analyses presented so far have the disadvantage of relying on aggregate data. Consequently, while we might find that the formal

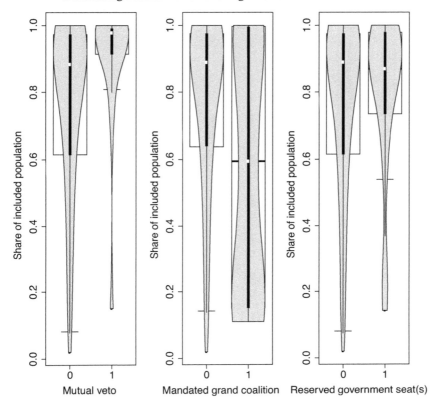

Figure 5.2 Formal governmental power-sharing institutions and practices (share of population)

institutions reserve executive seats for particular actors and that two ethnic groups share power, it could be that no ethnic group benefits from these reserved seats, either because the provision was not implemented or was granted to other ethnic groups or political actors. These difficulties can be circumvented with information on which, if any, ethnic groups were the intended beneficiaries of particular formal institutional provisions.

5.2.2 Group-level analysis

While offering information about formal power-sharing institutions in constitutions and peace agreements, the IDC data (Strøm et al., 2017)

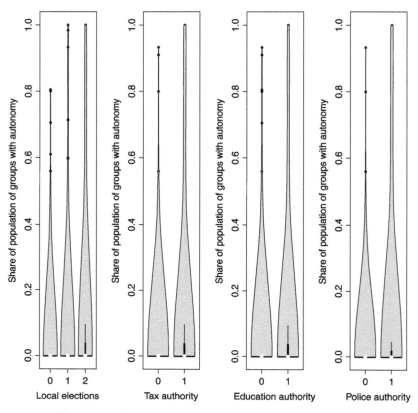

Figure 5.3 Formal territorial power-sharing institutions and practices (share of population)

says nothing about which actors or groups might profit from these provisions. In an additional data collection effort, we coded each power-sharing feature of the IDC data that we analyze in the current book (see Chapter 4) and assessed whether a specific ethnic group was explicitly granted governmental power sharing or implicitly affected by territorial power sharing through its settlement area.[2]

---

[2] Regarding formal governmental power-sharing institutions, we relied on the relevant passages in constitutions and peace agreements to assess whether a particular provision explicitly mentioned an ethnic group or an organization representing the latter's interest. We also consulted the coding notes available through the IDC dataset (see Strøm et al., 2015). Our coding is conservative in the sense that if, for instance, a constitution refers to the inclusion of the second strongest party in a government, we did not code this as

Since Our data collection effort shifts the unit of analysis to group-years. This allows us to assess in greater detail how formal institutional provisions translate into practices. Figure 5.4 depicts this relation for formal governmental power-sharing institutions. Since Table 5.2 indicates that these provisions are very rare in constitutions and peace-agreements, it is clear that only a few ethnic groups are selected for the three provisions that we retain. The figure also highlights that while\the presence of each of the three provisions slightly increases the chances that the targeted ethnic group is included in government, this effect is very small. More specifically, the likelihood that an ethnic group is part of the central government is only slightly smaller in the absence of these provisions, which is a situation that characterizes the vast majority of all group-years.[3] Figure 5.4 also suggests that governmental power-sharing practices are often present even in the absence of explicit formal rules. This implies that power-sharing practices are most often induced through other means.[4]

Figure 5.5 shows that the relationship between formal provisions for territorial power sharing and practices at the group-level is much stronger than in the case of governmental power sharing. For each of the four indicators for formal territorial power-sharing institutions we find that their presence for a particular ethnic group increases significantly the chances of the group enjoying regional autonomy in practice. While the overarching conclusion based on each of the four panels of Figure 5.5 is largely the same,[5] some interesting particularities are

empowering an ethnic group, as the second strongest party can change from election to election. For territorial power-sharing institutions we assessed whether the territories that obtained more authority in the three domains covered and elected their official representatives were the exclusive settlement area of an ethnic group coded in EPR. It bears noting that we did this only for groups that according to the EPR coding rules could profit from regional autonomy, namely those not enjoying monopoly or dominant status at the central level. To assess whether such territories exist, we relied on the GeoEPR dataset (Wucherpfennig et al., 2011) and information provided by Deiwiks, Cederman and Gleditsch's (2012) dataset on administrative units. We are grateful to Elise Clerc and Martina Dominković who have helped us in this coding effort.

[3] Thus, unsurprisingly, the χ^2 statistic is even so low in one of the three panels in Figure 5.4 that the chances of erring by rejecting the null-hypothesis of no relationship between formal provisions and institutions is close to one, while for the two other ones a relationship is clearly present.

[4] This might also be one of the reasons why Pospieszna and Schneider (2013) find no relationship between their indicator for governmental power-sharing institutions and the inclusion of a rebel group (i.e., power-sharing arrangement in the terms used by Pospieszna and Schneider, 2013) in the aftermath of a conflict. In addition, a proportional representation system as formal power-sharing institution can at best be considered as "soft" (Gates and Strøm, Forthcoming-b).

[5] The χ^2 values for the four underlying cross-tabulations are each large and allow us to reject the null-hypothesis with considerable confidence.

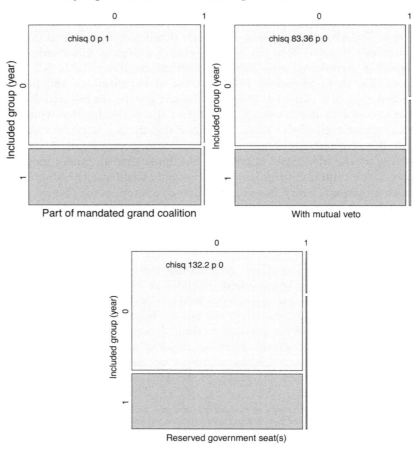

Figure 5.4 Formal governmental power-sharing institutions and practices benefiting ethnic groups

worth highlighting. First of all, the panel depicting the relationship between the type of offices elected at the regional level and regional autonomy clearly shows that legislative and executive elections (third bar in the first panel of Figure 5.5) make practices of regional autonomy more likely. It bears noting that only elections to the legislature (second bar in the first panel of Figure 5.5) make regional autonomy slightly less likely than the absence of elections (first bar). Second, regarding the

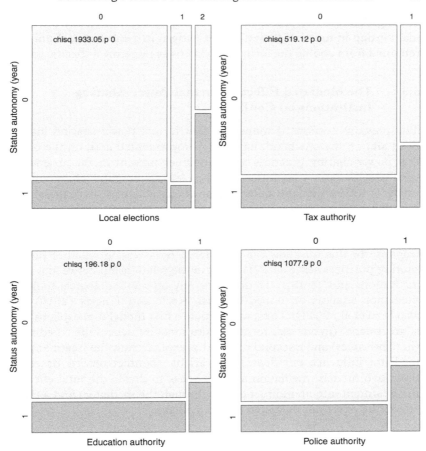

Figure 5.5 Formal territorial power-sharing institutions and practices benefiting ethnic groups

effects of different types of authority, we find that granting an ethnic group police authority in its settlement area increases its chances of profiting from regional autonomy the most. Interestingly, this type of authority also appears to be the most widespread. Third, and finally, each of the four panels of Figure 5.5 highlights that even in the absence of formal territorial power sharing granted to specific ethnic groups, some groups enjoy regional autonomy in practice. This most likely relates to our conservative coding of formal power-sharing institutions at the group-level: Except if a specific ethnic group was clearly the dominant group in terms of its settlement pattern in a sub-national unit, we refrained from coding the formal provisions as targeting a specific group.

5.3   The Mediated Effect of Formal Power-Sharing Institutions on Conflict

The previous sections demonstrate that formal power-sharing institutions are, on the one hand, not always implemented and, on the other, that power-sharing practices are sometimes present in the absence of such provisions in constitutions and peace-agreements. These empirical facts leave open the question, however, whether, as suggested by Figure 5.1, formal power-sharing institutions mostly affect the likelihood of a conflict onset through power sharing practices or whether these formal institutions influence conflict onsets through other channels. A response to this question can be offered by assessing whether power-sharing practices serve as a mediator in the relationship between formal institutions and conflict. To do so we rely on methodological tools for mediation analysis developed by Imai, Keele and Tingley (2010) (see also Imai et al., 2011). Thus, we estimate a first model that explains how a "treatment" (in our case formal institutions) influences the "mediator" (here practices) and a second model that explains how the treatment and mediator influence our dependent variable (conflict onset). Based on these two models, mediation analysis seeks to divide the total effect of the treatment into an indirect effect (through the mediator) and a direct effect (the effect not mediated by the mediator).[6]

5.3.1   Country-level analysis

In order to formally assess whether Master Hypothesis 2 is valid, we also need to decide what measures we use for the formal power-sharing institutions and which ones for practices. To measure formal institutions, we rely on the latent variables that we estimated in Chapter 4. They

---

[6] In what follows we draw heavily on Bormann et al. (2019) who present the results of such a mediation analysis at the country-level with the indicators for "inclusive" and "dispersive" formal power-sharing institutions to explain conflict onset. Our analysis differs from the previous study in three ways. First, in addition to country-level analysis, we present group-level results. Second, we use our IRT latent variables for formal power-sharing institutions, which rely on a more persuasive measurement model and allow us also to take account of missing data in a more convincing way. Finally, as missing data is also prevalent in our other explanatory variables, we rely on multiple imputation (King et al., 2001) to construct several complete datasets (using the R-package mice and estimate our mediation models on each of them before combining the results.

Formal governmental power sharing, practices and ethnic conflict

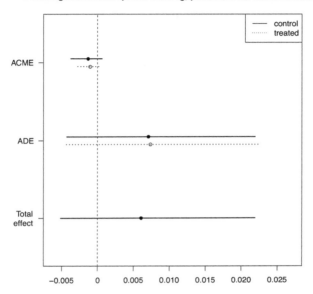

Figure 5.6 Mediated effect of formal governmental power-sharing institutions on conflict onset

summarize the information from three, respectively four indicators for governmental, respectively territorial power-sharing institutions. As indicator for power-sharing practices, we rely on the share of the population belonging to ethnic groups that are part of a governmental, respectively territorial power sharing (see Chapter 4). In the mediation analysis, we refer to formal power-sharing institutions as the treatment, while the practices serve as the mediator.

Figure 5.6 depicts the results of the mediation analysis for the effect of governmental power sharing on ethnic conflict onset.[7] In line with the results reported in Bormann et al. (2019) we find a mediated effect of formal power sharing through practices that is small and negative.[8] The confidence intervals for the mediated effects span from −0.002 to 0.000 (control group), respectively −0.003 to 0.000, thus overlapping

---

[7] As these estimates of the mediated and direct effects rely on two regression models, we report the results for the latter in the online appendix.

[8] Recall that the results reported here differ from those published in Bormann et al. (2019) because we use a different measure for formal power-sharing institutions, and resort to multiple imputations to deal with missing data in our other covariates.

with zero. On the other hand the direct effect is positive, with large confidence intervals. Thus, while in terms of magnitude the direct effect is clearly more important, the albeit relatively small mediated effects can more easily be distinguished from a null effect.

This result also has to be considered in the context of Bormann et al.'s (2019) additional findings, which indicate that these effects become much starker when distinguishing between conflicts that take place among power-sharing partners and those opposing an ethnic group in power to an excluded one. More specifically for the latter type of conflicts, formal governmental power sharing has a strong positive effect mediated through practices, while for the second type an equally strong negative effect appears.[9]

Figure 5.7 depicts the same mediated and direct effects for the formal territorial power-sharing institutions on territorial ethnic conflict onset. Again we find a mediated effect that is slightly negative, but this time the value of zero is almost in the middle of the confidence intervals. For the direct effect we find again a larger, positive one with, as before, a all ef large confidence interval.

Thus, we are able to confirm that these institutions mainly work through practices for formal governmental power-sharing institutions, Yet, this claim is on weaker ground for territorial power sharing.[10] This might be so because territorial power sharing exerts its strongest effect in conjunction with governmental power sharing (see Master Hypothesis 5), especially in post-conflict settings (Master Hypothesis 3).[11] The analyses presented here offer more solid support for the claim that formal power-sharing institutions operate, if at all, through practices to affect the likelihood of an ethnic conflict onset.

---

[9] We refrain from replicating the more nuanced analysis of these different types of conflicts, as it implicitly introduces information at the group-level in the analysis, but only for the dependent variable. A much more useful way to deal with this issue is to carry out the analysis at the group-level as we do below. This becomes possible thanks to the aforementioned additional data.

[10] It is interesting, again, to compare our findings to those reported by Pospieszna and Schneider (2013), who find that regional autonomy is not more likely in federal countries that have experienced conflict , and that regional autonomy actually increases conflict recurrence in such settings.

[11] Foreshadowing our treatment of Master Hypothesis 5 in Chapter 8, we carried out two additional mediation analyses while separating the observations in cases where a previous conflict had already occurred and those where this was not the case. In line with our findings reported in Chapter 8, we find that a slight negative mediated effect appears in the latter setting, while a conflict-inducing mediated effect for formal territorial power-sharing institutions appears in post-conflict settings.

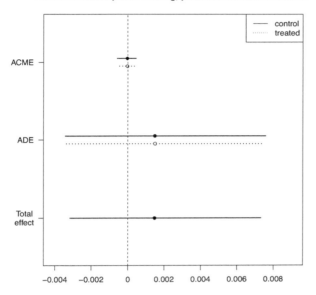

Figure 5.7 Mediated effect of formal territorial power-sharing institutions on conflict onset

5.3.2   Group-level analysis

The country-level findings reported above suggest that formal power-sharing institutions do not exert effects on conflict onset independently of power-sharing practices. As mentioned above, however, such analyses come with the drawback that we cannot directly distinguish which ethnic groups are involved in a conflict. Nor do they assure that formal provisions actually do target specific ethnic groups. Thus, in what follows we replicate the analyses reported above with data at the group-level. Again, we do so by first estimating two IRT models, this time relying on group-level data. This allows us to generate a group-level distribution of the two latent variables for formal governmental and territorial power sharing.[12]

---

[12] In the online appendix to this chapter we provide information on the distribution of the substantively most interesting estimated parameters, namely the item-difficulty and item-discrimination parameters.

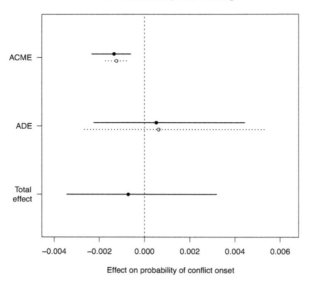

Governmental power sharing

Figure 5.8 Mediated effect of formal governmental power-sharing institutions on conflict onset estimated with group-level data

Figure 5.6 depicts the results of our mediation analysis for the effect of formal governmental power-sharing institutions. As expected, based on our discussion above and the results reported in Bormann et al. (2019), we find strong evidence that formal institutions only operate through practices when it comes to explaining conflict onset. More specifically, this figure reveals a negative and statistically significant mediated effect from formal power-sharing institutions through practices on conflict onset. The remaining direct (or independent) effect is estimated to be slightly positive, but the confidence intervals are large and include the value of zero. Thus, behind the total effect, which is slightly negative, there is a powerful and significant mediated effect.

This result constitutes powerful evidence for Master Hypothesis 2. At the same time, it casts doubt on most of the recent literature on power sharing. which has come to adopt an increasingly institutional perspective. As Figure 5.8 clearly shows, the overall effect of formal institutions (Total Effect) is indistinguishable from zero. Only once we consider that these formal institutions operate through practices are we able to demonstrate that formal power-sharing institutions actually reduce the likelihood of conflict.

Territorial power sharing

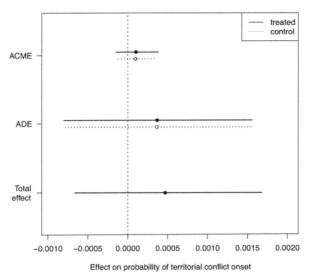

Figure 5.9 Mediated effect of formal territorial power-sharing institutions on conflict onset estimated with group-level data

While these results support our theoretical expectations, the ones pertaining to formal territorial power-sharing institutions are less supportive. Figure 5.9 shows that the mediated effect of formal territorial institutions on conflict onset is small, positive and statistically insignificant. The direct effect, however, is larger and also positive, although it fails to reach statistical significance even by a larger margin. Yet, it is premature to draw any final conclusions since it is likely that this finding has to be evaluated in the context of results reported in Chapter 8 and related to Master Hypothesis 5, namely that the effect of territorial power sharing depends, in part, on governmental power sharing.

Despite these weak results from the mediation analyses on territorial power sharing, it is important to underline that all our mediation analyses reported in this chapter support the first part of Master Hypothesis 2. If power-sharing institutions have an effect on conflict onset this effect only appears when the mediation through practices is taken into account. The strongest evidence for this effect is provided by our analyses of governmental power sharing at the group level. There we have clear evidence that formal provisions only affect conflict onsets through their effects on power-sharing practices.

5.4   Relative Effects and Endogeneity

Despite these promising findings regarding the mediated effect of formal power-sharing institutions, two issues remain unaddressed. First, as our discussion of Figure 5.1 highlights, we are also interested in knowing the extent of the effect of power-sharing practices on conflict which is unrelated to formal power-sharing institutions. Second, our analysis has so far focused on Hypothesis 2 rather than on the other master hypotheses. This is especially problematic in the case of Master Hypothesis 4. In fact, the endogenous nature of both formal power-sharing institutions and power-sharing practices could in principle invalidate our findings. While refraining from deploying our two endogeneity strategies in this chapter, we nevertheless provide a discussion based on sensitivity analyses, which should dispel most endogeneity concerns (see the online appendix). For both of these additional analyses we limit ourselves to the group level since the data at this level affords us the most direct assessment of the interplay between formal institutions and practices.

Yet, this section first addresses the question how much of the effect of power-sharing practices on conflict onset is due to formal institutions, and how much occurs through other means. To answer this question we rely on the constituent regression models that underlie the mediation analyses. Based on these equations, and relying on simulations, we generate datasets under various scenarios, most notably a scenario where no formal institutions are present, and a scenario where the existing institutions reduce conflict only through power-sharing practices. By comparing the average predicted differences in the probability of conflict, we can assess by how much the conflict probabilities change due to the different channels.[13]

Figure 5.10 displays three changes in the average predicted probabilities of a conflict onset. At the bottom, the figure shows the total effect for governmental power-sharing practices on conflict. We can divide this total effect in a part that is completely due to institutional provisions and another that is unrelated to these institutions. As the figure clearly shows, the overall effect of governmental power-sharing practices is negative and statistically significant. In addition, this effect, which is again statistically significant, is almost exclusively due to practices that are unrelated to formal institutions. The effect due to institutions, while negative as well, is much smaller and fails to reach statistical significance.[14]

---

[13] In the online appendix we provide a detailed description of the procedure.

[14] When comparing Figure 5.10 to other figures reporting the results of our various mediation analyses, it should be noted that the effects reported are not the same. This is due to our focus on substantive effects in the present analysis.

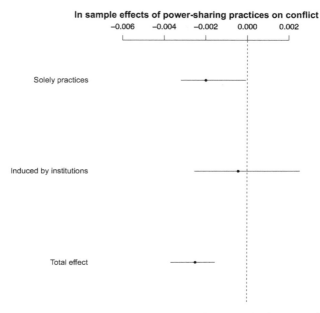

Figure 5.10 Effects of governmental power-sharing practices due to formal institutions and other factors

For the sake of completeness we provide a similar analysis for the effect of territorial power-sharing practices in Figure 5.11. Not surprisingly, given our mediation analysis, the total effect of territorial power-sharing practices on conflict onset is positive, but estimated with considerable uncertainty. The part of this effect that is induced by institutions is close to zero, which implies that the positive effect of territorial power-sharing practices on conflict onset is induced by other means than formal institutions.

Having assessed the relative importance of the effect of power-sharing practices induced or not induced by formal institutions on conflict, we can now turn to the most serious challenge for the analyses presented in this chapter, namely endogeneity. As we argued in previous chapters, the endogenous nature of both formal institutions and practices poses a major challenge to assessments of the consequences of power sharing. Here we assess the likelihood that the results of this chapter are affected by endogeneity. Such a sensitivity analysis is possible with tools provided by Imai et al. (2011) in the context of mediation analyses (for a related approach in other analyses, see Oster, 2016). More specifically, Imai et al. (2011, 770) discuss in detail that the results of mediation analyses

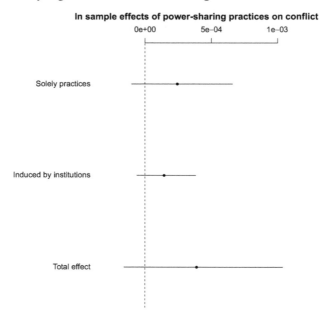

Figure 5.11 Effects of territorial power-sharing practices due to formal institutions and other factors

such as those reported in this chapter provide unbiased estimates of the causal effects as long as the so-called "sequential ignorability" assumption holds, which they describe as follows:

First, given the observed pretreatment confounders, the treatment assignment is assumed to be ignorable – statistically independent of potential outcomes and potential mediators. This part of the assumption is often called no-omitted-variable-bias, exogeneity, or unconfoundedness. ... The second part ... implies that the observed mediator is ignorable given the actual treatment status and pretreatment confounders.

If this assumption is violated then the error terms in the two equations estimated for the mediation analyses will be correlated. This offers a way to assess how the estimated mediated effects are affected by this correlation. Thus, Imai et al. (2011) propose a sensitivity analyses which rely on estimating the changes in the mediated effects for various values of the correlation between the two error terms. If the estimated effect barely changes, it implies that endogeneity concerns are hardly an issue.

In the online appendix to this chapter we report on a set of such sensitivity analyses for the two main analyses carried out with our group-level data. While these analyses show that, as those reported by Bormann et al. (2019), the estimates of our mediated effects are quite sensitive to the correlation in the error terms, the sign and direction of the effect is unlikely to be affected. Like Bormann et al. (2019), we argue that the correlation between the two error terms is most likely positive. Such a positive correlation would imply that unobserved confounders that make power-sharing institutions and practices more likely also increase the risk of conflict. Substantively this implies that governments introduce formal institutions and practices due to these confounders, especially for groups that are more likely to engage in conflict.

As our sensitivity analyses show, however, the mediated effect of power-sharing institutions through practices would be even stronger if such a positive correlation were to exist. Only in the case of a negative correlation does our estimated mediated effect disappear or reverse its sign. Thus, we are reassured by these sensitivity analyses, which tell us that the likely endogeneity of power-sharing institutions and practices is unlikely to affect our conclusions regarding the mediated effect of power-sharing institutions.[15]

5.5   Conclusion

In broad terms, the goal of this chapter has been to evaluate Master Hypothesis 2, which holds that formal power-sharing institutions influence conflicts mainly, if not exclusively, through their effects on power-sharing practices in addition to the latter's independent impact. The first part of this chapter evaluates whether and why our argument might hold. First, formal power-sharing institutions are not always formally implemented as our analysis clearly demonstrated. Second, in addition to not being implemented, formal power-sharing institutions often fail to result in practices that accommodate ethnic groups. Third, practices that accommodate ethnic groups often emerge even in the absence of formal institutional provisions. These three points highlight that the

---

[15] Bormann et al. (2019) discuss an additional challenge to our conclusion that formal power-sharing institutions operate exclusively through practices when affecting conflict onset, namely that the causal order is reversed. To address this issue, they consider models in which power-sharing practices affect, possibly, through power-sharing institutions conflicts. Their results suggests that in this case the mediated effects are indistinguishable from zero, while the direct effects, i.e., the effects from power-sharing practices on conflict, are clearly statistically significant.

exclusive institutional focus typically present in existing studies of the effect of power sharing is likely to be misleading.

Having set the analytical stage in the first part of the chapter, we then assessed more systematically how formal institutions affect the likelihood of conflict onset through practices or other channels. Throughout our analyses, whether focusing on governmental or territorial power sharing, whether using country- or group-level data, a common theme emerges: If formal institutions affect conflict onset at all, this effect is mainly mediated through power-sharing practices. We found the strongest, mediated effects for formal governmental power-sharing institutions. In contrast, the effects for territorial power sharing are less clear-cut. For governmental power sharing we have also been able to show that the effect of practices on conflict onset depends less on formal power-sharing institutions than on other factors. This result underlines even more forcefully our argument that practices are playing a pivotal role in the link between power sharing and conflict.

6 Endogenizing Governmental Power Sharing and Its Effect on Civil War*

In examining the linkage between power sharing and civil war, the previous chapters have presented initial evidence that power sharing seems to reduce the risk of conflict. More specifically, we have shown that this occurs primarily through power-sharing practices (see Master Hypothesis 2). However, our mediation analyses also highlighted two important caveats. First, the channel through which formal power-sharing institutions translate into behavioral practices is porous: *de jure* institutions frequently fail to result in behavioral practices. Second, power-sharing practices often arise even in the absence of formal institutions. In short, formal power-sharing institutions are neither necessary, nor sufficient, in generating power-sharing practices. Our focus in this and the remaining chapters of Part II, therefore, lies primarily on the effect of power-sharing practices on civil war, starting with an in-depth exploration of the effect of governmental power-sharing practices in this and the following chapter, followed by an assessment of the effect of territorial power-sharing practices in Chapters 8 and 9.

As discussed in Part I of this book, the claim that governmental power sharing can help secure peace in ethnically divided societies remains controversial (see Master Hypothesis 1a). This is despite immediate policy relevance for the prospects of many countries, including contemporary Iraq or Syria. In part, the controversy is driven by a narrow focus on those cases that have collapsed into large-scale violence such as Lebanon, Rwanda, Yugoslavia, Zimbabwe and others. Skeptics warn that power sharing tends to deepen pre-existing divisions, undermine cross-cutting cleavages, and encourage the escalation of crises between rivaling groups, making it an "impediment to peace" (Rothchild and Roeder, 2005a, 29). Yet, there are at the same time many examples of successful power sharing, including South Africa, Indonesia, Northern

---

* This chapter was previously published as an article, see Wucherpfennig, Hunziker and Cederman (2016).

Ireland or even Belgium and Switzerland, and power sharing has become increasingly common in recent decades (Gurr, 2000*a*; Strøm et al., 2017). Thus, other academics and policy makers are more optimistic about the stabilizing effect of power sharing, contending that power sharing produces peace by facilitating cooperation, reducing grievances and providing positive payoffs from peace (e.g. Lijphart, 1977; Hartzell and Hoddie, 2007; Mattes and Savun, 2009; Gurr, 2000*b*; Cederman, Gleditsch and Buhaug, 2013).

6.1   The Challenge of Endogeneity

Does governmental power sharing spur or reduce civil conflict? Despite the immediate policy importance of this question, we are still lacking systematic, unbiased evidence that could yield a clearer picture and guide policy-makers. Although a complete, rather than selective, sample can help to answer this question, reasonable doubt remains. Perhaps the most powerful criticism of analyses that identify a peace-inducing effect of power sharing points to reverse causation. Indeed, if the anticipated consequences of power sharing affect governments' decisions on whom to include in the first place, then studies that falsely assume ethnic inclusion to be an exogenous "treatment" may generate biased and misleading inferences (Fearon, Kasara and Laitin, 2007; Fearon, 2010; Blattman and Miguel, 2010). Previous studies have paid limited attention to problems of reverse causation, even though power sharing is widely considered a deliberate policy tool for conflict management. Rodrik (2012, 139) warns that where "policies are not random but are used systematically by governments to achieve certain ends," standard regression techniques are ill-suited to evaluate their effectiveness.

Indeed, a burgeoning literature suggests that institutional arrangements are endogenous to the threat of violent conflict (Acemoglu and Robinson, 2006; Boix, 2003; Svolik, 2012). Thus, in further probing Master Hypothesis 1a, a key objective of the current and subsequent chapters is to tackle the challenge of endogeneity brought about by concerns over reverse causation. Here we follow up the brief introduction of Master Hypothesis 4 in Chapter 3. Briefly, if power-sharing practices are adopted at least in part in anticipation of their effect on future conflict, then it is no longer straightforward to evaluate the causal effect of such practices. As we argue below in greater detail, addressing this challenge requires a deeper understanding of the conditions under which ethnic groups are invited to participate in power-sharing arrangements and when they are obstructed from doing so, that is, when they remain excluded. Focusing on governmental power sharing, this and the following chapter explore two ways of approaching this. Each of these has different strengths and weaknesses, but together they yield a strikingly coherent picture that further corroborates our argument that behavioral governmental power sharing *causes* peace.

In this chapter, we study and subsequently exploit how differences in colonial governance systematically affected which ethnic groups became part of the post-colonial government in former French and British colonies. As we show below, the specifics of this argument allow us to devise a credible instrumental variable (IV) that can be used to retrieve an improved, if not unbiased, estimate of the effect of power sharing on conflict during the post-colonial period. However, this approach is naturally limited to post-colonial countries, and, by design, also restricted to a mere cross-section. As an alternative that offers broader coverage across space and time, the second approach, which will be the focus of the next chapter, explores an actor-centric perspective by studying a simple formal model. This highlights the conditions under which governments are likely to share power with a domestic challenger depending on the threat of violence. We then derive a statistical "strategic selection" model that closely mirrors the theoretical model, thereby directly incorporating endogeneity. Before detailing these approaches to tackle the challenge of endogeneity, we first discuss in greater detail the consequences of how ignoring endogeneity is likely to result in biased estimates.

Although the link between ethnic groups' access to power and civil conflict appears strong and robust, it is not immune to criticism. This particularly relates to problems of endogeneity, which may bias the empirical estimates. Broadly speaking, endogeneity occurs when an alternative causal pathway between the treatment and outcome exists but has not been accounted for in empirical modeling. Specifically, such bias occurs if the treatment variable is itself responsive to the outcome (i.e., reverse causation), or if an unmeasured confounding factor affects both the treatment and the outcome (i.e., omitted variable bias). Econometrically, these scenarios imply that the correlation between the treatment variable and the stochastic component is non-zero, thus leading to biased estimates.

Despite increasing scholarly awareness, problems of endogeneity continue to undermine current research on civil war (Blattman and Miguel, 2010). Critics of the link between power sharing and peace point to reverse causation as the key threat. If inclusion in governmental power sharing is pursued in part with an eye to its anticipated consequences, then a causal arrow operates from (potential) conflict to power sharing. This makes it difficult to discern the actual effect of power-sharing practices on conflict because the anticipation of conflict determines whom governments include in power sharing in the first place, and who remains excluded. How this potential source of endogeneity affects empirical estimates depends on the manner in which governments deal with potentially dangerous groups:

1. *Co-optation: inclusion of potential belligerents.* According to this scenario, governments include those groups with the largest conflict potential and exclude groups that are unlikely to rebel to begin with. This will be the case if governments generally seek to avoid conflict, and expect that co-opting potential trouble-makers through inclusion in the government will reduce the overall conflict risk. In other words, "governments tend to calibrate the level of exclusion to what they can get away with" (Fearon, 2010, 19). If this mechanism applies, "naïve" comparisons of the frequency of rebellion by included and excluded groups will *underestimate* the peace-inducing effect of inclusion. The reason is that even though inclusion actually reduces conflict risk, only groups that are particularly conflict-prone for reasons other than power access are being included (cf. Svolik, 2009).

2. *Risk diversion: exclusion of potential belligerents.* Another possibility is that governments strategically exclude those groups with the highest conflict potential as a means to divert risk. This is the exact opposite of the above scenario. One possible explanation for this logic is that governments assume that exclusion *reduces* conflict risk, perhaps because potentially belligerent groups are then denied access to state resources that could be used for mobilization. Alternatively, governments may exclude conflict-prone groups even though they believe that exclusion increases conflict risk because they fear coup d'états by included rivals more than they fear civil wars by excluded rivals (Roessler, 2011; Svolik, 2009). In both scenarios "naïve" comparisons of the frequency of rebellion by included and excluded groups will *overestimate* the peace-inducing effect of inclusion, because conflict-prone groups tend to be politically excluded.

To understand the reasoning underlying these arguments more clearly, we return to the medical analogy that we introduced in Chapter 1. Compared to most other people, hospital patients generally suffer from poorer health. The corresponding naïve conclusion would be to infer that hospitalization is detrimental towards one's state of health. Needless to say, such inference omits that poor health is usually the cause of the medical treatment in the first place. Once this reverse causality is factored in, the correct inference is of course that hospitals are generally health-improving. Analogously, following scenario 1, more conflict-prone groups (i.e., ill patients) may be more likely to be included (i.e., hospitalized) in the first place, thus understating any conflict-dampening (i.e., healing) effect.

3. *Unobservable Confounders.* Finally, the estimates presented in the studies that link exclusion to internal conflict could suffer from endogeneity in the form of omitted variable bias if exclusion were to correlate with unobservable confounders that independently drive the probability of conflict. In this context, Fearon (2010, 20) stresses opportunities to rebel, such as group size, peripheralness, and mountainous terrain.

Again it is critical to theorize the potential consequences of this type of endogeneity. If omitted variables that make rebellion more feasible correlate positively with exclusion, then the exclusion-conflict finding will at least in part be spurious, that is, overestimated. As such, this scenario bears some resemblance to the "exclusion of belligerents" mechanism if factors of opportunity operate in part *through* exclusion.

In this chapter, we develop the first of the two approaches that address these issues. Following up the introductory discussion in Chapter 3, we rely on an instrumental variable logic that exploits differences in the ways France and Great Britain governed their colonial territories with respect to pre-existing ethnic structures. Specifically, we argue that the British approach toward customary institutions systematically empowered peripheral ethnic groups as compared to their French-ruled counterparts. As a result, the former groups were much more likely to become part of power-sharing arrangements in the post-colonial state. Since this differential within-logic operates independent of conflict, we are able to instrument for initial inclusion, which in turn allows us to retrieve an improved estimate of the effect of governmental power sharing on post-colonial conflict. This approach also informs about how the conflict potential of particular groups affected whether they were included in or excluded from power-sharing arrangements.

The basic idea behind the instrumental variable approach is to identify a variable, referred to as the *instrument*, that correlates with the potentially endogenous regressor, but is otherwise unrelated to the dependent variable (for an overview, see Sovey and Green, 2011). Put otherwise, in order to assess the validity of the exclusion-conflict nexus, we need to articulate a causal pathway that directly affects inclusion but is otherwise unrelated to conflict.

6.2   Explaining Ethnic Power Access

We introduce an argument that relates the ethno-political power constellation in post-colonial states to differences in colonial policy between the French and British empires. Whereas the present European ethno-political power constellation emerged from an extensive period of state-formation and nation-building, this is not the case for most post-colonial states. Here, particular groups' chances of gaining access to state power in the post-independence period depended heavily on colonial policy, which typically treated its subjects very differently conditional on ethnic affiliation (Horowitz, 1985; Young, 1994; Reno, 1995).

Our argument follows a sizeable literature that traces the long-term effects of colonial rule on a variety of contemporary outcomes, especially economic development (e.g. Acemoglu, Johnson and Robinson, 2001; Hariri, 2012). In particular, it is often argued that European metropoles employed distinct strategies in governing their overseas dependencies, which in turn impacted differently on subsequent economic development (Englebert, 2000; Lange, Mahoney and vom Hau, 2006; Mahoney, 2010; de Sousa and Lochard, 2012), democratic survival (Bernhard, Reenock and Nordstrom, 2004), coups (Jenkins and Kposowa, 1992), or conflict (Blanton, Mason and Athow, 2001; Lange and Dawson, 2009). Our argument concerning the ethno-political power constellation in post-colonial states explicitly builds on such differences between empires, but also makes specific predictions about geo-political patterns *within* post-colonial states. It proceeds in two steps. First, a stylized comparison of colonial rule between the two most important colonizers, France and Great Britain, demonstrates how these empires differed systematically in their manner of dealing with customary institutions and local autonomy, which both shaped ethno-political configurations. Second, we discuss how the locally confined consequences of these different modes of colonial governance carried over to the post-colonial state and affected which groups gained access to power after the colonizers' retreat.

6.2.1   Colonial period

It is often argued that whereas the British adhered to "indirect rule," the French relied on "direct rule" (Jenkins and Kposowa, 1992; Miles, 1994; Bernhard, Reenock and Nordstrom, 2004; Lange, 2004; Lange, Mahoney and vom Hau, 2006).[1] Scholars have, however, been

---

[1] Defining these concepts, Gerring et al. (2011, 377) argue that "a 'direct' style of rule features highly centralized decision-making while an 'indirect' style of rule features a more decentralized framework in which important decision-making powers are delegated to the weaker entity."

debating whether the difference between 'French direct rule' and 'British indirect rule' is historically accurate. In fact, there is evidence that both the British and the French relied at least in part on both principles (see Herbst, 2000; Lange, 2009). The problems relating to this distinction stem at least partially from attempts to characterize entire colonies even though both forms of rule were often applied in the same country (Crowder, 1964; Lange, Mahoney and vom Hau, 2006). Indeed, given the vastness of the colonial empires and the relatively small number of colonial administrators, ruling indirectly through a principal-agent structure was often the only feasible way of making peripheral areas governable at all, while a strong colonial presence at the center generally favored direct rule (Mamdani, 1996; Herbst, 2000; Gerring et al., 2011). Acknowledging these arguments, we contend that France and Britain differed systematically in both the *frequency* and especially the *manner* in which they implemented indirect rule in practice. In the following, we elaborate on these differences by focusing on two key factors that affect the ethno-political landscape, namely (1) customary institutions and (2) local autonomy.

First, sharp differences characterize the empires' approaches with respect to customary institutions. The British tended to keep pre-colonial power structures in place wherever possible. Formulated eloquently by Lord Lugard (1922) as the *de facto* doctrine for governing the empire's colonies, *British* indirect rule left local administration to native chiefs, kings, or other authorities with traditional claims to power, allowing them to rule in a largely autonomous manner as long as they cooperated with colonial officials (Lange, 2004; Crowder, 1964). In contrast, French colonial rule relied heavily on the principles of *centralization* and *assimilation*. The French empire generally organized the local administration of its colonies with little regard for pre-existing institutions, and minimized the degree of local decision-making in favor of centralized planning even where indirect rule was applied (Mamdani, 1996).

Thus, under French indirect rule, local conditions and institutions were often deliberately ignored. Local leaders primarily served the function of "agent[s] of the administration" (Crowder, 1968, 187), and in order to ensure loyalty with the empire, the French not only chose as their agents "those from the ruling lineage who spoke French and were known to be loyal to France, but often they imposed men without any traditional right to rule. These included clerks, old soldiers, and in some instances even personal servants of administrators" (Crowder, 1968, 190). Indeed, in selecting their agents, the French were more concerned about potential efficiency than legitimacy.

This does, however, not imply that the French refrained from employing locals in administrative positions within the French colonial apparatus. On the contrary, (Richens, 2009) shows that the ratio between European colonial administrators and the local African populace did not differ significantly between French and British possessions in Africa. However, whereas the British typically employed traditional authorities to reign over their own tribal communities, the French recruited native administrators rather than traditionally legitimized rulers to act as representatives of the colonial empire. Hence, British indirect rule meant the "incorporation of indigenous institutions – not simply individuals – into an overall structure of colonial domination" (Lange, 2004, 906).

A second distinctive property of British indirect rule was the comparatively large degree of autonomy that was granted to local agents, including "executive, legislative, and judicial powers to regulate social relations in their chiefdoms" (Lange, 2004, 907). Local agents had the obligation to collect taxes for the administration and to follow the guidelines set by the British Resident, but remained largely autonomous otherwise (Crowder, 1968, 217–218). This concentration of power within a single position has led Mamdani (1996) to describe the system of governance that would emerge from *British* indirect rule as "decentralized despotism."

In contrast, a key objective of French colonial policy was to fully integrate overseas colonies into the French state. In the words of Arthur Girault, who contributed to shaping French colonial policy in the late nineteenth century, the "[c]olonies 'are considered a simple prolongation of the soil of the mother country,' merely as 'départements more distant than the rest'" (quoted in Lewis, 1962, 132). Consequently, the political administration of the colonies was aimed to mirror the centralized French system, while leaving little room for local idiosyncrasies. Moreover, such centralization implied that decision-making was carried out at the highest possible level and that local administrators' duty was merely to implement these decisions. Native administrators in French colonies were expected to execute orders from the French *Commandant de Cercle* in accordance with a strictly hierarchical chain of command, Senegal being a notable exception (Crowder, 1968; Calori et al., 1997). In fact, the French actively prevented local concerns from entering the decision-making process by frequently rotating colonial governors and administrators, leaving them with little time to learn the local language or ethnography (Cohen, 1971, 504).

These distinct strategies of colonial rule created very different ethno-political configurations in British and French colonies. The British strategy of supporting traditional rulers and granting them significant authority led to the emergence of networks of powerful rural despots who controlled ethnically delimited constituencies. In contrast, the French approach of abandoning traditional institutions and centralizing decision-making was much less conducive to rural administrators building their own ethnically determined power bases. As a consequence, at the time of independence, political power was much more consolidated in the form of ethnically delimited chiefdoms in British colonies than it was in their French counterparts.

6.2.2   Post-colonial period

Next, we discuss why and how the ethno-political landscapes shaped during colonialism carried over to the post-colonial state and affected which ethnic groups were able to fill the emergent power vacuum at the center. In former British colonies, where political power in the periphery was in the hands of largely autonomous ethnic leaders, peripheral ethnic groups were more likely to gain access to power in the newly independent states than comparable groups in former French colonies.

At the time of independence, urban elites who had spearheaded the struggle for independence against their colonial rulers found themselves in competition over which group, or coalition of groups, would achieve control of the post-colonial state apparatus. In this struggle

the lines of cleavage were drawn not so much on ideological, class, economic, or professional differences as on ethnoregional divisions [...]. It was, therefore, imperative for the western-educated elements to strike a deal of co-operation with the traditional authorities who would supply the vote. (Azarya, 2003, 12–13)

Where extant, these competing elites could secure their place in power by cooperating with rural ethnic power holders who were able to quickly mobilize support, in the form of votes or otherwise. This was the case especially in former British colonies, where autonomous ethnic leaders had consolidated power thanks to British indirect rule and its focus on customary institutions. In exchange for support, urban elites offered these ethnic leaders a say in the central government, and ensured that the latters' hold on power in their respective chiefdoms was secure (Mamdani, 1996; Kenny, 2015). As we will show in greater detail below, this is well illustrated by the example of Nigeria, where the indirectly ruled Hausa-Fulani from the Northern part of the country together with the Igbo provided the basis for the electoral victory of a coalition led by the People's Congress (NPC) in 1959 (Horowitz, 1985). In Burma, non-democratic elite-level bargaining resulted in the inclusion of representatives of the relatively small Shan and Kachin groups from the North of the country by Burmese state builders, led by General Aung San, in the Panglong Agreement of 1947 (Callahan, 2003).

In contrast, in French colonies, where there were fewer rural power holders who could quickly provide support (in the form of votes or otherwise) to ambitious urban elites, political competition was focused more exclusively on the urban center. Thus, because they lacked the network of decentralized despots present in the British colonies, rural ethnic groups in former French colonies were rarely represented in the central institutions of newly independent states, as illustrated by Mali, Algeria and Vietnam, among others. Analyzing the presence of state institutions in rural Côte d'Ivoire in the 1960s and 1970s, Boone (1998, 11) observes that

Even as the administrative grid tightened over the countryside, there were few official sites, positions, or organisations in the rural areas that offered local people direct access to state resources, or that invited them to use proximity to the state to enhance their own local standing.

In sum, our argument broadly supports the notion that the legacy of the colonial state was regularly carried forward into the post-colonial state through "natural inertial forces" as shown by Young (2004, 29) and Mamdani (1996). Whereas in the British cases the newly independent centers often interacted with the peripheries through a network of political machines operating via patronage, the French post-colonial states were largely absent in rural areas. Thus, at the time of independence, in the British cases, peripheral ethnic groups played a strong role vis-à-vis urban groups, since rural ethnic leaders had consolidated constituencies and an autonomous power base. In contrast, in the French cases, peripheral ethnic groups were generally substantially less likely to be represented in the central states' governments, since they were less salient to urban elites in the competition over the state apparatus. These expectations are visualized in Figure 6.1.

6.2.3   Large-n analysis

This section presents large-n evidence in order to demonstrate that the probabilistic logic postulated above holds *ceteris paribus* across a large number of observations. This establishes our instrument for the later

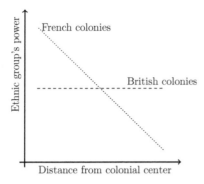

Figure 6.1 Colonial rule and group power access

parts of the chapter. In line with the instrumental variable approach, the primary purpose of these analyses is to demonstrate an *independent effect* of our colonial legacies argument with respect to the inclusion of particular groups. In addition to the statistical analyses presented here, we also probe several select cases, including Algeria, Nigeria, and Burma, to illustrate the plausibility of our argument. Space limitations prevent us from discussing particular cases in detail here; however, a series of case vignettes and indicative maps is available in the online appendix to this chapter.

As before, our primary source is the Ethnic Power Relations dataset, which offers data on ethnic power sharing at the group-level (see Chapter 4).[2] Wucherpfennig et al. (2011) provide a spatial extension named GeoEPR that codes the geographic settlement areas for regionally confined groups. We use these geo-spatial data to derive our measure of peripheralness. Finally, in order to identify colonial legacies, we combine EPR with the ICOW Colonial History Data Set (Hensel, 2009).

Using these data, we analyze the subset of groups with distinct settlement patterns[3] in Asian or African countries that gained independence from either France or Britain after 1945.[4] We omit groups from countries that broke away from other colonies because we are primarily interested in the stylized differences between the main colonial empires, and because other empires (e.g., Belgium or Portugal) were

---

[2] The current analysis is based on an earlier version (EPR-ETH, v. 2) of the data that covers the period 1946–2009.

[3] For example, ethnic groups in Burundi and Rwanda are coded as not settling in distinct geographic areas in GeoEPR (Wucherpfennig et al., 2011).

[4] This leads us to exclude, e.g., South Africa.

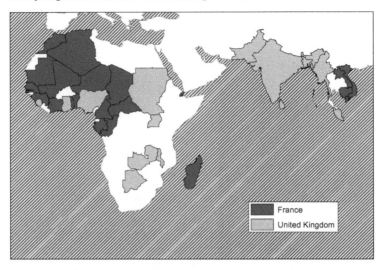

Figure 6.2 Countries included in our analyses

generally too small to offer meaningful geo-political within-variation.[5] Moreover, we exclude Latin America, as well as Rhodesia/Zimbabwe[6] from our sample since their status as settler colonies has led the ethno-political configuration at the time of independence to be shaped predominantly by the monopolization of power by European elites, rather than colonialist strategies of rule.

Given our interest in the effects of colonial strategies on post-colonial conflict through the initial ethno-political configuration left after decolonization, our dataset is a cross-section of 169 politically relevant ethnic groups in 36 post-colonial countries in Africa and Asia at the time of independence of their host country. A map of the countries included in our sample is given in Figure 6.2.

Next, we turn to the operationalization of our key variables. Because of its extractive nature, colonialism generally extended its reach from the coast towards the hinterlands.[7] Thus, we conceptualize peripheralness as the relative distance from the coast and construct our measure by

[5] Though see the online appendix for further discussion and analyses.

[6] South Africa is excluded because it gained independence pre-1945.

[7] This is well illustrated by the fact that the vast majority of colonial railroad lines – which served the purpose of exploiting natural resources – run perpendicular to the coast toward the interior (van de Walle, 2009, 317).

calculating the distance between each group's settlement area (centroid) and the colonial center, that is, the coast. For landlocked countries without direct access to the sea, we subtract the minimum (country) distance to the coast in order to arrive at a standardized measure. We then use the natural logarithm of the measure.

In terms of econometric modeling, our argument can be represented as the interaction between the colonial ruler and the physical location of the group with respect to the colonial center. In addition, we include the constitutive terms of the interaction term, that is a (binary) indicator for the respective colonial power and the (continuous) measure of remoteness (Braumoeller, 2004; Brambor, Clark and Golder, 2006).

The instrumental variable approach requires us to establish an independent effect of the instrument (see discussion below). We therefore consider other, confounding mechanisms that are likely to affect an ethnic group's access to state power and include a number of theoretically relevant control variables. The model features both country-level and group-level covariates. As regards the latter, a key variable is the relative size of a group, since larger groups can *ceteris paribus* be expected to be more influential. Thus, we use the ethnic groups' relative demographic size with respect to their host country's entire population, taken from EPR. Based on our theoretical discussion, as well as the case vignettes, factors like mass and concentration are also likely to be critical. In order to capture geographic concentration, we include the area of a group's settlement, as well as the area of the country (both in km^2, logged), since it can be expected that larger countries tend to contain more peripheral areas. We also include logged population and GDP per capita data for the year of independence. Finally, we account for instances in which independence was achieved by violent means, again relying on data by Hensel (2009).

The estimation results are given in Table 6.1. We compare two specifications: a conventional model that reflects the standard center-periphery logic (Model 1), and the full structural model that captures the logic of the ethno-political legacies of French and British rule through an additional interaction term (Model 2). This comparison yields interesting results. Model 1 suggests that there is neither a straightforward center-periphery effect, nor that British and French colonial rule differ with respect to the prospects of a group being included in the initial post-colonial government. However, these results only stand at first sight. Once the logic of differential colonial legacies is factored in, a more nuanced picture emerges that is strongly in line with our theoretical expectations. This is visualized in Figure 6.3. Here, the left panel depicts the predicted probabilities that a given group is

Table 6.1. *Explaining initial inclusion*

	(1) Center-periphery	(2) Differential legacies
British colony	−0.03	−3.72*
	(0.33)	(1.45)
Log distance to coast	−0.02	−0.55*
	(0.18)	(0.24)
Log distance to coast × British colony		0.68*
		(0.27)
Groupsize	2.30*	2.33*
	(0.95)	(0.93)
Log group area (km^2)	0.06	0.10
	(0.14)	(0.14)
Log country area (km^2)	−0.33	−0.34
	(0.19)	(0.18)
Log population	0.20	0.18
	(0.11)	(0.11)
Log GDP per capita	0.34	0.24
	(0.23)	(0.24)
Violent independence	0.23	0.23
	(0.34)	(0.34)
Constant	−1.88	1.72
	(2.49)	(2.67)
Observations	169	169
Log likelihood	−98.18	−94.34

Robust standard errors clustered by country in parentheses
* $p < 0.05$, ** $p < 0.001$

included in the initial post-colonial state as a function of the colonizer and peripheral remoteness.[8]

The plot closely mirrors our theoretical expectations (recall Figure 6.1). We find that groups in former French colonies follow a center-periphery logic, that is, the more peripheral a group, the less likely

---

[8] Rather than generating predicted values for imagined cases that set the remaining variables to arbitrary values (such as the mean), we prefer the "average effect in the population" (i.e., our dataset) (Gelman and Hill, 2007; Hanmer and Kalkan, 2013) across 1,000 draws from the estimated parameter distribution of Model 2. These were obtained by sampling 1,000 sets of values from the estimated parameter distribution of Model 2. For each (real world) observation from our dataset, we then computed the mean predicted values at different values of the colonizer dummy, distance to the coast, and their interaction term by using each of the sampled parameter sets.

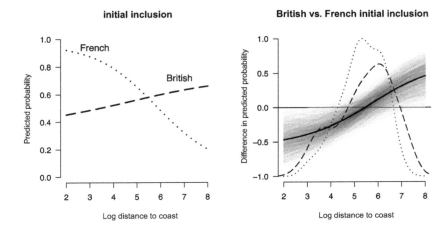

Figure 6.3 Ethnic groups' power access in the initial post-colonial period as a function of colonial legacy and location

it is to be included in the initial post-colonial state. By contrast, in line with our argument concerning the British implementation of indirect rule, this does not hold for groups in former British colonies, where peripheral groups stand a good chance of being included, especially in comparison to French groups.

The right panel in Figure 6.3 depicts the predicted probabilities of an ethnic group's post-colonial inclusion, differentiating between French and British colonies. The solid black line represents the difference between the predictions from the left panel, while the grey lines display the variation across simulations.[9] The figure demonstrates that the differences between groups in former French and British colonies are substantial and systematic, both at the center and in the periphery. Overlaid are density plots of the distributions of ethnic groups in former French and British colonies in terms of their relative location. These show that former French and British colonies are very similar in terms of geographic composition, and that large parts of the empirical cases are affected by the differential.

Turning to the control variables, as expected, large populations and higher GDP per capita tend to increase initial inclusion, but neither of these effects is statistically significant. However, we find a strong and

---

[9] Discarding the top and bottom 2.5 percent, this corresponds to a 95 percent confidence interval.

significant effect for group size. Somewhat surprisingly, group settlement area seems largely irrelevant. However, groups in particularly large countries are less likely to be included, although this effect is, by a very small margin, statistically insignificant. Finally, whether colonial independence was achieved in a violent manner or not does not have a significant effect. In sum, we find considerable empirical evidence consistent with our theoretical argument concerning the differential ethno-political legacies of French and British rule as a strong and systematic driver of the initial power constellation in post-colonial states.

6.2.4 Case illustrations

We also provide a series of brief case vignettes that illustrate the plausibility of our theoretical argument for select cases. Since our key argument about the ethno-political legacies of French and British rule builds on a spatial logic, we provide a series of maps that chart the geographic settlement patterns of groups that were included in the initial post-colonial state, and those that were not. To reiterate, in the former French colonies, we expect peripheral groups to be less influential.

Figure 6.4 shows that in Algeria the Arabs settled towards the coast gained the upper hand during the process of decolonization and took control of the post-colonial state (dotted shading), while Berbers were excluded from power (lined shading). Indeed, shortly after independence, Arabic became the sole official language and linguistic and cultural expressions of Berber were forbidden by the Arab-dominated ruling party *Front de Libération Nationale* (Lauermann, 2009, 42–43).

Mali is another case that illustrates this center-periphery logic (see Figure 6.5). Peripherally settled Arabs/Moors and Tuareg were faced with domination by the post-colonial regime under the leadership of Modibo Keïta. Mali also shows that our argument is not confined to countries with direct access to the sea. Indeed, similar patterns can also be found elsewhere, including Chad, the Central African Republic, Madagascar, Morocco, Niger, Togo, and Vietnam, where groups located closer to the center of colonial activity were able to take control of the post-colonial state.[10]

---

[10] Visual inspection across cases also suggests that the center-periphery logic is driven by scale; it affects primarily large countries. In line with assimilative strategies, broad power-sharing regimes that included many or all groups in the initial post-colonial state emerged in many of the *small* French ex-colonies, including Congo, Guinea, Mauritania, and Senegal. This is not surprising, since the colonial gradient can be expected to operate in absolute distance, and geographic differences in terms of differential power access are generally less likely in smaller countries.

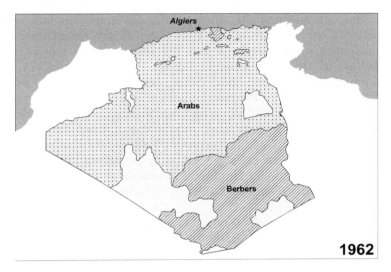

Figure 6.4 Ethnic groups' power access at the moment of independence in Algeria
Note: Dotted shading depicts included groups, lined shading depicts excluded groups.

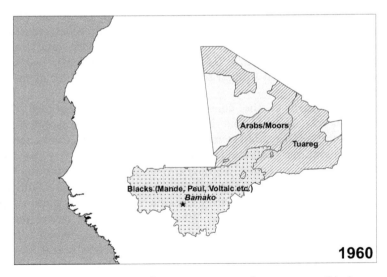

Figure 6.5 Ethnic groups' power access at the moment of independence in Mali
Note: Dotted shading depicts included groups, lined shading depicts excluded groups.

Having illustrated the ethno-political geography of former French colonies, we now turn to the states with a British colonial past. A brief qualitative survey confirms that the spatial distribution of excluded groups in British ex-colonies follows the center-periphery logic to a much lesser degree than in the countries that broke away from France. Our argument concerning the ethno-political legacies of British colonial policy is well illustrated by Nigeria, a paradigmatic case of British indirect rule given it was here that Lord Lugard's strategy was originally applied. The center of political and commercial colonial activity was clearly located at the coast, especially in Lagos. Accordingly, coastal ethnic groups faced very favorable socio-economic opportunity structures (Diamond, 1994a), especially the Yoruba (Horowitz, 1985, 151).

By contrast, members of northern groups were disproportionately poor and uneducated (Horowitz, 1985, 152). Moreover, compared to the South, where English was the language of administration and Western religion and education were promoted, "British officials administered the North through Hausa language and sought to preserve the region's social structure and institutions" (Diamond, 1994a, 26). Thus, despite their peripheral location and socio-economic disadvantage, the British approach to colonial governance offered comparatively favorable political conditions to the northern groups. In particular, the British policy of ruling through traditional ethnic authorities created strong incentives for political consolidation within the large and fragmented Igbo and Fulani groups (Horowitz, 1985, 149–150), preparing the path for strong and unified representation at the center at the time of independence.

With regard to the consolidation of ethnic identities, Diamond (1994a, 67) explains that Northern Nigeria was characterized by a "steep and finely graded status hierarchy, which tended to be reproduced over generations" and that its "authoritarian character . . . was deepened by colonial indirect rule." Diamond (1994a, 67) also notes that "because the youth [in Northern Nigeria] were groomed for political office by the colonial administration," they became influential in national politics after the end of colonial rule. When Nigeria gained independence, the Northern People's Congress-led coalition (NPC), which represented Hausa-Fulani and Igbo, was able to secure electoral victory in 1959, in part because the directly ruled Southern region was more factionalized, as well as because the Northern region was actively supported in the electoral process by the departing colonial authority as a means of

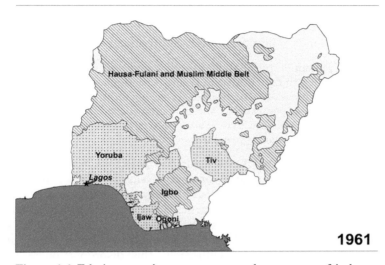

Figure 6.6 Ethnic groups' power access at the moment of independence in Nigeria
Note: Dotted shading depicts included groups, lined shading depicts excluded groups.

counter-balancing the South (Ankomah and Price, 2005). Thus, a coalition of Hausa-Fulani and Igbo was able to take control of the newly independent government as depicted in Figure 6.6.

Northerners distant from the coast were favored also in several other British colonies in West Africa, including Ghana and Sierra Leone (Horowitz, 1985, 447), but this pattern was by no means confined to Africa alone – it can also be found in Asia. In India, the British elicited collaboration from some Muslim groups, especially the Punjabi. Not surprisingly, in newly independent Pakistan, the Punjabi located in the North (and thus far away from the coast) gained the upper hand, which culminated in the relocation of the capital from coastal Karachi to Islamabad. Indeed, Wright (1991) explains that this process shifted the location of the "core" from the South to the North.

In Burma, the British divided their rule between the lowlands and the hills. This division made it most convenient for the imperial authorities to administer or even exploit the diversities rather than attempt to integrate the groups into a common political entity (Lange, Mahoney and vom Hau, 2006, 1447). Specifically, the British delineated a region for administering the lowland, predominantly Burman and Mon peoples, and allowed retention of local power structures in the diverse uplands. Thompson (1995, 273) argues that

Colonial promotion of the minorities as a source of support against majority populations led to the creation of groups with rising levels of educational and career expectations. It also resulted in an administration that separated the majority Burman population – the most influenced by Western colonialism – from most of the people who were allowed to retain their traditional views of and attitudes toward authority structures.

More importantly, the struggle for power in post-colonial Burma primarily hinged on military prowess (Callahan, 2003). In this respect, it is significant that the British strategy of "divide and rule," which included a ban on Burman participation in the army, gave the ethnic peripheral minorities, such as the Karen, Kachin, and Chin, a major military advantage over the lowland Burman population (see especially Callahan, 2003, 33–36). Ultimately, this disproportionate influence forced the builders of post-independence Burma to address the ethnic divide. The Panglong Agreement of 1947, which brought together the Burman state builders led by General Aung San with representatives of the Shan, Kachin, and Chin, was the fruit of these efforts (Walton, 2008). While the Karen, who fought a secessionist war of independence, as well as other numerous ethnic minorities were excluded, the Panglong Agreement hinged on a federal compromise that featured both far-reaching autonomy for the three invited hill peoples together with representation in the central government. Although the Burman-dominated government was to gradually chip away the concessions until Ne Win's military coup of 1962, which ended the remainders of peripheral influence on the government, the Karen, Kachin, and Chin did not rebel until their downgrading was becoming a fact (see, e.g., Callahan, 2003, ch. 7). Thus, in line with our argument concerning indirect rule, the relatively small Shan and Kachin groups in the North of the country enjoyed access to the executive in the initial post-colonial period (see Figure 6.7).[11]

---

[11] However, in contrast to most other cases, the initial post-colonial ethnic power configuration in Burma did not last particularly long, and was reversed in the late 1950s when the Shan and Kachin groups were removed from power (see, e.g., Callahan, 2003, ch. 7).

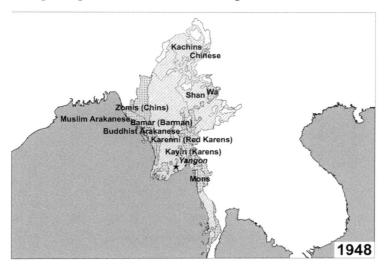

Figure 6.7 Ethnic groups' power access at the moment of independence in Myanmar
Note: Dotted shading depicts included groups, lined shading depicts excluded groups.

6.3   Explaining Conflict

In this section, we detail how the differential between French and British rule can be exploited to assess the validity of the nexus between ethnic power access and conflict. We begin by noting that the *conditional* effect of a group's relative location on inclusion, depending on the colonizer, is fundamentally different from the *uniform* center-periphery gradient established by the literature on conflict. Indeed, peripheralness is widely argued to be conducive to conflict (e.g. Fearon and Laitin, 2003). As such, the differential logic established above operates *independently* of conflict.

How can this information be used to study post-colonial conflict? Whereas existing work relies on time-varying data on political status that incorporates the risk of endogeneity (as discussed above), we focus on the snapshot of the initial post-conflict constellation, which allows us to overcome such problems. More specifically, our conflict analyses rely on a *cross-sectional* design that regresses whether a group was involved

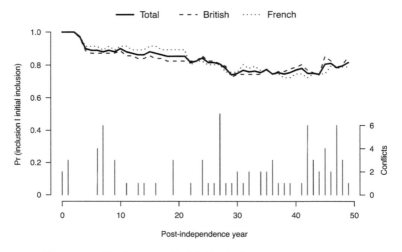

Figure 6.8 Persistence of initial inclusion

in civil conflict during the post-colonial period (i.e., from the time of independence until 2009) on initial power status.[12]

This cross-sectional design makes sense because the initial constellation in newly independent states is remarkably persistent (van de Walle, 2009, 321) and can therefore serve as a reasonable proxy for later constellations. To briefly elaborate, under the principle of nationalism, ethnic identities manifest themselves when group members hold key positions in the administration or army, since in-group recruitment is possible. This in turn secures the group's position in the long-run. We therefore argue that due to in-group recruitment, power configurations tend to be quite persistent across time (Rothchild, 1981; Wimmer, 1997).

The claim that power access is persistent across time can be evaluated empirically. Based on time-varying group-level EPR data, Figure 6.8 displays a group's yearly probability of being included given that it was included in the initial post-colonial power constellation. As can be seen, inclusion is highly persistent: with a .85 probability initially included groups will also enjoy access to state power fifty years later. Thus, due to this persistence, inclusion in the *initial* post-colonial state is likely to have long-term consequences for the political status of ethnic groups. Moreover, Figure 6.8 also demonstrates that there is no obvious pattern for the timing of post-colonial conflicts.

---

[12] Thus, by design our analyses cannot speak to the timing or dynamics of conflict.

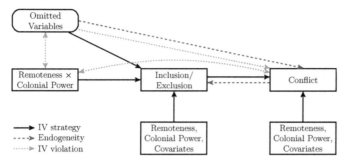

Figure 6.9 Identification strategy

Our full identification strategy is visualized in Figure 6.9. We treat the interaction effect between the colonial powers and our measure of remoteness as the instrumental variable to overcome possible endogeneity problems depicted by the dashed arrows.[13] The figure also highlights those pathways (dotted arrows) that could undermine the validity of the instrumental variable setup. We discuss these in detail below.

6.3.1   Data, method and results

Our measure of conflict is a dummy indicating whether an ethnic group has ever experienced ethno-nationalist conflict during the period between independence and 2009.[14] Because the dependent variable (conflict) and the endogenous regressor (inclusion) are both binary, a non-linear model is appropriate.[15] Thus, we rely on a seemingly unrelated bivariate probit estimator. This is a framework suitable for the analysis of two processes with dichotomous outcomes for which the error terms are correlated. Maddala (1983, 122) shows that the binary dependent variable of the first equation can be an endogenous regressor in the second equation (see also Wooldridge, 2010, 594ff.), and that a model specified in this way yields consistent estimates. The estimator has thus been used widely in political science in this form

---

[13] See Auer (2013) for an analogous research design.

[14] It is derived from the group-specific dataset ACD2EPR that links the UCDP/PRIO conflict data (Gleditsch et al., 2002) to EPR groups via the datasets by Wucherpfennig et al. (2011) and Cunningham, Gleditsch and Salehyan (2009). See also Chapter 4.

[15] As is well known, conventional instrumental variable techniques, in particular projection methods like two-stage least squares (2SLS), do not carry over to the case of limited dependent variables, especially when the endogenous regressor is not continuous (Rivers and Vuong, 1988). Indeed, such a two-stage logit/probit is generally inconsistent (Wooldridge, 2010, 597).

(Smith, 1999; Sondheimer and Green, 2010; Christin and Hug, 2012; Maves and Braithwaite, 2013).

Intuitively, the bivariate probit models the correlation between unobserved factors that simultaneously determine both access to state power and conflict through the coefficient ρ, thus capturing the relationship between the two processes. This allows for concrete interpretations with respect to endogeneity: whereas a negative ρ would suggest evidence in favor of the exclusion-of-belligerents mechanism, a positive ρ is consistent with the opposite mechanism, that is, the inclusion of belligerents.

In estimating the bivariate probit model, we specify two jointly estimated equations. The equation explaining inclusion is specified in the same way as Model 2 in Table 6.1. For the conflict equation, we rely on the same set of covariates, but instead of the interaction term between the colonial powers and remoteness we include the endogenized regressor, ethnic inclusion. Our main results are contained in Table 6.2. The upper half of the table displays the first set of equations that explain the endogenous variable ethnic inclusion, analogous to the analysis conducted above. The lower half of the table contains the equations in which conflict is the dependent variable.

For the purpose of comparison, Model 3 displays the estimates from two separate probit models that neglect the possibility of endogeneity, while Model 4 is the bivariate probit. Thus, the first part of Model 3 is a repetition of Model 2 in Table 6.1. Having discussed the inclusion equation in the previous section, we focus on the conflict equation displayed in the lower part of the table. The control variables indicate that there is some evidence in favor of a center-periphery gradient, although the effect is not statistically significant. Nevertheless, groups in former British colonies are statistically less likely to fight. Population size and per capita GDP show the expected signs, but neither is significant at conventional levels. We find no effect for group settlement or country area. Somewhat surprisingly, the coefficient for group size is negative, but also insignificant and reversed in the bivariate probit. Finally, where colonial independence was achieved in a violent manner, post-colonial conflict is less likely.

Turning to our main variable of interest, power status, we find a strong negative effect of ethnic inclusion on conflict. Based on the naïve assumption of exogeneity, Model 3 suggests a negative and highly statistically significant effect that matches the findings of Cederman, Gleditsch and Buhaug (2013, Ch. 3). Explicitly accounting for endogeneity, Model 4 reports an even stronger effect for this coefficient. In keeping with the inclusion-of-belligerents mechanism, this result reflects a larger

Table 6.2. *Full results*

	(3) Separate probits	(4) Bivariate probit
Eq 1: Explaining inclusion		
British colony	−3.72* (1.45)	−4.28** (1.27)
Log distance to coast	−0.55* (0.24)	−0.65* (0.22)
Log distance to coast × British colony	0.68* (0.27)	0.77** (0.23)
Groupsize	2.33* (0.93)	1.75 (0.92)
Log group area (km^2)	0.10 (0.14)	0.15 (0.13)
Log country area (km^2)	−0.34 (0.18)	−0.40* (0.18)
Log population	0.18 (0.11)	0.18 (0.13)
Log GDP per capita	0.24 (0.24)	0.26 (0.23)
Violent independence	0.23 (0.34)	0.23 (0.33)
Constant	1.72 (2.67)	2.51 (2.59)
Eq 2: Explaining conflict		
Inclusion	−0.73* (0.30)	−2.03** (0.25)
British colony	−0.68* (0.33)	−0.48 (0.25)
Log distance to coast	0.20 (0.18)	0.16 (0.11)
Groupsize	−0.91 (1.00)	0.46 (0.69)
Log group area (km^2)	−0.11 (0.14)	−0.05 (0.11)
Log country area (km^2)	0.15 (0.19)	−0.08 (0.15)
Log population	0.14 (0.14)	0.23* (0.12)
Log GDP per capita	−0.13 (0.29)	0.06 (0.20)
Violent independence	−1.53* (0.53)	−1.12* (0.50)
Constant	−2.73 (2.64)	−2.30 (1.74)
Observations	169	169
ρ		0.94
Prob > χ^2		0.03
Log likelihood	−94.34/−76.22	−168.09

Robust standard errors clustered by country in parentheses
* $p < 0.05$, ** $p < 0.001$

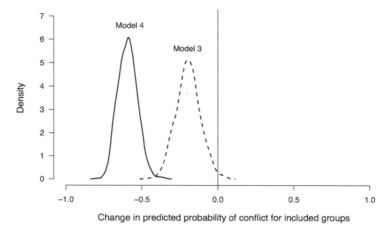

Figure 6.10 Marginal effects of inclusion on conflict, based on uncorrected and corrected Models 3 and 4 in Table 6.2

marginal peace-inducing effect of inclusion on conflict than identified by previous studies on the topic. Figure 6.10 visualizes this finding in terms of conflict probabilities. Simulating the effect for ethnic groups contained in our dataset by means of average predictive comparisons (Gelman and Hill, 2007), on average, a change from exclusion to inclusion decreases the predicted conflict probability by around 20 percent under the naïve model (Model 3). Once we account for endogeneity (Model 4), this difference roughly triples in magnitude to more than 60 percent. In short, we find that once the exogenous part of inclusion has been isolated, its peace-inducing effect becomes much more pronounced.

The coefficient ρ measures the correlation between the error terms, that is, possible endogeneity. The coefficient is positive and thus in line with the inclusion-of-belligerents logic, since stochastic factors that predict inclusion also have a positive effect on conflict. Moreover, ρ is also statistically significant at $p = .027$ (Wald test). In sum, we find considerable empirical support for the inclusion-conflict linkage.

6.3.2   Validation and sensitivity analyses

How credible is this result? In this section, we briefly describe a series of validity checks of our instrumental variable approach, as well as some sensitivity analyses. Due to space limitations, these are discussed in more detail in the online appendix.

In order for our colonial argument to serve as a valid instrument that can account for potential endogeneity, it must meet two key criteria. First, it should have sufficient *instrument strength* in explaining ethnic inclusion after controlling for covariates. Above, we provide theoretical and empirical evidence that this is indeed the case. Second, it must meet the *exclusion restriction* by precluding any correlation between the instrument and the error term (see gray dotted arrows in Figure 6.9). Specifically, the exclusion restriction will be violated if *and only if* any of the following conditions apply (Wooldridge, 2010, 89–90):

1. There exists reverse causation between the conflict potential of groups and systematic differences in the direction of the center-periphery logic.
2. The instrument correlates with an omitted determinant of conflict.
3. The instrument has an effect on conflict through an omitted variable (i.e., a variable other than inclusion).

Thus, the exclusion restriction imposes no restriction on potential correlation (or causation) between the instrument and any observed variables, provided they are included in the model.

According to condition 1, our argument will be void if the British empire deliberately chose to colonize areas with potentially belligerent groups in the periphery, while the French followed the reverse strategy. This seems highly unlikely since borders of colonized territories were typically demarcated arbitrarily, and often prior to explorations on the ground (Herbst, 1989, 2000; Englebert, Tarango and Carter, 2002).

Condition 2 arises if a causally deeper omitted variable correlates with the instrumental variable. A possible violation along these lines might stem from the fact that many former French colonies are Sahel-Saharan states whose peripheral groups are likely to be poorer and thereby more conflict-prone. Thus, peripheralness in French colonies, which corresponds to our instrument, could correlate with the error term through poverty as an omitted variable. Yet, controlling for underlying group-level economic and climatic preconditions that can be expected to impede economic development makes no difference to our results. In Models 5–9 of the online appendix, we account for the share of a group's territory used for agricultural production, agricultural territory *per capita*, soil quality, latitude, as well as a dummy for North Africa as additional controls. Although measures proxying for underdevelopment generally lower the prospects of inclusion, we consistently find that this occurs independently of our proposed instrumental variable logic, thus further supporting our main result that inclusion breeds peace.

Condition 3 requires us to consider potential consequences of the instrument that do not operate through inclusion. Specifically, it is possible that the type of colonial rule not only shaped the political, but also the economic center-periphery gradient in post-colonial states. In this case, peripheral groups would be relatively more developed in British colonies than in French colonies, again resulting in a problematic omitted variable that correlates with the instrument. However, there is no evidence for such an effect, because our instrument does not explain economic development at the level of ethnic groups (see the online appendix).

Two additional arguments could be made to undermine the validity of our findings. These further elucidate the role of the covariates included in the model. First, Posner (2005) argues that British indirect rule led to the genesis of smaller, rather than larger, ethnic groups. This is because the British mode of governance incentivized chiefs to underscore their local identities and cultures in order to maximize their legitimacy. By extension, this could result in more peripheral groups. While it is true that groups in British colonies are slightly smaller on average (but not more peripheral, see densities in Figure 6.3), we emphasize that we find no evidence that group size is determined by a center-periphery logic, neither unconditionally, nor differentially between the empires.

Second, one might wonder whether the colonizers continued to have an impact during the post-colonial period. For example, French foreign policy towards its former colonies has arguably been more proactive than its British counterpart. If this entails the systematic protection of governments, then excluded groups might be deterred from challenging the state. Substantively, this argument implies that inclusion should be more persistent in French colonies. However, Figure 6.8 indicates that the persistence of power access at the group-level does not differ between the two empires. More importantly, this objection hinges on between-empire effects, yet these are systematically accounted for through the dummy for colonial empire (which incidentally is not the instrument). In short, *by design* our findings must stem entirely from *differential* variation *within* French and British colonies, respectively.

Beyond these considerations, our results also hold in a series of sensitivity tests. First, we find that controlling for, or limiting the sample to, countries with coastal access does not alter the main findings. Second, we obtain similar results using alternative instruments (distance to major city) or alternative estimation techniques (two-stage estimation). Third, using alternative dependent variables that capture conflicts within post-colonial states, as well as ten years after their independence, we show that the peace-inducing effect of inclusion operates both immediately and in the long run. Other historical aspects, such as the duration of colonial rule or the strength of pre-colonial institutions, do not impact our main findings.[16] We also control for the influence of ethno-political contextual factors, such as the number of groups in the country as well as the share of included groups other than the group itself, again finding no substantial differences in our main results. Finally, we provide some evidence that "other" colonizers seem to have followed the British model (Mamdani, 1996, 86).

6.4   Conclusion

In line with Master Hypothesis 1a, we find strong and systematic evidence that – at least for the post-colonial world – inclusion in governmental power sharing systematically reduces the likelihood that ethnic groups become involved in ethnic civil war. Our instrumental-variable analysis confirms Master Hypothesis 4, because we have found that governments tend to co-opt potential rebels rather than excluding them. Yet, by design the identification strategy and findings are restricted to former colonies and hinge on the assumption that inclusion is highly persistent over time. In other words, questions regarding external validity remain. Moreover, the precise mechanisms by which a group's threat-potential affects the government's decision calculus to included or exclude it in a power-sharing arrangement are only crudely identified. In the next chapter, we therefore explore a more fine-grained approach that intends to complement our analyses of the post-colonial world by means of an explicit (formal) theoretical model.

---

[16] In a response to McAlexander's (2020) attempt to reanalyze Wucherpfennig, Hunziker and Cederman (2016), Wucherpfennig and Cederman (Forthcoming) propose a new instrument based on pre-colonial statehood.

7   The Strategic Logic of Governmental Power Sharing and Civil War*

In this chapter, we explore an actor-centric approach that emphasizes strategic interaction and offers an alternative to IV-estimation to pursue the evaluation of Master Hypothesis 4. We proceed in two steps. First, we introduce a simple formal model that captures the most important strategic dimension and highlights what is crucial for reverse causation: The conditions under which governments are likely to share power depending on the level of threat posed by a domestic challenger. As we have shown in Chapters 3 and 6, previous research on the origins of power sharing highlights *either* (1) government incentives for the *co-optation* of threatening challengers through power-sharing arrangements (e.g. Magaloni, 2008), *or* (2) *risk-diversion* by means of exclusion so as to avoid perilous infighting (cf. Roessler, 2011). Treating these as distinct theoretical possibilities, important consequences for the direction of the resulting bias emerge (Fearon, 2010).

Rather than favoring either consideration at the expense of the other, the model presented here unifies these mechanisms and shows that both have their place – depending on the challenger's level of threat as well as the government's ability to provide credible guarantees. Briefly, conflict-prone groups are generally likely to be co-opted through power sharing. However, this is no longer true when the challenging group is overwhelmingly strong, and thus cannot be co-opted. In this case, which is empirically rare, the government is better off diverting the risk and maintaining minority rule, as exemplified by the Syrian Alawite regime of Bashar al-Assad.

In a second step, the chapter provides a novel statistical estimator that closely mirrors the strategic logic of the theoretical model (cf. Signorino, 1999), but also accounts for the selection on unobservables. The estimator directly incorporates – and thereby endogenizes – the government's strategic decision calculus of whether or not to share power with an ethnic group, depending on its level of threat. This allows

---

* This chapter was previously published as an article, see Wucherpfennig (2021).

us to retrieve an improved, if not unbiased, estimate of the effect of power sharing. Applied to data at the level of ethnic groups around the globe since World War II that includes information about their inclusion in power-sharing arrangements as well as involvement in ethnic civil conflict (Vogt et al., 2015), we find strong evidence that governments do indeed strategically use power sharing as a way of managing the risk of conflict. In short, power sharing is systematically endogenous to conflict as suggested by Master Hypothesis 4. Nevertheless, we find that power sharing works much better than its reputation, and is on average a suitable means to secure peace in multi-ethnic states. These results hold up to several robustness checks, thus confirming Master Hypothesis 1a.

7.1   Reverse Causation

The question whether power sharing systematically limits or provokes conflict lends itself to quantitative investigation, but the possibility of reverse causation renders this a difficult problem for empirical analysis. Although many authors are aware of the issue (e.g. Walter, 2002; Roeder and Rothchild, 2005; Hartzell and Hoddie, 2007), almost all quantitative studies effectively assume that power sharing is an exogenous regressor and unrelated to the threat of future conflict.[1] Conceptually, this stands in marked contrast to how practitioners view power sharing: as a policy tool to manage future conflict. In other words, power sharing is applied systematically in anticipation of its prospects to keep the peace. Neglecting reverse causation is thus likely to induce bias, a research problem that can be traced back to Riker (1980), and is echoed in, recent research on the origins and effects of political regimes (e.g. Pepinsky, 2014).

To the best of our knowledge, only two studies on power sharing make a concerted effort to address problems of endogeneity by pursuing an instrumental variable approach, which is arguably the standard approach to overcome such problems in observational studies (Sovey and Green, 2011). In a pioneering effort, Cammett and Malesky (2012) instrument for proportional representation on the basis of a diffusion logic in neighboring states. However, their sample is restricted to negotiated settlements after civil war, thereby excluding both peaceful instances as well as other civil war outcomes.[2] In the previous chapter, we explored

---

[1] These studies assume that the problem of endogeneity can be "controlled away" through covariates, hinging on the strong assumption that the list of confounders is both fully observable and complete.

[2] In addition, Betz, Cook and Hollenbach (2018) show that such a spatial instrument is flawed to begin with.

an approach that exploits differences in colonial governance to explain inclusion in the post-colonial period, but this study is merely a cross-section of ethnic groups in former French and British colonies at the time of decolonization. In short, we are still missing a comprehensive, global assessment across space and time in order to overcome the limitations imposed by previous studies. Arguably this gap has been difficult to address, because persuasive instrumental variables are notoriously hard to come by in this field of research (Fearon, Kasara and Laitin, 2007). Thus, as an alternative way forward, we use the present chapter to leverage an actor-centric approach that sees power sharing as emerging from the strategic interaction between ethnic groups.

Addressing the problem of endogeneity in the application of power sharing as a policy tool is equivalent to understanding the origins of such regimes. We argue that the key question amounts to understanding why and when governments are willing and able to share power with an ethnic group, depending on the threat posed by the group. Using this agency-lens, we build on the critique outlined above and examine jointly the causes and consequences of *de facto* power sharing at the group-level. In doing so, we draw on recent literature that highlights how power sharing is a strategic tool used by regimes around the globe.

In this context, we introduced two key mechanisms in Chapters 3 and 6. The first, which we have referred to as *co-optation*, recognizes that for incumbent regimes, power sharing is a strategy to avoid popular uprising when exclusion is too risky and therefore not feasible (Przeworski and Gandhi, 2006; Gandhi, 2008; Magaloni, 2008; Svolik, 2012; Roessler, 2016). In this case, the ruling group delegates state benefits and power positions to selected groups as a way of appeasing or buying off potential challengers. In short, power sharing is used as a means of grievance-reduction (cf. Chapter 3). The second mechanism, which we have labeled *risk diversion*, occurs within power-sharing coalitions and captures the commitment problem that arises when members of a power-sharing arrangement face incentives to monopolize power by removing their ruling partners from the government through infighting or coups (Magaloni, 2008; Roessler, 2011; Svolik, 2012). Empirical analyses suggest that some formal institutions, including legislatures, parties and even elections, can help overcome this dilemma (Przeworski and Gandhi, 2006; Boix and Svolik, 2013), while Walter (1997) highlights the role of third-parties – especially peacekeepers – in enforcing the terms of a power-sharing agreement. Recognizing their conceptual similarity, henceforth we simply refer to both as credible institutions.

The logics of co-optation and risk-diversion have important consequences for causal inference. According to the co-optation perspective, governments exclude other groups wherever possible, while including only threatening groups. In this case, the peace-inducing effect of power sharing is likely to be underestimated. By contrast, if governments exclude potential belligerents to avoid infighting, the opposite is true, and empirical estimates will be overly optimistic (Fearon, 2010), which is what we found in our colonial approach presented in the previous chapter. Below we present an integrated theoretical and empirical analysis that investigates the conditions under which either mechanism is likely to prevail, thereby providing a more complete picture.

7.2   Theoretical Model

We rely on a game-theoretic model to demonstrate the strategic logic of power sharing. For the purpose of tractability, the model is a first-cut and deliberately simple. It builds on the arguments about co-optation and risk-diversion described above, and assumes complete and perfect information.

The model integrates and formalizes the arguments about co-optation and risk-diversion described above, and assumes complete and perfect information. The extensive form of the game is displayed in Figure 7.1. The game features two actors i: the *government* (G), and a rivaling domestic *group* (R) (cf. Boix and Svolik, 2013). The two actors compete over a metaphorical pie (normalized to a value of 1) that symbolizes the incompatibility, that is, control over the state's executive. The government moves first and either excludes (E) the group from power entirely, or grants a fixed share of its power (PS) to the group. Subsequently, after either government action, the group either accepts the government's action and remains peaceful ($\neg F$), or seeks an alternative outcome by resorting to fighting (F).

The payoffs are assigned as follows: If the government successfully excludes the group $\{E, \neg F\}$, it keeps the full pie 1 and the group receives

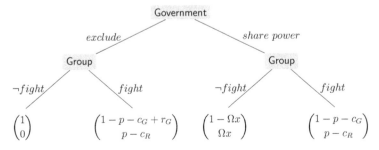

Figure 7.1 Extensive form

a payoff of 0. Naturally, this is the preferred outcome for the government. However, the group may not accept being excluded, and can challenge the incumbent by fighting $\{E, F\}$. Following standard practice, we model this conflict as a costly lottery. Here, the group wins the full pie with probability $p \in [0, 1]$, whereas G's probability of winning is $1 - p$. Thus, p is a measure of group strength relative to the government. Both actors have to bear a cost of fighting, denoted as $c_i > 0, i \in \{G, R\}$. Finally, to reflect that some governments may have incentives to fight early challengers so as to deter others (Walter, 2009; Tull and Mehler, 2005b; Spears, 2000), we add a reputation benefit, denoted $r_G \geq 0$, to the government's payoff when fighting excluded groups.

On the right side of the tree the government gives up some of its control over the state's executive and grants a power-sharing concession to the group. We denote this concession as $x \in (0, 1)$, but assume that its value is fixed. In case the group chooses to accept this power-sharing arrangement $\{PS, \neg F\}$, a potential commitment problem holds that the concession may be revoked. Indeed, the government generally faces incentives to renege on the arrangement should a favorable opportunity arise (Walter, 1997; Magaloni, 2008). Thus, the value of the concession x is conditioned by an institutional context, denoted as $\Omega \in [0, 1]$. If $\Omega = 1$, the commitment problem is non-existent and the government's offer to share state power is entirely credible so that the group has nothing to fear. In theory, if $\Omega = 0$, the government is entirely unable to commit to power sharing, and any arrangement is void, and effectively worthless (i.e. state failure). Higher values of Ω thus represent more credible "promises." R's payoff from peaceful power sharing is therefore Ωx, whereas this value is subtracted from the pie in G's payoff, that is, $1 - \Omega x$. Thus, by considering the full range of institutions, my approach goes beyond (and complements) pioneering work by Roessler and Ohls (2018) who address ethnic power sharing in weak states characterized by a strong commitment problem.

Finally, if the group is still not satisfied with this arrangement, power sharing breaks down and infighting among the power-sharing partners takes place $\{PS, F\}$, which modeled as a costly lottery as before. However, because concessions have taken place, the government can no longer collect reputation benefits for being tough.

Given complete and perfect information, the model can be solved by backwards induction. Thus, we assume that each player knows the other's payoffs, and vice-versa. The solution concept is therefore the subgame perfect equilibrium. The key is that we need to understand what keeps a group from fighting. The central intuition is that power sharing can achieve this, but only under credible institutions *or* if neither side has a high chance of winning and conflict is sufficiently costly.

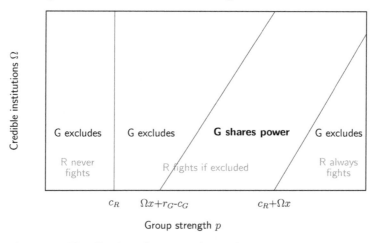

Figure 7.2 Visualization of comparative statics

The results are also displayed graphically as a summary in Figure 7.2.[3] Here, the x-axis represents a series of thresholds for the group expressed in terms of the parameter p, the group's relative strength. The y-axis denotes different levels of institutional credibility, (i.e. the parameter Ω). The different regions of the figure depict the actors' equilibrium paths according to the logic of backwards induction. In the following, we discuss five main results.

We begin by analyzing the conditions under which groups are willing to fight, along with the government's best response. In general, the group's decision to fight depends on whether the parameter p is larger than some threshold (as given along the x-axis in the Figure).[4] Depending on this threshold, groups will either (1) never fight ('weak groups'), (2) always fight ('overwhelmingly strong groups'), or (3) fight only if excluded ('moderately strong groups').

1. Weak groups. The group's threshold for fighting depends on the probability of winning relative to the costs of fighting. Therefore G never fights if $p \leq c_R$. Intuitively, *when facing weak, non-threatening groups, the government's preferred strategy is to deny power sharing and exclude the group so as to maximize the spoils.*
2. Overwhelmingly strong groups. Some overwhelmingly strong groups, however, will always fight in order to monopolize the spoils, regardless of the government's action, and especially when the institutions are not credible. For such groups the threshold for fighting, p, depends

---

[3] The figure depicts scenarios for which $\Omega > 0$, i.e. no state failure.
[4] In setting (strict) equalities, we assume that ceteris paribus R prefers $\neg F$ to F, and G prefers E to PS.

on how large the costs of fighting, c_R and expected value of power-sharing, Ωx are. This equilibrium result is intuitive in the sense that strong groups will prefer the gamble of war over the gamble of power sharing, especially when the latter is associated with a high risk of losing the concession due to a looming commitment problem. Given complete and perfect information, the government anticipates this behavior by the group. Knowing that the group will always fight, it is better off by excluding the group (since $r_G \geq 0$). *Thus, if the condition is met that the group will always fight, the government will engage in risk-diversion and never share power (c.f. Roessler, 2011).*

3. Moderately strong groups. If R's strength p lies in between the threshold of never fighting and the threshold of always fighting, that is, $c_R + \Omega x > p > c_R$, then the R will only fight if G maintains exclusion. In other words, power sharing can prevent moderately strong groups from fighting. Recognizing this co-optation device, the government will consider sharing power at the cost of a smaller share of the pie. So when does power sharing make sense for the government? To analyze this question, we define a critical value of the relative strength p^* with strict equality:

$$p^* = \Omega x + r_G - c_G. \tag{7.1}$$

At this critical value, the government is indifferent between exclusion and granting power sharing. If $p \leq p^*$, the government will prefer exclusion even though the group will resort to fighting. By contrast, to prevent conflict the government will have to offer the concession of power sharing. The government will do so if $p > p^*$. In other words, power sharing is attractive to the government when faced by moderately threatening challengers. More so, the model presented here implies that power sharing will not even be offered unless the government is faced by a militarily strong challenger. In short, *power sharing is a strategy of co-optation* to keep a domestic group from fighting where they otherwise would.

Next, we examine more closely the conditions for and consequences of power sharing.

4. Contrary to much of the literature – but in line with Boix and Svolik (2013) and Roessler and Ohls (2018) – Figure 7.2 shows that power sharing can be sustained if institutions are minimally credible, provided that neither the government nor the group is overwhelmingly strong. In other words, under weak institutions power sharing

can exist in equilibrium if it is *self-enforcing through a mutual threat,* that is when both parties are roughly equal in their thresholds for fighting.

However, fostering credible institutions can help bring about power sharing – and thereby peace – under specific conditions, namely when the challenging group is overwhelmingly strong, and the government is a minority. In Figure 7.2 this means moving from the lower right corner to the upper right corner.

5. Finally, in the model groups never fight when included in a power-sharing arrangement, but only if they are excluded. In short, according to the theoretical model, power sharing is associated with peace.

In sum, the theoretical model details the core strategic logic of power sharing in the face of civil war. It offers a unified account that comprises both the logics of co-optation and risk-diversion in the same model, and thus speaks to the question when and why governments are willing and able to share power with a domestic challenger depending on the level of threat. This question, we had argued, is key to addressing head-on the empirical challenge of reverse causation. Thus, we now turn to the second step of my empirical strategy and develop a statistical estimator that mirrors the theoretical model, thereby directly incorporating reverse causation. This allows us to test specific predictions, as well as the formal model in general.

7.3   Empirical Estimation of the Game

At a basic level, the theoretical model suggests that the decision to enact a power-sharing arrangement and the decision to fight are strategically interdependent. In this case, conventional estimators, such as logit or probit, can lead to serious bias (Signorino and Yilmaz, 2003). To overcome such problems, we derive a statistical model that includes the government's decision to grant power sharing or to exclude, and the group's decision to accept this choice or to resort to fighting as endogenous choices. Moreover, by explicitly modeling how the government strategically anticipates the group's response, we are able to deal with endogeneity problems that arise from strategic interaction (Signorino, 1999; Carter and Signorino, 2010).

The theoretical model depicted in Figure 7.1 assumes that neither the government nor the group make any errors in their decision-making – which we relax in order to derive the statistical model. Specifically, we make the plausible assumption that both actors are boundedly rational

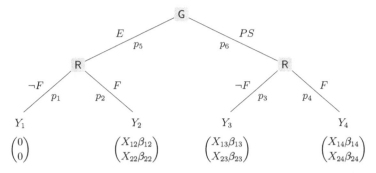

Figure 7.3 Empirical model

(Simon, 1955) by erring stochastically in making the optimal choice. Assuming a particular probability distribution for the actors' error terms, we derive a variant of the quantal response equilibrium (QRE) solution concept (McKelvey and Palfrey, 1995; McKelvey and Palfrey, 1998). The QRE includes the subgame perfect equilibrium solution concept as the special case in which neither actor makes errors (Signorino, 1999). The statistical model is therefore structurally consistent with the theoretical model, but also more general because it allows for the possibility that, at times, errors in decision-making occur.[5] Overall, this allows us to estimate the players' utilities directly from empirical data.

We introduce the logic of the statistical model by deriving for each player latent variables that reflect the differences in utilities from the relevant choice alternatives (with error). The notation is depicted in Figure 7.3. The players choose their actions based on the expected difference in utilities (with error). For G this means deciding between excluding the group or sharing power

$$\Delta(U_G) = y_G^* = U_G(PS) - U_G(E) + \epsilon_G \tag{7.2}$$

while for R this means deciding between staying peaceful and resorting to arms

$$\Delta(U_{R,E}) = y_{R,E}^* = U_{R,E}(F) - U_{R,E}(\neg F) + \epsilon_{R,E}$$

$$\Delta(U_{R,PS}) = y_{R,PS}^* = U_{R,PS}(F) - U_{R,PS}(\neg F) + \epsilon_{R,PS} \tag{7.3}$$

depending on whether G previously played E or PS. The conventional strategic estimator would then assume that the four possible outcomes $Y_1, \ldots, Y_4$ arise as the joint probabilities of the players' actions (Signorino, 1999; Carter, 2010). However, Leemann (2014) explains that

---

[5] In addition, we allow for these errors to be correlated; see below.

this implies the problematic assumption that the error terms between the players are uncorrelated, (i.e. $corr(\epsilon_G, \epsilon_{R,E}) = corr(\epsilon_G, \epsilon_{R,PS}) = 0$), which is likely to induce selection bias (Signorino, 2002). Following Leemann (2014), the strategic selection estimator derived here avoids this problem by allowing for the government's and the groups' error terms to be correlated via a bivariate distribution. As detailed below, this is critical to overcome endogeneity problems when estimating the effectiveness of the government's choice with regard to the probability of conflict. The estimator can be considered a hybrid of the conventional strategic estimator (Signorino, 1999) and a Heckman sample selection probit (Boyes, Hoffman and Low, 1989). Specifically, the four possible outcomes given by the joint probabilities of the players' actions are modeled as:

$$\{E, \neg F\} : P(Y_1) = \Phi_2(-\Delta U_G; -\Delta U_{R,E}; \quad \rho_1)$$
$$\{E, F\} : P(Y_2) = \Phi_2(-\Delta U_G; \quad \Delta U_{R,E}; -\rho_1)$$
$$\{PS, \neg F\} : P(Y_3) = \Phi_2(\quad \Delta U_G; -\Delta U_{R,PS}; -\rho_2)$$
$$\{PS, F\} : P(Y_4) = \Phi_2(\quad \Delta U_G; \quad \Delta U_{R,PS}; \quad \rho_2) \tag{7.4}$$

where Φ_2 is the bivariate standard normal cumulative density function with correlation ρ. This means that we assume the players' errors to follow a normal distribution. Put differently, the conventional strategic probit estimator is nested in our approach as the special case where $\rho_1 = \rho_2 = 0$.[6]

Drawing on Equations 7.2 and 7.3, the next step is to reformulate the estimator given in Equation 7.4 in terms of utility over outcomes:

$$P(Y_1) = \Phi_2\Big(p_1 U_G(Y_1) + p_2 U_G(Y_2) - p_3 U_G(Y_3) - p_4 U_G(Y_4); \quad U_R(Y_1) - U_R(Y_2); \quad \rho_1\Big)$$
$$P(Y_2) = \Phi_2\Big(p_1 U_G(Y_1) + p_2 U_G(Y_2) - p_3 U_G(Y_3) - p_4 U_G(Y_4); -U_R(Y_1) + U_R(Y_1); -\rho_1\Big)$$
$$P(Y_3) = \Phi_2\Big(-p_1 U_G(Y_1) - p_2 U_G(Y_2) + p_3 U_G(Y_3) + p_4 U_G(Y_4); \quad U_R(Y_4) - U_R(Y_3); -\rho_2\Big)$$
$$P(Y_4) = \Phi_2\Big(-p_1 U_G(Y_1) - p_2 U_G(Y_2) + p_3 U_G(Y_3) + p_4 U_G(Y_4); -U_R(Y_4) + U_R(Y_3); \quad \rho_2\Big)$$

where

$$p_2 = 1 - p_1 : p_2 = \Phi\Big(U_R(Y_2) - U_R(Y_1)\Big)$$
$$p_4 = 1 - p_3 : p_4 = \Phi\Big(U_R(Y_4) - U_R(Y_3)\Big) \tag{7.5}$$

---

[6] Signorino (1999) and others typically use a denominator of $\sqrt{2}$ to reflect variances of $\sigma = 1$, but this is for identification only and makes no difference other than scaling the estimates (Leemann, 2014, 377–378).

Written this way, the log-likelihood function is simply the joint probability of the outcomes:

$$\ell\ell = \sum_{i=1}^{N} \log P(Y_1)^{Y_1} + \sum_{i=1}^{N} \log P(Y_2)^{Y_2}$$

$$+ \sum_{i=1}^{N} \log P(Y_3)^{Y_3} + \sum_{i=1}^{N} \log P(Y_4)^{Y_4}. \qquad (7.6)$$

Using covariates to parameterize the players' utilities over outcome in the usual way, this function can then be optimized using standard maximum likelihood estimation. For example, we parameterize $U_G(Y_2)$ as $Z_{12}\gamma_{12}$, and $U_R(Y_2)$ as $X_{22}\beta_{22}$ (see Figure 7.3).

7.3.1   *Sources of Bias: Strategic expectations and sample selection*

Before detailing our choice of variables to parameterize the players' utilities, we discuss how the estimator given in Eq. 7.5 directly incorporates strategic expectations: the government's choice is based on a comparison between the utilities for the respective outcomes that are associated with choosing E, i.e. $U_G(Y_1)$ and $U_G(Y_2)$, and choosing PS, that is, $U_G(Y_3)$ and $U_G(Y_4)$. Once the government has made a choice, it is up to the group to decide which outcome materializes. Since this is not a fully random choice, the government weighs the utility of each outcome by the (anticipated) choice probabilities of the group (denoted $p_1,\ldots,p_4$). In other words, the government makes expected utility calculations that incorporate the probabilities that the group will remain peaceful or decide to fight.

By contrast, given that the rivaling group moves last, its decision calculus does not factor in any anticipated government *reaction*. However, those groups that choose between staying peaceful and fighting under exclusion might be systematically different from those that are granted power sharing, and some of these differences might not be fully observable to the analyst. This could lead to selection effects that bias the estimates for the group's utilities. Referring to the conventional strategic estimator (i.e. Eq. 7.5 with $p_1 = p_2 = 0$) Leemann (2014, 374) explains that

Compared to nonstrategic estimators, strategic models are even more prone to selection effects. First, external shocks or omitted variables can lead to correlated errors. Second, because the systematic parts of actors' utilities usually overlap on certain key variables, the two sets of explanatory variables are correlated. As a result, both the systematic and the stochastic components can be correlated.

However, given that the estimates for the first mover are computed based on the potentially biased predicted probabilities of the second actor, we also generate biased estimates for the first actor.

Thus, while strategic action affects the government's estimates, selection bias affects the group's estimates. Indeed, both potential causes for selection bias are plausible in the context of the current application.[7] For example, in the theoretical model, the parameter p (denoting the relative balance of power between the group and the government) is relevant to both players and therefore operationalized empirically through the same covariate (see below). This creates overlap on a key variable. Similarly, despite careful attempts to accurately specify the model, it is plausible that omitted variables or external shocks render some groups more or less prone to conflict, which affects their likelihood of being included in a power-sharing arrangement. The estimator derived above explicitly addresses these problems by allowing for correlated errors, thereby generating consistent, unbiased and efficient estimates in the presence of both selection bias and strategic action.[8] This will be of particular importance when we use the estimator to obtain an estimate of the effectiveness of power sharing as a means of preventing civil conflict by comparing the group's predicted probabilities to fight depending on the government's choice.

7.3.2   Data

The EPR dataset is particularly suitable for our purposes because it offers a measure of *de facto* executive power at the group-level. Depending on the country, this is either the presidency, the cabinet, or senior posts in the administration, including the army. Moreover, it is noteworthy that EPR is time-variant in its coding, that is, it captures major shifts in the power constellation across time. To re-iterate, EPR distinguishes between three major types of access to power based on whether the group (1) rules alone, (2) shares power, or (3) is excluded from executive power. The second type of power access captures *de*

---

[7] For analytical tractability the estimator assumes that the players are not aware of the correlation between error terms, unlike the estimator proposed by Signorino (2002). Monte Carlo analyses by Leemann (2014) suggest that this assumption makes little difference even if the DGP is based on a 'known' correlation.

[8] Strictly speaking the estimator does not require an exclusion restriction. Although the theoretical model predicates that some covariates are only relevant for G (which could be considered quasi instruments), identification is secured through non-linearities arising from strategic interaction and/or bivariate normality in errors, much like in a bivariate probit model (Wilde, 2000).

facto executive power-sharing arrangements, regardless of whether such arrangements arose due to formal rules or not. Thus, groups that share power enjoy meaningful representation, while excluded groups have no regular representation within the country's executive.

We use these group-level data to construct yearly group-government dyads based on all groups that are either included in a power-sharing arrangement or excluded. We consider 'the government' to be all groups which are not excluded, minus the group itself if the group is part of a power-sharing arrangement. Groups which rule alone cannot fight the state by definition and are therefore dropped from the analysis as no meaningful dyad can be constructed in such cases (Cederman, Wimmer and Min, 2010).[9]

7.3.2.1 Decision variables Directly reflecting the theory, the distinction between exclusion and power sharing is used as the government's decision variable. To capture the group's decision to fight (or remain peaceful), we rely on a group-level coding of the outbreak of civil conflict that is based on the Uppsala Conflict Data Programm's Armed Conflict Dataset, which requires at least twenty-five battle-related deaths in an intrastate conflict between a government and a non-governmental party in one calendar year (Gleditsch et al., 2002). Specifically, the ACD2EPR dataset provides a mapping of each conflict onset onto corresponding EPR group(s), provided that the rebel organization recruited from and claimed to operate on behalf of the group (Wucherpfennig et al., 2012).[10] Overall, there are 221 group conflict onsets and 10,409 group years of power sharing (out of a total of 29,145 observations) in the data. Jointly, the variables for exclusion/power sharing and conflict onset yield the four outcomes of the theoretical/empirical model.

7.3.2.2 Empirical specification of utilities In specifying government and group utilities, our general strategy is to strictly follow the theoretical model given in Figure 7.1 and operationalize each pay-off component through one or more relevant covariates. In short, we attempt to approximate the logic of the theoretical model as closely as possible. Since the strategic selection estimator adds considerable complexity in terms of computational demands and interpretation, a parsimonious specification is essential.

---

[9] However, these groups represent the government for groups from the respective countries.

[10] This includes violent coups that exceed the battle-related deaths threshold, but excludes non-violent ones.

To allow for identification, we need to set the utility of at least one outcome per player to zero. This provides a baseline for each player, and all other estimates will have to be interpreted relative to this base category. Given the theoretical model, the straightforward choice for the group is to set $U_R(Y_1) = 0$, since this outcome is also zero in the theoretical model. Because the government only compares its own utilities, we can simply normalize by subtracting a value of 1 from each of its payoffs, thereby also setting $U_R(Y_1) = 0$ (see Figure 7.1). As a result, we specify three sets of covariates per player.[11] Rather than discussing the parameterization of each utility separately, we discuss how each payoff component is operationalized, with the understanding that the full parameterization of each utility then follows directly from Figure 7.1.

Relative Group Strength p. To capture this parameter, we rely on the group's *demographic balance* relative to the government. For an excluded group i, this is computed as $p_{E,i} = s_i/(s_i + \sum_j s_j)$, where s denotes the group's relative share of the population as provided by EPR and j denotes all (other) groups that currently hold executive power. For groups included in power sharing this is $p_{PS,i} = s_i/\sum_{j \neq i} s_j$ (see Buhaug, Cederman and Rød, 2008). Constructed this way, $p \in (0, 1)$, which correctly reflects the theoretical model. Relying on demographic shares as a measure of strength is widely accepted (Bhavnani and Miodownik, 2009; Cederman, Gleditsch and Buhaug, 2013) and has several advantages, including that it is available at the level of ethnic groups.

Cost of fighting c_i. Following standard practice, we use GDP per capita (Gleditsch, 2002) to operationalize the (opportunity) cost of fighting for both actors (see Fearon and Laitin, 2003). In addition, we include the logged number of years since the last conflict (peaceyears), as well as a dummy variable for previous conflict.

This allows us to distinguish between pre- and post-conflict situations, while also addressing issues of event and duration dependence (Carter and Signorino, 2010). It can be expected that opportunity costs in post-conflict situations are lower, for example due to the availability of trained fighters and small arms, or feelings of revenge. Following Cederman, Gleditsch and Buhaug (2013), we also include a dummy for ongoing conflict during the previous year, reflecting lower mobilization costs.

Reputation benefits r. Governments should be more inclined to accept fighting when doing so can deter future challengers. In other words, they will benefit more from risking exclusion where they are faced with a large

---

[11] Strictly speaking, $X_{23}\beta_{23}$ is subsumed in $X_{24}\beta_{24}$ in our empirical estimation, but this merely changes sign, as can be seen in Equation 7.3.

number of potential challengers, especially early on (see, e.g., Tull and Mehler, 2005a; Walter, 2009). In order to operationalize this argument, we rely on the logged number of excluded groups in the country, interacted multiplicatively with the dummy for previous conflict.

We now turn to the part of the model that is most difficult to operationalize, namely the size of power sharing concessions and how credible these concessions are, that is, the commitment problem.

Credible institutions Ω. The theoretical model highlights how institutions lend credibility to the promise of power-sharing concessions, which is critical given that incentives to renege will likely prevail. While operationalizing this commitment problem is challenging, we exploit the insight that particular institutions may serve as a constraint on the government's ability to renege on the promise of power sharing. In particular, it can be expected that constraints on the central executive (i.e. the government), for example through legislatures or an independent judiciary, will make power sharing more credible to the challenger. Following this line of reasoning, we use the XCONST dimension ("executive constraints") of the Polity IV data (Marshall, Gurr and Jaggers, 2017) to capture the degree to which institutions are credible.[12] XCONST is a 7-point scale that captures "the extent of institutionalized constraints on the decision-making powers of chief executives" exercised by "accountability groups", such as legislatures in Western democracies, "the ruling party in a one-party state, councils of nobles or powerful advisors in monarchies, the military in coup-prone polities, and in many states a strong, independent judiciary" (Marshall, Gurr and Jaggers, 2017, 24). Higher values denote larger constraints on the executive. Alternative operationalizations of Ω are considered in the robustness analyses.

Share of power x. Finally, we require an indicator of the size of the concession that the government transfers to the group – the share of state power the group holds under power sharing. Empirically, it is difficult, if not impossible, to measure this aspect independently of the relative strength parameter p, especially counterfactually for groups not currently included in a power-sharing arrangement. We therefore make the additional assumption that in the empirical model, x is also

---

[12] We follow Gleditsch and Ruggeri (2010) and replace periods of interregnum with the minimum value so as to maximize the number of observations, and especially conflict onsets. Substantively, periods of interregnum are associated with great uncertainty, effectively preventing credible commitment.

captured by the group's demographic share relative to the government. This is empirically warranted, since Francois, Rainer and Trebbi (2015, 465) convincingly show that within African power-sharing arrangements "political power is allocated proportionally to population shares across ethnic groups."

7.3.3   Main results

We estimate the model using standard maximum likelihood techniques with an analytical gradient and strict convergence criteria to ensure optimization. Table 7.1 contains the estimation results. Following (Carter, 2010), we present more conservative (non-parametric) bootstrapped standard errors derived across 500 iterations. In general, for the statistical model to be consistent with the formal model, the (non-interacted) coefficients associated with each payoff component should be consistent with Figure 7.1. A close examination of the results reveals that, on the whole, the theoretical model is largely supported, since most estimated coefficients show the expected sign. Moreover, compared to a standard strategic estimator that does not allow for correlation between the error terms, the strategic selection estimator fits the data significantly better as suggested by an increase of fifteen in the log-likelihood value (for two additional degrees of freedom).[13]

Before turning to the two core questions about (1) the strategic origins and (2) the effects of power sharing on conflict, we briefly comment on the players' utilities. According to the strategic selection model, governments are more inclined to fight a rivaling excluded group in conditions of low GDP per capita, shortly after a previous conflict, and when there is an ongoing conflict that involves another group. Moreover, in line with reputation arguments we find that governments benefit from fighting in the presence of multiple challengers, especially early on.[14] When the rivaling group is included, however, the government's utility for fighting increases when GDP is low and the longer peace has endured. Here too, ongoing conflict with another group elsewhere raises the government's utility for fighting. Turning to the group's utilities, for a

[13] Note that coefficients for $U_G(E,F)$ and $U_G(PS,F)$ appear large, but this is because these utilities are scaled by very low baseline probabilities of fighting, i.e. $p2$ and $p4$ (see Eq. 7.5).

[14] For post-conflict situations, the relevant effect is the sum of the coefficient for the number of excluded groups and the interactive term, i.e. $243 - 204 = 39$, which is substantially smaller.

Table 7.1. *Player utilities for statistical strategic selection model*

	$U_G(E, F)$	$U_G(PS, -F)$	$U_G(PS, F)$	$U_R(E, F)$	$U_R(PS, -F)$	$U_R(PS, F)$
Constant	-1550.72 (777.76)	-7.14 (3.50)	1175.75 (310.71)	-2.69 (0.03)		-2.89 (0.07)
Relative balance	22.33 (15.73)	7.11 (1.58)	-3044.65 (783.73)	-0.09 (0.02)		0.28 (0.04)
Log GDP per capita	-3.20 (1.12)		-119.45 (29.73)	0.01 (0.00)		-0.03 (0.00)
Log peaceyears	-1.74 (0.83)		61.53 (15.66)	-0.01 (0.01)		0.00 (0.00)
Previous conflict	1382.73 (705.51)		-133.34 (42.69)	0.92 (0.06)		0.02 (0.01)
Conflict with other group	242.60 (21.73)		213.29 (47.42)			
Log num. excl. groups	13.71 (4.82)					
Previous conflict × log num. excl. groups	-204.31 (20.52)					
XCONST		-0.17 (0.05)			-0.07 (0.01)	
Relative balance × XCONST		1.73 (0.17)			0.04 (0.01)	
$\rho 1$	-0.23 (0.09)					
$\rho 2$	0.16 (0.07)					
Log likelihood	-13334.61					
Observations	29734					

Bootstrapped standard errors in parentheses

rivaling group that is excluded, high GDP increases the utility of conflict, as do enduring peace and the absence of prior conflict. When the group is part of a power-sharing arrangement, fighting can be beneficial when GDP is low, when the group has fought before, and after long lapses of peace.

7.3.4 Origins of power sharing

Building on these estimated utilities, we now shift the focus to two core questions. First, under what conditions are governments likely to share power with a rivaling group? Second, accounting for this endogenous choice, does power sharing limit (or spur) the risk of armed civil conflict? With regard to the former question, the key insight of the theoretical model has been that the threat of conflict informs the government's choice whether to share power with the group, and that this is conditioned by how credible the promise of power sharing is for the group. Reflecting this, Figure 7.4 uses the strategic selection model to generate predicted probabilites for the government's choice as a function of how strong the group is relative to the government (the parameter p operationalized as the relative demographic balance), as well as the credibility of the institutions (Ω operationalized as

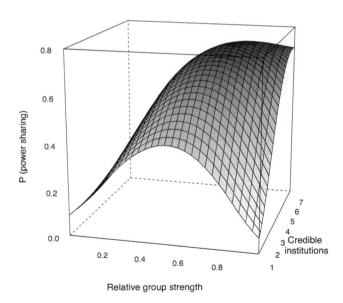

Figure 7.4 Estimated probability of power sharing

executive constraints). This goes beyond existing work (including the previous chapter), which has focused on weak institutional contexts, especially Africa (Roessler, 2016), providing a comprehensive account that covers a wide range of (global) settings. Strikingly, the figure bears a close resemblance to the equilibrium results of the theoretical model (see Figure 7.2). In particular, the statistical model likewise predicts that weak groups generally have a low probability of being part of power-sharing arrangements. Theoretically, this is because these groups do not pose a credible threat to the government, and thus there is no need to accommodate them. As groups get relatively stronger, power sharing becomes more likely, as suggested by the theoretical argument regarding co-optation. Under strong institutions, this monotonic relationship prevails, such that very large groups are almost certainly included in power sharing. However, in anarchic environments where the government cannot credibly commit to the promise of power sharing, this relationship only holds up to a point. Here, overwhelmingly strong groups feature a declining probability of being part of power-sharing arrangements, in line with our arguments concerning risk-diversion. As a result, when there exists a strong commitment problem, the relationship between relative strength and power sharing follows an inverted U-shape.

The vertex of this curvilinear relationship is estimated where the group and the government are roughly at parity, suggesting that power sharing can emerge endogenously even under conditions of anarchy. In this case, power sharing is self-enforcing through a mutual threat (cf. Roessler, 2011). The figure shows how improving the quality of institutions (i.e. moving towards the back of the cube) can make power sharing possible even in constellations where one side is vastly superior in strength.

In sum, the analysis so far strongly suggests that governments use power sharing in ways that follow a strategic logic. This overall picture is consistent with the estimated correlation between the players' stochastic components of their utilities: While the correlation coefficient ρ_1 is negative, ρ_2 is positive, suggesting that powerful groups are generally more likely to be offered power sharing. Substantively, this mirrors the findings derived from the colonial approach in the previous chapter.

7.3.5 Effect of power sharing on conflict

By accounting for the conditions under which power sharing is likely to emerge, it becomes possible to retrieve an unbiased estimate of the effect

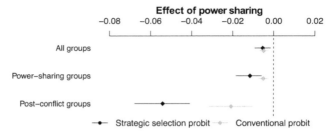

Figure 7.5 Estimated effect of power sharing

of power sharing on conflict. Based on the statistical model, this corresponds to the counterfactual of how a given group would have behaved had the government chosen differently. Thus, we compare predicted probabilities of fighting given either exclusion or power sharing, using this formula

$$P(F|PS) - P(F|E) =: \frac{\widehat{P(Y_4)}}{\widehat{P(Y_3)} + \widehat{P(Y_4)}} - \frac{\widehat{P(Y_2)}}{\widehat{P(Y_1)} + \widehat{P(Y_2)}} \qquad (7.7)$$

across groups in the sample (see Equation. 7.5).

Figure 7.5 depicts this estimate as the black dots (along with 95 percent confidence intervals) for a variety of scenarios. The gray diamonds denote the corresponding estimated effects derived from a standard probit that was calculated using all covariates (including interaction terms; results not shown) that are also included in the strategic selection estimator. All estimates were derived as average predicted probabilities, meaning that they reflect quantities of interest for real-world observations (i.e. combinations of values on the covariates) which are actually in the (sub-)sample (Hanmer and Kalkan, 2013).

The first two estimates correspond to the global average effect of power sharing on civil conflict. As can be seen, the strategic selection estimator yields a negative effect that is also statistically significant. Moreover, comparison to the "naïve" probit estimate suggests that the failure to account for strategic selection (i.e. endogeneity) leads to an underestimation of this pacifying effect by almost 20 percent.

The next two sets of estimates examine two concrete questions. First, has power sharing kept the peace in those instances where it has been applied? To address this question, we generate average predicted probabilities for all groups in the sample which are included in power sharing. This analysis suggests that, on average, power sharing has kept the peace. Second, by singling out the relevant observations, we ask whether power sharing is generally also suitable in post-conflict situations (see Master Hypothesis 3). Again the answer is a clear 'yes', as implied by a sizable negative estimate. Moreover, in both scenarios, the pronounced difference compared to the "naïve" estimates further underlines the risk of underestimating the effectiveness of power sharing and suggests that it has been or could be particularly beneficial.

In order to ensure that these results are not idiosyncratic, we conducted a number of robustness analyses. These are presented in the online appendix. First, we examined whether the results also hold for a more restrictive dependent variable that captures governmental conflicts only (rather than also territorial ones). Although the standard errors are slightly larger, the key findings are similar. Second, we employed an alternative operationalization of the commitment problem, using the 'political constraints index' from Henisz (2000), which attempts to identify underlying political structures and measure their ability to support credible policy commitments. Again, the key results are qualitatively unchanged. Finally, we explored whether the results are driven by the specific cases studied in the colonial approach presented earlier, that is former British and French colonies. However, such concerns are not warranted. Re-estimating the model without these cases again does not affect the results.

7.4   Conclusion

Whether governmental power sharing is a suitable means to secure peace in multiethnic states has been the subject of intense scholarly debate. In this chapter, we have highlighted how insufficient attention to reverse causation due to strategic interaction can hamper sound inference. Our analysis has demonstrated that examining the specific conditions under which domestic challengers are accommodated through co-optation (power sharing) or excluded so as to divert risk by governments yields a more complete picture compared to existing work which so far has treated the two in isolation. Building on these insights, the chapter has directly addressed endogeneity concerns about the effect of power sharing on conflict, finding a peace-inducing effect (see Master Hypothesis 4). In other words, the evidence presented here suggests that critics of power sharing are likely to have overstated their case, at least in part because of insufficient attention to endogeneity.

In general, as anticipated by Master Hypothesis 1a, the result that governmental power sharing is robustly associated with peace is encouraging from a policy-making perspective, precisely because it is a political decision that can be implemented also in the short-run – unlike other risk factors, such as underdevelopment, low state capacity or the country's topography which are much harder to manipulate (cf. Fearon and Laitin, 2003). In most cases, then, inter-ethnic conflict can and should be resolved through political compromise. However, our findings indicate that such a compromise should not be taken for granted, and that its accomplishment may hinge on the credibility of the promise of shared government and as such on the environment in which this promise is made. In this regard, strengthening institutions will be particularly effective in cases of minority rule in order to prevent challengers from resorting to violence.

The Syrian case in the midst of the Arab Spring is a good example. Observing that other regimes in the region were faced with demands for greater inclusiveness, and that these demands were often pursued by violent means, a preemptive strategy for the regime of Bashar al-Assad would have been to accommodate previously excluded groups, especially the Sunnis. However, our analysis suggests that fears of future reprisals due to a vastly unfavorable balance of power between the ruling Alawite minority (13 percent of the country's population) and the Sunnis (65 percent) made this impossible, especially because the regime could not credibly commit that such an arrangement would actually endure. Fueled by this mistrust, gaining full control over the Syrian state through military victory thus became the opposition's objective. Moreover, according to the model analyzed in this chapter, by providing weapons to the Syrian Free Army external states only made things worse, precisely because the Assad regime and the loyal Alawite minority anticipated future reprisals if previously excluded groups were to become empowered. Importantly, this dilemma arose not just because of the demographic imbalance, but also because of a lack of an enforcement mechanism that would have made power sharing credible to the Sunni majority.[15]

To end civil wars and to keep post-conflict peace, (UN) peacekeeping has become the standard policy prescription by the international community. Theoretically, this is justified because peacekeepers can help overcome commitment problems, thereby enabling lasting peace agreements (Walter, 2002). But peacekeeping does not need to be restricted to (post-) conflict situations; in principle it can also work preemptively. So far, the United Nations Preventive Deployment Force (UNPREDEP) in the Republic of Macedonia has been the only 'proactive' mission in a country deemed to have a high risk of conflict outbreak. The results of our analysis suggest that such missions – by providing

---

[15] Syria scores a 3 ("slight to moderate limitation") for executive constraints in 2010.

credible institutions that make power sharing possible – could prove particularly helpful in countries seeking to peacefully transition out of minority rule.[16] Arguably, external "help" of this kind could have made a difference in Syria, too.

While we believe to have shed new light on an established question by disentangling some important aspects about the (two-way) relationship between power sharing and civil war in multiethnic states, the approach pursued in this chapter is not without limitations. These should be addressed by further research. For example, our approach does not account for the possibility of non-violent coups as an additional mode by which governments may lose power.[17] Although many instances of infighting originate from coups – especially since the threshold for conflict onset is low at twenty-five battledeaths in our data – non-violent coups are currently subsumed under the 'peaceful power sharing' outcome. Given our focus on the effect of power sharing on violence, this is a reasonable first cut, but future work should explore this in more detail. Moreover, future research should investigate the role of repression in maintaining exclusion since repressive regimes can increase the cost of rebellion, although maintaining the necessary apparatus implies costs for the regime, too.

For now, we conclude that our evidence directly speaks in favor of a policy alternative that contradicts current claims that, in order to curb ethnic civil war, one has to strengthen existing strongmen, "un-mix" ethnic groups entirely through partition (Chapman and Roeder, 2007; Kaufmann, 1996), or even "give war a chance" (Luttwak, 1999). Rather, our main results support the intuitive and normatively desirable principle according to which compromise in the form of power sharing more often fosters peace than spurs inter-ethnic conflict.

---

[16] Conceptually, this means that peacekeepers help moving from the front right-hand corner to the back right-hand corner in Figure 7.4.

[17] Roessler (2011) considers coups, but his approach is problematic for at least two reasons. First, his approach sees civil war (exclusively driven by exclusion) and coups (exclusively driven by power sharing) as the *only* threats governments face, and these are mutually exclusive. Thus, his approach conceptually omits many prominent infighting cases, such as Lebanon, Rwanda, Yugoslavia or Zimbabwe. Second, his data conflate inter- and intra-ethnic coups.

8   The Effect of Territorial and Governmental Power Sharing on Civil War*

While the previous two chapters focused exclusively on governmental power sharing, the current chapter extends the analysis to territorial power sharing. Thus, the main goal of the chapter is to test Master Hypothesis 1b. Governments typically invoke such arrangements in large and ethnically diverse countries, where centralized rule is difficult to implement. Adopting the same approach as in Chapter 6, we will continue to address issues of endogeneity by testing Master Hypothesis 4 with instrumental variables, while turning to strategic estimation in the following chapter. In addition, we will also evaluate the difference between pre- and post-conflict phases (Master Hypothesis 3) and the interaction between governmental and territorial power sharing (Master Hypothesis 5). With respect to the former, it is important to realize that territorial power sharing is often implemented together with its governmental counterpart. In fact, Master Hypothesis 5 postulates that it is precisely this combination that facilitates peace as opposed to the use of territorial power sharing alone. Finally, this chapter will also systematically study the different effects of power sharing before and after the first outbreak of conflict (see Master Hypothesis 3).

For reasons of tractability, we start the next section by analyzing the effect of territorial power sharing on conflict while assuming that territorial autonomy can be treated as exogenously given. In line with Master Hypothesis 4, the remainder of the chapter then relaxes this preliminary assumption by introducing an instrumental variable strategy that is similar to the one we applied to post-colonial conflict in Chapter 6. In the spirit of Chapter 7, the next chapter proposes an extended strategic-estimation framework that allows us to analyze governments' offering of autonomy as a strategic choice. This model also enables us to consider group claims that aim for not only territorial power sharing but also outright secession.

---

* This chapter draws heavily on Cederman et al. (2015).

8.1   The Combined Effect of Territorial and Governmental Power Sharing before and after Conflict

The turbulent and partly violent breakup of Yugoslavia and the Soviet Union in the early 1990s gave decentralization along ethnic lines a bad name. As we showed in Chapter 2, some scholars argue that offering ethnic groups regional autonomy triggers secessionist conflict, and therefore they reject ethnic federalism as a method of conflict resolution (e.g., Brubaker, 1996; Bunce, 1999; Snyder, 2000; Cornell, 2002). Other scholars, who typically focus on a wider set of cases, are much more optimistic about the stabilizing effect of decentralization. In their view, such arrangements do not merely function as grievance-reducing concessions, but also as effective modes of governance in ethnically divided societies (e.g., Lijphart, 1985a; Gurr, 2000b; Hechter, 2000).

Is territorial power sharing as perilous as its critics have claimed? To find out, we present an empirical evaluation of the effect of regional autonomy on internal conflict. Based on the general arguments of this book, we contend that the skeptics have overstated the case against autonomy policies.

In the following, we will focus our main attention on territorial, rather than governmental, conflict. A territorial rebellion concerns a specific territory that constitutes a part of the country in question. In contrast to governmental conflict, which relates to incompatibilities at the level of sovereignty of the entire state, territorial conflicts are fought over the control of a home region of a particular population, usually consisting of an ethnic group. The resident population may advance claims for autonomy, but it is also possible that the group's demand extends to full independence through secession.

8.1.1   Theoretical claims

In keeping with the reasoning advanced in the Chapters 2 and 3, we expect that territorial conflict can be particularly effectively mitigated through territorial power sharing. However, as we have seen, it would be a mistake to consider autonomy arrangements of this type independently of governmental power sharing. Indeed, as noted in Chapter 3, it is perfectly possible for regional autonomy to coexist with power sharing at the central level, as illustrated by Yugoslav and Indian federalism, as well as current power-sharing arrangements in Bosnia and Herzegovina, Ethiopia and Nigeria.

Going beyond the preliminary analysis presented in Chapter 4, Master Hypothesis 5 demands that we consider the full set of interactions between territorial and governmental power sharing. For this reason, it is useful to study the influence of power sharing in three mutually exclusive categories, namely cases involving (1) governmental power sharing only, (2) territorial power sharing only, and (3) those cases where both kinds of power sharing are present at the same time. Following from our theoretical reasoning presented in Chapters 2 and 3, we expect all three power-sharing configurations to be beneficial compared to cases where no power sharing arrangement is invoked. However, based on Master Hypothesis 5 we postulate that the combined effect is more powerfully and robustly pacifying than territorial power sharing alone. As argued in Chapter 3, it can be expected that both types of power sharing are necessary to give potential secessionists a stake in the cohesion of the polity (see also McGarry and O'Leary, 2004). We summarize these arguments in our first four hypotheses:

Hypothesis 8.1. Groups that are granted governmental but not territorial power sharing are less inclined to rebel than those that enjoy neither.

Hypothesis 8.2. Groups that are granted territorial but not governmental power sharing are less inclined to rebel than those that enjoy neither.

Hypothesis 8.3. Groups that are granted both territorial and governmental power sharing are less inclined to rebel than those that enjoy neither type of power sharing.

Hypothesis 8.4. Groups that are granted both territorial and governmental power sharing are less inclined to rebel than those that enjoy only territorial power sharing.

Once an armed conflict erupts, however, it drastically changes the relationship between the group and the incumbent government. Indeed, the effectiveness of governments' concessions to ethnic groups may well depend on whether their relationship has been peaceful thus far. In other words, what works as a preventive measure before the outbreak of violence may be less successful in a post-conflict setting.

In fact, by introducing Master Hypothesis 3 in Chapter 3, we have already acknowledged that the potential of power sharing as a means of pacification may be profoundly affected by the first emergence of violent conflict. There, we argued that prior instances of fighting make subsequent onsets more likely because they poison intergroup relations, radicalize both sides, and strengthen their combat capacity in the long run. In short, uncurbed vengefulness and lingering radicalization, together with an opportunity structure conducive to violence, are a potent cocktail for recurrent conflict (see also Collier et al., 2003; Walter, 2004).

For these reasons, and to render Master Hypothesis 3 more precise, we postulate the following:

Hypothesis 8.5. Groups that have rebelled in the past are more likely to rebel again compared to those that have not.

Focusing on territorial conflict specifically, we now proceed to explore how past violence influences the pacifying effect of governmental concessions, as stated by H8.1–8.4. We consider the logic of grievance-reduction and that of confidence building (see Chapter 3). Analyzing each of the three mechanisms that were introduced in Chapter 3 in turn, our analysis considers how prior conflict modifies the pacifying impact of both territorial and governmental power sharing:

Post-conflict concessions in a climate of hatred and vengefulness. Territorial power sharing by itself in a post-conflict context is likely to be afflicted by two types of problems known from the literature on federalism (Bednar, 2008, 68). In the absence of safeguards, the central government may encroach on the authority of the regionally based group, and, conversely, the region could fail to fulfil its obligations. Several scholars highlight that the latter problem may lead to the "ethnic capture" of regional institutions, and thus to secessionist tendencies (e.g., Roeder, 2007). Building on Riker (1964), Filippov, Ordeshook and Shvetsova (2004) emphasize that one way of avoiding such transgressions from tearing a federation apart is to ensure that politicians have stakes both at the regional and central levels, for instance through political parties. As these problems are more prevalent in a post-war setting, such safeguards linked to regional autonomy operate less effectively, as illustrated by the Naga and Manipuri insurgencies in India, the Moro secessionist conflict in the Philippines or the patchy implementation of ethnic federalism in Ethiopia (Ghai, 2000). Along similar lines, McGarry and O'Leary (2005, 15) argue that

federalism is about "shared-rule" as well as "self-rule", and the relevant constituent entities and peoples are likely to want a federal government that represents them, that is inclusive and, indeed, consociational. National minorities excluded from the federal government will be less inclined to promote their interests (see also Kymlicka, 1998).

Whether federal or not, the central state needs to create incentives for potentially separatist politicians demonstrating that working within the system yields political advantages, both for their personal careers and for the groups that they claim to represent (see, e.g., Riker, 1964; Filippov, Ordeshook and Shvetsova, 2004; Bednar, 2008). Such incentives were introduced in post-conflict Nigeria, where the victorious Gowon government followed what Bah (2005, 93) calls an "inclusionary approach" and "generous post-war reconciliation" that included general amnesty, reintegrated the secessionist Igbos in the Nigerian civil service and rehabilitated some of the destroyed areas. More than forty years after the end of the Biafran War, violence has still not recurred along the original conflict lines. Likewise, the successful inclusion of the Punjabi-Sikhs in the federal Indian government further illustrates the positive effects of combined regional autonomy and full inclusion after a conflict (Guha, 2008).

For these reasons, we conclude that grievance-reduction and confidence-building efforts to overcome the hostility of past conflict require a compromise at the level of central government rather than mere decentralization of authority within a regional framework.

Post-conflict concessions and extremist splintering. We have argued that past conflict tends to produce organizational factions on both sides, some of which may refuse to give up the fight for full independence. Under such circumstances, it does not take much for one small extremist faction to sabotage attempts to reach compromise, as the peace process in the southern Philippines has shown. The 1996 Jakarta agreement granting meaningful autonomy to the Moro people was signed by the Moro National Liberation Front (MNLF) but its rejection by the more radical, independence-seeking Moro Islamic Liberation Front (MILF) resulted in continued armed insurgency (Bertrand, 2000).

It is therefore essential that any grievance-reducing settlement be as inclusive as possible. If offered not until the outbreak of violent conflict, territorial power sharing could be destabilizing by dividing the self-determination movement:

An early, generous offer of autonomy, made before extreme separatist organizations outflank moderate leaders, may avert secession. A similar offer, made after separatist violence has broken out, may well do what opponents of concessions fear: it may testify to the weaknesses or vacillation of the central government and the success of the separatist, thereby fortifying their will to fight on. (Horowitz, 1985, 625)

Failed negotiations with the center can produce frustrations that could be exploited by radical separatists (Bakke, 2015). Furthermore, winning over the hearts and minds of extremists is very difficult if merely regional autonomy is on offer since this will be seen as "too little, too late" once the relationship between the group and the government has turned violent. Without credible commitments that the state will not renege on its autonomy promises (Lake and Rothchild, 2005), why should extremists be satisfied with a consolation prize that does not even guarantee them decisive influence over the central state institutions, let alone full independence? Moreover, territorial power sharing can more easily be used for mobilization purposes by ethnic populists if they are detached from states' central decision-making mechanisms (Bunce, 1999; Snyder, 2000). Where ethnic and regional boundaries overlap, intense competition between regional parties may also facilitate ethnic outbidding because regional parties competing for the same electorate may adopt increasingly extreme views to attract votes away from other regional parties (Brancati, 2006, 658). Relying on explicit evidence that organizational fragmentation fuels conflict, Cunningham (2011) argues that fragmented self-determination movements are more likely to respond violently to governmental concessions than are united ones (see also Bakke, 2015).

Of course, governmental power sharing can also break down because of extremist posturing following conflict. Nevertheless, as suggested by the confidence-building logic, such arrangements leave less room for separatist activism and makes pragmatic politicians more successful. Thanks to their influence within the state's central executive, moderate group representatives not only have more of a personal stake in the future of their country, but are also more likely to claim ownership of national policies by showing that they can deliver favorable policy outcomes:

If the rebels are represented at different levels of government their enemies cannot decree or implement policies without their consent. Under these conditions, the rebels' enemies will be unable to pursue any policies, whether military, economic, cultural, or relating to autonomy and federalism, that are detrimental to the rebels. The sharing of decision-making power helps ensure that other kinds of power sharing are implemented and opens up the possibility for both groups to shape future policies. (Mattes and Savun, 2009, 742)

Thus, as long as the ethnic group remains excluded from national executive influence, there should be ammunition for confrontational and extremist agitation, especially if the central government subjects it to unfavorable policies. In contrast, central power sharing can be expected to have a more pervasive pacifying impact even in post-conflict situations, precisely because it involves the former belligerents in central decision-making: "The more integrated the rebel group is in the political system, the less incentives it will have to disrupt it" (Mattes and

Savun, 2009, 742). Evidence for this claim is provided by the successful integration of the former belligerent Igbo in Nigeria after the Biafran War (Bah, 2005) or the coming into power of the Tigrayan People's Liberation Front (TPLF) after the ousting of Mengistu in Ethiopia (Young, 2006). In these cases, a combination of grievance-reduction and confidence-building helps prevent splintering and radicalization of the state-challenging side.

Post-conflict concessions and secessionist capacity building. Finally, we investigate whether territorial or governmental power-sharing conces- sions influence secessionists' mobilization capacity. While far from all autonomy rights create a government in waiting, devolution reforms set up decision-making institutions and resources that can be exploited by secessionists to support renewed fighting if their increasingly radical demands are not satisfied. For example, in the northeastern region of India, separatists were rewarded with the creation of Nagaland and Manipur as full-fledged states of the Indian Union in 1963 and 1972 respectively. However, despite being granted substantial autonomy, armed groups in these states subsequently radicalized their demands and continued to fight as "some of the most sophisticated militant outfits in the region in terms of their access to weapons and funding, level of training, and network of safe areas" (Lacina, 2009, 1014). As we have seen, several authors contend that regional autonomy along ethnic lines tends to empower separatist politicians:

Many institutions of partitioned decisionmaking, such as the powers of autonomous homelands in ethnofederal states, can be abused by regional leaders, including ethnomilitary warlords, to press the central government for further devolution and to extract income that can be invested in future fighting capacity. (Rothchild and Roeder, 2005a, 37)

In contrast, governmental power sharing increases the need to bargain and coordinate policies on a daily basis as opposed to creating a separate compartment of governance. This confidence-building logic in turn increases transparency in interactions between the government and former rebels, thus making it harder for either side to rebuild preemptive military capability (Hartzell and Hoddie, 2003). Following the Tuareg rebellion in the 1990s in Mali, high-ranking rebel officers were appointed to leadership positions in the army and were also assigned to key non- military government positions. Transparency and coordination were also increased by the peace processes in El Salvador, Mozambique, and Djibouti, where former rebel armies were integrated into the national armed forces and participated in the non-violent political process

(Glassmyer and Sambanis, 2008). After civil wars, security guarantees through power-sharing arrangements are not sought merely by the former rebels, but also by the incumbents to state power:

Former combatants require assurances that no single group will be able to use the power of the state to secure what they failed to win on the battlefield, and perhaps threaten the very survival of rivals. Institutional choice in this environment is driven by the need to protect the interests of all signatories to the agreement. Power sharing serves as the mechanism that offers this protection by guaranteeing all groups a share of state power. (Hartzell and Hoddie, 2003, 319)

Furthermore, in most cases, rebel fighting capacity depends critically on mobilization. As we have argued above, far-reaching concessions granting previously excluded groups influence at the center can also be expected to make separatist recruitment efforts more difficult. In this sense, grievance reduction should decrease mobilization capacity (Cederman, Gleditsch and Buhaug, 2013, Ch. 3).

Our discussion of the three mechanisms suggests that governmental and territorial power-sharing arrangements will have different effects depending on whether they are introduced preventively before or reactively after a conflict. Based on these insights, we can therefore reformulate our expectations concerning prior conflict and concessions by breaking up hypotheses H8.1–8.4 depending on whether or not conflict has already occurred between the group and the government. We start by covering the pre-conflict situation:

Hypothesis 8.1a. Before the outbreak of the first conflict, groups that are granted governmental but not territorial power sharing are less inclined to rebel than those that enjoy neither.

Hypothesis 8.2a. Before the outbreak of the first conflict, groups that are granted territorial but not governmental power sharing are less inclined to rebel than those that enjoy neither.

Hypothesis 8.3a. Before the outbreak of the first conflict, groups that are granted both territorial and governmental power sharing are less inclined to rebel than those that enjoy neither type of power sharing.

Hypothesis 8.4a. Before the outbreak of the first conflict, groups that are granted both territorial and governmental power sharing are less inclined to rebel than those that enjoy only territorial power sharing.

The next set of hypotheses applies to situations that have already turned violent:

Hypothesis 8.1b. After the outbreak of the first conflict, groups that are granted governmental but not territorial power sharing are less inclined to rebel than those that enjoy neither.

Hypothesis 8.2b. After the outbreak of the first conflict, groups that are granted territorial but not governmental power sharing are less inclined to rebel than those that enjoy neither.

Hypothesis 8.3b. After the outbreak of the first conflict, groups that are granted both territorial and governmental power sharing are less inclined to rebel than those that enjoy neither type of power sharing.

Hypothesis 8.4b. After the outbreak of the first conflict, groups that are granted both territorial and governmental power sharing are less inclined to rebel than those that enjoy only territorial power sharing.

Based on Master Hypothesis 3 we expect that, once violence emerges in a relationship, attempts to pacify through inclusive measures encounter different, and often more difficult, challenges. More specifically, however, territorial power sharing can be expected to lose its pacifying effect if autonomy concessions are not backed up by governmental power sharing at the center (see Master Hypothesis 5), thus casting doubt on H8.2b. In other words, after conflict, governmental power sharing is the only mode of ethnic inclusion that robustly prevents renewed violence and it can be postulated to pacify more effectively than territorial power sharing on its own (see H). In essence, on its own, regional autonomy is likely to be "too little, too late."[1]

So far we have analyzed how ethnic representation at the regional and central levels influences the prospects of peace. Going beyond this relatively static perspective, we derive a hypothesis that focuses on changes in the provision of autonomy. Previous research on ethnic conflict suggests that conflict becomes much more likely if the group in question loses its current power status. Such downgrading is known to trigger violent reactions in the immediate period after the reversal (Petersen, 2002). Within a broad macrohistorical context, Hechter (2000) associates nationalist mobilization in general, and peripheral nationalism in particular, with the shift from indirect to direct rule. With respect to political violence, Cederman, Wimmer and Min (2010) and Cederman, Gleditsch and Buhaug (2013, Ch. 4) find strong evidence that civil war onsets are considerably more likely during a two year

---

[1] See also the related finding by Pospieszna and Schneider (2013), who show that regional autonomy adopted in a post-conflict setting does not have pacifying effects.

period following a status loss. Specifically relating to regional autonomy, McGarry and O'Leary (2009, 11) argue that conflict is likely to follow if governments attempt to revoke already granted autonomous rights: "To an important extent, secession and violence in the territory of many failed federations followed directly from attempts by certain groups to centralize these federations." They conclude that violence is not so much caused by decentralization as by its opposite, centralization. Prominent examples of retraction and failure of autonomy arrangements that contributed to fueling conflict include the Kurds in Iraq and the Southern groups in the Sudan (Weller, 2005; O'Leary, 2012), Punjab and Kashmir in India (Singh, 1993), Eritreans in Ethiopia (Negash, 1997) as well as the Kosovars in Yugoslavia, where Milosevic's efforts to recentralize the country included the revocation of the autonomous status of Kosovo in 1990 (Gagnon, 2004). Grievances over this downgrading turned into open conflict a few years later. Drawing on their own data on territorial claims and concessions, Sambanis and Zinn (2006) find that the imposition of direct rule through the revocation of autonomous rights increases the risk of secessionist conflict. This reasoning can be formalized in the following way:

Hypothesis 8.6. Groups whose territorial power-sharing rights have recently been revoked are more likely to rebel than those that have not experienced such status loss.

8.1.2   Empirical analysis

Having stated our theoretical claims, we now turn to the empirical evidence needed to evaluate their validity. To a large extent, we build directly on our group-level baseline models that were introduced in Chapter 4. The EPR dataset offers the necessary measures of both territorial and governmental power sharing. The main dependent variable can be derived directly from the Uppsala Conflict Data Program's notion of territorial incompatibility. Finally, the ACD2EPR mapping provides the corresponding coding of conflict onsets at the level of EPR groups (Wucherpfennig et al., 2011).

Since the current task is to model territorial conflict, we restrict the sample to groups whose settlements are concentrated in a part of their respective countries' territories, as specified by the GeoEPR dataset. As it can be expected that there are important differences between world regions, we run all models with world-region fixed effects.[2]

---

[2] We rely on Fearon and Laitin's (2003) definition that divides the world into the West, Eastern Europe and the Former Soviet Union, Asia, North Africa and the Middle East,

Furthermore, to better capture the logic of territorial conflict, we add the following control variables: First, we control for federal institutions at the country level, as defined by Bednar (2008). Second, our analysis also controls for the ethnic structure of the state as a whole as well as for an important interaction effect applying to states with many ethnic groups. According to Walter's (2009) strategic logic, the number of excluded groups should be negatively related to the risk of conflict since governments facing many ethnic groups will be less willing to make concessions to single groups in order to deter consequent challenges or further demands by other groups, as illustrated by Moscow's hard line in dealing with the Chechens' claims.[3]

Having described the coding of the main variables, we are now ready to analyze the probability of conflict onset in response to specific power-sharing configurations. Building on the group-level models introduced in Chapter 4, Table 8.1 introduces a first set of models that are restricted to territorially relevant groups as described above. Model 1 reveals that governmental power sharing seems to have a conflict-reducing effect that is statistically significant. The effect of territorial power sharing is also negative, but a 95 percent confidence interval fails to exclude zero. In order to test our first batch of hypotheses, Model 2 introduces the three mutually exclusive categories of power-sharing configurations that distinguish between cases with governmental but no territorial power sharing, cases with territorial but no governmental power sharing, and cases with both types. The corresponding coefficient estimates give support for H8.1–8.3 because all three cases are associated with negative and significant conflict-dampening effects. However, there is no evidence that territorial and governmental power sharing together would be any more effective than each component on their own. In both models, we also find strong support for the independent effect of prior conflict (H8.5) and downgrading through revocation of autonomy (H8.6). In contrast, status loss in terms of central executive power does not appear to influence the risk of territorial conflict. Otherwise, the control variables behave roughly in accordance with the baseline models as presented in Chapter 3.

Sub-Saharan Africa, and Latin America, using the West as the reference category. Note that adding these regional dummies leads to a problem of complete separation, as no territorial conflicts occurred during the period of observation. Thus, in the analyses reported in this chapter observations from Latin America are excluded. In the online appendix we offer reanalyses while relying on Gelman and Hill's (2007) Bayesian logit model. We employ the same model to allow for integrating the groups with dispersed settlement patterns in analysis (see the online appendix to this chapter).

[3] This variable enters the analysis in logarithmic form together with a dummy variable to handle cases where the number of excluded groups is zero.

Table 8.1. *Explaining onset of territorial conflict*

	(1) Terr. conflict onset	(2) Terr. conflict onset
Gov. power sharing	−1.474*** (0.317)	
Terr. power sharing	−0.489 (0.321)	
Only gov. power sharing		−2.355** (0.808)
Only terr. power sharing		−0.872* (0.359)
Gov. & terr. power sharing		−1.375** (0.429)
Postwar period	1.523*** (0.306)	1.510*** (0.298)
Gov. downgrade	−0.262 (0.446)	−0.269 (0.448)
Terr. downgrade	1.714*** (0.475)	1.659*** (0.476)
Rel. group size	4.799* (1.913)	4.099* (1.819)
Rel. group size^2	−9.547** (3.015)	−8.543** (2.876)
Federal state	0.822* (0.367)	0.802* (0.353)
Log excl. groups	−0.430** (0.148)	−0.422** (0.151)
Log country GDP, lag	−0.228 (0.201)	−0.179 (0.202)
Log country population, lag	0.217* (0.085)	0.230** (0.082)
Ongoing conflict	0.418 (0.293)	0.363 (0.301)
Constant	−4.599* (1.935)	−5.081** (1.946)
Observations	25139	25342
Pseudo R^2	0.180	0.186

Standard errors in parentheses
$^+ p < 0.1$, $^* p < 0.05$, $^{**} p < 0.01$, $^{***} p < 0.001$

As a next step, we analyze the effect of power-sharing configurations before and after the outbreak of the first internal conflict and in so doing test the hypotheses H8.1–8.4a,b. Table 8.2 introduces the results of this exercise. Model 1 presents the results for the entire world.

Table 8.2. *Explaining onset of territorial conflict before and after first conflict*

	(1) Terr. conflict onset	(2) Terr. conflict onset
Only gov. power sharing prewar	−2.115* (0.893)	
Only terr. power sharing prewar	−1.500*** (0.418)	−1.098** (0.393)
Gov. & terr. power sharing prewar	−1.153+ (0.600)	−0.724 (0.743)
Only gov. power sharing postwar	−2.585** (0.946)	
Only terr. power sharing postwar	−0.393 (0.405)	−0.701 (0.448)
Gov. & terr. power sharing postwar	−1.466* (0.650)	−3.260*** (0.982)
Postwar period	1.445*** (0.375)	1.974*** (0.454)
Gov. downgrade	−0.271 (0.450)	0.533 (0.585)
Terr. downgrade	1.648*** (0.479)	1.206+ (0.707)
Rel. group size	3.955* (1.828)	1.544 (3.335)
Rel. group size^2	−8.507** (2.923)	−4.370 (6.289)
Federal state	0.770* (0.364)	0.580+ (0.335)
Log excl. groups	−0.374** (0.144)	−0.589*** (0.108)
Log country GDP, lag	−0.184 (0.200)	−0.145 (0.139)
Log country population, lag	0.203* (0.082)	0.183* (0.092)
Ongoing conflict	0.353 (0.293)	0.648* (0.309)
Constant	−4.751* (1.982)	−3.415* (1.488)
Observations	25342	11933
Pseudo R^2	0.189	0.237

Standard errors in parentheses

+ $p < 0.1$, * $p < 0.05$, ** $p < 0.01$, *** $p < 0.001$

Corresponding to prewar situations, the first three coefficients in the Table reveal that all three configurations are associated with reduced conflict, thus confirming H8.1b–8.3b. Yet, contrary to our expectations given by H8.4b, a combination of territorial and governmental power sharing does not seem to be more effective as a peace strategy than autonomy on its own. In contrast, the results for groups that have rebelled in the past are entirely in line with our theoretical expectations. Whereas governmental power sharing still exerts a negative effect on onset, thus confirming H8.1b, the same thing cannot be said for territorial power sharing on its own. While the coefficient is negative, it is very small and cannot be safely distinguished from no effect. Importantly, however, we can be much more confident that the combination of territorial and governmental power sharing is associated with conflict reduction (cf. H8.3b). We get strong effects for a history of rebellion and territorial downgrading, in agreement with H8.6. Again, the estimation of the confounding variables does not offer any major surprises.

Model 2 reruns the same model for a more restrictive sample in an attempt to explain the outbreak of territorial civil wars in Eurasia. Because of the reduced sample size, it is impossible to estimate the effect of governmental power sharing.[4] In contrast, the effect of territorial autonomy is still robust before the outbreak of the first case of large-scale violence. However, the most important finding is that combined territorial and governmental power sharing appears to be particularly effective as a conflict resolution method in this part of the world.

Our findings up to this point suggest that territorial power sharing on its own is probably not a robust mode of securing peace in situations which have seen a history of violent conflict, at least without the support of governmental power sharing at the central level. While this is entirely in line with our theoretical expectations, we have said nothing about substantial effects that should be expected for groups that could benefit from such provisions. To explore these important counterfactuals, we rely on "average predictive differences" proposed by Gelman and Hill (2007, 466). Instead of comparing predicted probabilities for some imagined case by, for example, holding all variables at their mean, this method is based on calculating the predicted changes in probabilities for all relevant cases in the sample. Thus, we sampled 1,000 values from the estimated parameter distribution of Model 1 in Table 8.2 and computed the predicted probability of conflict in two scenarios for all group-years for which an upgrade to territorial or governmental power sharing was possible. The first scenario assumes that no such upgrade

---

[4] It turns out that Sub-Saharan Africa is the region that drives this result.

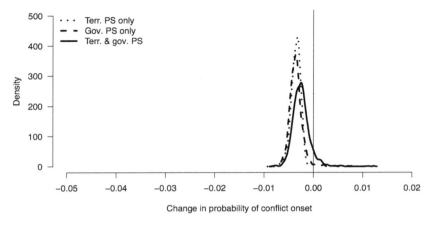

Figure 8.1 Effect on conflict of territorial and governmental power sharing (PS) in pre-conflict periods

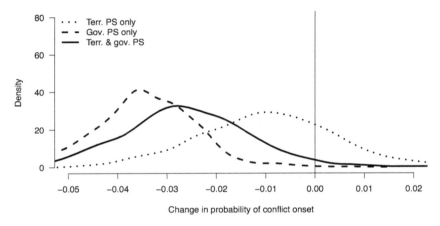

Figure 8.2 Effect on conflict of territorial and governmental power sharing (PS) in post-conflict periods

occurred, whereas the second one assumes that either type of power sharing, or their combination, was granted. The differences in these probabilities were then averaged for each parameter set. The density of these "average predictive differences" are depicted in Figures 8.1 and 8.2 for the pre-conflict and post-conflict situations respectively, thereby addressing Master Hypothesis 3.

Focusing on pre-conflict settings, Figure 8.1 shows that both territorial and governmental power sharing reduce the probability of conflict onset, with the latter category divided into two subcategories. While governmental power sharing without autonomy appears to be more effective than regional autonomy and governmental power sharing with autonomy, the latter two also produce more peaceful outcomes than would be the case in their absence. Once we turn to the post-conflict cases, however, it becomes clear that governmental power sharing continues to exert a powerful negative effect on the onset probability, whether it is combined with autonomy or not (see Figure 8.2). As is the case in pre-conflict settings, virtually all average changes in probability are within the negative range, thus clearly separated from zero. For regional autonomy without central power sharing, however, the picture is less clear-cut. In this case, the distribution straddles zero, with a considerable share of the mass above zero. This result suggests that, on average, ethnic decentralization is likely to be too little, too late for peace building, unless combined with governmental power sharing (see Master Hypothesis 5). More generally, we find that power sharing provisions exhibit substantially large effects in postwar situations, although these are associated with higher degrees of uncertainty.[5] Thus, contrary to the autonomy skeptics' claims, we find that such provisions – especially central governmental power sharing – are crucial in conflict-ridden situations (see Master Hypothesis 3).

8.2   Accounting for Endogeneity: An Instrumental Variable Approach

In the previous section, we again assumed ethnic groups' access to power to be exogenous. Master Hypothesis 4 suggests that this assumption is potentially problematic if governments' decisions to offer groups concessions through either type of power sharing are made in anticipation of future conflict. In other words, the values of our main explanatory variables are not randomly assigned and could therefore be at least partially dependent on a given group's conflict propensity (see Fearon, Kasara and Laitin, 2007, 193). As argued in Chapter 3 and shown empirically for governmental power sharing in two previous chapters, this type of bias could lead to either an underestimation or an overestimation of the causal effect of power-sharing institutions.

---

[5] Statistically, this follows from the positive coefficient for the postwar variable, which shifts the linear predictor to the steeper regions of the non-linear logit link function, thus resulting in larger marginal effects.

If opportunistic governments attempt to prevent anticipated conflict by appeasing potential "troublemakers" through self-determination, the conflict-dampening effect of governmental power sharing will be underestimated. Such a pragmatic approach of co-optation is invoked by representatives of dominant ethnic groups who prefer to keep as much of the state's resources as possible, while at the same time making concessions in the name of inter-ethnic peace.

The opposite approach of risk diversion applies in situations where the government tries to preempt anticipated conflict by excluding, rather than including, threatening groups. Such precautionary measures could be implemented in order to prevent ethnic competitors from wielding influence from within governmental institutions. Applying this argument to Sub-Saharan Africa, Roessler (2011, 313) suggests that "ethnic exclusion serves as an expedient mechanism to eradicate perceived enemies." As opposed to the previous scenario, this logic would imply that the pacifying influence of both territorial and governmental power sharing may have been overestimated.

In order to account for this, we again turn to instrumental variable approach before proceeding with strategic estimation in the next chapter. As in Chapter 6, this means that we have to articulate a causal pathway that directly affects territorial power sharing but is otherwise unrelated to conflict risk. There can be no doubt about the difficulty of fulfilling the criteria given by the exclusion restriction.[6] A definitive answer to questions relating to endogenous institutions would therefore require a more sophisticated research design than can be provided in this section of the book, although we propose an instrument that at least alleviates some of these concerns. An effective instrument needs to vary across groups, since much of the variation in regional autonomy is among groups and not countries. Our starting point is therefore Sambanis and Milanovic's (2014) straightforward observation that only sufficiently large groups can credibly demand, and expect to be granted, autonomy. However, large groups are also more likely to experience conflict because their size facilitates mobilization. Thus, group size alone cannot serve as an instrument as it affects not only autonomy demands (Sambanis and Milanovic, 2014, 18) but also conflict propensity (Cederman, Wimmer and Min, 2010, 96).

---

[6] Evaluating extant work, Sambanis and Milanovic (2014, 9) argue that "no prior study of the effects of decentralization ... has proposed a valid instrumental variable approach to estimate the causal effect of (expected or actual) conflict on decentralization or vice versa."

Opting for a similar approach as the one we used in the instrumental-variable analysis in Chapter 6, we instead exploit systematic differences in governance between former French and British colonies resulting from their respective colonial heritages (Horowitz, 1985; Young, 1994; Blanton, Mason and Athow, 2001). Mirroring the centralist system of France, the French approach to colonial governance relied on a high degree of centralization, and so it is no accident that autonomous arrangements are particularly rare in states that experienced French colonial rule (Strang, 1994; Le Vine, 2004). In contrast, the British adopted a much more pragmatic attitude that directly built on pre-existing customary institutions and frequently included the use of "indirect rule," which explains why decentralization along ethnic lines remains a common response to ethnic diversity in countries with a British colonial past.[7] Consequently, in former British colonies larger groups should be more likely to enjoy regional autonomy than similar groups in former French colonies. Thus, the interaction between group size and the identity of the colonial empire constitutes an instrument that is unlikely to have an effect on conflict except through autonomy.

Our approach finds support in the literature on colonial powers. Calori et al. (1997, 691) note that the British, primarily interested in defending and expanding their commercial interests, "relied heavily on local self-government and indirect rule when controlling their colonial empire." The French, by contrast, "centralised decisions concerning their colonies, implemented actions by means of decrees and edicts, attempted to control local affairs by placing their own in local positions of power, in much the same manner as Louis XIV did with his use of "intendents" and Napoléon did with his use of "préfets." Whereas the French encouraged local elites to assimilate to French culture, the British retained and empowered local chiefs by giving them far-reaching autonomy including the authority to collect taxes (Crowder, 1968; Lange, 2004).

As mentioned above, these differences in the style of governance shaped the institutional characteristics of former colonies in systematic ways, as emphasized by O'Leary (2001, 280):

Multinational federalists have been influential in the development of federations in the former British empire, notably in Canada, the Caribbean, Nigeria, South Africa, India, Pakistan and Malaysia. They influenced Austro-Marxists and Marxist-Leninists, and have had an enduring impact on the post-communist development of the Russian Federation, Ethiopia and the rump Yugoslavia.

---

[7] Obviously, as discussed in Chapter 6, this difference between the two colonial empires concerns the general governance tradition. In terms of implementation, there was considerable variation within the empires themselves and even within specific colonies (Herbst, 2000; Lange, 2004).

By contrast, autonomous arrangements are particularly rare in states that experienced French colonial rule (Strang, 1994; Le Vine, 2004).

Consequently, combining the observations with regard to group size and type of colonial rule, we expect territorial autonomy to be more likely for populous groups in former British colonies. After all, regional autonomy is especially hard to justify for very small groups, even in this setting. In former French colonies, however, population size should not increase the likelihood of gaining regional autonomy. In other words, the French inclination for centralization can be expected to disadvantage those groups for which regional autonomy is otherwise most feasible. However, this does not affect small groups for which autonomy is not feasible to begin with. This logic creates systematic and increasing differences between groups in former French and British colonies depending on their size.

We exploit this difference by constructing our instrument as the interaction between the indicator for British colonial past and the territorial size of the group's settlement area. As opposed to using group size or colonial heritage on their own, this combined variable is not related to conflict in any obvious way, except through the autonomy mechanism. Relying on this identification strategy, we examine a sample comprised of all territorially distinctive ethnic groups in postcolonial states with either a French or British colonial history.[8] The approach is far from ideal because our exogenous mechanism applies only to a much smaller sample than the global one we relied on above. This in turn forces us to assume away the important distinction between prewar and postwar effects that we analyzed in the first part of this study (see the online appendix for details). Yet, these simplifications seem reasonable in view of our main goal, namely to assess the general direction of a possible endogeneity bias as regards autonomous institutions.

Analogous to Chapter 6, we first present a cross-sectional analysis that focuses on the initial ethno-political constellation after the country's independence. We employ a similar specification as for our analysis on governmental power sharing. This is given in Table 8.3. For the top half of the table the dependent variable is territorial power sharing. These models capture the conditions under which governments grant autonomy. Model 1 is a baseline model. Model 2 includes the interaction term between the colonizer and the group's settlement area. Figure 8.3 visualizes these effects, demonstrating that a large settlement area is associated with a high probability of being granted territorial power sharing for groups in former British colonies, while the opposite is true

---

[8] We drop European settler colonies from the sample (e.g., South Africa and Zimbabwe).

Table 8.3. *Accounting for endogeneity: static models*

	(1) Probit	(2) Separate probits	(3) Bivariate probit
Equation 1: Territorial power sharing			
British colony	0.380	−5.507**	−5.123*
	(0.543)	(1.802)	(2.375)
Log area	0.095	−0.404**	−0.219
	(0.113)	(0.155)	(0.232)
British col. × log area		0.613***	0.524*
		(0.168)	(0.226)
Log country area	−0.163	−0.041	−0.015
	(0.163)	(0.159)	(0.172)
Log GDP	0.021	0.016	0.065
	(0.357)	(0.451)	(0.412)
Log population	0.337*	0.259*	0.272*
	(0.137)	(0.129)	(0.130)
Group size	0.170	0.173	−0.076
	(0.160)	(0.202)	(0.267)
Constant	−4.000	−0.204	−2.432
	(3.454)	(4.083)	(4.430)
Equation 2: Territorial conflict			
Terr. power sharing		0.033	−1.272[+]
		(0.313)	(0.694)
British colony		0.041	0.122
		(0.403)	(0.377)
Log area		−0.134	−0.098
		(0.125)	(0.104)
Log country area		0.147	0.098
		(0.202)	(0.104)
Log GDP		−0.336	−0.293
		(0.270)	(0.311)
Log population		0.146	0.221[+]
		(0.134)	(0.125)
Group size		−0.627	−0.422
		(0.521)	(0.539)
Constant		−0.142	−0.808
		(3.135)	(3.011)
ρ			0.803
			(0.480)
Observations	162	162	162

Standard errors in parentheses
[+] $p < 0.1$, * $p < 0.05$, ** $p < 0.01$, *** $p < 0.001$

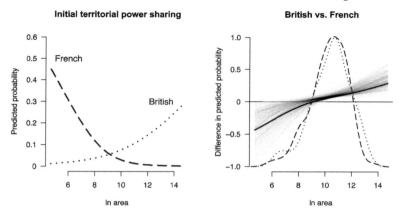

Figure 8.3 Explaining initial territorial power sharing

for groups in former French colonies (left panel). Moreover, the right panel demonstrates that this difference is particularly pronounced for groups with large settlement areas.

Having validated our instrumental logic, we turn to examining the effect of territorial power sharing on (post-colonial) conflict. The estimates for this dependent variable are given in the lower half of Table 8.3. In order to allow for a direct comparison, the lower half of Model 2 is a separate probit analysis that does not endogenize territorial power sharing. As in Chapter 6, we capture endogeneity with a bivariate probit model (see Model 3) that instruments for territorial power sharing, thus yielding unbiased estimates if all the underlying assumptions are fulfilled (Maddala, 1983).

In analogy to the results of our instrumental variable approach in Chapter 6, the findings of Model 3 offer strong support for the opportunistic interpretation of governments' approach to ethnic diversity. Compared to the naïve analysis in Model 2, which fails to detect an effect of territorial power sharing on conflict, the impact is strongly negative and clearly significant when endogeneity is accounted for. In other words, in line with Master Hypothesis 4, naïve analysis underestimates the effect of territorial power sharing, suggesting that groups with a higher potential for conflict are more likely to be appeased through this type of power sharing.

Moving beyond a simple cross-sectional specification, in Table 8.4 we also examine a time-series cross-sectional version of this instrumental variable approach. The model specification is very similar to the models in Tables 8.1 and 8.2, with the main difference being that we drop as

Table 8.4. *Accounting for endogeneity: dynamic models*

	(1) Probit	(2) Separate probits	(3) Bivariate probit
Equation 1: territorial power sharing			
British colony	0.464 (0.317)	−4.745** (1.748)	−5.175** (1.771)
Log area	0.076 (0.082)	−0.359[+] (0.198)	−0.390[+] (0.208)
British col. × log area		0.520** (0.194)	0.566** (0.199)
Rel. group size	−0.837 (1.640)	−0.977 (1.621)	−0.973 (1.617)
Rel. group size^2	−0.031 (1.896)	0.020 (1.994)	−0.058 (1.906)
Log country population, lag	−0.064 (0.180)	−0.020 (0.188)	−0.016 (0.212)
Log country population, lag	0.433*** (0.129)	0.356*** (0.101)	0.356*** (0.108)
Log country area	−0.184 (0.206)	−0.019 (0.126)	−0.017 (0.143)
Constant	−3.591 (2.959)	−0.994 (2.698)	−0.732 (2.813)
Equation 2: territorial conflict			
Terr. power sharing		−0.151 (0.120)	−0.830** (0.280)
British colony		0.183 (0.247)	0.276 (0.253)
Log area		−0.029 (0.078)	−0.003 (0.081)
Rel. group size		−1.764 (1.422)	−1.806 (1.414)
Rel. group size^2		1.160 (1.496)	1.083 (1.510)
Log country GDP, lag		−0.101 (0.083)	−0.093 (0.093)
Log country population, lag		0.113* (0.055)	0.199*** (0.051)
Log country area		0.034 (0.118)	0.005 (0.125)
Constant		−2.294 (1.628)	−2.958 (1.893)
ρ			0.445* (0.214)
Observations	10877	10877	10294

Standard errors in parentheses
[+] $p < 0.1$, * $p < 0.05$, ** $p < 0.01$, *** $p < 0.001$

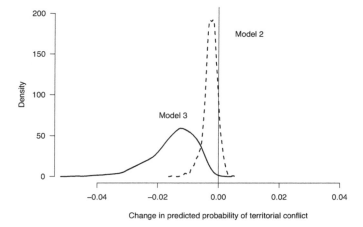

Figure 8.4 Marginal effect of territorial power sharing, based on uncorrected and corrected Models 2 and 3 in Table 8.4

many of the potentially endogenous variables as possible, including the postwar variable and its interactions with the power status variables. The variables measuring ongoing conflict and the downgrading variables are also removed, as is the number of excluded groups. Given the argument about groups' settlement areas, we add a measure for the size of the country. As in the previous tables, we do not show the coefficients for the peace-year variables.

The setup of Table 8.4 is identical to Table 8.3, with the upper half denoting equations that model the determinants of territorial power sharing for a given group, while the bottom half denotes the equations for territorial conflict. Models 1 and 2 demonstrate that accounting for the differential logics within French and British colonies, respectively, yields a pattern that is in line with the cross-sectional analysis presented above; groups in former British colonies are systematically more likely to enjoy territorial power sharing the larger their settlement area.

Instrumenting territorial power sharing in this way has dramatic consequences for the estimated effect of territorial power sharing on territorial conflict, as can be seen by comparing the lower part of Table 8.4 in Models 2 and 3. Relying on the same counterfactual method as in the previous graphs of this chapter, Figure 8.4 plots the predicted effect of territorial power sharing on conflict for the naïve analysis of Model 2 (dashed line) and the instrumented one of Model 3 (solid line). The former density distribution indicates that in the uncorrected analysis, autonomous arrangements have a weakly negative influence that is hardly distinguishable from zero. Once reverse causation is taken into account in Model 3, however, the distribution shifts left into the clearly conflict-dampening domain of the graph.

Provided that these results are representative of the global sample of groups, we conclude that our analysis in the previous section has tended to underestimate the actual pacifying effect of decentralization. Much does speak for the sample being representative, since French and British ex-colonies feature a large number of diverse countries including many important conflict cases. Furthermore, our endogeneity analysis can be seen as a tough test since it covers Sub-Saharan Africa, a region where, according to Roessler (2011), the opposite tendency should apply.

In sum, this section offers a systematic if somewhat incomplete confirmation that territorial power sharing is most likely to be invoked in cases where the potential for conflict is high, as argued by McGarry and O'Leary (2009) and Grigoryan (2012). Indeed, the evidence suggests that these scholars are right, thus implying that our quantitative analysis of autonomy's pacifying influence is erring on the safe side.

8.3 Conclusion

Focusing on regional autonomy arrangements, we have investigated to what extent, and in what form, territorial power sharing mitigates civil conflict (see Master Hypothesis 1b). Our point of departure has been past research indicating that exclusion of ethnic groups triggers internal conflict (see Chapter 3). As we have argued, however, such results do not automatically imply that regional inclusiveness will guarantee peace, especially if the relationship between an excluded group and the incumbent government has already seen violence. In such situations, we have found that, on its own, regional autonomy is likely to be "too little, too late." It is too little because only full inclusion through governmental power sharing reduces conflict propensity significantly (see Master Hypothesis 5); and it is too late since regional autonomy could be effective, but only if offered in a timely, preventive fashion before group-government relations turn violent (see Master Hypothesis 3).

Although these findings fall short of an across-board endorsement of territorial power sharing as a conflict resolution tool, they differ significantly from studies that depict ethnic decentralization, and especially ethnofederalism, as inherently pernicious and destabilizing, typically arguing in favor of partition or even ethnic dominance. Here, we have presented a disaggregated and more balanced framework that produces encouraging results. First, we find that territorial power sharing can serve a useful conflict-preventing purpose that keeps a group-government relationship peaceful, a role that the critics often overlook. Second, in stark contrast to the critics' admonitions, there is no support for a clearly conflict-fueling influence of regional autonomy even in post-conflict situations. Third, our analysis indicates that ethnic inclusion at the center can effectively pacify previously violent relationships. Thus, if regional autonomy is to be offered, it should be combined with governmental power sharing as recommended by McGarry and O'Leary (2009). Fourth, and finally, our efforts to take the endogeneity of autonomy concessions into account in post-colonial settings indicates that governments typically offer such accommodation in order to dissuade threatening groups from resorting to violence, which in turn implies that we have been erring on the safe side with our causal inferences (see Master Hypothesis 4). If anything, the actual pacifying effect of decentralization is likely to be even more powerful than uncorrected analysis suggests.

These are important empirical results that directly contradict claims that no solution short of partition can possibly improve the situation (e.g., Kaufmann, 1996; Chapman and Roeder, 2007). In addition to individual rights, regional autonomy offers an appealing alternative to groups' remedial right to secede since its geopolitical effects are considerably less destabilizing (Buchanan, 2004). All in all, our main results uphold the intuitive and normatively attractive principle according to which ethnic inclusion produces peace.

9 The Strategic Logic of Territorial Power Sharing, Secession and Civil War

In the previous chapter, we introduced models of territorial power sharing, including instrumental variable analysis similar to that presented in Chapter 6. This approach suffers from the same limitations that led us to introduce a strategic model in Chapter 7. In this chapter, we will make a parallel effort to put our evaluation of the effect of territorial power sharing on a more dynamic and actor-based footing (see Master Hypothesis 1b).

As we have argued, claims to self-governance by territorially concentrated ethnic groups are at the core of the political debates and struggles in many countries, including current-day Iraq, Syria, Nigeria, the United Kingdom, Spain, and Ukraine. Faced by the prospects of state disintegration or civil war, the governments of these countries are confronted with the complex question of how to respond to such demands. In the hope of placating separatists, governments often offer autonomy to disgruntled minorities. However, there is no guarantee that such concessions will have the desired effects. Indeed, states sometimes fall apart despite, or perhaps even because of, wide-ranging decentralization along ethnic lines, as illustrated by the former Soviet Union and Yugoslavia.

In this chapter, we address this central research question by demonstrating that the existing literature has paid insufficient attention to the theoretical and empirical implications of strategic interactions between groups and governments. Governments face a strategic trade-off: Concessions may undermine their power, but a refusal to accommodate self-determination movements could trigger violence. Indeed, decisions to grant self-governance are likely shaped by reactions to separatists' anticipated actions. Can the government afford to remain unrelenting and set a precedence, while risking civil war? And what would happen should violence break out? Moreover, just as governments consider the consequences of territorial power sharing, groups strategically choose whether to make demands for self-determination.

For instance, one may expect that more influential or powerful groups will make bolder claims. Facing such claims, the government may believe that it is likely to face an opponent that is difficult to vanquish in a conflict, and therefore make concessions, in agreement with Master Hypothesis 4 and the findings of the previous chapter.

In view of such strategic interactions, we argue that the consequences of autonomy can hardly be fully understood in isolation from its generative process. Since strategic anticipation reverses the causal arrow, it also renders demands for self-governance endogenous. To be sure, scholars have viewed regional autonomy and secessionist politics through the lens of strategic interactions for some time (e.g., Hechter, 2000; Walter, 2006a, 2009). Yet, few have explicitly modeled the resulting interdependencies. Nor did the previous chapter attempt to model specific interactions among actors.

Responding to these difficulties, this chapter proposes an alternative approach to reverse causation and endogeneity that renders explicit the actors' actions and motivations. Along the lines of Chapter 7, the present analysis builds on a simple game-theoretic model that captures the strategic choices of governments and self-determination movements, including autonomy concessions and full-blown secession. The game makes explicit the sequence of interaction and highlights the logic of strategic anticipation. We then use the theoretical model to derive an estimator that is consistent with our game-theoretic model and that generates our empirical results, again relying on Signorino's (1999) "statistical strategic models."

Overall, our results highlight the importance of strategic interdependencies between the rebels' and governments' actions. Most importantly, the findings show that granting territorial power sharing to groups seeking self-determination decreases the likelihood of violent conflict, thus corroborating Master Hypothesis 1b and the results of the previous chapter. Furthermore, the findings show that territorially concentrated ethnic groups tend to calibrate the extent of their demands on the basis of their bargaining power (i.e. the level of threat they pose), but also how they expect the government to respond to these demands. We also find that governments are more likely to grant concessions to threatening groups, but these responses are constrained by further strategic considerations, especially concerns about reputation when demands by other groups could be incentivized through concessions (cf. Walter, 2006a).

The strategic approach also enables us to test more specific propositions about what drives the strategic relationship between autonomy, secession, and conflict. For example, while oil deposits in an ethnic group's settlement area induce governments to reject demands for secession, this also leads rebels to more frequently request secession. Similarly, we find that government facing a high number of territorially concentrated groups are more reluctant to make concessions. This, in turn, makes rebel groups more likely to accept the *status quo*.

The chapter is structured as follows. In the next section we evaluate the literature on autonomy, secession and conflict to highlight the main arguments and gaps that still persist. Based on this review of the literature, we then introduce an extensive form game that captures the interaction between an ethnic group and a central government. In the following two sections we present the empirical model, along with the data we use to estimate the effect of these two actors' choices, as well as our empirical results. The final section concludes by summarizing our findings and sketching further avenues for research.

9.1   Territorial Power Sharing, Secession and Conflict

We situate our approach in the broader context of the literature on decentralization and conflict. Adding causal depth to the main research question on the effect of autonomy, we add two additional research questions to the agenda:

1. Does territorial power sharing contain or fuel conflict?
2. What explains governments' reactions to demands for self-governance?
3. What explains the demand for self-governance?

Although each research question corresponds to a particular scientific debate, we contend that arguments about strategic interaction imply that these questions – and especially the effect of territorial power sharing – can hardly be addressed properly in isolation. Our main research question asks whether territorial power sharing affects the conflict proneness of ethnic groups in a society. Scholars stressing the pacifying effect of autonomy typically build (directly or indirectly) on Tiebout's (1957) classical framing of decentralization as a mode to resolve conflicts over public goods provision in a way that addresses heterogeneous preferences between regions of a country. By extending policy responsiveness to as many people as possible, grievances can be avoided and peaceful avenues for political change provided to potential secessionists (Hechter, 2000; Bakke and Wibbels, 2006). Skeptics retort that autonomy and federalism, especially along ethnic lines, risk deepening already existing cleavages (Kaufmann, 1996; Chapman and Roeder, 2007; Roeder, 2007) while equipping groups with resources that can be used to fuel separatist campaigns, possibly even violently (Snyder, 2000; Roeder and Rothchild, 2005). However, most of this literature, whether based on qualitative case studies or quantitative analysis, treats the level of decentralization as exogenously given, and thus rarely addresses the question why governments grant autonomy in the first place.[1]

In order to address the main research question, we need to address the second core research question, because an assessment of autonomy's effect on conflict cannot treat governmental choice to grant autonomy as if it were exogenous. Many scholars explicitly or implicitly acknowledge that regional autonomy and federal arrangements are, at least in part, adopted in order to placate minorities and pacify center-periphery relations. Yet, if this is the case, decentralization efforts by governments are endogenous and cannot be assumed to be adopted without considerations about the prospects of violence. Sambanis and Milanovic (2014, 1845) describe these obstacles blocking sound causal inference:

This problem of endogeneity arises in some form in every study of the relationship between conflict and autonomy, or decentralization and any other policy outcome because changes in the level of decentralization are likely to reflect the government's expectations about how they will affect the risk of conflict or the policy outcome in question.

Arguing that no viable instrumental variable capable of solving the endogeneity problem econometrically can be found for autonomy or any other type of decentralization, Sambanis and Milanovic (2014) limit themselves to articulating correlational claims while deliberately refraining from causal interpretations. Their analysis reveals strong correlations between relative regional income, regional population share, natural resource endowment and regional inter-personal inequality on one side and demand for regional autonomy on the other.

Consequently, even if we are only interested in the first core research question on the overall effect of autonomy, the second question examining the origin of such institutions, also has to be addressed (see Lustick, Miodownik and Eidelson, 2004). This is because governments are

---

[1] The broader literature on federalism and decentralization examines why such schemes are originally introduced, but is seldom directly linked to the conflict research (for recent excellent reviews of this literature, see Weingast, 2005; Rodden, 2006; Beramendi, 2007; Bednar, 2011; Beramendi and León, 2015). It is worth noting that due to his exclusion of demands for regional autonomy as a campaign strategy, Roeder (2018) in his recent book on "National Secession" cannot directly address our main research question. Relatedly, Siroky (2011), while focusing his discussion of secession on the secessionist group and the government (in addition to the international arena) does not explicitly address the intertwined nature of these main levels.

likely to have forward-looking expectations as regards groups' actions. Unfortunately, however, governmental responses to territorial claims for self-governance have attracted surprisingly little attention in the conflict literature (Cunningham, 2014, 77).[2] Because the literature on grievances and inequality has focused on conflict as an outcome while treating ethnic inclusion and decentralization as exogenous, we know relatively little about what motivates states to grant regional autonomy to potential or actual secessionist movements. Given the inherently strategic nature of the second question, it is natural that the best-known work in this area is inspired by game-theoretic reasoning (for a broader review of this literature, see Walter, 2009). Highlighting the importance of reputation in a bargaining context, Walter (2006a) analyzes the government's decision-making when faced with secessionist bids (see also Jenne, Saideman and Lowe, 2007).[3] Considering the risk of state collapse and conflict, governing elites in large multi-ethnic states will be reluctant to make concessions to any of the state's ethnic minorities since such moves may embolden others to follow suit (see also Roeder, 2018).[4]

Grigoryan (2015) proposes a game-theoretic model that focuses on how governments respond to "restive ethnic minorities." The model extends Fearon's (1998) application of the commitment problem to secessionist conflict, in order to explain why governmental responses to minorities' demands vary from state to state. The argument is that state elites may well prefer to coerce separatist groups the weaker the state is and the more likely the group is to receive support from third parties, such as ethnic kin. Although the study makes a valuable contribution to theory-building, it does not fully explore the comparative statics implied by the model, and the empirical evaluation is limited to selected case studies.

By modeling explicitly the ethnic group's choice to mobilize, Grigoryan (2015) also directly addresses our third core research question on the causes of territorial claims or demands. Compared to the second one, the question dealing with what inclines groups to make claims for self-determination is relatively well covered in the literature. Classical

---

[2] There is considerable literature on state repression in the more general sense (for an excellent review of this literature see Davenport, 2007).

[3] Bunce (2004) discusses cooperation and conflict between the center and periphery of multiethnic states (for a more extensive treatment, see Bunce, 2003). In her study of India, Lacina (2015) offers a more comprehensive discussion of the same relationship (see also Lacina, 2014, 2017).

[4] Walter (2006a, 2009, Chapter 5) also offers an empirical study that addresses the third question, but fails to link it to her work on the second question (for an extension of this author's main argument, see Schädel, 2016).

contributions by Gurr (1993) and Horowitz (1985) highlight grievances and discrimination as possible causes that prompt ethnic groups to mobilize along separatist lines (for an overview, see Cederman, Gleditsch and Buhaug, 2013). Recentralization, such as withdrawal of regional autonomy, can also serve as a strong trigger for peripheral mobilization (e.g., Hechter, 2000; Jenne, 2006).[5] Besides political marginalization, scholars have also analyzed economic inequality as a motivation for secessionist campaigns, both for groups that are poorer (Hechter, 1975; Horowitz, 1985; Dower and Weber, 2015) and wealthier (e.g., Gourevitch, 1979; Collier and Hoeffler, 2006; Hale, 2008; Morelli and Rohner, 2015) than the country average.

Beyond these grievance-based accounts, there are studies that focus on the opportunities of ethnic groups to build support for their separatist bids. Such factors include demographic concentration (e.g., Toft, 2002; Weidmann, 2009), and the group's relative power compared to the incumbent government (e.g., for the case of secessionism, see Sorens, 2012). As with the analyses of the overall impact of territorial power sharing on conflict, endogeneity poses difficulties for the studies of the demand for sovereignty as well. Indeed, most scholars treat secessionist motivations as exogenous and generally do not fully capture the strategic logic of state-minority politics.

This survey of the literature reveals that there are several challenges to confront. First, due to its endogenous nature, any empirical analysis of the consequences of autonomy necessarily also requires addressing the two other questions, which are causally antecedent. Yet, such an integrated approach has rarely been pursued, and if so, typically only at the level of theory, as illustrated by the work of Walter (2009) and Grigoryan (2015).

Second, the empirical literature tends to conflate explanations of self-determination demands with accounts of armed conflict (see, e.g., Collier and Hoeffler, 2006). Clearly, in agreement with recent work on non-violent conflict (e.g., Chenoweth and Lewis, 2013), studies of separatist politics systematically need to separate the third question about demands from the first one about political violence, since making demands is not the same thing as engaging in violent conflict (Cetinyan, 2002).

Finally, the literature often confuses demands for secession with less encompassing claims for autonomy. Although movements may be split as regards to these objectives, both between factions and over time

---

[5] Lacina's (2015) work emphasizes that power struggles within the periphery and their relationship to the central government affect the likelihood of conflict.

(Cunningham, 2014), these are distinct options. Some movements may strategically express secessionist demands in order to secure autonomy.[6] Thus, as reflected by our third core question, a complete model of secessionist politics would need to include demands for autonomy and secession as distinct moves.

In summary, we conjecture that an examination of the effect of decentralization and territorial autonomy on conflict needs to pay close attention to reverse causation induced by strategic independence. This is because groups can be expected to calibrate their demands depending on the level of threat they pose, but also on what they can reasonably expect to extract. Governments, on the other hand, are likely to react strategically to such demands by granting concessions only to the extent that this proves necessary in order to avoid conflict, while keeping a close eye on avoiding reputation costs that would incentivize further challengers. Ultimately these arguments suggest that autonomy appeases groups and thus tends to be granted to conflict-prone groups. As we detail below, omitting these strategic dynamics is likely to induce bias in empirical analyses. The next section therefore lays out an actor-centric approach that renders these general ideas more concrete within a framework that allows for a theoretically derived empirical estimation approach.

9.2   A Strategic Model

This section models the strategic origins of regional autonomy and secession, along with their consequences in terms of armed conflict. By laying out a structured sequence of actions, we attempt to overcome the main shortcomings identified in the previous section by relying on an approach very similar to the one used in Chapter 7. Addressing the main research question by taking into account the two additional ones mentioned above, the model makes explicit several aspects highlighted by the theoretical discussion above. This has several advantages. First, choices by the central government and a group potentially seeking self-determination are theorized to be interdependent, given the structure of our game tree. In other words, implementations of territorial power sharing through regional autonomy, for instance, are explicitly modeled as governmental reactions to demands by an ethnic group. This allows us to address issues of endogeneity head-on. Second, demands for secession can be met with offers of autonomy, and such offers can be

---

[6] In his model, Grigoryan (2015) also refrains from making this important distinction, while Roeder (2018) evacuates campaigns for autonomy completely from his approach.

accepted or challenged through secession, as suggested by the Scottish and Catalan independence campaigns. To allow for this, our model distinguishes between demands of secession or autonomy even though they are frequently conflated in the literature. Finally, the model makes explicit that group demands for autonomy or secession, as well as governmental responses, occur in the shadow of bargaining power. In other words, the shadow of future conflict looms directly over the scope of groups' demands, as well as governmental responses.

9.2.1   *Extensive-form game*

Based on these core ideas, we propose a succinct extensive form game that stylizes the interaction between a domestic group which we refer to as the potential rebels (r) and a central government (c), and which serves as the basis for our statistical model. Figure 9.1 visualizes the sequence of play that ends with ten distinct outcomes, indicated through circled numbers. To aid subsequent discussion, we reference each decision node through boxed Roman numerals.[7]

In a first move (node $\boxed{\text{I}}$), the potential rebels may either demand autonomy or secession, or make no demand, thereby accepting the *status quo* and ending the game at outcome ④. These demands by groups may be formulated through violent or non-violent campaigns (Chenoweth and Lewis, 2013; Sambanis, Germann and Schädel, 2018) or, for secessionist demands, simply in declarations of independence (Coggins, 2011; Regan and Wallensteen, 2013; Griffiths, 2015).

If the rebels' demand for secession is accepted, the game ends with outcome ⑦,[8] while in all other cases the governments decide how to respond to these demands by either rejecting them, or granting autonomy or secession (nodes $\boxed{\text{II}}$, $\boxed{\text{III}}$). Subsequently, in nodes $\boxed{\text{IV}}$, $\boxed{\text{V}}$, $\boxed{\text{VI}}$, and $\boxed{\text{VII}}$ the rebels can respond to the government's action by deciding whether to escalate the conflict and respond by violence (outcomes ①, ③, ⑥ and ⑨) or simply accept and back down (outcomes ⓪, ②, ⑤, ⑧).

Set up in this way, the model closely reflects the three research questions formulated above. At the empirical level, the interactions presented in Figure 9.1 have so far been studied almost exclusively in

---

[7] In the figure we subscript the boxed Roman numerals with the abbreviations for the actors involved. Strictly speaking this representation depicts a stage of a possibly infinitely repeated game. It also bears some resemblance to Hale's (2008) simple games and Grigoryan's (2015) more elaborate game.

[8] This assumption, is justified through Tir's (2005) empirical finding that secessions conceded by central governments remain peaceful.

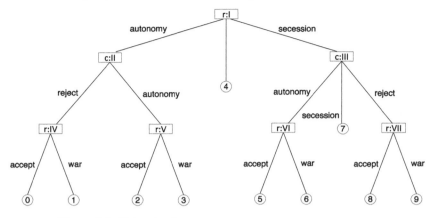

Figure 9.1 Extensive form game

what might be considered reduced-form models (i.e. single equation models that generally omit endogenous relationship).[9] A more direct way to assess the effects of the various elements of our game, especially with regard to interdependent choices, is to rely on a strategic statistical model as proposed by Signorino (1999).

The underlying idea of this technique is to write down a statistical model that mirrors a particular extensive form game (see also Chapter 7). Using a game with complete and perfect information as a starting point, the approach assumes that the actors make small errors when making choices at their respective decision nodes, thus generating probabilities associated with each action.

By parameterizing the utilities of the various outcomes for each player using empirical data, the effect of variables on choice probabilities can be estimated and the latter be calculated. If we assume that the errors made by the actors are independently and identically distributed according to a type 1 extreme value distribution, the functional form for determining the probabilities corresponds to a logit specification.

The probability of a particular outcome occurring is then given by the joint probability of the constituent actions, that is, by multiplying the choice probabilities of each action leading from the initial node [I] to the particular final node corresponding to an outcome. We illustrate this approach with the probabilities associated with the left-most final nodes

---

[9] As Carrubba, Yuen and Zorn (2007) remind us, however, especially if we are to take seriously strategic interaction, such a model would have to specify the comparative statics implications in a particularly careful manner.

in Figure 9.1. As by assumption the errors made by each actor at each decision node are independent, we can derive the probability of ⓪ as follows:

$$p(\text{⓪}) = p(autonomy_r) \times p(reject_c|autonomy_r) \times p(accept_r|reject_c, autonomy_r)$$
$$(9.1)$$

Starting with the last probability, we note that conditional on having reached node $\boxed{\text{IV}}$, the probability of ⓪ is determined solely by r and given by a comparison between the groups' utilities associated with the 'available' outcomes:

$$p(accept_r|reject_c, autonomy_r) = p\big(U_r(\text{⓪}) - U_r(\text{①}) > \epsilon\big) \qquad (9.2)$$

Proceeding analogously for node $\boxed{\text{V}}$ yields the conditional probability $p(accept_r|autonomy_c, autonomy_r)$. Using these conditional probabilities as weights, we can calculate the expected utility for the two actions c has at node $\boxed{\text{II}}$.

$$p(reject_c|autonomy_r)$$

$$= p\Big[\big(p(accept_r|reject_c, autonomy_r) \times U_c(\text{⓪})$$

$$+ \big(1 - p(accept_r|reject_c, autonomy_r)\big) \times U_c(\text{①})\big)$$

$$- \big(p(accept_r|autonomy_c, autonomy_r) \times U_c(\text{②})$$

$$+ \big(1 - p(accept_r|autonomy_c, autonomy_r)\big) \times U_c(\text{③})\big) > \epsilon\Big]$$
$$(9.3)$$

Moving up one step in the game using analogous calculations for $p(autonomy)$, we obtain a specification for the unconditional probability $p(\text{⓪})$ (see Equation 9.1). Proceeding for all final outcomes in the same way we obtain equations for all probabilities associated with each final outcome, which allows us to formulate the appropriate likelihood function as the joint probability over the outcomes. It also allows us to estimate the effects of various variables on the utilities attached to the final nodes, and thus on the decisions depicted in the game tree by the two actors.[10]

---

[10] In the context of a strategic game with two actors and two decision nodes, Leemann (2014), proposes a model with correlated errors. We refrain from following Leemann's (2014) suggestion and note that reduced form estimations that dominate in this field of research rely on the same assumption. In addition, Leemann's (2014) estimator does not guarantee equilibrium behavior by all actors involved.

Set up this way, the estimator captures interdependence and strategic anticipation in a way that closely resembles conventional backwards induction. For example, in instances where r moves last (i.e., decides whether to raise arms), in the preceding move the government c will weigh each choice alternative (and the associated utilities that follow) by the (expected) probabilities with which r is likely to react.

9.2.2   Data

Estimating a strategic model of the type depicted in Figure 9.1 requires a considerable amount of *actor-specific* data. In particular, we require data on the trajectories of play, that is, the various outcomes, along with data for each player's utility associated with these outcomes. Combining two recent datasets makes it possible to analyze empirically how the various decisions by groups and government interact. As before, we rely on the "Ethnic Power Relations" (EPR) dataset (see Vogt et al., 2015) as our point of departure from which we identify the relevant actors. EPR provides a global list of politically relevant ethnic groups worldwide from 1946, as well as information on their access to power. These data allow us to identify those groups which control the "central government," but also those groups that could plausibly put forward demands for territorial self-governance, here referred to as "the rebels." In constructing our sample of potential rebels, we assume that only groups that are territorially relevant and do not control the state as a monopoly or dominate in the executive (i.e. groups that do not rule alone) are affected by the strategic interaction outlined above. In addition, EPR also provides a group-level coding of civil conflict through the ACD2EPR dataset (Wucherpfennig et al., 2012). We augment these ethnic group-year data with information from Sambanis, Germann and Schädel's (2018) data on Self-Determination Movements (SDM), which provides a direct mapping of self-determination movements to EPR groups. Given the temporal coverage of these data, this results in a sample spanning from 1946 until 2012.[11]

9.2.2.1 Dependent variable Our dependent variable corresponds to the various final outcomes of our theoretical model, as illustrated in Figure 9.1 and is constructed from our combined dataset. Within our sample, we consider all ethnic groups that have engaged in a campaign for autonomy (as per the SDM data) to have put forward demands for

---

[11] In the online appendix, we provide a list of all countries appearing in our analyses, and the number of group-years that they contribute to our data.

autonomy at node $\boxed{1}$, leading to the left part of the tree. If no conflict occurs after a rejected demand, the group-year is treated as final outcome ⓪, while conflictual instances are classified as final outcome ①.[12] Groups that are granted autonomy during their campaign for autonomy and fail to initiate a violent conflict are assigned to final outcome ② in the year of the governmental concession, while instances of conflict onset after autonomy was granted are captured in final outcome ③. Groups that do not put forward any demands are captured in final outcome ④. Implicitly this outcome serves as our baseline category.

Secessionist campaigns (as coded in SDM) lead groups down the right part of the game tree. Final outcome ⑤ captures situations in which the government offers regional autonomy to a group that subsequently remains peaceful, while final outcome ⑥ designates those situations where conflict occurs. If such a secessionist demand is accepted, this leads to final outcome ⑦ and subsequently drops from the analysis.

Finally, if a government does not react to a demand for secession, the absence of a conflict onset leads us to assign the respective group-year to final outcome ⑧, while the conflictual instances lead to final outcome ⑨.

9.2.2.2 Theorizing and operationalizing the payoffs Formulated as a likelihood function for the outcomes, the strategic-estimation approach assumes that the utilities that rebels and the government derive from particular outcomes can be parameterized through particular observable variables. Drawing on the theoretical accounts discussed above, we propose that the payoffs (i.e. utilities) for both actors are composed of five main theoretical elements. These can be considered as latent variables in our empirical analyses. Table 9.1 lists the theoretical payoff components along with the observable variables that we use for parameterization in the statistical model.

First, where *autonomy* is realized, this is likely to be considered a benefit for the rebel group, but a cost for the government. Specifically, we assume that autonomy is particularly valuable for an ethnic group that profited from such an arrangement in the past, but lost it in the meantime (this factor is also highlighted by Jenne, 2006; Walter, 2006a, 2009; Sorens, 2012). In addition, we posit that on average granting autonomy is less costly for the government of countries with a federal system (cf. Lacina, 2014), but benefits the affected rebel group.

---

[12] Following standard practice, group-years of ongoing conflicts are omitted from the dataset, as conflict onset and continuation are likely to be affected differently by explanatory factors.

Table 9.1. *Operationalization of payoffs and theoretical expectations*

Payoff component	Variables for r	Exp. payoff	Variables for c	Exp. payoff
Autonomy	Federal system	+	Federal system	−
	Group previously lost autonomy	+		
Secession	Oil in ethnic group's settlement	+	Oil in ethnic group's settlement	+
	Dispersed settlement pattern	−		
War costs	Number of previous wars	−	Log of GDP per capita	−
	Excluded group	−	Democracy (Xpolity2)	+
	Peace years	NA		
Pr(r wins war)	cross-border ethnic kinship	+	Cross-border ethnic kinship	−
	Power balance	+	Power balance	−
	Relative wealth of group	+	Relative wealth of group	−
Reputation costs	Duration group is excluded	+	Number of challengers	+
		+	Number of groups w/ autonomy	−

Second, *secession* is likely to have a similar structure of costs and benefits. Following a series of authors including Collier and Hoeffler (2006), Walter (2009), Sorens (2012), and Morelli and Rohner (2015), we expect that natural resources within the secessionist group's settlement area, oil in particular, are likely to increase the value of a secession, while imposing high costs on the government. Conversely, for a group whose settlement pattern is dispersed, the value of secession is likely to be smaller.

Third, following a large literature on bargaining approaches to conflict we acknowledge that *war is costly*. If the rebel group chooses to fight, then both government and rebel group incur war costs. For the rebel group we assume that previous conflicts lower material, military and mobilization costs thanks to infrastructure deriving from prior campaigns. Exclusion from central executive power further facilitates mobilization of support for a war against an oppressive government, as implicitly argued for secessionist claims by Sorens (2012, 46f). For the government we postulate that economic development reduces the costs of war[13] and that audience costs make wars in democracies particularly costly.[14]

Fourth, in the event of a conflict, the outcome is rendered as a *costly lottery* over victory or defeat. Given the complementary nature of the outcome probabilities in a dyadic setting, we formulate the probabilities of achieving military victory from the viewpoint of the rebels. We join authors such as Walter (2009) and Grigoryan (2015) in claiming that groups with transborder ethnic kin, as well as those with a larger relative share of the population, have better chances for military success in territorial conflicts (see also Jenne, 2006). In addition, we consider the group's economic wealth as an additional factor influencing the likelihood of war victory.[15]

Finally, both rebels and governments are likely to face *reputation costs*. We anticipate that rebel groups that make demands and back down after a rejection by the government face reputation costs. We consider these costs to be especially high if an ethnic group has been excluded from power for a long time.[16] Similarly, offering concessions to rebel groups induces reputation costs for the government, since this demonstrates to other potential challengers that concessions can be obtained (Walter, 2009, 68f). Consequently, we follow her approach by using the number of potential challengers to operationalize reputation costs for the central government. We argue, however, that if a government has already granted autonomy to other groups in the past, then offering such a concession to an additional one is likely to induce lower reputation costs as compared to a situation where several groups already profit from autonomy (cf. Lacina, 2015).

---

[13] For a similar argument about secession, see Sorens (2012, 44f).

[14] Griffiths (2015) makes a similar case for the way in which democratic governments deal with secessionist demands.

[15] Several authors also mention economic development as a factor influencing the likelihood of demands for autonomy (e.g., Sambanis and Milanovic, 2014) or secession (e.g., Sorens, 2012, 32f), but do not explain through what mechanism this occurs. We explicitly argue that wealthier groups have better chances of winning in a war.

[16] We conceptualize this variable in two different ways for groups demanding secession and autonomy. For the former we count the years since a group has not had access to executive power at the central government. For the latter we also consider being a junior partner in government as a case of limited executive power. We motivate this difference by the fact that the EPR data on regional autonomy assume that such concessions are only relevant for excluded groups, as well as junior partners in government. In addition, this different conceptualization also renders the estimation easier, because it ensures that there is an implicit exclusion restriction for each decision-node.

Table 9.2. *Outcomes, payoffs and observations*

Outcome	Payoff for r	Payoff for c	n
⓪	- reputation costs	0	1941
①	- war costs + p(r wins war)* autonomy	- war costs − p(r wins war)* autonomy	22
②	autonomy	- autonomy − reputation costs	1421
③	- war costs + p(r wins war)* autonomy	- war costs - p(r wins war)* autonomy − reputation costs	13
④	0	0	29456
⑤	autonomy - reputation costs	- autonomy − reputation costs	468
⑥	- war costs + p(r wins war)* secession	- war costs − p(r wins war)* secession − reputation costs	17
⑦	secession	- secession − reputation costs	8
⑧	- reputation costs	0	1203
⑨	- war costs + p(r wins war)* secession	- war costs − p(r wins war)* secession	67

In terms of data sources, variables pertaining to group status can be constructed on the basis of the EPR dataset (see Chapter 4) and its GIS extension, GeoEPR (Wucherpfennig et al., 2011). We complement these data with information on federalism by Bednar (2008), the level of democracy from Vreeland's (2008) modified Polity measure (Marshall et al., 2002), the presence of oil in an ethnic group's settlement (Hunziker, 2014), group-level economic indicators (Cederman, Weidmann and Bormann, 2015), and ethnic kinship (Cederman et al., 2013). A table of descriptive statistics can be found in the online appendix.

Having detailed the payoff components both conceptually, as well as in terms of observable variables, Table 9.2 details how we compose the actor's payoffs for each outcome. In combination with the specific parameterization proposed above, this determines how we specify the statistical model. As particular payoff components appear in different utilities assigned to final outcomes (e.g. war costs for the rebels), we estimate one set of coefficients for the explanatory variables pertaining to a particular latent variable (i.e. payoff component). The final column of the table also denotes the number of group-years per outcome.

9.3   Empirical Analysis

Although previous scholarship on strategic estimation relies on frequentist approaches, we here estimate our model in a Bayesian framework for two main reasons. First, the distribution of observations over the ten final outcomes is highly unequal, with some nodes appearing only very infrequently among the observed outcomes, as the last column in Table 9.2 illustrates. As a result, standard maximum likelihood estimation frequently generated instances of quasi-complete separation. The Bayesian approach avoids such problems.

Second, the indicator on relative economic wealth at the group-level suffers from considerable missing data.[17] To address this issue we include an imputation step which estimates a model linking all of our independent variables with the GDP per capita of each group. For groups and years for which this information was missing we drew from the estimated posterior distribution of the dependent variable of this auxiliary regression[18] and used the predictions to calculate the relative wealth for each ethnic group. These values were then imputed for the missing values during each sampling iteration (see Lunn et al., 2012).

In discussing the results, we follow the game structure given in Figure 9.1, thereby addressing directly the three research questions that have guided our analysis. We focus on substantive effects in terms of probabilities that the actors will take particular actions.[19]

9.3.1   What explains the demand for self-governance?

In accordance with the sequence of play in our model, we begin with our third research question which asks about the conditions under which groups put forward demands for self-governance, and if so, whether to opt for autonomy and secession (node Ⅰ). At a basic level, our argument about strategic interaction holds that groups anticipate how governments will respond to their demands, and therefore calibrate their demands accordingly. Evidence to this effect is depicted in Figure 9.2, which shows the average predicted probabilities of the rebels demanding either autonomy or secession as a function of the anticipated reaction by the government along two dimensions: how likely it is that the government

---

[17] As Cederman, Weidmann and Bormann (2015) show, for smaller and regionally not concentrated groups, estimating group-level GDP is particularly difficult.

[18] Estimations were carried out with JAGS (Plummer, 2010) while using diffuse uninformative priors. We use 185,000 draws from two chains of the posterior distribution after discarding 1000 burn-ins and thinning to obtain 1000 draws. The R-hat statistic proposed by Gelman and Rubin (1992) suggests convergence, with the exception of some coefficients linked to the imputation step, which is likely to be inconsequential.

[19] We provide and discuss the estimated coefficients in the online appendix.

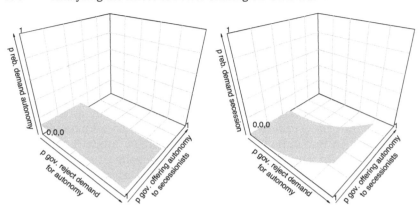

Figure 9.2 Average predicted probabilities of rebels' demands as a function of (anticipated) government's responses

will give in to demands for autonomy (see node $\boxed{\text{II}}$), and how likely it is that the government will grant autonomy if the group demands secession (see node $\boxed{\text{III}}$).[20]

The figure illustrates that the rebels' demands are sensitive to the government's anticipated reactions. More specifically, the left panel shows that rebel groups are deterred from demanding autonomy if they anticipate that such demands will be rejected. At the same time, if governments become more likely to offer autonomy to secessionists, demands for autonomy become slightly less frequent.

The right panel demonstrates that demands for secession hinge on the government's accommodating stance. As the government becomes increasingly likely to reject demands for autonomy, the likelihood of secessionist demands increases. Similarly, though much less strongly, if counter-offers of autonomy by the government become more likely, secessionist demands increase as well.

While these basic insights already suggest that groups formulate demands for self-governance in a way that is consistent with our strategic expectations, it is useful to examine what drives such behavior. Based on the estimates of our statistical model, it is possible to assess how

---

[20] The probability of the group making no demands (outcome ④) is simply the complement of these two probabilities. For node $\boxed{\text{III}}$ we set the probability of accepting secession to .5. Thus, we are looking at a moderately tough government. As a consequence of fixing this probability, the remaining probabilities for c are bound, as can be seen in the Figure 9.2.

specific variables affect the likelihood of particular demands. This allows us to examine the decision calculus more directly. Figures 9.3 and 9.4 therefore depict the average differences in the predicted probability of rebel groups requesting autonomy, secession or accepting the status quo as a function of continuous and binary covariates, respectively.

If groups articulate demands on the basis of expectations about the government's response, then arguably the best information available concerning the prospects of being successful is to observe other groups in the country. In particular, if other groups already enjoy autonomy, then such self-governance is evidently feasible as the government must have given in previously. This, in turn, incentivizes "deprived" groups to raise demands to "catch up" and join the ranks of self-governing groups. In keeping with this argument, we find that a higher number of groups with autonomy in the country strongly raises slightly the odds of a group putting forward demands for autonomy as well (see Figure 9.3), while lowering the probability that the group will demand to secede. Indeed, we find a similar pattern of behavior for groups in federal states, while groups that lost autonomy are likely to demand that the previous status is restored (see Figure 9.4).

However, according to reputation theory (Walter, 2006a) there are limits to what governments can afford to give away. Thus, the flipside of the previous argument is that devolving power to groups ultimately risks state erosion, and so governments facing a high number of potential challengers can be expected to remain unrelenting in order to deter future demands. This anticipation of a reluctant government should also lead to high number of challengers reducing the probability of a group demanding either autonomy or secession, arguably because the government will be less likely to yield in the first place. Our findings suggest, however, that rebel groups hardly adjust their demands to this logic.

Beyond these reputation dynamics as drivers for strategic demands, we also find that groups whose settlement areas contain oil deposits are more likely to demand secession, while being slightly more reluctant to request autonomy (see Figure 9.4). This supports Collier and Hoeffler's (2006) claim regarding the role of natural resources in secessionist wars.[21] Relatedly, we find that the relative wealth of ethnic groups does

---

[21] Our result, however, is more specific, as it shows that secessionist demands are more likely in this scenario, but not necessarily conflicts. The latter depend on the government's reaction to these demands and the rebels' reaction as we will see below.

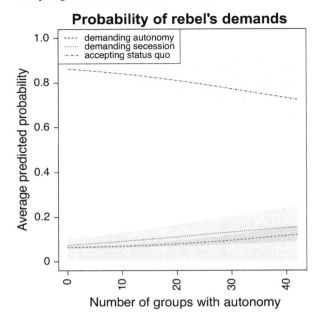

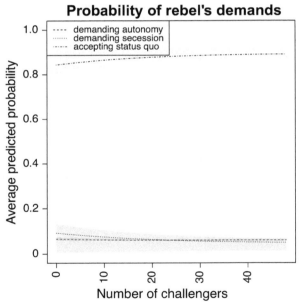

Figure 9.3 Average predicted probabilities of groups making demands (node $\boxed{\text{I}}$) for continuous variables
Note: (and 95% credible intervals)

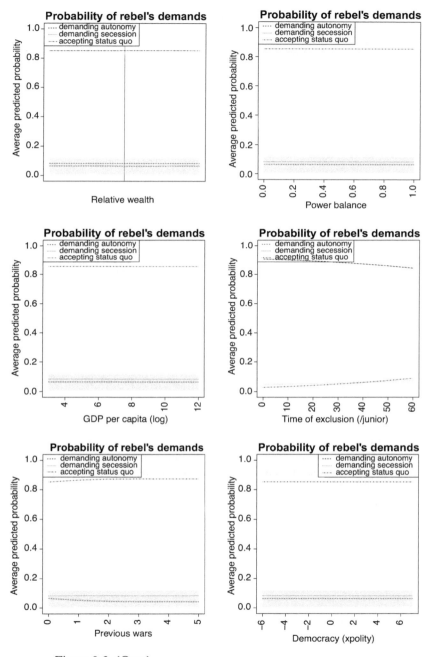

Figure 9.3 (*Cont.*)

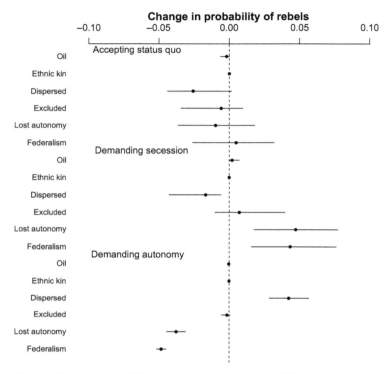

Figure 9.4 Average differences in group's probabilities of making demands (node $\boxed{\text{I}}$) for binary variables
Note: (95% credible intervals)

not seem to affect whether a group makes either type of demand, nor does the power balance nor GDP per capita (see Figure 9.3).[22]

Excluded groups appear to be reluctant to ask for autonomy, while this variable has only a small positive effect on demands for secession (see Figure 9.4).[23] However, if an ethnic group has been excluded from

---

[22] As these latter covariates influence the probability of the rebels' winning a possible conflict, this suggests that this probability only has a reduced effect on a rebel group's choice of demands. Our findings also run counter to Sambanis and Milanovic's (2014) emphasis on economic factors in their correlational analysis. As our results seem to suggest, when the strategic interdependencies are taken into account, economic factors explaining the demand for self-determination (with the exception of oil deposits) largely vanishes. Similarly, our empirical finding contrasts with results from Jenne (2006, 22), who finds that economically advantaged groups are much less likely to engage in self-determination campaigns (see also Walter, 2009; Sorens, 2012).

[23] This is linked to the fact that counter to our expectations excluded groups appear to face higher war costs. This result contradicts in part Sorens's (2012, 60ff) who finds

power for a longer period of time, the probability that it will demand either secession or autonomy decreases. As we assume that the length of this time period affects the reputation costs of the rebel groups (for which we find a negative effect), this implies that as the reputation costs of backing down after a rejected demand decrease, rebel groups become more "demanding."

Finally, contrary to our expectations, ethnic groups with geographically dispersed settlement patterns are more likely to ask for autonomy. However, such groups are less likely to demand secession.[24]

In summary, our analysis – in response to the question of what explains the demands of rebel groups – confirms that strategic interdependence is of great importance. The rebels' anticipation of the government's responses influences considerably the rebels' demands. This also transpires in the impacts of the substantive variables. Above all, a rebel group acting in a context with many other potential challengers anticipates that the government will be less accommodating and thus becomes less likely to advance self-determination claims.

9.3.2   What explains governments' reactions to demands for self-governance?

We now turn to our second research question, which asks about the conditions under which governments react to groups' demands by either granting autonomy or secession, or denying such demands. So far we have argued that whether groups make particular demands depends in part on the governments' expected reactions. We expect that the government will form similar forward-looking expectations before reacting to self-determination demands. In particular, we expect the government's decision calculus to be influenced by the aim of maintaining state integrity and preventing conflict, while at the same time maximizing the political spoils for the ruling group. We show that it can be difficult to simultaneously realize these aims.

In line with the previous section, in Figure 9.5 we begin by examining how the government's anticipation of the rebels' reaction affects the responses to demands for self-governance. The top left panel considers the left part of our game tree and depicts how the expected probability of the rebels resorting to fighting after the government's decision to reject

---

that the power of ethnic groups affects their demand for secession. It should be noted, however, that Sorens (2012, 58) uses the relative population size as indicator for power.

[24] Since our estimated coefficients indicate that dispersed groups benefit less from both autonomy and secession, the contrasting effects of these types of demands are likely due to the strategic interdependencies between the rebels and government.

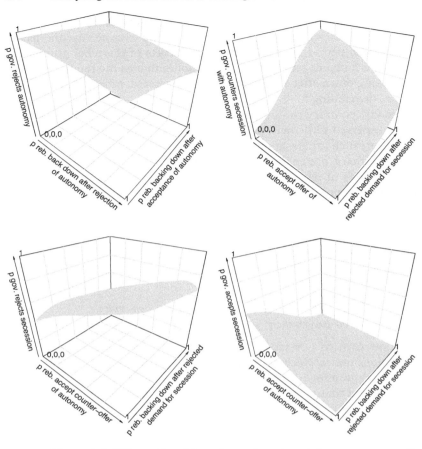

Figure 9.5 Effects of anticipated reactions by rebels on government's decision

(node Ⅳ) or accept a demand for autonomy (node Ⅴ) influences the government's choice (node Ⅱ). In partial agreement with our expectations, we find that governments are more likely to grant autonomy when they expect that doing so will keep the group from fighting. At the same time, however, as rebels become more likely to back down after a rejected demand for autonomy, the government becomes less likely to reject such demands.

The remaining panels address the right part of the game tree (node Ⅲ). The top right panel considers how the prospects of violence affect the government's decision to placate secessionist demands by a counteroffer of autonomy. Interestingly, such a counteroffer is most likely if secessionists are likely to back down, even if such a counteroffer is unlikely to be accepted.

The decisions whether to accept or reject demands for secession are depicted in the lower two panels. The left panel shows that the likelihood of rejection is quite high and increases as the rebels become more likely to accept counteroffers of autonomy. Consequently, if they are willing to accept a compromise, governments react by adopting a tougher negotiation position, while at the same time becoming more accommodating to secessionists. However, the panel to the right shows that the acceptance of secession by governments is not a very likely course of action in general, and is only more probable if rebels themselves are unaccommodating. If the rebels are likely to accept the government's counteroffer of autonomy, governments are much less willing to accept secession.

Together, the evidence presented in Figure 9.5 corroborates our argument about strategic interaction, especially the finding that governments systematically make concessions in the form of offering and granting autonomy as a means of securing peace. As before, we now examine in more detail what drives these dynamics by considering the substantive effects of our covariates on the government's decisions. This analysis highlights important ways in which governments can be constrained in the choices.

Figures 9.6 and 9.7 highlight that the government's reaction to demands for self-government is mostly driven by the political and territorial configuration that induces reputation concerns for the government. As the number of potential challengers increases, the government is more likely to reject demands for either autonomy or secession. To understand why, we observe that self-determination concessions increase the reputation costs, thus making accommodation less attractive to governments. This result supports Walter's (2006a) argument that governments tend to offer fewer concessions if the number of potential challengers is high. Thus, contrary to Forsberg (2013), whose study focuses on post-conflict arrangements, we find support for Walter's (2006a) reputation effect in a broader set of cases (see also Sambanis, Germann and Schädel, 2018; Bormann et al., 2019). On the other hand, as the number of groups with regional autonomy increases, governments become more likely to offer autonomy to secessionists but also more likely to reject demands for secession or autonomy. Again, this confirms our expectation that an increasing number of groups with regional autonomy decrease the reputational costs for governments when being accommodating.

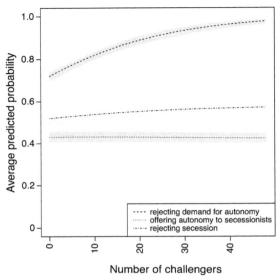

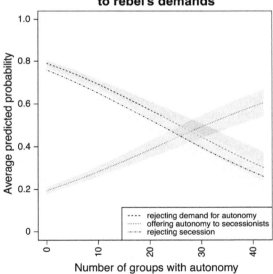

Figure 9.6 Average predicted probabilities of governmental concessions for continuous variables
Note: (95% credible intervals)

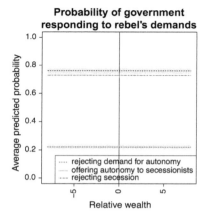

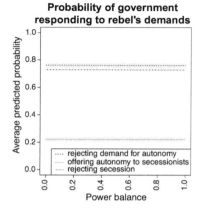

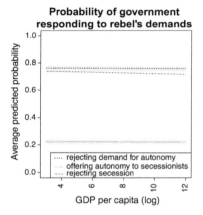

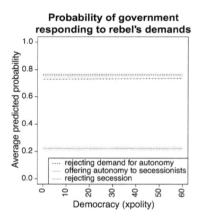

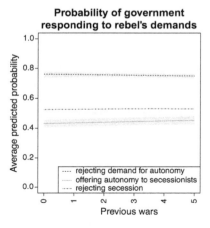

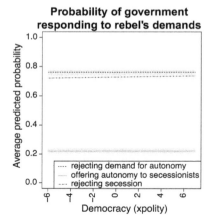

Figure 9.6 (*Cont.*)

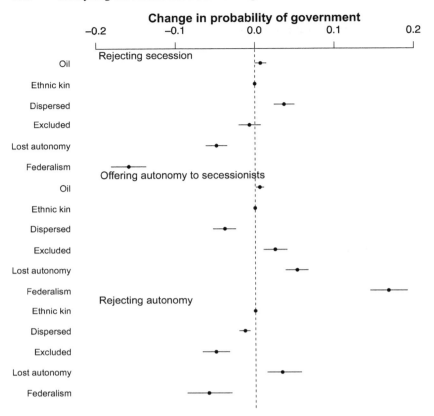

Figure 9.7 Average differences in predicted probabilities for governmental concessions for binary variables
Note: (95% credible intervals)

In Figure 9.7 the effect of federalism stands out. Governments in federal systems are more likely to accept such demands for autonomy as the costs of offering autonomy are lower in such systems according to our estimated coefficients. When facing a secessionist group, governments in federal states are much more likely to counter demands with an offer of autonomy. Here, again the lower costs of offering autonomy in federal systems comes into play, as we expected.

Groups that are territorially dispersed and make demands for secession, on the other hand, face resistance from the government. As Figure 9.7 shows, for such groups the probability that the government rejects their secessionist demand is higher, while the likelihood of a counteroffer of autonomy is lower. Similarly, secessionist demands by groups settled in areas with oil deposits are more likely to be rejected. At the same time, however, counteroffers of autonomy are also more likely. All these effects illustrate again how governments anticipate how secessionists will react to the former's response when deciding on the appropriate response.

The remaining substantive effects depicted in Figures 9.7 and 9.6 are less pronounced. Contrary to Griffiths (2015), we find no evidence that democratic countries respond differently to demands for self-determination compared to autocratic ones. This is linked to the fact that, counter to our expectations, democracies appear to face only slightly lower costs when engaging in a war. Also, and in keeping with Walter's (2009, 90f) null finding, we find no evidence that economic characteristics of the territory settled by a self-determination movement and other economic factors affect the level of accommodation offered by the government. The reason for this null effect is that the relative economic standing of groups only slightly affects the probability of the rebels winning a war. Similarly, the economic well-being of a country increases the costs for the government of waging war, but not to such an extent that it affects its accommodation decisions.

In summary, as is the case with the rebels' demands, strategic anticipation is also influential in the explanation of the government's reaction to demands for self-governance. Although often constrained by concerns about reputation, governments grant or offer autonomy to domestic challengers in order to co-opt groups and keep them from fighting. In general, governments are very unlikely to accept secession, and if they do, they do so if the rebels are anticipated to be uncompromising. Similarly, through these anticipated reactions, territorial characteristics of the rebel groups and the political context that the government faces play important roles in explaining the actions of the government.

9.3.3   Does territorial power sharing contain or spur conflict?

Our initial starting point has been that arguments about strategic interdependence between groups and governments suggest strongly that decentralization is endogenous. Having modeled its generative process, we are now ready to return to the main research question and to evaluate the effect of autonomy on conflict. We focus squarely on how decentralization strategies by the government affect the odds that groups will resort to fighting.[25]

---

[25] We discuss the effects of exogenous factors in the online appendix to this chapter.

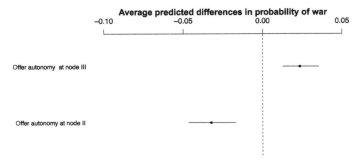

Figure 9.8 Effect of autonomy concessions
Note: (and 95% credible intervals)

We evaluate the effect of autonomy by considering counterfactual decisions by the group to fight given different choices in terms of decentralization by the government. Figure 9.8 shows average predicted differences in probabilities at the two nodes where the government may offer autonomy. The figure shows that offering autonomy to groups making this demand decreases the likelihood of conflict. In other words, this estimate (counterfactually) compares group behavior in node IV to how the group would have behaved in node V.

We find a different effect for offers of autonomy to secessionists when comparing counterfactual behaviour in node VI and VII. If we calculate these average predicted differences in probabilities it transpires that offering autonomy increases the chances of war.[26] In summary, addressing endogeneity driven by strategic interaction head-on yields strong and uniform support for the notion that decentralization in the form of granting autonomy to ethnic groups has a systematically pacifying effect on conflict.

The analyses underlying Figure 9.8 also allow us to derive a further test of Master Hypotheses 3 and 5. More specifically, the changes in the predicted probabilities of conflict depicted in the figure above can also be calculated for different scenarios depending on whether a rebel group has been engaged in previous conflicts or whether it is enjoying governmental power sharing. Figure 9.9 depicts how the average predicted probability changes after a concession of autonomy by government as a function of

[26] As our data contain no offer of secession to a secessionist groups that led to conflict, we cannot offer the same analyses for such cases (for an analysis of the reasons for this, see Tir, 2005). One indication that demands for secession are a riskier business is that the probability of conflict after secessionist demands is four times higher than after a demand for autonomy (i.e., 0.04 instead of 0.01).

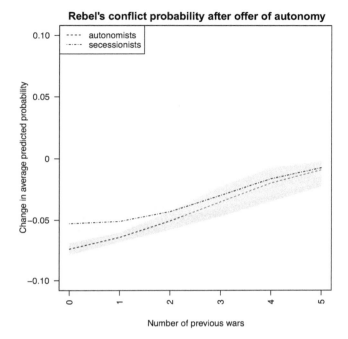

Figure 9.9 Effect of autonomy concessions as a function of the number of previous wars
Note: (and 95% credible intervals)

the number of previous wars a group has fought. As such concessions can be made both to autonomists and secessionists, we depict these changes of predicted probabilities for both types of groups. As the figure clearly shows, the strongest pacifying effect of autonomy concessions appear if a group has not been involved in a previous conflict. On the other hand if a group has been engaged in several previous conflicts, then autonomy concessions reduce the chances of conflict only marginally. This trend holds for autonomists, but is reversed for secessionists. Figure 9.9 reveals that autonomy concessions by governments increase the chances of a conflict for secessionists, particularly if these groups have not been involved in more than two or three previous conflicts. Thus, again, our analysis indicates that the effect of territorial power sharing differs between pre- and post-conflict situations.

Figure 9.10 displays the results of a test of Master Hypothesis 5. More specifically it depicts how autonomy offers reduce the probability of conflict for autonomists and secessionists, and whether it is combined

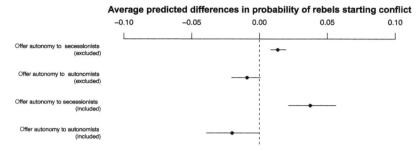

Figure 9.10 Net effect of autonomy concessions
Note: (and 95% credible intervals)

with governmental power sharing or not. While a concession of autonomy reduces the conflict probabilities only when rebels demand for
autonomy, with respect to Master Hypothesis 5, it is, however, more
notable that the conflict-reducing effect of territorial power sharing is
stronger if combined with governmental power sharing (i.e., the group
being included in government). For secessionists, surprisingly, offering
autonomy is most conflict-prone if they are included in government and
less so if they are excluded Thus, again our analysis taking into account
the strategic interactions about rebel groups and governments offers
some support for Master Hypothesis 5.

In summary, these final analyses based on our statistical strategic
model confirm that confidence and credibility are important mechanisms to consider when analyzing the effects of power sharing. More
specifically, our analyses show that autonomy offers reduce the likelihood
of conflict, but this reduction may be reversed if the credibility of the
offer is questionable. Hence, if a government makes concessions to
a group that has already been in conflict several times, such concessions often fail to instill confidence in the rebels. Conversely, offering
autonomy to a group reduces the chances of a conflict especially if the
group is also part of a governmental power-sharing arrangement. Such
offers instill much more confidence in the rebels that the autonomy
arrangements will not be rescinded in the near future.

9.4   Conclusion

Understanding whether, how, and why specific institutional arrangements generate peace ranks among the top research problems in political
science. Yet, evaluating their effects is almost always complicated by
the problem of endogeneity (see Master Hypothesis 4). Put simply, if

institutions are not assigned randomly as in a laboratory experiment, but are the result of political choices, then we have reason to believe that their origins are causally related to what they are supposed to achieve. Thus, the key question is "how to distinguish effects of institutions from those of the conditions that give rise to them" (Przeworski, 2004, 527).

In analogy to the modeling effort presented in Chapter 7, this chapter has sought to increase causal depth by analyzing the process that brings about outcomes of self-governance, autonomy and secession for territorially concentrated ethnic groups. By explicitly modeling the interdependencies of a central government and a rebel group in their bargaining over self-determination, and by relying on an estimator that directly accounts for this interaction, we shed new light on key findings in the literature. In this sense, the strategic modeling presented here complements the instrumental variable analysis of the previous chapter.

Needless to say, the current analysis also has limitations and calls for additional comparative interpretations that relate it more closely to the existing literature. For instance, unlike McGarry and O'Leary (2009) we have not considered how territorial concessions interact with concessions at the central level of government, but treated the latter as exogenously given. Similarly, we have not analyzed the level of support in the international community, as argued by Coggins (2011). Indeed, more work is required to compare our estimation results more directly with studies relying on reduced form models.

Despite these limitations, our results provide more solidly grounded answers to our three main research questions. With respect to our last core research question, we find that the feasibility of self-determination projects plays an important role. Indeed, dispersed groups are much less likely to demand secession. Similarly, groups with oil deposits on their settlement areas are more likely to be secessionist, without being more prone to demand autonomy. This is compatible with the argument proposed by Collier and Hoeffler (2006), although we record no other effects for economic variables. Finally, a group having had autonomy in the past but having lost it, is much more likely to demand it again, than other groups with no such experience.

As regards our next core research question on government responses, there is support for Walter's (2006a) claim regarding reputation costs as measured by the number of challengers. We find that a larger number of challengers decreases the probability that a government accepts demands by self-determination movements.

Turning to our main results regarding conflict we find that oil on the territory of a secessionist group reduces considerably the likelihood that a demand rejected by the government will lead to a secessionist war initiated by the rebels. Showing that oil deposits make secessionist claims more likely, our results suggest that in this link, the government's reaction to secessionist demands plays a crucial role.

For the central question whether autonomy and secession actually pacify or deteriorate relations between government and rebels, we find consistent effects that speak in favor of territorial power sharing's pacifying impact, thus confirming the findings of the previous chapter (see Master Hypothesis 1b). Whether granting autonomy to secessionists or offering it to groups that demanded it, such concessions on average decrease the likelihood of conflict outbreak, though to different degrees.

Part III

Power Sharing and Civil War in Time and Space

10   The Diffusion of Power Sharing*

The empirical analysis in the second part of the book attempts to find out whether governmental and territorial power sharing practices live up to their pacific promise in multi-ethnic systems. In the third and final part of the book we zoom out from the meso-level perspective that pits governments against groups by considering larger comparisons in time and space. Whereas the present chapter traces the diffusion of power sharing practices around the world, the following chapter analyzes long-term trends in inclusive practices and conflict patterns. Finally, in Chapter 12, we sum up what this book tells us about theory and policy.

By asking why governments may have an incentive to include potentially oppositional groups in the first place, the previous empirical chapters found that, in most cases, such inclusive policies tend to prevent or reduce conflict. The endogenization of governmental inclusion decisions serves an obvious inferential purpose, but the question of what brings about power sharing has so far not stood at the center of our attention. In fact, this is a generally understudied question. Most of the empirical literature on various types of power sharing considers their consequences in terms of democracy and political stability.

Here we follow up the analysis in Part II by considering how factors outside states' borders may influence their decisions to include or exclude ethnic groups within their borders. The descriptive statistics shown in Chapter 4 indicates that there is considerable differences between world regions as regards the level of ethnic groups' inclusion in the central executive. The general results derived in the previous

---

* This chapter is an updated version of a previously published article, see Cederman, Gleditsch and Wucherpfennig (2018). We thank for extending the analysis to 2017.

analytical chapters thus risks masking considerable heterogeneity. While some areas have experienced major gains, such as Sub-Saharan Africa, others have seen hardly any improvement at all, as illustrated by the Middle East and north Africa (see especially Figures 4.3 and 4.4).

The fact that inclusion and power sharing, and their opposite, ethnic dominance, appear to be regionally clustered constitutes a puzzle. Thus, it may not be enough to explain ethno-political constellations based on a "closed-polity" model, and arguments about transnational diffusion are likely to complement such research. Existing studies that have opened up the state in the search for explanations of inclusive practices have either assumed a global diffusion of norms (e.g., Meyer et al., 1997), or limited themselves to specific regions, such as the Balkans (e.g., Mylonas, 2012; Weiner, 1971). In short, we are lacking a systematic study on the transnational determinants of ethnic inclusion.

The literature on democratization has demonstrated explicitly the role of diffusion patterns in relation to internal causes (Gleditsch and Ward, 2006). Inspired by these approaches, but without equating ethnic inclusion and nation-building with democracy a priori, we investigate to what extent diffusion mechanisms can account for the increase of ethnic inclusion. We do so by assessing whether an Open-Polity Model (OPM) adds explanatory power to the baseline constituted by a Closed-Polity Model (CPM).

Accounting for how ethnic dominance gives way to power sharing, and the reverse, our findings indicate that the relevant diffusion processes operate most prominently at the level of world regions rather than globally or between territorial neighbors. The more inclusive the region, the more likely becomes a shift to power sharing. Conversely, shifts away from inclusion to dominance are more likely in regional settings where ethnic exclusion is more common, although there are fewer transitions to exclusion in the post-World War II period and this finding is less certain from a statistical point of view.

The chapter is structured as follows. We first review existing domestic explanations of inclusion in the literature and build on these to set up the CPM. We then draw on studies covering the diffusion of democracy to develop the propositions for the OPM. The following section introduces our data and explores patterns therein, thus preparing the ground for empirical evaluation of the CPM and the OPM. In addition, we present effect analysis and discuss a number of case illustrations. The concluding section summarizes our results and discusses their importance for theory and policy.

10.1 Explanations of Ethnic Power Sharing in the Literature

Broadly speaking, existing scholarship can be classified as either *closed-polity* approaches, which seek explanations within the state itself, or *open-polity* accounts, which explain inclusion as the result of transnational factors and processes. We briefly summarize the closed-polity studies before turning to research that goes beyond purely domestic explanations.

Ethnic diversity plays an important role in explanations of ethnic inclusion, either as a root cause of inclusion, or as an intermediate variable. Either way, the central importance of ethnic diversity for a government's decisions to include or exclude ethnic groups is intuitive and straightforward. Indeed, in ethnically homogeneous states, the need for ethnic power sharing never arises in the first place. In instances where the population aside from a dominant group is very small and marginal, shifts toward ethno-political pluralism make little sense.

Viewing ethnicity as being inert and deeply rooted in history, primordialist scholarship tends to be pessimistic about the prospects for power sharing, primarily because ethnic cleavages are assumed to be associated with deep mistrust (e.g., Connor, 1994; Geertz, 1963). Modernist theories also assume that ethnic diversity plays a role, but view such patters as products of state formation and other political processes, rather than as immutable structures. Adopting an explicitly constructivist perspective, these theories stress how political institutions, including education, language and religious policies in state bureaucracies, contribute to ethnogenesis and assimilation (e.g., Gellner, 1983). European history shows that state-centric nationalism has tended to produce more inclusive, civic identities through assimilation as opposed to unification or separatist types of nationalist mobilization, which are more closely associated with ethnic nationalism (Hechter, 2000).

Other explanations highlight democracy as a source of inclusive politics. Strictly speaking, both democracy and power sharing in multi-ethnic states are about inclusion, although inclusion concerns individuals in the former case, and ethnic groups in the latter case. The main logic stresses that ethnic minorities enjoy more freedom to organize in democracies, and thus cannot be suppressed as easily (e.g., Diamond, 1994*b*). Doing well in political competition in democracies may require a broader support base, and this can encourage coalitions and collaboration across ethnic groups. Thus, it seems reasonable to expect elites in democracies to be less likely to cling to ethnic dominance when there is significant diversity (Gurr, 2000*b*).

Finally, existing work has implicitly treated ethnic inclusion as a tool of conflict-management, based on either past or anticipated conflict. One important question is whether governments tend to include or exclude ethnic groups that they expect could rebel in the future. For example, Roessler (2011) argues that elites in Africa tend to exclude potential coup-makers even at the risk of triggering peripheral war. Although this logic may apply to some cases, especially in Sub-Saharan Africa, our analyses in Chapters 6 and 7 indicate that governments more generally include potentially threatening groups.

Having briefly summarized the most prominent closed-polity accounts of ethnic inclusion, we now turn to mechanisms proposed to explain inclusive and exclusive practices in open polities. Clearly, these perspectives are less numerous and influential than those that focus on explanatory factors internal to the state. Generally, this class of explanations tends to trace normative change at the global level toward more inclusive practices. The global polity school of Meyer and collaborators 1997 postulates a sweeping macro-historical process, propagating a "rational world culture" across the globe since the age of the Enlightenment.

At the regional level, explanation of ethnic groups' power access typically show how groups with transnational ethnic kin risk being excluded on grounds that their loyalty is questioned. In a classical study of the "Macedonian syndrome," Weiner (1971) shows how a climate of suspicion and paranoia led to increasing polarization both within and between Balkan states in the first half of the twentieth century. Governments will exclude, and possibly even discriminate, groups that are ethnically linked to rival states with which the host state has ongoing rivalries (Mylonas, 2012). However, these conjectures are yet to be tested beyond particular historical cases.

10.2   From Diffusion of Democracy to Diffusion of Inclusion

In order to extend the theoretical and empirical scope, we shift the attention to the democratization literature to establish more depth in terms of possible diffusion mechanisms. This allows us to highlight several important parallels in terms of the drivers of both democracy and inclusion.

Scholars have noted that many of the domestic conditions held to favor democratization change slowly over time or fail to stack up with periods of important transitions, and suggested that the likelihood of a transition in one country changes in response to international factors and events in other states (see e.g., O'Loughlin et al., 1998; Starr, 1991). Moreover, transitions to democracy are not a one-way street, and for much of twentieth century forms of autocratic rule such as one-party states also appeared to diffuse.

Gleditsch and Ward (2006) argue that although the specific trajectories of individual transitions are extremely diverse, they can be subsumed under a simple framework focusing on power, mobilization, and the preferences of important actors, where democracy emerges as a rational compromise when no single actor is able to dominate. They relate the diffusion of democracy to how linkages to external actors and events influence the relative distribution of power and the preferences of relevant groups in conflict over political institutions (see also Simmons, Dobbin and Garrett, 2006).

Outside actors can promote democratization by providing assistance to reform efforts and undermining autocratic rulers. More generally, external shocks may alter the domestic distribution of power, and the impact is likely to be particularly dramatic when there are shifts and upheavals in neighboring entities and protest emulates efforts elsewhere. Schelling's (1971) "tipping model" and the idea of cascades have often been applied to fall of socialism in Eastern Europe (see also Kuran, 1991).

The prospects for democratization also depend on the perceived benefits and costs of particular institutional arrangements. Many powerful actors traditionally resisted democratization over fears of the consequences of unmitigated popular rule (see Muller, 1999). However, resistance declines as elites observe that democracy in other countries did not lead to the expected disastrous outcomes. Moreover, maintaining autocratic rule becomes more costly as other countries democratize and remaining autocrats are more likely to be subjected to sanctions and ostracized as remnants of illegitimate rule. Conversely, the temptation to restrict governmental access is higher in neighborhoods dominated by ethnic exclusion. In general, countries are likely to be judged as particularly bad offenders in terms of violating human rights and discriminatory practices based on how they fare relative to other putatively similar neighboring states (see Bell et al., 2014; Gleditsch and Ward, 2006).

In principle, the mechanisms highlighted by diffusion scholars in general, and by students of democratization in particular, could plausibly also apply to transitions to ethnic inclusion. Successful transitions to inclusion in other states may inspire excluded groups to make similar demands and emulate the strategies of contestation that have proven effective elsewhere. Governing coalitions are also likely to become less resistant to granting inclusion if they observe that the consequences of shifting away from exclusion in other states have been less dire than feared. Finally, states that engage in significant exclusion are more likely to look worse, or stand out more to outsiders, in comparison to other states as exclusion becomes less common in other states they are likely to be compared with. This may in turn translate into sanctions for maintaining exclusion or incentives to offer inclusion in terms of improved relations or acceptance in more discriminating international organizations.

However, there are also some limits to the direct analogies to experiences from democratization. Whereas democratic rule is essentially a universal norm, applicable to all countries, countries are likely to face less uniform expectations about power sharing given variation in ethnic demography, as ethnic inclusion or exclusion requires some degree of diversity in the first place.

10.3   Introducing the Closed-Polity and Open-Polity Models

In this section, we derive a series of testable hypotheses that summarize the theoretical expectations of both the closed-polity and the open-polity perspectives. Rather than levels of ethnic inclusion, we aim to explain the timing of shifts from ethnic dominance to shared rule, and vice versa. We refer to these as inclusive and exclusive shifts respectively.

10.3.1 Closed-polity hypotheses

To establish a baseline for these transitions, the first step is to take ethnic diversity into account. Building on our discussion about ethnic homogeneity, we expect ethnically diverse countries to experience more transitions to power sharing than uniform ones. We use low ethnic fractionalization as a proxy for the processes that have created greater ethnic homogeneity. Based on this reasoning, we derive our first pair of hypotheses describing transitions between ethnic dominance and power sharing:

Hypothesis 10.1a. Ethnic diversity increases the probability of inclusive shifts.

Hypothesis 10.1b. Ethnic diversity decreases the probability of exclusive shifts.

Our account of the literature reminds us that the link between democracy and power sharing is complex. Clearly, there is no one-to-one relationship between democracy and ethnic inclusion. Some democracies discriminate along ethnic lines, such as Estonia and Israel, while some non-democracies practice extensive power sharing, as illustrated by African cases of ethnic inclusion around charismatic political leaders, such as Omar Bongo in Gabon and Mathieu Kérékou in Benin. Furthermore, stable democracies may be less likely to see change in their demos configurations. Yet, on the whole, it can be expected that the chances of inclusive transitions would be higher in democratic states with competitive elections, and such environments also tend to be characterized by a political culture that supports the willingness to make compromises and seek consensus solutions (Gurr, 2000a, 2000b). To cover transitions in the other direction, we postulate that autocratic polities will typically be more exposed to the risk of coups and political purges that initiate ethnic dominance. Again, we summarize these expectations with a second set of hypotheses:

Hypothesis 10.2a. Democracy increases the probability of inclusive shifts.

Hypothesis 10.2b. Democracy increases the probability of exclusive shifts.

Work on democratization stresses that transitions to democracy are less difficult when countries have previous experiences with democratic rule, as these imply that institutions and organizations can be reestablished and do not need to be created from scratch (see e.g., Dahl, 1971; Gleditsch and Ward, 2006; Huntington, 1991). By analogy, countries that have previously had power sharing can be expected to be more likely to return to such arrangements. Based on historical path-dependence, we would expect that inclusive shifts are more likely in countries with a history of inclusion. Without institutional or normative legacies, power sharing will be more difficult to devise or develop, and proposed arrangements will often run into ideological opposition. Thus, we propose the following two hypotheses:

Hypothesis 10.3a. Previous inclusion increases the probability of inclusive shifts.

Hypothesis 10.3b. Previous exclusion increases the probability of exclusive shifts.

Finally, we expect shifts in ethnic power structures to be more likely under political instability or change. Political leader changes provide opportunities for leaders to broaden coalitions, through including other groups, as well as opportunities to impose greater dominance. Based on the extensive literature on power sharing as part of post-conflict settlements, we expect changes toward inclusive arrangements to be especially common in countries that have already experienced, or are currently experiencing civil war. Beyond post-conflict cases, political elites may seek to form grand ethnic coalitions as a way to prevent future conflict. As illustrated by many cases in Sub-Saharan Africa, peace agreements typically try to avoid conflict-inducing "spoiler" effects by embracing inclusive solutions (Stedman, 1997). In other cases, previous conflict may motivate leaders to opt for imposing control through ethnic dominance, as illustrated by Rwanda. We summarize this reasoning with a combined hypothesis:

Hypothesis 10.4. Political instability increases the probability of both inclusive and exclusive shifts.

10.3.2   Open-polity hypotheses

Turning now to the open-polity perspective, we formulate hypotheses at three levels of diffusion, namely globally, between territorial neighbors, and at an intermediate level, within world regions. Each of these levels constitutes a plausible context within which diffusion mechanisms may be operating. For all these settings, we postulate that the external level affects both included and marginalized groups. While dominant ethnic elites come under pressure to open the doors to previously excluded ethnic groups, representatives of groups that are deprived of governmental representation could be encouraged to redress their situation. However, this dynamic could also be reversed if repeated shifts toward higher levels of exclusion inspire further moves toward ethnic dominance.

In principle, decentralized learning and emulation may drive such a process by prompting ethnically exclusive regimes to become more inclusive, but as with democratization, such reforms typically encounter considerable resistance from incumbent power holders. Previously dominant ethnic elites may have much to fear from sharing power with potentially vengeful and assertive counter-elites (Roessler, 2011). In such cases, entirely voluntary mechanisms may not be enough to effect change. Instead, inclusion is more likely to flow from imposed diffusion pressures exerted by external actors, such as international organizations and power states. Motivated by a strong normative commitment and/or by strategic self-interest, these external actors will attempt to influence the behavior of domestic actors, especially the government in question, by appealing to norms, by socializing them, and by setting incentives that reward inclusive behavior while punishing exclusive moves. Again, it is also possible that illiberal powers will try to reward exclusive and discriminatory, rather than liberal, policies by undermining the influence of liberal organizations that are perceived to stand in the way of narrowly ethno-nationalist definitions of "sovereignty."

We start by considering diffusion at the global level. Along the lines of Meyer et al. (1997), it is possible to interpret the increasing adoption of inclusive practices as a part of a world-wide emulation of dominant models of governance. To some extent, international organizations, especially the United Nations, could drive such a trend through incentives and sanctions, but Meyer et al.'s argument stresses a more informal mechanism that operates primarily through emulation by local elites. Constructivist scholarship has done much to analyze this type of normative evolution with respect to governance forms (see e.g., Dobbin, Simmons and Garrett, 2006; Finnemore and Sikkink, 1998). As a part of a general trend toward liberal values in world affairs, such a macro-historical diffusion process, can be expected to trigger shifts to inclusion if the world becomes more inclusive in general (Simmons and Elkins, 2004). Conversely, an illiberal counter-trend could provoke moves toward ethnically exclusive rule. We formulate these expectations in the following way:

Hypothesis 10.5a. Higher global inclusion increases the probability inclusive shifts.

Hypothesis 10.5b. Higher global inclusion decreases the probability exclusive shifts.

Rather than being a truly global phenomenon, the diffusion effect could also be limited to emulation and learning between territorial neighbors. There is considerable heterogeneity across different parts of the world, and this is difficult to reconcile with the idea of universal influences affecting all countries alike. To a large extent, the "Arab Spring" of 2011 illustrates this pattern of diffusion between neighboring states. Starting in Tunisia, the wave of protest against the ruling dictatorships spread like a forest fire from country to country in the Middle East, but had only limited impact in other parts of the world such as East Asia. Previous studies of the diffusion of democracy have typically operationalized and found support for such processes at the level of contiguous states (Gleditsch and Ward, 2006; Kopstein and Reilly, 2000). Subscribing to a similarly decentralized approach to diffusion, Kuran (1998) proposes a model of "dissimilation" that explains how an ethnicization of politics leads to divergent identification patterns spreading across state borders through demonstration effects and reputational mechanisms.

In order to instrument for power sharing, Cammett and Malesky (2012) assume that such institutions tend to spread in states' geographic neighborhoods. To our knowledge, their study is the only example of a formal investigation of diffusion of power sharing, although the diffusion mechanism is primarily introduced for methodological purposes, rather than being defended as a central theoretical component in their argument. Again, it is reasonable to expect the mechanism to operate both in expanding and contracting inclusion. Indeed, there may also be "countervailing incentives" that demonstrate how ethnic inclusion may spread based on negative experiences with exclusion or positive experiences with inclusion (see e.g., Fearon, 1998, 112–113). As authoritarian neighborhoods are likely to hamper democratization, the same would hold for the adoption of inclusive practices and institutions.

Thus, we postulate a neighborhood-level version of our diffusion account according to which the adoption of power sharing in one country sets the incentives for both governments and representatives of excluded groups to follow suit in neighboring states. In principle, such a diffusion scenario could be compatible with imposed diffusion, especially in case of asymmetric neighborhood relations involving powerful states. Yet, the most likely setting features voluntary learning or emulation. Again, we summarize our expectations with a pair of hypotheses:

Hypothesis 10.6a. Higher neighborhood inclusion increases the probability inclusive shifts.

Hypothesis 10.6b. Higher neighborhood inclusion decreases the probability exclusive shifts.

Finally, we consider the possibility that the relevant diffusion mechanisms occur between countries in broader regions or groupings that are larger than states' immediate geographical neighborhoods, but more confined than the global level. Rather than diffusing evenly, "modular" political phenomena tend to spread among regions or states that share common institutional, historical and cultural characteristics (Beissinger, 2007). There are many possible ways to identify distinct regions in the international system, including structural similarity (e.g., similar language or regime type), formal organizations (e.g., the OECD), and geographical proximity between states. In an early study of regions in world politics, Russett (1967) examined clustering in political, social and economic characteristics through factor analysis to identify how countries map into similar regional groupings. To a large extent, the regions derived tend to be clearly geographically confined, reflecting the common history and origins of conventional world regions. Moreover, interactions tend to be higher among proximate states (Bergstrand, 1985), and formal organizations without universal membership are often defined on a regional basis (Powers and Goertz, 2011). As such, we focus on conventional definitions of geographical regions.

In the case of democratization, diffusion has followed wavelike processes that are mostly confined to specific world regions that exhibit such similarities, such as Southern Europe, Eastern Europe or Latin America (Huntington, 1991). Focusing on "democratization from above," Pevehouse (2005) argues that regional organizations reinforce such a process by legitimizing transitional regimes and by imposing pressure on elites in authoritarian member states, who may also feel reassured enough by organizational protection to acquiesce to the transition process.

We propose that larger geographic regions constitute important reference categories for the diffusion of inclusion as well. Drawing on Pevehouse's theory, a first set of causal mechanisms postulates that regional organizations use targeted policies to pressure or entice incumbent regimes to become more ethnically inclusive, through incentives, persuasion and socialization that prompt change and lock it in through institutional safeguards. While the goal of ethnic inclusion is typically an explicit principle of the organization itself, the actual compliance with the norm among the member states is crucial for this type of regional spread. As in the case with democracy, world regions diverge drastically in their level of ethnic inclusiveness and so do the regional organizations themselves. The degree of interventionism in the area of minority politics varies from stronger norms of non-interventionism, as illustrated by the Association of Southeast Asian Nations (ASEAN), to more interventionist organizations, such as the European Union and the African Union.

In addition to "inclusion from above" through formal institutions, there is a second set of more informal mechanisms that operates at least partly without the direct support of regional organizations. In such cases, early and successful adopters are likely to take the lead in promoting inclusive norms, usually due to a combination of moral commitment and strategic self-interest in order to lock in the reforms in the original adopting country (Beissinger, 2007; Spruyt, 1994). Post-Apartheid South Africa illustrates how a pioneering state is inclined to externalize its own success story by promoting power sharing as a solution in post-conflict situations.

On the receiving side, the effectiveness of diffusion depends crucially on the compatibility of the diffusing norms with local habits and inclinations (Acharya, 2004). Mehler (2016) argues that the adoption of inclusive practices depends both on norm-infusing external actors and the receiving actor, in this case the incumbent government. In world regions, such as Africa, where power sharing is compatible with the traditional, paternalistic governance styles, we can expect inclusive practices to spread more readily than in areas that are more strongly committed to ethnic nationalism. For example, Rothchild and Foley (1988) report that "political incorporation of all major social interests" constitutes the main approach to politics in most African states.

As is the case with the consolidation of democracy (Pevehouse, 2005, Chap. 6), regional institutions also contribute to preventing reversals away from ethnic inclusion. If key members' commitment to inclusion wavers, thus weakening the organization's influence, an illiberal snowball process could be set in motion that would create a region-wide return to exclusive ethno-nationalism that triggers a general shift toward exclusive policies and possibly even discrimination of ethnic minorities.

We summarize our theoretical expectations at the regional level with a final pair of hypotheses:

Hypothesis 10.7a. Regional inclusion increases the probability inclusive shifts.

Hypothesis 10.7b. Regional inclusion decreases the probability exclusive shifts.

10.4   Conceptualizing and Measuring Ethnic Inclusion

Having laid out our theoretical conjectures about the factors and processes driving shift to and away from ethnic inclusion, in this section we introduce our main data sources. We also present some descriptive statistics that highlight important variation across space and time. Our measure of ethnically inclusive regimes is based the Ethnic Power Relations (EPR) data (see Chapter 4).[1] Based on the EPR data, we define ethnic inclusion at the state or country level based on whether power is shared between two or more ethnic groups. More specifically, a country with two or more groups sharing power (as either junior or senior partners) is considered to have inclusion. Likewise, a country

[1] Here we use a version of the dataset that covers the period from 1946 to 2017.

is considered to have exclusion if the state is controlled by a single group. The measure is binary in that countries either have inclusion or exclusion. However, a country with inclusion or power sharing could still have additional individual groups that remain inclusion.[2] Beyond the EPR coding of group status we use two important additional criteria to identify transitions and levels of inclusion in other states. The EPR data focus on inclusion at central government level, and the inclusion of a party representing an ethnic group in the government coalition is a sufficient condition for inclusion by our criteria. However, we do not code the exit of such a party as a transition back to exclusion unless the group becomes actively discriminated against. For example, the Democratic Union of Hungarians in Romania was a junior partner in many government coalitions since 1996, but we do not code a return to exclusion when the party becomes part of the opposition as happened after the 2012 legislative elections. This can be seen as analogous to the role of turnover as a litmus test for democracy. Many see democratic transitions as incomplete unless there has been an actual turnover where previous autocratic incumbent coalitions voluntarily leave office after a defeat (e.g., Przeworski et al., 2000). However, the victory of a party associated with individuals from an old autocratic coalition such as former members of Communist parties does not by itself imply a return to autocracy unless leaders actually move to undermine democratic institutions. Most regions include both countries where ethnicity is relevant and countries where it is not according to the EPR data. Although countries where ethnicity is irrelevant may not exert much of a pull towards inclusion in other states they cannot be characterized as states with exclusion and are also unlikely to deter inclusion. In order not to exaggerate the extent of inclusion by restricting rates of inclusion to only states where ethnicity is relevant we treat all countries where ethnicity is irrelevant as implicitly included when calculating regional rates of inclusion.

We first examine the proportion of states with inclusion as defined above over the period 1946–2017. Figure 10.1 indicates the proportion included for for all countries, suggesting a clear increase over time. Although the population of states also changes over the period, especially with the introduction of new independent states during

---

[2] We have also considered an alternative measure of inclusion further requiring that power sharing must encompass at least 50 percent of the population of relevant groups. In practice, however, power sharing involving less than 50 percent of the population (inclusive minority rule) tends to be rare, and only one such case exist in 2013, namely Nepal, where the included groups are just short of 50 percent. In other words our results do not change much with a stricter size requirement, and we focus only on the simple power sharing measure here.

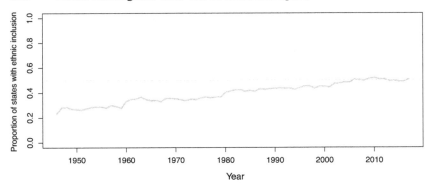

Figure 10.1 Proportion included, 1946–2017

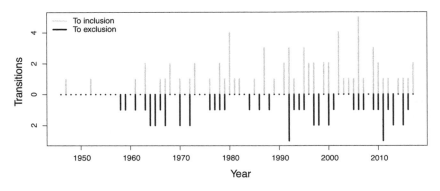

Figure 10.2 Transitions to/from inclusion, 1946–2017

decolonization, we see a similar positive trend if we focus only on countries in continuous existence since 1946.

Figure 10.2 plots the actual transitions between states in individual countries to/from inclusion over time. This does not suggest a simple pattern, where all transitions cluster in specific time periods, although there is some evidence for a peak in transitions away from inclusion in the 1960s and 1970s and a larger number of transitions to than away from inclusion in the post-Cold War period. Over the entire period we have 70 transitions from exclusion to inclusion and 49 transitions from inclusion to exclusion.[3]

The global trends mask considerable geographical variation and differences across regions.

---

[3] Beyond changes for individual group the EPR data also allow for changes in the group composition, but only 11 transitions to/from inclusion coincide with such group changes. Notably, in the 1994 transition in South Africa, Blacks as an excluded group is transformed into 9 distinct included groups.

Table 10.1. *Ethnic inclusion and regime type*

	Exclusion	Inclusion
Non-democracy	2895	1886
Democracy	1653	1213

Mapping the spatio-temporal distribution of inclusion provides an overview of the variation across space and time. Figure 10.3 depicts four global snapshots. It is clear from this that there has been a clear increase in inclusion and shifts away from ethnic dominance among African states and to some extent Latin America as well. However, in other regions such as Europe we have seen far fewer changes. The maps indicate spatial clustering within these broader geographical regions at specific time points, as countries with inclusion tend to be surrounded by other countries with inclusion and changes in places with exclusion appear to take place on a geographically clustered basis, with groups of contiguous countries likely to change status between different time periods.

Before delving into our empirical analysis, in Table 10.1 we also look at the relationship between our inclusion vs. exclusion measure and other types of political representation and status. It is straightforward to show that inclusion is *not* simply synonymous with political democracy. Inclusion is slightly more common than democracy over the whole period (41 percent) than democracy (37 percent),[4] Exclusion is more common among non-democracies, but even for democracies the countries with inclusion remain in a minority over the period. Indeed, across our sample, just over half of the observations (53.7 percent) are on the diagonal of the table, attesting to how we see many cases of inclusion outside democratic regimes and many ethnically exclusionary democracies. In short, inclusion is different from political democracy.

Ethnic inclusion can be more or less encompassing, and ethnic dominance can be more or less exclusionary. However, the density distribution of inclusion for the share of included population across democracies, non-democracies, countries with power sharing, and countries with dominance by a single group all have a clear peak in the upper end of the distribution, indicating that the included groups tend to be numerically large and that the excluded population share tends to be relatively small in all countries. However, non-democracies and countries without power sharing regimes have a smaller peak at the high end a more noticeable tail over lower values of inclusion toward the left.

[4] We define democracy as having a value of 6 or above on the 20 point Polity scale, see Jaggers and Gurr (1995).

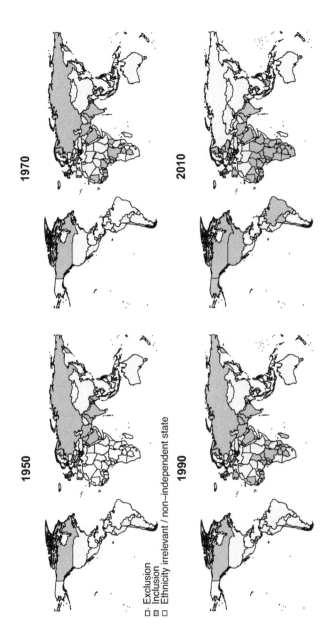

1950

1970

1990

2010

□ Exclusion
■ Inclusion
□ Ethnicity irrelevant / non–independent state

Figure 10.3 Ethnic inclusion and exclusion, 1950–2010

10.5   Operationalizing the Closed- and Open-Polity Models

Before turning to the OPM, we need to establish an analytical baseline, which is the task of the CPM. Our derivation of hypotheses from the CPM identifies classes of properties that are likely to shape exclusion and the resistance or willingness to transition to a power sharing regime, such as ethnic demography, political institutions, security and conflict.

Under the heading of Hypotheses H10.1a and H10.1b, we have argued that more diverse countries should be more likely to see demand for power sharing than less diverse countries, and the value/cost of accepting/resisting such agreements should also depend on diversity. For our measure of ethnic demography we use the fractionalization (ELF) index as a simple measure of the diversity of a country, based on the Herfindahl–Hirschman index (Hirschman, 1964). More specifically, the ELF index is defined as $1 - \sum_{i=1}^{N} p_i^2$, where p_i is a measure of relative size as a proportion of all the N groups in a country. Higher values indicate a more heterogenous population, split among a larger number of significant groups. Low values indicate lower heterogeneity, as a single large group p_i^2 approaches one, or very small groups have only a limited impact on the overall index value. We measure group sizes using shares in the EPR data, after normalizing so that all politically relevant groups in a country in a given year sum to 1.[5]

According to H10.2a, democratic institutions and political competition should also increase willingness to power sharing and decrease resistance, and vice versa (H10.2b). To operationalize democracy, we consider whether a country has democratic political institutions, using a binary indicator of whether the country has a Polity value of 6 and above. We use values at the beginning of the year, based on the Polity 4d data, since the EPR data look at the ethnic-power relations in place on 1 of January of each year.

Transitions may be more or less likely, depending on previous trajectories or consolidation effects (see H10.3a and H10.3b). We consider a binary measure indicating whether a country has previously had inclusion or a power sharing regime up to $t-1$ for transitions to inclusion (and previous exclusion for transitions to inclusion). We further also consider the length at time at the observed state at $t-1$, entered as a cubic specification to allow for a non-monotonic relationship (Carter and Signorino, 2010).

---

[5] We have also considered a number of other plausible measures of ethnic demography and political status, including the overall number of groups, the number of excluded groups, share included population, as well as a possible non-monotonic relationship with fractionalization. However, all of these fail to improve the fit of the model of transitions from exclusion to inclusion over a model with the simple fractionalization measure. Many criticisms of the ELF measure in studies of conflict are not directly relevant here, since we look at different outcome, i.e., inclusion.

Finally, in order to evaluate H10.4, we consider two measures for political instability. First, we look at whether countries experienced a change in the leader in the prior year, based on the Archigos data (Goemans, Gleditsch and Chiozza, 2009). Second, we look at two measures indicating violent civil conflict. We flag all post-conflict periods, where a country has previously seen an ethnic civil war, based on the ACD2EPR data linking the actors in the Uppsala Armed Conflict data to ethnic groups in the EPR data through ethnic claims on behalf of specific groups (Wuucherpfennig et al., 2012). We also consider whether a country has an ongoing ethnic civil war.[6]

Ethnic inclusion may also be affected by various other country characteristics such as the level of development or country size that may also be spatially clustered. We thus consider a country's GDP per capita and population size, using the most recent version from the Expanded Trade and GDP data (Gleditsch, 2002). We log the absolute values, as we would expect the impact to be proportional to the base so that the impact of a given absolute difference should be relatively less important with higher base values.

The features above together constitute the CPM, in the sense that they only consider features within individual countries. We then compare this to the OPM that captures how the likelihood of transitions depend on inclusion and power sharing in other states. We analyze connections at all three levels. The *global* level encompasses all other countries in the world, and our measure for a given country i indicates the global proportion of all other countries in the world, expect for i itself (see H10.5a and H10.5b). To test H10.7a and H10.7b, we then consider a measure of inclusion for other states within a country's geographic *region*, separating between the Americas, Europe, Sub-Saharan Africa, Middle East and North Africa, Asia, and Oceania.[7] Finally, in order to evaluate H10.6a and H10.6b, we consider the share of inclusion among *neighboring countries*, using a 500 km buffer around the outer boundaries of a state based on the CShapes data (Weidmann, Kuse and Gleditsch, 2010).

We recognize that the distinction between internal and external factors is slightly ambiguous here, since many of the internal factors emphasized in the Closed-Polity Model may themselves reflect international factors, such as democracy, political development, and even civil war. However, a comparison of the two models will allow us to examine to what

---

[6] We have also considered the length of time that a country has remained at peace, either since a previous conflict or independence. However, we found that this did not appear to make a notable contribution after considering the other conflict and security related measures, and do not report this result here.

[7] This is consistent with the operational definition of region used in other studies, e.g., (Pevehouse, 2005).

extent levels in other states appear to have an additional influence on transitions, once we consider domestic factors.

It is now time to consider how specific factors affect the likelihood of transitions from exclusion to inclusion and vice versa. We rely on a two-way transition model between binary states, similar to the models used in studies of transitions to and from democracy. In brief, we estimate the likelihood of one state conditional on the previous state in two separate models, that is,

$$Pr(y_{i,t} = 1 \lfloor y_{i,t-1} = 0) = \frac{1}{1 + e^{-}\mathbf{X}\beta}$$

and

$$Pr(y_{i,t} = 0 \lfloor y_{i,t-1} = 1) = \frac{1}{1 + e^{-}\mathbf{X}\gamma}.^{8}$$

10.5.1 Empirical results

We first estimate the CPM. The first column in Table 10.2 displays the estimates of a model of transitions to inclusion in a country with exclusion at time $t - 1$ while the second column displays the estimates for transitions from inclusion to exclusion. It is clear from comparing the results in the two columns that the estimates from transitions in one direction are not simply the mirror image of transitions in the other direction.[9] We comment first on the estimates for transitions to inclusion.

As expected by H10.1a, we find a significant positive coefficient for the ELF index in the first column, indicating that transitions to inclusion are more likely in more diverse countries. For democracies we find a positive coefficient suggesting that these are more likely to see transitions, but this effect is not statistically significant at conventional levels, thus offering only weak support for H10.2a.[10] In keeping with H10.3a, the coefficient for previous inclusion is large, which suggests that the likelihood of transitions is much higher if a country has previously had inclusion. By contrast, there is much less evidence for an effect of time at

---

[8] This transition model can also be estimated as a single equation with interaction terms between the right hand side covariates and lagged values. However, since the variance in limited dependent variables must be assumed for identification, joint estimation and separate models will yield identical results.

[9] More technically, although the coefficients in a model predicting $Pr(y_{i,t} = 1)$ and $Pr(y_{i,t} = 0)$ by definition would be symmetric (since one event is simply the inverse of the other), this it is not the case for a first order transition model between states from $t - 1$ to t. Note that the samples are defined by state at $t - 1$, and thus differ, and we can have more transitions in one direction than the other.

[10] Our substantive results do not change when we replace the binary democracy measures with the full Polity scale or alternative democracy measures from the V-dem project.

Table 10.2. *Closed-Polity Model of transitions*

	Dependent variable:	
	Trans. to inclusion (1)	Trans. to exclusion (2)
ELF	3.075***	−3.238***
	(0.689)	(0.822)
Democracy	0.361	−0.589
	(0.341)	(0.390)
Leader change	2.508***	1.988***
	(0.289)	(0.318)
Postconflict	0.533	−0.172
	(0.333)	(0.409)
Ongoing civil war	0.112	0.146
	(0.484)	(0.546)
Ln GDP pc	−0.204	−0.094
	(0.171)	(0.174)
Ln population	−0.267**	−0.066
	(0.113)	(0.139)
Previous inclusion	1.823***	
	(0.336)	
Previous exclusion		0.277
		(0.374)
Constant	−3.123*	−1.158
	(1.760)	(1.905)
Observations	4,013	3,009
Log likelihood	−241.674	−190.142
Akaike Inf. Crit.	507.347	404.284

Note: * $p < 0.1$; ** $p < 0.05$; *** $p < 0.01$

inclusion, and the polynomial terms are not jointly statistically significant (not shown). With regards to H10.4, we find a large positive coefficient for leader change. This suggests that expansion of a coalition to ethnic inclusion is much more likely in these situations, and that we rarely have transitions under the same ruling leader. For post-conflict periods we find a positive coefficient, consistent with H10.4, but the coefficient is not statistically significant. For ongoing civil war we find a positive and insignificant coefficient. Of the remaining control variables, both GDP per capita and population size have negative coefficients, but only the latter is statistically significant. In sum, there is some support for domestic factors affecting the likelihood of transitions to inclusion, as ethnic diversity, episodes of leader change, and previous inclusion make transition more likely, but the effects of political stability in terms of civil conflict and democracy are at best modest.

Turning to transitions from inclusion to exclusion, the second column reveals much fewer consistent influences. The negative sign for ELF indicates a symmetric effect, in that transitions away from inclusion to exclusion are much less likely in more diverse countries, thus corroborating H10.1b. Consistent with H10.4 we find a positive coefficient for leader change, which suggests that these also make exclusive shifts more likely. The signs for democracy, post-conflict periods and ongoing civil war are consistent but not significant. None of the other factors are statistically significant, including previous exclusion. Moreover, the estimate for the intercept is considerably larger than for inclusion, indicating generally higher baseline transition probabilities.[11]

In the first column of Table 10.3 we expand the CPM to form the OPM by adding a term for inclusion at the global level, not counting observation i itself (see H10.5a).[12] This addition returns a positive coefficient, which implies that countries may be more likely to see transitions when the global level of inclusion is higher. In the second and third column of Table 10.3 we consider a term comparing inclusion among neighbors within a 500 km buffer (H10.6a) and a term indicating the proportion of inclusion within the geographical regions, respectively. Both coefficients are positive and highly statistically significant. The other results do not change notably when adding expanding the CPM to an OPM, save for that the post-conflict term becomes marginally significant in some specifications. Hence, the transnational features seem to capture something distinct from the purely domestic characteristics.

---

[11] We have also considered a number of alternative specifications, but found no evidence that these changed the main findings or improved model fit. Again, we found no evidence for a clear relationship between time since conflict and transitions. There is no evidence for transitions being more common following elections or transitions to democracy.

[12] The model stipulates transition probabilities conditional on pre-determined levels among reference units rather than a fully spatial model of simultaneous transitions. For inclusion/exclusion, simultaneous transitions are rare – less than 10 percent of transitions to inclusion occur in the presence of a simultaneous transition in a neighboring state, and less than 2 percent of observations with a transition to inclusion in a connected state actually see a transition. Simultaneity could also be an issue if we expected strategic behavior where countries enact transition in anticipation of others, but this does not seem applicable here. Finally, it is difficult to include temporal autocorrelation in spatial limited dependent variable models. We consider only first order transitions. Higher-order transition models tend to be overparameterized, and rarely fit better than first order models (Berchtold and Raftery, 2002), controlling for time at state.

Table 10.3. *Open–Polity Model of transitions*

	Dependent variable:							
	Transition to inclusion				Transition to exclusion			
	(1)	(2)	(3)	(4)	(5)	(6)	(7)	(8)
Global inclusion (−i)	6.817** (2.822)			2.362 (3.169)	3.989 (2.747)			6.090* (3.110)
Neighb. inclusion (−i)		1.922*** (0.505)		0.744 (0.749)		−0.383 (0.651)		0.848 (0.865)
Regional inclusion (−i)			3.312*** (0.729)	2.252** (1.139)			−1.124 (0.925)	−2.876** (1.419)
ELF	2.983*** (0.698)	2.925*** (0.713)	2.998*** (0.695)	2.909*** (0.713)	−3.258*** (0.830)	−3.224*** (0.819)	−3.215*** (0.821)	−3.165*** (0.831)
Democracy	0.102 (0.356)	0.557 (0.356)	0.613* (0.363)	0.607 (0.397)	−0.626 (0.385)	−0.421 (0.393)	−0.552 (0.394)	−0.455 (0.395)
Leader change	2.555*** (0.290)	2.482*** (0.301)	2.655*** (0.301)	2.525*** (0.307)	2.025*** (0.320)	1.874*** (0.325)	1.976*** (0.319)	1.927*** (0.329)
Post conflict	0.547 (0.340)	0.740** (0.354)	0.584* (0.341)	0.625* (0.358)	−0.308 (0.414)	−0.190 (0.417)	−0.189 (0.406)	−0.414 (0.421)
Ongoing civil war	0.157 (0.491)	0.210 (0.488)	0.089 (0.480)	0.174 (0.489)	−0.005 (0.555)	0.148 (0.548)	0.089 (0.550)	−0.302 (0.589)
Ln GDP pc	−0.292* (0.173)	−0.171 (0.170)	−0.087 (0.169)	−0.165 (0.179)	−0.121 (0.173)	−0.122 (0.185)	−0.202 (0.196)	−0.342 (0.213)
Ln population	−0.248** (0.115)	−0.245** (0.115)	−0.278** (0.112)	−0.238** (0.116)	−0.050 (0.137)	−0.064 (0.145)	−0.082 (0.141)	−0.058 (0.144)
Previous inclusion	1.279*** (0.396)	1.602*** (0.357)	1.388*** (0.353)	1.250*** (0.413)				
Previous exclusion					−0.029 (0.426)	0.387 (0.397)	0.412 (0.384)	0.209 (0.440)
Constant	−4.809** (1.883)	−4.330** (1.773)	−5.269*** (1.815)	−5.541*** (1.931)	−2.381 (2.053)	−0.837 (2.139)	0.272 (2.255)	−0.654 (2.333)
Observations	4,012	3,905	4,012	3,905	3,009	2,886	3,009	2,886
Log likelihood	−238.751	−224.020	−231.223	−220.807	−189.078	−183.417	−189.399	−180.581
Akaike Inf. Crit.	503.502	474.040	488.446	471.614	404.156	392.835	404.797	391.163

Note: * $p < 0.1$; ** $p < 0.05$; *** $p < 0.01$

While indicating that it is possible to find evidence consistent with all of the three different levels, the above results do not directly speak to whether one level is more relevant than another. The global level of inclusion has the highest coefficient, but the model for regional inclusion has a lower log likelihood or better overall fit. Comparing the individual models also does not allow considering the degree of overlap or complementarity between the measures.

In column four we add all the terms to the model simultaneously. The coefficient for regional inclusion remains positive and statistically significant, while the coefficient for neighboring inclusion is reduced noticeably in size. The coefficient for global inclusion remains large, but the standard error is also large, which reflects a much less consistent influence.[13] We see these results as suggesting that the relevant linkages for ethnic inclusion are not fully global, but broader than the relations to immediate neighboring countries that have been stressed in some studies of diffusion in transitions to democracy. This is consistent with the idea that governments base their approach to ethnic inclusion on expectations shaped by other countries in larger regions, and a possible influence of regional organizations below the global level.[14]

Turning to transitions to exclusion in the subsequent columns of Table 10.3, we find much less clear support for strong predictors of exclusive shifts as well as evidence for clear differences between the CPM and the OPM. The term for global inclusion consistently has the wrong sign compared to H10.5b, indicating that greater global inclusion makes transitions to exclusion more likely.[15] While diffusion among neighbors cannot be separated from zero, the regional term is significant and has the expected negative sign, thus yielding support for a symmetric effect where countries are less likely to see transitions away from exclusion when direct or regional neighbors have higher rates of inclusion, as anticipated by H10.7b.

---

[13] The term for global proportion could plausibly be associated with time trends. However, estimating the model with a linear time trend yields a positive but not significant coefficient, and does not change the conclusion for the other level of inclusion terms.

[14] We have also considered a number of specifications, reflecting alternative mechanisms or possible confounders, but found no evidence that these changed the main findings or improved model fit. First, there is no evidence that countries with transnational ethnic kin were more likely to see transitions, irrespective of whether the kin group is included or not. Second, we could not find any evidence that peacekeeping operations or other external interventions had a clear impact on transitions, or that including these reduced the impact of the inclusion term. Finally, although the European Union may respond to ethnic discrimination (e.g., Kreutz, 2015), these actions are not associated with a consistent higher likelihood of transitions.

[15] The odd coefficients in Models 5 and 8 could be a reflection of the mostly linear upward trend of inclusion which correlates strongly with a time trend, see Figure 10.1.

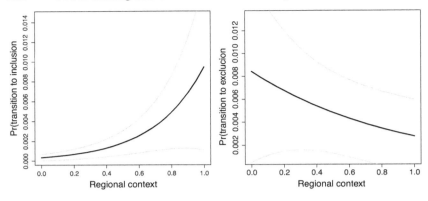

Figure 10.4 Transitions to inclusion/exclusion by regional context

10.5.2 Substantive effects

Logit coefficients indicate effects on the log odds of the response and are difficult to interpret directly in substantive terms, since the substantive impact on the probabilities of the response depend on the values of all factors affecting the baseline odds. To evaluate the effect of differences in the regional environment on transitions from exclusion to inclusion we estimate the predicted likelihood for a median profile, letting the neighboring and regional environment change from zero to universal inclusion rates. To ensure realistic scenarios we consider the median values for observations with exclusion at $t-1$. The left plot in Figure 10.4 plots the implied marginal effect, with a 95 percent confidence interval for the predicted values, and the transition probability for a profile with the median values among countries with exclusion as a dashed line. Although the likelihood of transitions at the median is very small, there is a strong relative change in the likelihood over variation in the regional context, and transitions become consistently more likely in an environment with more inclusion.

Since the baseline likelihood of transitions also changes with other factors in the model, the net impact of differences in other countries will also be large in a scenario where change is more likely. In Nigeria in 1996, following other changes in the region, the predicted probabilities of a transition to inclusion exceed 0.35. Nigeria does indeed see a transition to power sharing in 1999 in our data, with the transition to democracy and a government including parties representing the previously excluded Yoruba.

Turning to transitions from inclusion to exclusion, we find similar results, where transitions to exclusion become less likely in a local environment with higher rates of inclusion. However, the error bands are much wider in this case than in the case of transitions to inclusion. Note also that the higher constant term implies a higher likelihood of transitions, possibly indicating greater volatility in transitions to exclusion depending on whether smaller groups are included or not. Yet, since there are few other things with clear influence on the baseline odds we do not see the same degree of variation in the predicted probabilities, and the observation with the highest transition probability (Central African Republic in 1987) is only about 0.112.

10.5.3 Case illustrations

Rather than affecting the entire world evenly, the regional effect driving inclusion operates especially strongly in two sets of cases. First, when the European Union started negotiating its eastern enlargement in the 1990s, it made both future aid and membership conditional on democratic norms that included minority rights and power sharing. As shown by (Wilkinson, 2005), this commitment to consociational principles of ethnic proportionality was explicitly incorporated into the conditionality principles and prompted policy changes in several cases. While improvements of minority rights benefited the Russians in Latvia and Estonia without bringing about power sharing per se, EU pressure helped bring about more inclusive rule in Romania and Bulgaria. Furthermore, it is likely that regional "top-down" diffusion made a big difference, because these transitions to inclusion occurred despite considerable domestic opposition (see also Brusis, 2003; Kelley, 2004). It is hardly surprising that our data record inclusive shifts in Slovakia, Bulgaria and Romania along these lines, although subsequently, there have been transitions away from inclusion. These reversals suggest that "inclusion from above" through EU conditionality may not be sustainable in the long run.

Another important set of cases can be found in Sub-Saharan Africa, which is the part of the world that has experienced the largest and most important increases in power sharing in recent years (Cheeseman, 2011; Mehler, 2009). More than any other event, the successful adoption of power sharing in South Africa after the fall of the Apartheid system reinforced this norm, promoted by the global salience of the struggle against the racist regime. Even though the 1994 transition in South Africa is normally thought of as an instance of democratization, the end of racial discrimination ushered in shared rule along consociational lines that was directly inspired by Lijphart's own writings on South Africa (Vandeginste, 2009).

The fall of socialism had a dramatic impact on the aims and strategies of both sides in the South African conflict. Until the end of the Cold War, the African National Congress (ANC) aspired to establish a socialist one-party state similar to those in power in most of its neighboring countries rather than a liberal democracy or system of power sharing. After the Soviet Union stopped funding the ANC in 1989, a negotiated transition with power-sharing similar to the 1979 Lancaster House Agreement in Zimbabwe became a more attractive option. Internal documents from the ANC explicitly acknowledge the impact on their strategy and aims:[16]

our historic conjuncture of the 1994 democratic breakthrough took place against the backdrop of ... the demise of socialism in the Soviet Union ... [which] altered completely the balance of forces in favor of imperialism (p. 160) ... The collapse of ... socialism influenced our transition towards the negotiated political settlement in our country (p. 189).

With regards to the National Party, the last white president de Klerk also notes that "the collapse of the Soviet Union helped to remove our long-standing concern regarding the influence of the South African Communist Party ...".[17] The decline in fear of communism in the region also decreased the willingness of key actors in Western states to overlook the Apartheid regime, and helped remove barriers to international pressure for reform.

After this important breakthrough, South African politicians such as Mandela and Mbeki played a prominent role as enthusiastic promoters of power sharing in their capacity as mediators in post-conflict situations in other parts of the Africa (Curtis, 2006), a role that was also assumed by other African statesmen (Cheeseman, 2011). After the death of Julius Nyerere, Nelson Mandela took the lead in the negotiations that ended the Burundian civil war with the Arusha Accords in 2000 (Vandeginste, 2009). According to Lemarchand (2006), his strong commitment to ethnic inclusion influenced the outcome of the peace negotiations decisively in a consociational direction. In the early 1990s, an earlier attempt to share power had been cut short by a Tutsi military coup that produced widespread political violence and volatility until the end of the decade.

---

[16] www.anc.org.za/docs/umrabulo/2015/ngc_disc_docsy.pdf

[17] Speech delivered at Stanford University, 29 January 2001, http://news.stanford.edu/news/2001/january31/deklerk-131.html.

In 1996, the Organization for African Unity (OAU) imposed sanctions on the coup-maker Pierre Buyoya, which increased the regional pressure on the ethnically exclusive regime (Mehler, 2013, 33). Unfortunately, while representing a major improvement over the violent 1990s, the power-sharing deal has failed to deliver long-term stability in Burundi. While the terms of Arusha are still formally valid, violent political protest flared up in 2015, followed by a failed coup attempt. However, so far, ethnic inclusion has helped prevent the recurrence of full-fledged civil war.

Liberia constitutes another clear example of transnational factors facilitating transitions to power-sharing (Adebajo, 2002; Ero, 1995; Sesay, 1996). Like the long-lasting conflict in Burundi, the Liberian civil war was in many senses a classical example of a conflict driven by competing claims for ethnic dominance. Since its foundation in 1847, Liberia was dominated by the Americo-Liberians, i.e., descendants of the freed slave settlers, despite constituting a very small share of the total population (only 2 percent in 1946). The 1980 coup by Samuel Doe transferred political dominance to the Krahn. The 1989 revolt by Charles Taylor pitted an alliance between the Americo-Liberians, Gio, and Mano against the Krahn and Mandingo. Whereas the UN and the OAU failed to provide a response to the conflict, a 1990 summit by the Economic Community of West African States (ECOWAS) set up a committee to promote a settlement and deploy a multinational peace-keeping force to Liberia, explicitly calling for "a broad-based interim government." Although the armed conflict continued, the international efforts helped facilitate the parties agreeing to a peace agreement and transnational government with participation by the different parties.

Although it is easy to find overt international influences in cases with direct foreign interventions, most transition to inclusion have taken place outside peacekeeping and foreign initiated negotiations. Guinea provides an example where international factors played a plausible facilitating role in promoting a transition to ethnic inclusion, even in the absence of overt intervention. Prior to 2008, the central government in Guinea had remained remarkably stable since independence, despite widespread instability and change in neighboring states (Arieff, 2009). The death of President Conté (in power since 1984) was followed by a coup, which unleashed a period of violent instability. Following voluntary mediation by the president of Burkina-Faso, the main parties agreed to a transition framework, which gave way to ethnic power sharing between all the relevant groups in the country (Witt, 2013). Although it is difficult to evaluate counterfactuals about transnational influences, a recognition of the benefits of inclusion in other states in the region likely supported the agreement to share power, and the likelihood of external condemnation and sanctions deterred efforts to strive for exclusive dominance (see also, Marinov and Goemans, 2014).

Of course, power-sharing arrangements in Sub-Saharan Africa have often been far from stable, as illustrated by recent events in Burundi and the break-up of the Sudan, following the externally prompted adoption of power sharing in 2006. In this part of the world, many regimes suffer from instability that may trigger infighting and conflict recurrence (Roessler, 2011; Spears, 2002). Yet, despite occasional reversals to instability and exclusion, our findings suggest that this does not prevent power sharing from gradually gaining ground in Sub-Saharan Africa, and our findings also suggest that if initial transitions to inclusion fail, they are more likely to be followed by a return to inclusion later.

10.6   Conclusion

Complementing the endogenization of power sharing in Chapter 7, the main aim of this chapter has been to offer a systematic analysis of the factors that affect where and when governments shift from ethnic dominance to inclusion aggregated to the country level. As anticipated, these determinants can be found both within and outside the state. While Chapter 7 and much of the previous studies have focused on domestic explanations, we have found strong evidence of a diffusion effect within regional contexts. Significantly, however, we have not been able to confirm any consistent spread at the global level, thus casting doubt on sweeping theories of an emerging world polity. The support for diffusion among contiguous states is also weaker than expected. To some extent, these effects can also be found in the opposite direction, from inclusion to exclusion, thus suggesting that there is a potential lock-in effect that prevents single countries in regions dominated by ethnic exclusion from adopting power sharing.

Contrary to ethnic diversity or other structural factors that are almost entirely beyond manipulation in the short run, inclusion is inherently a policy choice that can in principle be influenced. From a policy-making perspective, this makes our findings about the open-polity dimension particularly good news, since fostering power sharing and inclusion in one country is likely to have positive externalities in neighboring countries by raising the odds of similar arrangements being adopted there too. There may even be regional "tipping phenomena," otherwise seen in connection with democratization and the adoption of norms. Sub-Saharan Africa appears to have experienced such a wave of inclusion since the Cold War. Obviously, the open-polity perspective presented in this chapter shows that such snowballing effects could also feature illiberal waves toward ethnic dominance. For example, following the rise of right-wing populism targeting multi-ethnic and globalized governance, a drastic weakening of the European Union could remove critical pressures on members states in Eastern Europe, thus eroding the support for ethnic inclusion. We have already noted that the organization's liberal influence may be waning in Eastern Europe and beyond.

Given the link between exclusion and conflict, it is conceivable that the spread of inclusion helps to account for regions of peace as well. However, as we have highlighted, this is no one-way street. Spatial processes that operate in the opposite direct – shifts toward exclusion – ultimately risk creating not only clustering of exclusion, but also conflict, as illustrated by the Middle East.

Of course, we do not expect this analysis to be the final word on what explains ethnic inclusion. Future research will have to further unpack the causal mechanisms driving decisions to abandon or adopt exclusive practices. To be sure, we have made no empirical effort to distinguish between explanations that draw on emulation and learning. Nor have we attempted to separate those that stress voluntary demonstration effects from those that depend on international pressure through international organizations or great powers. For example, additional analysis is needed to tell whether the diffusion effects in Sub-Saharan Africa are driven by regional organizations, such as the African Union, or more informally organized post-conflict intervention offered by regional leaders volunteering as mediators.

While we have controlled for previous conflict, the endogenous relationship between exclusion and conflict would also need to be further analyzed. There is strong evidence suggesting that leaders in postcolonial states typically include those groups that are seen as potentially threatening, but these results have not yet been extended to other parts of the world (see especially Chapter 6). To fully endogenize inclusion and conflict, it would be useful to disaggregate the analysis of diffusion effects to the group level. This would also render possible a more nuanced analysis of mechanisms relating to transborder ethnic kin and irredentism (see e.g., Cederman et al., 2013).

11   Trends in Power Sharing and Conflict*

In view of the intense fighting in Ukraine, Syria, Iraq, South Sudan, and Yemen, to name a few ongoing or recent conflicts, it would seem that the world is degenerating into chaos and violence. Unsurprisingly, many observers have expressed such fears, including former United Nations General Secretary Ban Ki-moon, according to whom the world seems to be "falling apart."[1] Indeed, recent years have seen a weakening of the liberal world order and the revival of ethnic nationalism in Europe and elsewhere (see, e.g., Bonikowski, 2017; Cederman, 2019; Rachman, 2014).

Yet, in stark contrast to this bleak picture, many conflict researchers insist that both civil and interstate warfare have been declining in recent years. Responding to pessimistic projections about emerging chaos and conflict around the world, recent studies detect a steady decrease in political violence. In a magisterial survey, Pinker (2011) argues that the current trend toward pacification should be seen as a part of a general "civilizing process" that has its origins in prehistoric times. Focusing on more recent political conflicts, Goldstein (2011) attributes the global decline in armed conflict to the influence of peacekeeping and other more indirect interventions by international organizations. Pinker and Mack (2014) note that the media by definition will give more attention to violent events than peace or "things that don't happen." Given these biases, to avoid "less hyperbolic assessment ... [t]he only sound way to appraise the state of the world is to count." While highly publicized and enthusiastically received both inside and outside academia, the decline-of-violence thesis remains controversial. Most of the scholarly criticism concerns whether the measurements of the trend are correct, whether they hold for all types of conflict, and whether the process encompasses

---

* This chapter is an updated version of Cederman, Gleditsch and Wucherpfennig (2017) with more recent data added to the analysis.
[1] "Opening General Assembly debate, Ban urges leadership to move from 'turbulence' to peace." New York, September 24, 2014, UN News Center. www.un.org/apps/news/story.asp?NewsID=48808#.VDvba-cY7Fg

the entire globe (see, e.g., Braumoeller, 2013; Fazal, 2014; Harrison and Wolf, 2012; Levy and Thompson, 2013; Thayer, 2013). Yet, on the whole, the decline-of-violence thesis has so far fared quite well thanks to a spirited defense by Pinker and others, and has thus started to acquire the status of an established fact (see, e.g., Gleditsch and Pickering, 2014).

What is less clear is what particular mechanisms appear to be driving the decline. Because of the sweeping nature of the original claims, the literature has focused mostly on macro-level patterns featuring broad and somewhat diffuse claims about general political violence, rather than tracing the operation of specific causal mechanisms that trigger more precisely defined forms of conflict. For this reason, we focus on the recent trend in ethnic civil wars as a particularly important subclass of political violence. Civil wars have arguably caused the worst human suffering since the end of the Cold War. Civil wars furthermore remain an important international security concern; many international crises or wars have at least in part emerged out of ethnic civil wars, with World War I as perhaps the most prominent historical example (e.g., Gleditsch, Salehyan and Schultz, 2008). At the time of writing, there are concerns that the crisis in Crimea and Eastern Ukraine and unrest in Syria, Iraq and Yemen will escalate to larger regional conflicts.

In order to evaluate the dynamics of ethnic warfare, this chapter offers systematic and disaggregated tests of explanatory propositions as a way to come closer to a causal account of the decline-of-conflict thesis for ethnic civil wars. More specifically, we rewind the historical tape back to the first few years after the Cold War, since this was a particularly important juncture that puzzled experts on ethnic conflict. Several scholars reacted to the historically pivotal events in the former Yugoslavia and elsewhere in the post-communist world by extrapolating a "coming anarchy" of "tribal" fighting that would engulf the world (Kaplan, 1994; Walzer, 1992). A few years later, but still a good decade before the publication of Pinker's and Goldstein's books, Gurr (2000*a*) responded to these "doomsday" scenarios by arguing that since the mid-1990s, the frequency of ethnic conflict had actually declined considerably, and that this trend was likely to continue. He explained this declining trend by postulating the existence of a new regime of accommodation and compromise that helps prevent new conflicts and end ongoing ones.

With the benefit of almost two decades' worth of new data on ethnic civil wars and accommodation, we are now in a good position to evaluate whether Gurr was right, and especially whether he was right for the right reasons. In other words, we examine whether a new regime of accommodative politics can account for the frequency of ethnic conflict after the Cold War. To answer these questions, we use group-level data on ethnic groups' power access from the mid-1990s as well as data on peacekeeping operations. To anticipate, our findings provide ample support for the proposition that Gurr was right both about the decline of ethnic civil war and the postulated causes.

Clearly, a lot more than intellectual history of conflict research is at stake, because Gurr's analysis has major implications for our theoretical understanding of civil wars as well as the most appropriate domestic and international policies. In terms of theory, confirming his claims would lend support to a more general literature on grievances in civil wars that includes Gurr's own work (e.g., Gurr, 1993, 2000b) but also goes well beyond it (see, e.g., Part II of this book and Cederman, Gleditsch and Buhaug, 2013; Horowitz, 1985; Petersen, 2002)

Furthermore, whether Gurr was right for the right reason is of immediate relevance for policy since such a result underlines the conflict-dampening effect of concessions to, and compromises involving, ethnic groups that have hitherto been generally badly treated and excluded from effective representation and power. This stands in stark contrast to the alternative body of research that sees civil war exclusively as a problem of weak states, dismissing both the role of grievances for conflict as well as the potential for accommodation to help settle conflicts (Fearon and Laitin, 2003, 2004). Summing up the policy implications of the weak states' paradigm, Mack (2002, 522) notes that

If grievances have nothing to do with the onset of war, then seeking to assuage them via preventive diplomacy, conflict resolution and confidence-building strategies will do nothing to reduce the risk of armed conflicts. If Collier & Hoeffler and Fearon & Laitin are correct, and what counts is not grievance but the relative capabilities of rebels versus the state, then strategies of 'peace through strength', repression and deterrence would appear to be optimal prevention strategies.

In the following, we first briefly review the relevant literature on ethnic conflict, focusing on Gurr's own writings. We then proceed to set up testable hypotheses building directly from Gurr's thesis, which are then exposed to systematic tests based on recent data.

11.1   Literature Review

Even though much of the conflict research on civil war had seen the rivalry between the superpowers as a key source fueling conflicts (see, e.g., Buzan, 1991), the initial enthusiasm over the end of the Cold War quickly gave way to a new pessimism (see, e.g., Mearsheimer, 1990*a*,*b*; Mueller, 1994). Many argued that the stable and largely peaceful world of nuclear deterrence under the superpowers was being replaced by a new and more dangerous world with increasing ethnic warfare.

One of the most prominent contributions, Kaplan (1994, 45), warned of a coming anarchy where we would see "the withering away of central governments, the rise of tribal and regional domains, the unchecked spread of disease, and the growing pervasiveness of war." While Kaplan stressed environmental scarcity, others gave cultural and ethno-religious factors a much more prominent role in promoting conflict. For example, Huntington (1993, 71) argued that "conflicts among nations and ethnic groups are escalating" as cultural lines rose to prominence after the Cold War. This scholarly pessimism about a seemingly inexorable increase of ethnic conflict also became widespread among politicians and policymakers. US President Bill Clinton noted in his 1993 inaugural address that "the new world is more free but less stable. Communism's collapse has called forth old animosities and new dangers."[2] Former CIA director Gates (1993, A10) likewise argued stridently against the temptation to disarm after the end of the Cold War, highlighting how "the events of the last two years have led to a far more unstable, turbulent, unpredictable and violent world."

Given the current emphasis on the decline of war, these statements may seem excessively pessimistic in retrospect, but they accurately reflect the conventional wisdom at the time. Indeed, the premise that wars were becoming more common, and especially ethnic strife, was so commonly accepted that very few even bothered to present any empirical evidence to corroborate the claim. To our knowledge, the first statement in print suggesting that war may be declining rather than increasing after the Cold War is an early analysis of the Uppsala Armed Conflict Data (Wallensteen and Sollenberg, 1995). However, this assessment was limited to an analysis of a six-year period 1989–1994, and primarily discussed whether there was a trend rather than possible causes. The article received relatively limited attention, and the authors themselves appeared to downplay the significance of the finding by choosing to emphasize how it was premature to dismiss interstate war as obsolescent in a follow-up article published one year later (Wallensteen and Sollenberg, 1996).

An op-ed piece on a decline in warfare in the *Los Angeles Times* by Wilson and Gurr (1999) received more attention, including from

---

[2] See www.presidency.ucsb.edu/ws/?pid=46366.

policymakers.[3] However, this contribution also primarily noted the phenomenon itself, without much discussion of the specific causes, as did a similar later op-ed piece by Goldstein (2002). Gurr's (2000*a*) is the first effort to both comment on the declining frequency of ethnic conflict and attempt to explain the causes of this trend. Moreover, although many of the arguments invoked about accommodation as a solution to conflict are not necessarily new, Gurr (2000*a*) appears to be the first to note the increase in accommodation and explicitly state its importance for the future of ethnic conflict.

Gurr (2000*a*) based his evidence primarily on the Minorities at Risk data, an effort to document the political status and conflicts involving ethnic minority groups (for extended discussions of the MAR project Gurr, 1993, 2000*b*; Hug, 2013). Noting that the perceived eruption of ethnic violence in the 1990s actually was part of a longer-term trend that started in the 1950s, Gurr (2000*a*, 52) explicitly took issue with "the conventional wisdom ... that tribal and nationalist fighting is still rising frighteningly." Over the 1990s, the absolute number of active violence conflicts had fallen from the peak level, and a much larger number of conflicts had deescalated rather than escalated in severity. Gurr also noted that wars of self-determination, which tend to be particularly destructive, were increasingly solved by peace agreements. More generally, Gurr (2000*a*, 52) pointed to a new regime of accommodation, "where threats to divide a country should be managed by the devolution of state power and that communal fighting about access to the state's power and resources should be restrained by recognizing group rights and sharing power." Political tactics had become more widespread relative to violent tactics. Since mobilization tends to precede violent ethnic rebellion by several years, Gurr furthermore noted that "[t]he decline in new protest movements foreshadows a continued decline in armed conflict."

According to Gurr (2000*a*, 55), the decline of ethnic war was neither the result of "an invisible hand" nor of unintended developments and trends, but rather a causal outcome of concerted efforts to curb and prevent conflict by individuals, groups, and organizations. Many of the important features stressed by Gurr pertained to changes in the attitudes or behavior of governments, notably an increasing emphasis on the protection of minority rights, manifested in a decrease of active discrimination, an increase in political autonomy, and greater

[3] According to Andrew Mack (personal communication), this op-ed piece eventually reached the desk of then General Secretary of the United Nations, Kofi Annan.

accommodation of groups through power sharing. Although many of these changes were linked to the general increase in political democracy in the third wave of democratization, underfoot since the 1970s (see, e.g., Huntington, 1991), Gurr noted that even autocratic states had made efforts to accommodate minority groups, even if still restricting general political rights or resisting open political competition.

Another important reason underlying the decrease of ethnic conflict was the realization that conflicts over self-determination were costly and thus best solved through negotiations and efforts to reach agreements to prevent violence. Although it can be difficult for the antagonist to settle conflicts alone, for example, due to commitment problems (see, e.g., Walter, 1997), the scope for assistance from, and engagement by, regional and international organizations had expanded with the end of the Cold War and the superpower rivalry (see, e.g., Doyle and Sambanis, 2006).

Beyond commentary, the pessimism about the coming anarchy prompted a new wave of research on the causes of civil war, often informed by the notion that ethnic civil war essentially was a security dilemma comparable to interstate conflict under anarchy (see, e.g., Melander, 2000; Posen, 1993). This analysis may have seemed superficially compelling in the case of the former Yugoslavia, where the federal government disappeared and left the ethnic federal units in a position to confront one another. However, this is a rather questionable interpretation of the dissolution of the former Yugoslavia, which understates the extent to which Serbia continued to control the remnants of the federal institutions, including the Yugoslav National Army. More fundamentally, Yugoslavia is in many ways an atypical case where civil war arises as a federal state dissolves, whereas the more typical scenario in a civil war involves much weaker non-state challengers facing an established central government.

The image of the former Yugoslavia as a canonical case of ethnic conflict became much less prominent as the wars in the region eventually came to an end. Much of the subsequent research on civil war came to dispute the validity of ethnic civil war as a distinct category and reject the relevance of ethnicity and grievances for civil war altogether, instead highlighting how civil war fundamentally was a problem of weak states and rent-seeking activities (Collier and Hoeffler, 2004; Fearon and Laitin, 2003). In addition, the Minorities at Risk Dataset, the main data source used by Gurr (2000a), was subjected to a great deal of criticism for problems of selection bias. More specifically, since the dataset primarily covers disadvantaged minorities, it may be poorly suited to provide answers to many questions about the general relationship between ethnic relations and conflict (see, e.g., Hug, 2013). Consequently, the majority of empirical studies conducted during the early 2000s moved away from ethnic groups as the unit of analysis, focusing on country-level analyses instead (see, e.g., Fearon and Laitin, 2003).

However, a new wave of research, that also serves as the theoretical starting point of this book, has challenged the alleged irrelevance of ethnicity and grievances (see, e.g., Cederman and Girardin, 2007; Cederman, Gleditsch and Buhaug, 2013; Petersen, 2011; Regan and Norton, 2005). We extend this line of research to derive testable propositions based on Gurr's projections relating changes in accommodation and decreasing exclusion to the decline of civil war.

In the following three sections, we extend this line of research to derive testable propositions based on Gurr's projections. We argue that three propositions would have to hold if Gurr was right for the right reasons? First, there would have to be a decline in ethnic civil wars since the mid-1990s. Second, there would have to be evidence of an emerging regime of accommodation guaranteeing ethnic groups increased access to power and decreasing discrimination and exclusion. Third, and most importantly, we would expect the latter trend to cause the first trend, rather than being spuriously related or simply coinciding but unrelated trends.

11.2   Has Ethnic Conflict Declined since the Mid-1990s?

The first task is to establish to what extent ethnic conflict has actually declined since the mid-1990s. Although a large number of studies claim that there is an overall decline in civil war, other studies find that the decline is not uniform for all types of conflict and regions. For example, (Gleditsch, 2008, 702) notes that civil wars involving Muslim countries and/or Islamic opposition movements have remained relatively constant since the end of the Cold War. If ethnic conflicts are particularly intractable or difficult to avoid – as many pessimists would have us believe – then we may well have a persistence or increase in such conflict despite an overall decline in civil wars driven by other types of conflict such as a decline in Marxist rebellions. In order to examine trends for ethnic conflicts specifically we trace conflict trends at the group level with respect to conflict incidence, onset and termination. In short, we evaluate the following proposition:

Hypothesis 11.1. There has been a decline of ethnic conflict since the mid-1990s.

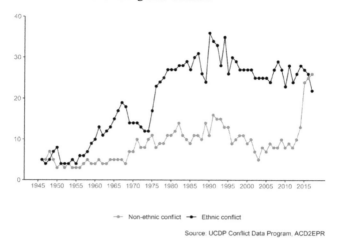

Source: UCDP Conflict Data Program, ACD2EPR

Figure 11.1 Number of ethnic and non-ethnic civil conflicts

To evaluate this proposition, we need group-level data on ethnic groups and their conflict behavior. As in previous chapters of this book, we use a conflict coding based on the ACD2EPR data, which map each rebel organization in the Uppsala Conflict Data Program's Armed Conflict Dataset (ACD) (Gleditsch et al., 2002) to the corresponding ethnic group in the Ethic Power Relations (EPR) data, if the rebel organization expresses an aim to support the ethnic group and group members participate in combat (Wucherpfennig et al., 2012). For convenience, we use the term ethnic civil war for all ethnic civil conflicts in the ACD dataset, which relies on a lower limit of twenty-five battle deaths.

Figure 11.1 displays the number of ethnic and non-ethnic civil conflicts since 1946. With a small spike during the mid to late 1970s – following the final phase of decolonization – there has been an increase in ethnic conflict until the early 1990s, very much in line with the observations made by many scholars at that time.[4] Likewise, non-ethnic conflict also increased until the same turning point. However, this increasing trend has not continued past the mid-1990s. Instead, ethnic conflict incidence has been declining since the mid-1990s – precisely the turning point that (Gurr, 2000a) pinpointed (indicated here by the

---

[4] We acknowledge that the incidence of ethnic conflict prior to decolonization may be underestimated in so far as most colonial conflicts could be deemed to involve an ethnic element. However, the lack of precise information on the political status and conflict participation by ethnic groups in colonies prevent us from a more systematic analysis of these conflicts at the group level.

Source: EPR, ACD2EPR

Figure 11.2 Number of ethnic groups in conflict

dashed vertical line). Moreover, as anticipated by Gurr, this declining trend has generally continued from the mid-1990s until our most recent data point in 2017.

It should be noted, however, that the decrease does not apply to non-ethnic conflict. In fact, they have been responsible for a major surge of civil conflict in the 2010s. Indeed, for most of the period since the early post-WWII period, ethnic civil conflicts have been more numerous than their non-ethnic counterparts. However, in recent years, the number of non-ethnic internal conflicts has surpassed that of ethnic ones. This situation stands in stark contrast to the end of the Cold War and the early post-Cold War periods that were dominated by ethnic conflict.

Yet, our conflict level statistics do not allow us to examine conflict trends relative to group characteristics. We instead turn to the group level, and examine the number of ethnic groups that are involved in civil conflict. Figure 11.2 displays the number of ethnic groups in conflict from 1946 through 2017. The picture is very similar to Figure 11.1. Again, the chart describes an increase in ethnic civil war until the mid-1990s, and a decline since this juncture. The latter trend is even more clearly visible based on group counts.

We further decompose conflict incidence by assessing the number of conflict onset per year (Figure 11.3), as well as the rate by which ongoing conflicts terminate (Figure 11.4). Figure 11.3 is also consistent with Gurr's prediction of a decline in ethnic conflict onsets since the end of the Cold War, despite a short-lived spike in 2011 reflecting several

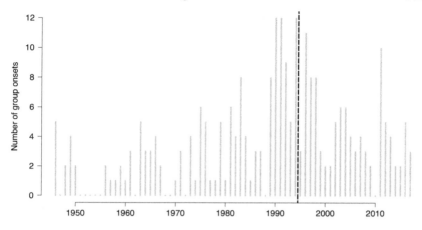

Figure 11.3 Onset of ethnic civil war

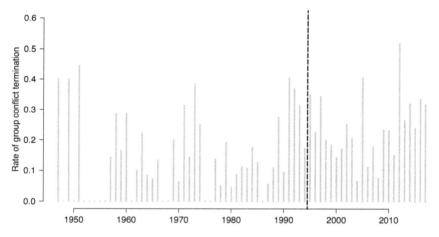

Figure 11.4 Termination of ethnic civil war

ethnic groups in the south of Sudan. The rate at which groups in conflict terminated fighting in Figure 11.4 is less straightforward, in part due to declining number of ongoing conflicts and thus fewer opportunities for termination. Until the 1980s, many years saw no groups terminating fighting at all, while the rate of termination has been more or less consistently high since the 1990s, broadly in line with Gurr's conjectures.

In summary, the empirical record offers an affirmative answer to our first question: the conflict trend since the mid-1990s has been mostly negative, both in terms of outbreak and ending of conflicts. With the first piece of Gurr's thesis in place, we now turn to the second question concerning trends of accommodation.

11.3   Has Accommodation Increased since the Mid-1990s?

The optimistic scenario sketched by Gurr hinges on several changes toward more cooperative and inclusive behavior. This section evaluates this emerging regime of accommodation favoring previously excluded or discriminated ethnic groups.

Hypothesis 11.2. There has been an increase of accommodation since the mid-1990s.

To facilitate precise empirical evaluation, we break up the overall claim into several-sub hypotheses, all of which concern the period since the mid-1990s:

Hypothesis 11.2a. Group rights have improved through reduced discrimination.

Hypothesis 11.2b. Governments have been more likely to grant territorial autonomy to previously powerless groups.

Hypothesis 11.2c. Governments have been more likely to include previously excluded groups in power-sharing regimes.

Hypothesis 11.2d. There has been a trend toward democratization.

Hypothesis 11.2e. There has been a trend toward more frequent peacekeeping operations.

We evaluate the first three using the EPR dataset, which provides a coding on whether the group in question rules alone (i.e., either monopoly or dominance), shares power, or is excluded from executive power. In assessing trends in power status, we here focus on the type of behavior that is most in line with the theoretical conjectures made by Gurr, as described in Hypotheses 11.2a–11.2e. Figure 11.5 shows changes in the power status of ethnic groups over time, depicting mean shares of population across countries. The world has clearly become more inclusive since the World War II, with the average share of

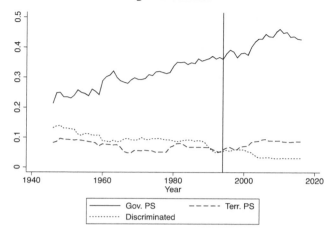

Figure 11.5 Trends in accommodation, such as power sharing (PS), and its opposite (discrimination) as average share of country population

countries' population enjoying governmental power sharing steadily increasing with the possible exception for the most recent years in the 2010s. Discrimination has also declined, while territorial power sharing has seen some increase since the mid-1990s.[5]

To study trends in democratization, we rely on the well-known Polity IV data. We here follow a conventional distinction between countries whose value lies above six (democracies), versus those whose value lies beneath (see Figure 11.6). As is well-known, there has been a steady increase in the share of democratic countries, especially since the end of the Cold War. Finally, Figure 11.7 displays the evolution of peace keeping operations over time, using Beardsley's (2011a) approach to extract missions with military deployment by the UN, a regional security organization or a coalition of states.[6] This indicates a qualitative shift in the number of peacekeeping missions around the end of the Cold War, when the reduced tensions between the superpowers expanded the room for peacekeeping in civil wars.[7]

[5] This figure does not depict political exclusion and discrimination due to colonialism since the EPR dataset only covers sovereign units. If these cases were considered, however, the trend toward inclusion would have been even stronger.

[6] We exclude interventions without the consent of the host countries and collective security actions with offensive aims such as the US-led UN force in the Korean War.

[7] While the number of operations has not changed much since 1996, the budgets have increased substantially in recent years (Hegre, Hultman and Nygård, 2019).

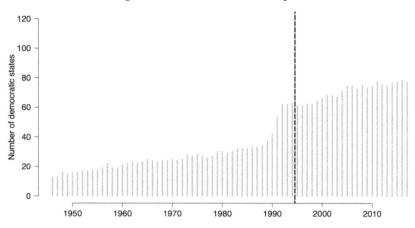

Figure 11.6 Trends in democracy

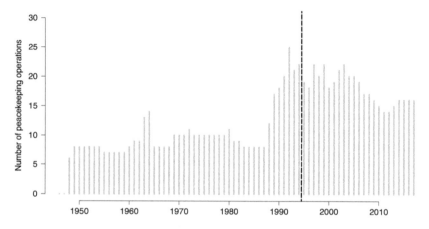

Figure 11.7 Trends in peacekeeping

11.3.1   Is increasing accommodation linked to the decline of ethnic civil war?

On the whole, the empirical record vindicates Gurr's claims about an increase in ethnic and political accommodation. Indeed, the trends that were already visible a decade after the end of the Cold War remain intact and have possibly been even stronger. This section addresses whether the increasing accommodation plausibly caused the decline of ethnic civil war. We unpack the aggregate trends and evaluate ethnic power access and conflict outcomes for individual ethnic groups. If Gurr's expectations are correct, groups that were granted improved power access or group rights should be less likely to experience violence than those who were not, and democratization and peacekeeping should exert a further influence. We test the following hypotheses for the onset (a) and termination (b) of ethnic civil war for the period from 1994 through 2017:

Hypothesis 11.3a. Strengthened group rights through reduced discrimination caused a decline of ethnic civil conflict.

Hypothesis 11.3b. Granting of territorial power sharing caused a decline of ethnic civil conflict.

Hypothesis 11.3c. Inclusion in power-sharing regimes of previously excluded groups caused a decline of ethnic civil conflict.

Hypothesis 11.3d. Democratization caused a decline of ethnic civil conflict.

Hypothesis 11.3e. Peacekeeping operations caused a decline of ethnic civil conflict.

These mechanisms could operate through either a decline in the probability of a conflict outbreak or an increased likelihood that conflicts will terminate. For peacekeeping, however, we do not expect to see any effects on conflict outbreak, since peacekeeping almost by definition is deployed to ongoing conflict to facilitate conflict termination.[8]

Our research design attempts to approximate counterfactual principles in that it identifies accommodative changes as treatments and restricts the sample to those groups that can enjoy such treatments, rather than comparing levels of accommodation across groups based on the full sample. This approach elucidates the consequences of increasing accommodation, which is precisely the gist of Gurr's reasoning. However, it should be noted that our analysis is of course quasi-experimental rather than strictly counterfactual since it rests on estimation without a truly randomized, experimental treatment, with all the limitations that this entails.

In keeping with this logic, we test our hypotheses with dummy variables for all group years following the accommodative event, while

---

[8] Peacekeeping may prevent regional conflict spillovers to other countries (Beardsley, Cunningham and White, 2015), but the only 'proactive' mission in a country deemed to have a high risk of conflict outbreak so far is the United Nations Preventive Deployment Force (UNPREDEP) in the Republic of Macedonia (see, e.g., Stamnes, 2004).

discarding from the treatment any years characterized by reversals and limiting the scope to the period after 1993 until and including 2017. To be precise, H11.3a is tested with a dummy variable that captures the granting of basic group rights by referring to group years following an upgrade from discriminated status. We consider all years following such changes if they occurred after 1993 and the group did not suffer discrimination again, which implies that all discrimination-free years following the first upgrade are considered as treatment.[9]

Following the same principles, our operationalization of H11.3b focuses on those groups that were previously completely excluded, but were subsequently granted regional autonomy after 1993. Here the treatment concerns upgrades to autonomous status rather than the granting of group rights. Analogously, we test H11.3c by restricting the sample to all excluded groups and those that were included after 1993, considering the latter groups as the treatment category. Furthermore, using a country-level measure of democracy, we evaluate H11.3d based on a democratization indicator that denotes cases where groups were residing in a country that underwent a transition to full democracy since 1993. In line with the previous change indicators, this one considers only the democratic years as the treatment following the initial democratization, thus dropping any reversals to authoritarian rule from the treatment category. Finally, in the case of peacekeeping (H11.3e), we rely on the country-level variable that we introduced in the previous section. Here the variable indicates if peacekeeping was implemented anywhere in the country.

In addition, we introduce a number of variables to control for important group-level and country-level properties:

- Relative group size based on the demographic estimates of EPR.[10]
- Past conflict indicating whether the group has rebelled against the government since 1946 or the independence of the country.

---

[9] All treatment years, which are not necessarily consecutive, are coded as one, and all other years are kept at zero. This means that we do not consider at all those cases that already enjoyed group rights in 1993 since these groups were already "treated." For example, if a group was granted rights in 2002 until 2005 and then again after 2009, the variable would be zero before 2002 and then one from 2002 through 2005, following by zeroes until and including 2008, and one thereafter.

[10] Relative group size $g \in [0, 1)$ comparing the population of the group G to the population of the incumbent I is defined as $\frac{G}{G+I}$ if the group is excluded and as G/I if the group is included.

Table 11.1. *Explaining onset of ethnic civil conflict*

	(1) Conflict onset	(2) Conflict onset	(3) Conflict onset	(4) Conflict onset
Group rights	−1.169* (0.513)			
Autonomy		−1.036 (0.699)		
Inclusion			−1.111* (0.525)	
Democracy				−0.709[+] (0.408)
Postwar period	0.527 (0.851)	1.533*** (0.466)	1.465*** (0.418)	1.462*** (0.369)
Log country GDP, lag	−0.581* (0.265)	−0.228** (0.074)	−0.279*** (0.073)	−0.210* (0.105)
Log country population, lag	0.463*** (0.121)	0.292* (0.116)	0.201* (0.083)	0.103 (0.105)
Rel. group size	7.577** (2.940)	2.343 (1.714)	3.399* (1.664)	2.956 (1.994)
Rel. group size^2	−5.147 (4.543)	−0.954 (2.284)	−2.269 (2.204)	−2.697 (2.708)
Constant	−3.052 (2.067)	−3.966** (1.425)	−2.716* (1.144)	−2.429[+] (1.349)
Observations	1956	7307	10046	8716
Pseudo R^2	0.199	0.245	0.250	0.179

Standard errors in parentheses
[+] $p < 0.1$, * $p < 0.05$, ** $p < 0.01$, *** $p < 0.001$

- Logged GDP per capita and logged population size at the country level, lagged (Penn World Table 7.0, see Heston, Summers and Aten, 2011).
- Number of years since the previous conflict for onset analysis, and number of years since the last peace spell, both entered as cubic polynomials (Carter and Signorino, 2010).

Table 11.1 presents results for onset and Table 11.2 results for conflict termination for all politically relevant EPR groups that can receive

Table 11.2. *Explaining termination of ethnic civil conflict*

	(1) Conflict end	(2) Conflict end	(3) Conflict end	(4) Conflict end	(5) Conflict end
Group rights	1.765*** (0.505)				
Autonomy		1.685*** (0.476)			
Inclusion			0.924* (0.365)		
Democracy				0.321 (0.394)	
Peacekeeping					0.361 (0.220)
Log country GDP, lag	0.030 (0.137)	-0.079 (0.105)	-0.026 (0.085)	0.027 (0.120)	-0.012 (0.090)
Log country population, lag	-0.109 (0.319)	-0.392*** (0.093)	-0.225* (0.097)	-0.450*** (0.101)	-0.278*** (0.078)
Rel. group size	-4.200 (4.443)	-1.824 (1.385)	-1.684 (1.376)	-2.135 (1.838)	-2.680+ (1.453)
Rel. group size^2	3.142 (4.140)	0.511 (1.865)	0.787 (1.596)	1.025 (1.982)	2.058 (1.537)
Constant	-0.422 (4.214)	3.612* (1.496)	1.485 (1.445)	2.924* (1.468)	1.924 (1.327)
Observations	272	570	705	648	833
Pseudo R^2	0.069	0.047	0.039	0.100	0.033

Standard errors in parentheses
+ $p < 0.1$, * $p < 0.05$, ** $p < 0.01$, *** $p < 0.001$

accommodation from 1946 through 2017. We report logit estimates with robust country-clustered standard errors. Ongoing conflict years were dropped from the onset analysis and peace spells from the termination analysis.

In keeping with Gurr's projections, Table 11.1 shows that the granting of group rights dampens the risk of conflict, although the coefficient does not quite reach significance at the level of $p = 0.02$ (see Model 1). Regional autonomy arrangements also have a negative estimated coefficient, but the estimate is not statistically significant and we do not have clear evidence that this affects the probability of conflict in a consistent manner (see Model 2).[11] Yet, groups included in power-sharing benefit from a lower conflict propensity, a result that is statistically significant at the $p = 0.03$ level (see Model 3). Democratization also appears to operate as anticipated by Gurr, but at a somewhat lower level of significance (see Model 4).[12]

To evaluate what these results mean in practice we compare simulations for two counterfactual scenarios: A world in which no accommodation takes place and a world in which group rights are strengthened by means of either ending discrimination, granting regional autonomy, inclusion or democratization. We assume that accommodation takes effect in 2008 and then we estimate the average probability of a group experiencing a conflict onset within ten years. Set up this way, the difference between the predictions for the two scenarios constitutes the long-term effect of accommodation.[13]

Figure 11.8 visualizes the predictions for Models 1–4, with the squares depicting the non-accommodation scenario, the circles representing the accommodation scenario. The difference between the two (i.e., the predicted change) is given by the diamonds. The figure demonstrates that accommodative politics is associated with considerably lower levels of conflict for affected groups. Indeed, our estimates suggest that on average groups that are no longer discriminated against are 15 percent

---

[11] It should be noted, however, that the current analysis does not explore the combination of territorial and governmental power sharing. In Chapter 8 we showed that territorial autonomy has a conflict-reducing effect in combination with power sharing.

[12] Since multiple groups may engage in the same conflict, there is a risk that the results might be driven by 'double-counting" of influential cases. However, our results are robust to a procedure that randomly keeps just one group from such instances.

[13] Specifically, we draw 1,000 sets of coefficients based on the original model estimates, and calculate predicted probabilities for each observation for the prediction period 2008 to 2017, assuming non-accommodation and accommodation respectively. We then calculate yearly averages, i.e., the mean predicted probability (Gelman and Hill, 2007, 406) for the relevant sample-year for a given draw, $\bar{p}_t$. The probability of experiencing at least one event during the ten year period, 2008–2017, is given by $1 - \prod_{t=2008}^{2017}(1 - \bar{p}_t)$. The expected change induced by accommodation is then computed as the first difference between the two estimates (again for each draw).

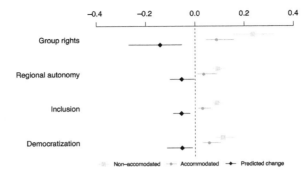

Figure 11.8 Predicted probabilities of at least one conflict onset during 2008 to 2017

less likely to experience conflict during the next decade. Inclusion can reduce this probability by 20 percent, while democratization leads to a reduction in risk by 27 percent.

In perfect symmetry to the onset models, the analysis of conflict termination relies on a dependent variable that marks the 'onset of peace" while dropping all peace years. Table 11.2 shows encouraging results for the link between group rights and war termination (see Model 1). Turning to Model 2, it is clear that autonomy has a major pacifying influence on ongoing civil wars. Model 3 suggests that offering power sharing to rebels could have a positive influence on conflict termination, a result that is significant at the $p = 0.05$ level.[14] In contrast to the onset analysis, however, democratization does not appear to be associated with a reduction in conflict at a level that can be separated from zero (see Model 4). Finally, Model 5 reveals that peacekeeping operations make conflict endings somewhat more likely, a finding that just barely misses significance at the $p = 0.1$ level.

Figure 11.9 visualizes our results in an analogous manner, depicting the mean probabilities for a group in conflict to terminate fighting within two years following a change towards accommodation in 2008. The groups that are no longer discriminated against are on average 45 percent more likely to terminate fighting within two years, while granting regional autonomy leads to an increase of 43 percent. The estimates for inclusion and democratization amount to 25 and 7 percent respectively.

[14] Yet, narrowing the focus to governmental conflict produces significantly stronger results. This is to be expected because governmental power sharing addresses the sources of conflict at the center of government.

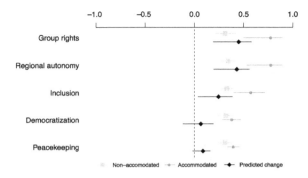

Figure 11.9 Predicted probabilities of conflict termination during 2008 or 2009

Finally, peacekeeping raises the probability of conflict termination within two years by 9 percent.

In general, these findings confirm Gurr's reasoning, and more generally those studies that argue in favor of the pacifying influence of accommodation and ethnic inclusion. For example, powerful arguments have been made in support of power-sharing arrangements, including regional autonomy (see, e.g., McGarry and O'Leary, 2009) and governmental power sharing (see, e.g., Lijphart, 1977; Mattes and Savun, 2009). Because all these institutions cannot as a rule be treated as random shocks or externally imposed factors, however, endogeneity remains a major challenge in this literature. In the absence of an identification strategy relying on an effective statistical instrument, the current study also does not offer a fool-proof way of circumventing these difficulties. Yet, it seems reasonable to assume that power sharing and similar concessions are primarily offered to groups that are potentially threatening and thus more likely to engage in armed conflict (see Chapters 6–9). If so, then inclusive moves are actually likely to be more effective than indicated by naive modeling on observed data. The same applies to peacekeeping operations, which are known to have been applied in more difficult cases rather than conflicts which are easy to settle (e.g., Fortna and Howard, 2008; Beardsley, 2011b).

The result showing that conflict varies with democratization is also of considerable theoretical interest. While previous studies link democratization episodes to the outbreak of civil war, these have typically focused on more limited liberalization processes leading to semi-democracy rather than full democracy (e.g., Cederman, Hug and Krebs, 2010; Mansfield and Snyder, 2005). In this sense, the current study is compatible with such findings, especially since incomplete democratization is not associated with a pacifying trend.

11.4   Conflict-Preventing and Termination-Promoting Accommodation since the Mid-1990s

In this section we examine in more depth some of the individual cases that underlie our statistical findings. Doing so allows us to go beyond statistical significance and examine if the highlighted mechanisms plausibly have had the impact that we claim. Table 11.3 shows the full set of possible combinations of the specific type of accommodation that we have highlighted (columns) and the different outcomes in terms of effects on onset, or the outbreak of new conflicts, or termination, or the settlement of ongoing conflicts (row). The cells of Table 11.3 indicate illustrative cases discussed in greater detail below in the text. We focus in particular on cases where we have seen conflict prior to changes towards greater accommodation, and our claims are better supported if we can substantiate that the changes plausibly have contributed to prevent outbreaks of new conflicts or settlements of ongoing conflicts.

11.4.1   Conflict-preventing accommodation

Our discussion of the cases starts with a survey of the effect of accommodative policies on the outbreak of ethnic civil war as formulated in hypotheses H3a–H3d, leaving the peacekeeping hypothesis H3e to be evaluated in the next subsection that focuses on conflict termination.

Group rights. Governments have been increasingly inclined to discontinue discriminatory policies since the mid-1990s and in such cases, new or renewed conflict has been very rare indeed. A case in point is the reduction of tensions in Liberia following the fall of Charles Taylor.

Table 11.3. *Examples of conflict-preventing and termination-promoting accommodation since the mid-1990s*

	Group rights	Autonomy	Inclusion	Democratization	Peacekeeping
Onset	Liberia, Nigeria	Kurds in Iraq	South Africa, Angola	Guatemala, Ghana	(•)
Termination	Tuaregs in Mali and Niger	Northern Ireland, Aceh	Bosnia	Burundi	Macedonia

After assuming office in 2006, Ellen Johnson-Sirleaf, who was subsequently awarded the Nobel Peace Prize, formed an ethnically inclusive government of technocrats (Dunn, 2010). According to Gerdes (2011, 51), "[r]oughly half the cabinet of early 2006 was staffed with individuals associated with ethnic groups that historically were underrepresented in government." Despite neopatrimonial tendencies, the elite bargain has helped prevent recurrence of conflict. Likewise, neopatrimonialism and corruption continue to haunt Nigeria, but the situation of the Ijaws in the Niger Delta has also improved considerably following the election in 2007. Thanks to more conciliatory policies in the Niger Delta and actual representation at the cabinet level, Ijaw demands have been at least partly met (International Crisis Group, 2007). Arguably, the Serb government's more lenient treatment of minorities following the fall of Slobodan Milosevic has not been followed by rebellion, although the Kosovo Albanians effectively seceded in 1999 after the war. The indigenous populations in Guatemala and El Salvador have also profited from upgraded group rights, as have the Berbers and Tuaregs in Libya, following the fall of Gadaffi. Likewise, in the wake of the US invasion in 2002, several Afghan groups, such as the Hazaras, Tajiks, Turkmens and Uzbeks, were liberated from severe discrimination imposed by the Taliban regime (Adeney, 2008). In all these cases, the previously discriminated groups have refrained from rebelling. The same cannot be said for situations where discrimination persists. In these instances, armed resistance against the government is much more likely.[15]

Regional autonomy. The results for Model 1 in Table 11.1 suggests a negative effect of the granting of regional autonomy, but although the coefficient has the right sign the large standard errors mean that the difference is not statistically significant. However, there are only three groups in our sample where a shift to regional autonomy is followed by new conflict outbreaks, namely the Bodo in India (2009 and 2013), the Dinka in Sudan (2011) and Catholics in Northern Ireland (1998). The last incident refers to the Omagh bombing, which was carried out by the splinter group the Real IRA in a deliberate effort to spoil the ongoing peace process. It was strongly condemned by the main republican organizations including Sinn Féin, and other republican organizations such as the Irish National Liberation Army declared a ceasefire, thus

---

[15] The main exceptions to the peaceful trend following the granting of group rights include the Tuareg rebellions in Mali and Niger. Yet, it has to be noted that the peace agreements were only partly implemented. Another case of recurrent conflict after the granting of group rights involves the Southern Mande in the Ivory Coast, but here the upgrade occurred through a coup rather than through accommodative moves on the part of the government and conflict resulted from a status reversal.

also demonstrating their commitment to the peace process. The Real IRA accepted responsibility three days after the attack, but at the same time apologized for the attack and stated that they did not intend "at any time to kill any civilians." As such, it is difficult to consider this an intentional effort to start a civil war. If anything, the clear sea change in attitudes by Republicans in Northern Ireland towards the use of violence after the Good Friday Agreement supports the claim that providing regional autonomy can help prevent future conflict outbreaks. Indeed, as we discuss below, granting regional autonomy was instrumental in achieving peace in the first place.

Inclusion. Several of the instances where group rights led to pacification coincide with the shift from exclusion to inclusion in power sharing regimes, such as the Liberian and Nigerian cases discussed above. Another set of trajectories that features upgrading from powerless status to inclusion in the executive through power sharing has also been mostly peaceful despite the fears expressed by various critics (see, e.g., Rothchild and Roeder, 2005*b*). In Eastern Europe, the European Union also contributed to more inclusive policies, as illustrated by the improved power access of the Hungarians in Slovakia and Romania, and the Turkish in Bulgaria (Bochsler and Szöcsik, 2013). An especially important case, given the troubling prehistory of conflict, has been the power sharing in Bosnia Herzegovina. While falling short of full integration and confidence-building, the ethnically inclusive institutions have managed to keep the peace after several years of bitter fighting and ethnic cleansing in the early 1990s (McMahon, 2004/2005; McCrudden and O'Leary, 2013). Below, in our discussion of conflict termination, we will return to this case. South Africa represents another impressive example where ethnic inclusion has succeeded in pacifying a long history of conflict. While post-Apartheid South Africa continued to be afflicted by problems of crime, poverty and corruption, conflict has been drastically reduced (Ikejiaku, 2009). Indeed, interethnic peace would hardly have been conceivable without far-reaching ethnic inclusion of previously excluded and oppressed groups. Another illustration of how ethnic inclusion can stabilize previously conflict-ridden countries is provided by the People's Movement for the Liberation of Angola (MPLA). Originally an Mbundu-Mestiço movement, this organization became increasingly successful in attracting support from other ethnic groups, especially from the Ovimbundu-Ovambo and the Bakongo groups (Roque, 2010). In post-conflict Angola the key route to political power is an MPLA affiliation. In this sense, the MPLA regime is no longer representing the interests of one ethnic group. Indeed, since 2006, the Angolan cabinet has comprised ministers from all three major ethnic groups. However, the overall stabilizing influence of power sharing is not limited to Sub-Saharan Africa: as already noted by Gurr, the fall of Suharto in Indonesia ushered in a much inclusive approach to ethnic minorities, which brought power access to previously excluded groups such as the Acenese, Bataks, Chinese, Minankabaus, Papuans, Sundanese and Malay. Below, we will return to the first of these groups in our discussion of conflict resolution. In the other cases, ethnic inclusion combined with decentralization has helped pacify ethnic power relations (Horowitz, 2013).[16]

Democratization. Guatemala provides an example where a transition to democracy is followed by no further conflict onsets in the country, and further inspection of the case suggests that democratization plausibly contributed to prevent renewed conflict. The shift to democratic rule in 1996 appears to have promoted the political influence and access of the country's indigenous Maya population. Although the civil war in Guatemala could be considered a Marxist insurgency or ideological conflict, it was clearly linked to the indigenous Mayan population through explicit claims and widespread recruitment. The umbrella organization known as the Guatemalan National Revolutionary Unity (UNRG) recruited disproportionately from the Mayan community over the course of the conflict. Many of the constituents' organizations emphasized the plight of the country's indigenous communities and the need for protection of their rights and land reform, especially the Guerrilla Army of the Poor (EGP) preceding the merger of the different groups.[17] Indigenous communities have gained greater access to central power in the aftermath of the transition, and President Alfonso Portillo included several indigenous members in his cabinet after his 1999 election victory. Democracy in Guatemala has survived important challenges, including high crime and the controversial 2003 presidential campaign by former General and President Ríos Montt. This latter involved extensive demonstrations both by supporters challenging attempts to ban him standing as a candidate and opponents holding Ríos Montt responsible for genocide. Of course, many contentious issues facing the Maya remain after democratization, such as the perceived threats

---

[16] Again, there is a short list of conflict onsets following power-sharing upgrades. We have already discussed the Tuaregs in Mali and the Southern Mande in a previous footnote. Other cases include the Tutsi-Banyamulenge in the Democratic Republic of the Congo in 2006, and the Dinka in the Sudan in 2011. While the former onset would have to be seen in a larger context involving "Africa's world war" (Prunier, 2009), the latter one was triggered by the secessionist struggle that gave birth to South Sudan the same year.

[17] See, e.g., the Guatemalan truth commission document 59, available at https://web .archive.org/web/20130506083412/http://shr.aaas.org/guatemala/ ceh/mds/spanish/anexo1/vol2/no59.html.

from mining companies to their rights and environmental degradation. However, many observers note that democratization has helped establish the indigenous as full citizens and helped indigenous groups more effectively pursue their interest through non-violent resistance vis-à-vis local authorities (Rasch, 2012).

There are many cases where democratization follows as part of a peace treaty between warring parties or even a peacekeeping mission with external support. Ghana represents a case where democratization arises without a formal settlement and without possible interference from effects of external support. Ghana is considered to have had a transition to full democracy in the Polity data on July 1 2001, and was very much introduced from above by former military ruler Jerry Rawlings. Ghana has a history of sectarian rule and coup d'etats. Rawlings – of mixed Ewe and Scottish ancestry – came to power through a military coup in 1979, ousting the previous Akan (Ashante) dominated leadership. Once in power, Rawlings proceeded to execute a large number of officers of Akan origins as part of a "house cleaning" exercise (see, e.g., Austin, 1985; Pieterse, 1982). The transition to democracy appears to have been effective in preventing military coups and ethnic polarization and establishing democratic control of the military in political life (Luckham, 1996). Although the main parties still have an ethnic partisan base, voting cannot be explained exclusively by ethnic affiliation, and there have been several transfers of powers since the transition without a resumption of violence. Some observers note that Ghana has managed to implement a system with elements of consociational democracy, by integrating members from different ethnic groups in the party leadership. Both the Ewe-dominated National Democratic Congress and Akan-dominated New Patriotic Party include members from all major groups in the national executive, and it is customary for presidents to include a running mate from other ethnic groups to enhance their appeal in democratic competition (Asante and Gyimah-Boadi, 2004). Moreover, there have been efforts to try to overcome regional inequalities that could fuel ethnic tensions. Ghana is widely considered to be one of the success stories of democratization in Africa. Indeed, Lindberg (2006) cites Ghana as one of the most consolidated and secure democracies in Africa. Thus, it can be concluded that democratization has helped make future sectarian coups and violence less likely in Ghana.[18]

---

[18] Beyond the general trend, we note that there are only two clear counterexamples of ethnic conflict breaking out following democratization over the period, the South Ossetians in Georgia and Diola in Senegal. Both are somewhat unusual and in our view do not clearly undermine our argument. The settlement area of the South Ossetian was largely not under the control of Georgia. Furthermore, Georgia is a borderline case

11.4.2 Conflict-resolving accommodation

The discussion above shows that there is plenty of supportive evidence for the link between ethnic concessions and the prevention of future conflict onsets. Is there a similar, conflict-reducing effect of accommodation during ongoing civil wars? Here the plausibility of the results in Table 11.2 hinges on a much smaller number of cases.

Group rights. Model 2 in Table 11.1 indicates that the granting of group rights increases the probability of conflict termination. In contrast to the other statistical findings, however, the causal mechanisms are not obviously accounted for by accommodative moves by governments. This applies particularly to the Tuaregs in Mali and Niger, the Tutsi-Banyamulenge in the Democratic Republic of Congo and several groups in Afghanistan in 2002, which were all heavily influenced by external processes. For example, fighting in Mali came to an end not so much due to the upgrading of group rights as thanks to the intervention of French forces. Possibly, the Ugandan government's more lenient approach to the Langi and Acholi from 2006 contributed to conflict termination in 2006 and 2011 (Lindemann, 2011). Yet, given the limited number of ongoing conflicts that could have been affected by improved group rights and the likelihood of recurrent onsets, it is safer to leave final conclusions concerning this influence to future research.

Regional autonomy. In contrast, the record is much stronger with respect to decentralization as a response to ongoing civil war. Again, the number of conflict cases is very limited, but in two of the three conflicts that coincided with decentralization moves, the granting of autonomy is strongly linked to an absence of new conflict outbreaks. Despite pessimistic references to autonomy as an "impossible solution" (Kaufmann, 1996), the "Good Friday Agreement" was signed in April 1998 and entered into force in 1999. This peace agreement paved the way for a successful peace process that led to the devolution of power to the Northern Ireland Assembly. At the same time, the agreement reaffirmed Northern Ireland's status as part of the UK, unless a majority of the Northern Irish votes against continued union. Both the parliament

of democracy, hovering around the threshold during the period (5 up to Jan/24/2004, 7 until Nov/6/2006, and then 6 at the time of the outbreak of the war). Senegal becomes democratic in 2000 and has a recurrence of the Casamance conflict in 2011. However, there was widespread concern at the time that President Wade was trying to hand over power to his son and to introduce questionable constitutional changes that he was later forced to abandon. See www.bbc.co.uk/news/world-africa-13887613. The conflict ends after the opposition wins competitive elections, and there has been no subsequent conflict since then (although the period is quite short). Thus, we conclude that neither seem very compelling counterexamples to our causal logic.

and the coalition government contained mechanisms guaranteeing the influence from both Catholic and Protestant parties. Additionally, the agreement also included provisions that the paramilitary groups should decommission all weapons within two years. While concerns remain as regards the extent to which the current institutional configuration will allow the previous conflict parties to fully transcend their previous hostility, this case of devolution has been widely heralded as a success (McCrudden et al., 2016).

The other important case where decentralization has helped terminate a long-standing conflict is the province Aceh of Indonesia. While external events such as the devastating tsunami of 2004 clearly played a role, it would be difficult to imagine a peaceful end to the secessionist struggle of the Acenese without far-reaching concessions on the part of Jakarta (Horowitz, 2013). In May 1999, after the fall of Suharto, Jakarta issued two laws on decentralization, one on regional government and one on center-region financial relations. The laws conferred significant autonomy to the regions (unlike the 1974 law), but similar to the 1974 "New Order" legislation, the focus was once more on district autonomy. In August 2001, President Megawati Soekarnoputri enacted the Law on Special Autonomy for the Province Naggro Aceh Darussalam (NAD). It offered broad autonomy to the Province of Aceh and a greater share of income from its natural resources, previewing a 70 percent share for Aceh's oil and gas revenues (Wennmann and Krause, 2009). Furthermore, it granted Aceh the right to establish its local government in line with local traditions and to base the legal system on the Sharia. On balance, it appears plausible that far-reaching governmental concessions helped bring a long and bitter struggle to a peaceful end.

Finally, the third conflict, during which decentralization occurred, involved the Bodo in India in their struggle for independence. In this conflict, however, autonomy concessions have not proven as successful as in the previous two cases, because fighting has recurred since the 1990s. Yet, it should be noted that Bodo territorial autonomy is not geographically fragmented and did not enter into force until 2003 because of fierce resistance by Bodo and Asseme extremists (Bhaumik, 2007).

Inclusion. The statistical evidence presented above lends some support to the claim that the granting of power sharing at the center has a pacific influence. Yet, the case-specific record is quite mixed, especially since external influences have been so strong that it is difficult to disentangle the impact of power sharing on peace and stability. Introduced through the Dayton Accords, power sharing in Bosnia Herzegovina illustrates this point. In this high-profile case that remains loosely confederal under international tutelage, it is even doubtful whether proper ethnic inclusion can be said to have been implemented (Schneckener, 2002). All the same, conflict recurrence has been avoided so far. External influence through the US-led military intervention in the fall of 2001 also complicates the evaluation of why the Hazaras, Tajiks and Uzbeks in Afghanistan stopped fighting the government. It is unlikely that they would have stopped without externally imposed regime change in Kabul, but it is also hard to see why they would have terminated their rebellion without gaining influence at the central level. In Burundi, the power-sharing agreement that was negotiated in Pretoria in 2002 has been relatively successful in keeping the piece, at least until the recent coup attempt in the spring of 2015. Exhibiting some resemblances with Lijphart's consociationalism, it is still open to interpretation whether relative post-war stability can be attributed to ethnic inclusion or to "generally favourable societal circumstances" (Lemarchand, 2007, 16). All in all, we conclude that in contrast to its strongly conflict-preventing effect, accommodation through power sharing may have contributed to ending at least some conflicts, but it rarely played the main role since many of these peace processes involved major external intervention.

Democratization. Burundi also provides an example where democratization in an ongoing conflict helped facilitate a settlement to the conflict. The transition to democracy recorded in the Polity on August 19 2005 is followed by a peace treaty and settlement, including all but one of the Hutu groups. Lemarchand (2007, 7) notes that Burundi unlike Rwanda recognizes "ethnic differences as a necessary condition to reconcile minority rights with the claims of the majority" and "exemplifies a highly promising effort to share power among a large number of parties, whose membership is sometimes mixed." National institutions such as the parliament and army have ethnic quotas to ensure over-representation and prevent ethnic dominance. The holdout PALIPEHUTU-FNL faction eventually agrees to a ceasefire and to become a political party, thus ending the active civil war in the country. Thus, in this particular case, we believe the evidence suggests that democratization helped bring the conflict to an end. Given the weak statistical pattern, however, it would be unwarranted to conclude that the introduction of democracy during ongoing civil wars is likely to end them in general.

Peacekeeping. Peacekeeping efforts have played an important role in settling ongoing conflicts and preventing escalation or recurrence. The 2001 Albanian revolt in Macedonia serves a good example of a deployment of peacekeepers that prevented escalation. The Albanian community in Macedonia has suffered extensive discrimination and marginalization since the country's indepencence in 1991. The 2001 revolt followed in the wake of the Kosovo Liberation Army (KLA) in neighboring Kosovo, and the National Liberation Army (NLA) in Macedonia drew on participants as well as arms and resources from the neighboring conflict. Although transnational conflicts are often considered particularly difficult to settle and prone to recurrence (e.g., Gleditsch, Salehyan and Schultz, 2008; Salehyan, 2009), there is some evidence that the external peacekeeping prevented the Albanian conflict in Macedonia from escalating to a major war and helped foster the Ohrid Agreement ending the conflict.

Although the original UN mission in Macedonia was withdrawn in 1999 (following a Chinese veto against its renewal), NATO and EU envoys encouraged the government to seek a political solution to the conflict in 2001 and sent representatives to the Ohrid discussions between warring parties. Once a framework agreement was reached, NATO supervised the de-arming of the NLA through the Operation Essential Harvest task force, deploying a contingent of almost 5000 soldiers.[19] The Ohrid agreement helped enhance the political influence of Albanian parties in Macedonia and become government coalition partners. In sum, we believe that peacekeeping helped foster an end to the conflict and prevent future recurrence of violence.

There is of course a large literature on peacekeeping, reaching somewhat divergent conclusions about wether peacekeeping works or not (see, e.g., Doyle and Sambanis, 2000; Paris, 2004). Much of the disagreement in the literature stems from different criteria for success. Peacekeeping is generally successful in that conflict recurrence is likely, but may not satisfy more encompassing criteria for success such as good governance and capacity to function without external support. There are also reasons to question whether any peacekeeping employment should have an effect, and some evidence suggests that missions need to be sufficiently large and well-resourced to reach their objectives (see Ruggeri, Gizelis and Dorussen, 2013). Bosnia Herzegovina could be considered a successful case of peacekeeping in that a large mission eventually helped terminate the conflict, while previous smaller efforts proved inadequate to deter aggression. However, Bosnia Herzegovina is less successful as the country remains split along ethnic lines and heavily dependent on foreign aid (Diehl and Druckman, 2012). Ultimately, peacekeeping

---

[19] www.telegraph.co.uk/news/1338179/Nato-launches-Macedonia-mission.html.

is also more likely to result in stable peace when accompanied by other trends fostering greater inclusion and accommodation such as decreasing ethnic discrimination and democratization.

11.4.3 Predicting conflict trends

The divergent claims on the future of ethnic conflict in the 1990s could be considered as forecasts. Gurr formed his predictions on the basis of explicit theory that relates changes in accommodation and exclusion. By contrast, many of the pessimists, including Kaplan, saw conflict as virtually inevitable and extrapolated a continuing steady rise of ethnic conflict into the future.

Treating these contrasting views as distinct conceptual models, the current analysis evaluates their ability to generate out-of-sample predictions. Turning the clock back to the mid/late 1990s, we focus on the information that was available to these authors at the time of writing. Restricting the analysis to conflict incidence, we estimate two simple statistical models that seek to reflect Gurr's accommodative politics and the time trend predicted by the pessimists.

The accommodative politics model builds on a binary measure of 'political inclusion' as its key variable (see Model 3 in Tables 11.1 and 11.2). By contrast, in keeping with the doomsayers' extrapolations, the trend model includes 'calendar year' as the central explanatory variable. In addition, both models include count variables for 'peaceyears' and 'waryears' to account for duration dependence. In short, each model contains three independent variables, two of which are identical across both models. We then estimate these models drawing solely on the historical data that was observable at the time of the debate, that is, data covering the period 1946–1999.[20]

Combined with new data for the post-Cold War period, the parameter estimates derived from our 'training' dataset can be used to generate in-sample predictions for the period 1946–1999, as well as out-of-sample predictions for the period 2000–2017. For each group-year, this yields the predicted probability of conflict incidence. It is then possible to aggregate by summing all group-level predicted probabilities for a given year. This transforms the group-year predicted probabilities into a global yearly predicted *count* of the number of ethnic groups

[20] Results for a sample 1946–1994 are virtually identical for both models (results not shown).

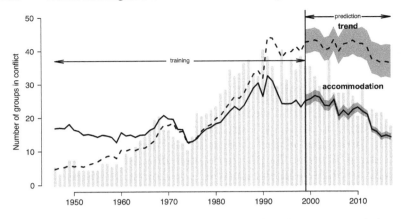

Figure 11.10 Out-of-sample predictions based on accommodative politics and trend

engaging in conflict. This is visualized in Figure 11.10. Here, the in-sample predictions from the training period are given by the dark solid line (accommodation), and the dashed line (trend). The out-of-sample predictions are provided with 95 percent confidence intervals.

The results are striking. The trend model performs better in-sample, mirroring relatively closely the rise in ethnic civil war until the early 1990s. By contrast, the accommodation model overpredicts conflict until the mid-1960s, while slightly underpredicting during the 1980s.[21] However, this performance pattern is sharply reversed for the out-of-sample prediction. Whereas the trend model vastly over-predicts the amount of ethnic civil war (orange), the theoretically driven specification focusing on ethnic exclusion correctly predicts a decline that started during the late 1990s and largely matches the empirical trend (gray barplot).[22] We emphasize that these predictions are theory-driven, thus allowing us to evaluate more closely the causal mechanisms behind the decline in conflict. In short, Figure 11.10 suggests that not only was Gurr right in anticipating a decline in frequency of ethnic civil war, but by pointing to the role of accommodation as a driving force, he appears to have been right for the right theoretical reasons.

---

[21] The root mean squared error (RMSE) is 4.53 for the accommodation model vs. 7.81 for the trend model, and the mean absolute percentage error (MAPE) is 0.27 vs. 0.77. RMSE $= \sqrt{\sum(y_i - \hat{y}_i)^2/n}$. MAPE $= \frac{1}{n}\sum|\frac{y_i-\hat{y}_i}{y_i}|$. Lower values indicate better predictions for both measures.

[22] RMSE: 13.73 vs. 5.37; MAPE: 0.51 vs. 0.16.

11.5   Conclusion

This chapter contributes to the recent literature on the decline-of-conflict hypothesis by focusing on the reasons for the decline of ethnic civil war. Our findings are largely compatible with Gurr's observations about "ethnic warfare on the wane" and stand in stark contrast to various pessimistic projections that were made in the early post-Cold War period and continue to be made about today's world. Along a number of empirical dimensions, we have found that this relatively optimistic perspective holds up well despite a surge in civil conflict in recent years. Ethnic, as opposed to non-ethnic, civil wars appear to have subsided after the mid-1990s, and this decline is at least partially attributable to an increase in governments' accommodative policies toward ethnic groups. We will return to the issue of non-ethnic conflict in the concluding chapter of this book.

Clearly, a lot more than intellectual history is at stake, as Gurr's arguments have major implications for our theoretical understanding of civil wars while offering clues about appropriate policies. Our findings support the general literature on grievances in civil wars that includes Gurr's own work (see, e.g., Gurr, 1993, 2000b) and many others (see, e.g., Cederman, Gleditsch and Buhaug, 2013; Horowitz, 1985; Petersen, 2002). The findings have relevance for policy in underlining how concessions to ethnic groups that have hitherto been generally badly treated appears to be associated with lower levels of conflict. This differs fundamentally from the alternative body of research that sees civil war exclusively as a problem of weak states, dismissing both the role of grievances for conflict as well as the potential for accommodation to help settle conflicts (e.g., Fearon and Laitin, 2003, 2004). Our analysis supports the conclusion that inclusive policies, whether based on group rights, autonomy, inclusion or democracy, constitute the safest path to peace (see also Mack, 2002).

Apart from the focus on ethnic civil conflict, our analysis has been limited to the period from the mid-1990s. A more profound treatment of the decline-of-war thesis would have to consider the entire post-WWII era as well. Preliminary analysis indicates that we get similar results if we extend the sample to the period from 1946. Yet, it could well be that the accommodation regime was less effective during the Cold War because power sharing and similar arrangements were simply not credible in the absence of strong third-party guarantees. Indeed, it would seem that power sharing in Bosnia-Herzegovina after the end of the Cold War would not have endured without massive external support. It is also possible that the pacifying behavioral norms flowing from the accommodation regime have lagged far behind their introduction. In any case, this chapter confirms Master Hypotheses 1a and 1b in a more recent context than the previous chapters, thus strengthening our confidence that shared power does secure peace.

These are important tasks for future research. For now, we conclude that there is ample evidence in support of Gurr's initial conjecture based on empirical data going back to the beginning of the post-Cold War period. Our findings reinforce more general claims about violence made by Pinker and Goldstein, but help go beyond sweeping claims and establish important reasons why ethnic civil conflict has declined. Furthermore, the results lend support to, and further illustrate more concretely, the consequences of the findings of Part II of the book.

12   Conclusions for Theory and Policy

In this concluding chapter of the book, we summarize what we have found in the previous chapters and discuss the theoretical significance and limitations of our findings. Furthermore, based on these reflections, we provide some recommendations for policy making.

12.1   Summarizing Our Main Results and Assessing Their Theoretical Significance

In this section we return to our master hypotheses that we introduced in Chapter 3. The most important overall finding relates to the effectiveness of power sharing (see Master Hypothesis 1). While the title of this book ends with a question mark, for most practical purposes this sign of punctuation can now be removed. Indeed, both in terms of governmental and territorial power sharing, we have found robust evidence that either set of practices tends, on average, to reduce conflict compared to situations characterized by their absence (see Master Hypotheses 1a and 1b respectively).

Of course, this main result reflects merely an average effect and thus by no means implies that power sharing should be viewed as a panacea that will always deliver peaceful outcomes. Indeed, there will always be cases and conditions where its pacifying impact is undermined and even reversed. Our analysis offers clues about situations where we would expect the challenges to be the most formidable.

All the same, our statistical approach casts doubt on sweeping, pessimistic accounts that view either governmental and/or territorial power sharing as uniformly conflict-inducing and damaging. In this sense, the main findings of this study invite us to be particularly skeptical about claims that compromise and negotiations will only make things worse and, therefore, one should, as a rule, "give war a chance" (Luttwak, 1999), while relying on ethnic "control" by one group (as analyzed by

Lustick, 1979), or, alternatively, opt for partition (e.g. Chapman and Roeder, 2007; Johnson, 2008; Kaufmann, 1996).

Our book considers systematically why such radical alternatives are likely to be counterproductive. In fact, the remaining master hypotheses are devoted to four main reasons why the literature has underestimated the usefulness of shared power as a pathway to peace.

According to Master Hypothesis 2, formal power-sharing institutions exert a pacifying effect primarily through the actors' practices. As shown by the empirical analysis in Chapter 5, the main channel from such institutions to peace runs through actually implemented and acted-on provisions while the *de jure* arrangements by themselves have little independent effect. The implementation of peace agreements, for example, is far from trivial, as illustrated by numerous deals that were never successfully implemented (Nilsson, 2008; Walter, 2002). Thus, the formal arrangements adopted in the 1990s in Zaire (Tull and Mehler, 2005*a*) were never implemented (see Strøm et al., 2017). Similarly, Masunungure (Forthcoming) describes in detail how the formal arrangements adopted in Zimbabwe were undermined by President Robert Mugabe (see also LeVan, 2011). Furthermore, even this perspective loses sight of the full potential of power-sharing practices, because there are also cases where inclusive behavior emerges even in the absence of formal institutions. Our results also indicate that such informal modes of power sharing contribute to peaceful outcomes, as illustrated by cases in Sub-Saharan Africa, such as Ghana or Benin.

Needless to say, we do not argue that formal institutions are inherently ineffective and should therefore not be studied. Quite on the contrary, their specific implementation is likely to affect outcomes in various ways as shown by Strøm et al. (2015). What we do question, however, is the growing tendency in the literature to focus exclusively on formal institutions, while paying little attention to actual behavior. As outlined in Chapter 2, this is a plea for a return to Lijphart's original focus on practices, although his own subsequent research drifted away from this priority in favor of a mostly institutional perspective. Our findings regarding the importance of practices are especially strong when it comes to governmental power sharing. As the practice of territorial power sharing almost by definition has to rely on some institutional bases, our measures of practices and formal institutions are much more closely linked.

The centrality-of-practices argument is presented in Master Hypothesis 2. A focus on practices, rather than a more narrowly construed analysis of formal institutions such as post-conflict agreements, encourages us to consider a wider spectrum of situations in which power sharing is likely to affect political actors' decision-making. In particular, it is crucial to analyze the link between power sharing and peace even before political violence erupts (see Master Hypothesis 3). Fortunately, in this book, we have been able to draw on general data about ethnic groups' access to power and their tendency to rebel that allow us to draw conclusions about the conflict-preventing impact of power sharing. In Chapter 7, we find that governmental power sharing is generally an effective mode of securing peace, across a wide range of scenarios, both before and after conflict. In Chapter 8, we detect a strong indication that territorial power sharing exerts a conflict-preventing effect before the first outbreak of armed civil conflict.

Because of these reasons, we feel inclined to second Gates et al.'s (2016) assessment that power sharing-studies need to be extended beyond the current focus on power sharing as an instrument of peace-keeping and peace-enforcement. Failing to heed this advice would lose sight of the overall effect of power sharing on outcomes of peace and war. This argument does not preclude more specialized studies of conflict resolution from being worthwhile. Yet, such analyses always need to be interpreted with an eye to the limitations as regards power sharing's full preventive potential, and the deeper question of causation pertaining to general reasons why power sharing is introduced in the first place. It goes without saying that studies that restrict the attention to the ending of conflict processes will never be able to offer a fully unbiased account of the effects of power sharing in the long run.

Perhaps the most important reason to study that entire cycle of power sharing and conflict, based on a full, global sample, relates to Master Hypothesis 4, which posits that power-sharing practices are endogenous to prospects of peace and risk of conflict. More specifically, we have expected governments to co-opt ethnic groups by offering them de facto power sharing wherever rebellion appears likely and the groups are relatively powerful and potentially threatening. Indeed, this is what we consistently find both with respect to government power sharing (see Chapters 6 and 7), and territorial power sharing (see Chapters 8 and 9).

If our findings had contradicted these expectations, the original inclusion-peace nexus would have been spurious. This is far from an academic eventuality, since scholars have outlined plausible conditions under which threatened governments may react with the opposite action, that is through risk diversion strategies that exclude potential "trouble-makers" rather than including them. As we have seen, Roessler (2016) outlines a scenario where African leaders prefer to throw opponents out of the cabinet even at the risk of triggering peripheral civil conflict rather than running the risk of a coup at the center of the country (see also Roessler, 2011). While our findings fail to find general support for such a logic of risk diversion even in post-colonial cases in Africa and Asia (see, e.g., Chapter 6), we identify a special case in which institutionally weak governments are confronted with extremely strong oppositional coalitions, as has been the case in the Syrian civil war since the early 2010s (see Chapter 7). In such cases, the governing elites are self-deterred from offering negotiations and compromise solutions because of an inherent fear of power sharing sliding into a condition of total power loss, with potentially fatal consequences for the incumbent elite.

As with endogeneity of governmental power sharing, we find very similar results for territorial power-sharing practices. Along the lines of Chapter 6, the analysis in Chapter 8 shows that autonomy and other types of territorial power sharing are more common in potentially conflictual instances than otherwise. Thus, in Chapter 9 we find that governments are more likely to counter secessionist claims with offers of autonomy if the claims come from a group that is excluded from power and resides in a settlement area that is endowed with oil. At the same time, due to reputation effects, governments are much less accommodating with respect to claims for autonomy and secession if their hold on power is challenged by a larger number of groups.

Finally, as stipulated by Master Hypothesis 5, we have argued that it is impossible to assess the consequences of territorial power sharing without paying attention to how such practices interact with governmental power sharing. In fact, the latter can be seen as a complement to the former by embedding potential secessionists in a framework that binds them and gives them a stake in the state's central institutions. Indeed, Chapter 8 offers clear evidence in favor of such a postulate. Especially in post-conflict situations, autonomy on its own may be "too little, too late" (see Master Hypothesis 3). As illustrated by Canada, Switzerland and Belgium, this double strategy has yielded peaceful outcomes in several multi-ethnic federations (McGarry and O'Leary, 2009). Arguably, the so far relatively stable Indian system that features both power sharing and democracy has also relied on this consociational combination (Lijphart, 1999), although this particular conclusion remains controversial (e.g. Wilkinson, 2000) and the sustainability of power sharing in India may now be in doubt (Girvin, 2020).

Together, the evidence speaking in favor of Master Hypotheses 2–5 goes a long way toward explaining why power-sharing skeptics have come to reject Master Hypotheses 1a and 1b. So far, we have summarized findings emanating from the chapters of Part II. Below, we will have reasons to return to the findings generated by the previous two chapters in the current part of the book. For now, we turn to a number of limitations and open questions that we have so far been unable to address.

12.2   Limitations and Ideas for Future Research

While analyzing power sharing and conflict, we have introduced a number of scope restrictions. The current section reminds us of these limitations and hints at extensions and research ideas that go beyond the current project.

The first obvious limitation concerns the dependent variable, which has remained conflict throughout the book. We maintain that this is a reasonable focus, since power sharing is typically resorted to primarily as an expedient to reduce or avoid conflict. All the same, shared power has consequences for a number of additional outcome dimensions, including perhaps most prominently democratic rule. In fact, as shown in Chapter 2, Lijphart (1969) introduced his original idea of consociationalism precisely to counter conventional majoritarian conceptions of democracy that dominated political science in the United States and the United Kingdom. A vivid debate about to what extent power sharing is truly compatible with different definitions of democracy has ensued with Lijphart, McGarry and O'Leary arguing forcefully in favor of such compatibility, on both normative and empirical grounds, and others, including, among others, Roeder and Rothchild (2005) and Horowitz (1985) against. For instance, a recent empirical study by Hartzell and Hoddie (2015) comes to the conclusion that power sharing helps generate, rather than undermines, democratic outcomes. Yet, other studies are less optimistic about the democratic qualities of shared power (for Africa, see Tull and Mehler, 2005a).

While this debate about the quality of governance is very important, our book deliberately sets the issue of democracy aside in order to focus on power sharing's pacifying effect. In particular, we refrain from normative assessments of power sharing practices or institutions. Thus, our main priority has been to evaluate whether power sharing has contributed to maintaining peace in Bosnia and Herzegovina while recognizing that the country's dysfunctional institutions fail to live up to anyone's standard of good governance. There is thus plenty of room for future research to take the quality of governance into account, especially since long-term stability hinges on the extent to which the broad majority of a country's population feels represented by its government. In fact, political stability, rather than conflict, both in terms of regime survival, and durability of state borders, belong to the outcome dimensions of interest. The economic performance constitutes another crucial dimension of system output that calls for systematic study (see for instance the related work on political and economic inclusion by Acemoglu and Robinson, 2006). Again, while considering these additional dimensions to be important in their own right, at the same time we posit that they are likely to be profoundly affected by the armed conflict. Democracy and development are both much harder to maintain in the presence of conflict.

Turning to the "treatment variable," we have introduced a number of limitations to concentrate the thematic scope of the book. Perhaps most importantly, we have analyzed power sharing along ethnic lines, while leaving aside non-ethnic cases. In principle, however, there is no reason to think that other deep divides, such as those emanating from classical ideological disagreements, for instance along the left-right axis, could not be subject to power sharing initiatives. In fact, the historical record offers a number of cases, including power sharing in Austria, Colombia, Cambodia, and El Salvador, where the main participants have been identified primarily in non-ethnic terms.

We believe that some of our fundamental findings concerning the advantages of decentralization are readily transferable to such cases (see, e.g., Cederman, 2019). All the same, more systematic research of such cases would be highly welcome. The most important large-N studies of power sharing, covering both pre- and post-conflict cases, do not draw an explicit distinction between ethnic and non-ethnic cases (see, e.g., Gates et al., 2016). There are, however, a series of informative case studies of non-ethnic cases of power sharing covering, for example, Colombia (Zukerman Daly, 2014), Cambodia (Leifer, 1992) and El Salvador (Wood, 2000). Thus future work should consider in a broader and systematic way how non-ethnic groups might become more peaceful through integration into the political system.

Other obvious limitations as regards the dimensions of power sharing include the realm within which power sharing is attempted. The current study has concentrated its analytical fire on political inclusion within the state's executive and delegation of power to its provinces because of their obvious centrality to the policy-making process, but additional types of political power sharing based on other branches of government also deserve to be systematically studied, including power sharing within regional and local bodies (see respectively Lacina, 2017; Vinson, 2017). In particular, power sharing within the military may offer important clues about the prospects of peace and conflict (see, e.g., Hoddie and Hartzell, 2003).

Beyond politics, power-sharing practices that promise to reduce other dimensions of horizontal inequality can also make a contribution to peace. For example, as illustrated by the successful experiment of power sharing in Aceh, revenue sharing has the potential of defusing ethno-regional resource conflicts (see, e.g., Wennmann and Krause, 2009). More broadly speaking, researchers and politicians have proposed arrangements in order to pool decision-making capacity in areas pertaining to resource allocation (e.g., Hartzell, 2019). Even in the area of cultural horizontal inequalities, such as the dimensions relating to language and religion, power sharing may offer compromise solutions that contribute to reducing conflict. Such measures include the recognition of minority languages, educational programs targeting disadvantaged groups, as well as extended symbolic recognition of religious holidays (see, e.g., Linder and Bächtiger, 2005; Langer and Stewart, 2013). In a particularly impressive, recent book, King and Samii (2020) offer a comprehensive account of how governments' recognition of ethnic groups' rights reduces conflict.

This brief discussion of additional inclusive dimensions makes immediately clear that the current monograph has only been able to offer an overall perspective that brackets specific details in terms of institutional features and their concomitant behavioral manifestations. The way that power-sharing practices are introduced is another important issue to consider.

Raising the question of how power sharing is initially introduced also points to the problem of overcoming resistance against ethnic majorities, or what Horowitz (2014) has termed the "adoption problem." The question of what makes such inclusive practices acceptable to the wider majority has received little previous attention in this book. Yet, an emerging literature on majority nationalism points to the destabilizing role of backlashes against power sharing, which may derail planned concessions to minorities and put pressure on governments to withdraw their existing group rights. A number of recent studies highlight the prevalence of majority backlashes against minority rights in the context of nation-building in the former socialist states of Central and Eastern Europe (Bustikova, 2014). Beyond these cases, an emerging literature analyzes instances of majority mobilization against Catalan autonomy rights in Spain (Cetrà and Swenden, 2020), the gradual advance of Hindu nationalism in India, which mobilizes against Muslim's citizenship rights and Kashmir's autonomy (Girvin, 2020), and the backlash between 1986 and 1995 among Anglophone Canadians against proposals for asymmetric autonomy for Québec (Basta, 2020).

Whereas many power-sharing initiatives originate within a particular political system, others are clearly imposed from abroad. Chapter 10 offers a discussion of the latter, but this analysis could in principle be combined with an assessment of how effective such "diffused" cases of power sharing are compared to endogenously developed norms and practices. In this respect, Chapter 11 yields some initial insights in that peace keeping operations appear to shorten ongoing conflict, but this result does not explicitly reveal if such external attempts came with power-sharing reforms. Finally, we have made no effort to separate cases where power sharing was introduced as a temporary way to (re)establish long-term democratic rule, as shown by the South African experience, from those where power sharing serves a permanent and inherent feature of the political system, perhaps best exemplified by Switzerland.

Having briefly discussed both the main outcome of interest and power sharing as its cause, we now consider the link between both. Building directly on our own previous work on inequality-induced ethnic grievances as important drivers of civil conflict, the theoretical framework of the current study proposes "anger reduction" as the central set of mechanisms that help to prevent and resolve conflict. Chapter 3 also introduces a complementary set of "fear-reducing" mechanisms to account for power sharing's pacifying effect. Rather than pitting these two mechanisms against each other, we have made an effort to connect both governmental and territorial power-sharing practices with both these mechanisms. This pragmatic theoretical perspective has the advantage of overcoming persistent theoretical opposition between explanations based on "grievances" and "opportunities" (Cederman and Vogt, 2017). While our theoretical arguments in Chapters 7 and 9 based on statistical strategic models make more room for an explicit opportunity logic in the spirit of Roessler's (2016) recent work, we have not made any systematic attempt to surgically operate out the empirical effect of either type of causal mechanism. Such an endeavor falls well beyond the scope of the present volume, but would be a worthy analytical objective of future studies since deeper knowledge about the way that shared power induces peace is of major policy relevance.

In terms of agency, our approach introduces simplifications in a Lijphartian manner in that we have treated entire ethnic groups as if they were unitary actors. While moving the research frontiers well beyond country-level studies that merely feature variables rather than actors, this formulation glosses over important within-group dynamics that may have considerable repercussions for peace and conflict. For example, radical elites within an ethnic group often resort to political violence in order to scupper peace agreements negotiated by more moderate members of the same group. Such "ethnic outbidding" through "spoilers" are known to undermine the effect of power sharing (e.g., Jarstad, 2008; Stedman, 1997) with recurrent or prolonged conflict as likely outcomes.

Furthermore, it is clear that Lijphart's group-reifying perspective relies on potentially elitist assumptions, implying that each group is well represented by its own group leaders who are equipped with a mandate to negotiate with other leaders in accordance with the "group's interests." It goes without saying that such a mandate can be abused and is not necessarily compatible with democratic representation. For this reason, some theorists argue that "true" power sharing has to be embedded within a democratic system. For example, McGarry and O'Leary (2009, 9) are reluctant to draw negative policy conclusions from the former Soviet Union and Yugoslavia and similar cases because these "failed federations were forced together. Thereafter, there was neither self-rule nor shared rule." Indeed, some observers regard contemporary power-sharing practices in Sub-Saharan Africa as a natural extension of clientilist governance that serves the corrupt interests of ethnic "chiefs" rather than the average members of their groups (see, e.g., Tull and Mehler, 2005*a*).

Finally, our empirical scope has been global, covering the entire period since World War II. While some of our illustrative cases and sensitivity analyses try to investigate whether our claims apply to subsets of this massive sample, the book thus covers a considerable chunk of human history that no doubt conceals plenty of spatial heterogeneity and temporal variation. For this reason, we very much welcome more contextually sensitive studies at lower levels of aggregation that are capable of offering more empirical nuance and precision than this book does. Research that looks more closely at the effects of power-sharing arrangements on groups that are not part of these arrangements would also be worthwhile. While our initial country-level analyses in Chapters 4 and 5 cover such effects, the subsequent chapters analyze the consequences of power-sharing arrangements for politically excluded groups.

Nevertheless, if interpreted with a healthy dose of caution, we believe that our general findings offer a reasonable first analytical cut that may prove more useful than highly aggregated "horse race" regressions confronting one set of proxy variables against another. In particular, by adopting a strategic perspective featuring ethnic groups as actors, we have made an effort to tease out the forward-looking logic inherent in many subnational decision-making situations. Yet, we will have to leave for future research to resolve whether our postulated mechanisms really hold once the black box is fully opened in specific cases.

12.3   Conclusions for Policy

Where do all these findings lead us in terms of policy making? Our main results align with the United Nations' Sustainable Development Goals (SDGs), especially with SDG 16, which promotes peace through inclusive institutions.[1] To some extent, our claims and results would kick in open doors with policy makers. Indeed, power sharing is typically considered to be a key component of any contemporary post-conflict compromise in deeply divided states (McCulloch and McEnvoy, 2018). In its explicit advocacy of inequality reduction through power sharing, the report on *Pathways for Peace* reflects this consensus closely (United Nations and World Bank, 2018). Nevertheless, Chapter 2 shows that the link between shared power and peace is still quite controversial among academic researchers. Thus, by presenting more solid evidence in favor of inclusive approaches to peace, we hope that the present book will help eliminate at least some reasons for this academic skepticism.

While criticism of specific implementations of power-sharing arrangements will no doubt still be called for, this book shows that there are good reasons for the positive consensus that currently dominates the policy-making community. By corroborating Master Hypotheses 1a and 1b, we have found strong support for a generally pacifying influence exerted by both governmental and territorial power sharing, sometimes in a powerful combination (see Master Hypothesis 5). As stated before, these are statistical results, which means that it would be a mistake to recommend practices of these kinds across the board without paying attention to the context of specific cases, but as power sharing of either kind serves as a reasonable starting point in the search for means to prevent or resolve civil conflict.

One of the most important findings concerns the importance of actually implemented provisions and behavioral practices rather than formal arrangements (see Master Hypothesis 2). The lesson to be learnt here is that general laws and peace agreements may turn out to be entirely ineffective if the parties fail to deliver in terms of implementation. This point is well known in the applied literature on conflict resolution (Jarstad and Nilsson, 2008; Walter, 2002), but appears to be less appreciated in the theoretical debates about the pros and cons of specific institutions. Thus, our book raises the question of how it can be ensured that power-sharing arrangements are implemented effectively,

---

[1] See www.un.org/sustainabledevelopment/peace-justice/.

and more generally, how power-sharing practices can be encouraged and fostered (e.g., Belmont, Mainwaring and Reynolds, 2002).

Hopefully, the current volume will also remind practitioners about the need to adopt a counterfactual perspective on inclusive practices. It is misleading and counterproductive to abandon power sharing as a pacifying tool merely because some power-sharing arrangements have been followed by political violence. The solid empirical support for Master Hypothesis 4 reminds us that power sharing is not introduced randomly, but governments resort to such practices if they expect trouble further down the line. Yet, this means that inclusive policies may be more effective than a simple correlation would lead us to think. After all, we will not abolish all hospitals just because people are more likely to die there than elsewhere. The reason, of course, is that the gravely ill are inclined to seek hospital treatment at a higher frequency than healthy individuals. By the same token, power sharing may still be our best hope to reduce conflict even if in many instances it turns out to be less successful, because the alternative of retaining an exclusive approach to governance is even worse.

Adopting an applied perspective based on recent trends, Chapter 11 confirms that liberal and inclusive practices have indeed brought significant peace dividends since the mid-1990s, despite a recent spike of non-ethnic political violence that has been mostly associated with the ascendance of jihadism in the 2010s. Thus, we should not let this recent surge of transnational conflict detract from the apparently successful pattern of decline in terms of ethnic civil conflict. Given the continued importance of this category of political violence, this is a positive development. Therefore, the priority has to be to maintain, and possibly even accelerate, this beneficial downward trend. The main way to sustain the decline of ethnic conflict centers on mechanisms relating to equality among ethnic groups, including the granting of governmental and territorial power sharing, but also of promoting group rights, democracy and multilateral intervention, such as peacekeeping. While measures promoting economic development and state capacity also help reduce conflict, progress toward pacification will not be effective without addressing issues relating to equality and justice. In these respects, our analysis is fully in line with the conclusions of the *Pathways for Peace* report (United Nations and World Bank, 2018).

More ominously, however, power sharing and other accommodative mechanisms and institutions that have been responsible for the decline of ethnic civil conflict are currently threatened by a surge of populist ethno-nationalism, which targets tolerance and inclusive policies toward ethnic minorities while at the same time opposing multilateral measures across the board. Should this political trend continue to entrench itself, it may well threaten the liberal regime that has brought about the reduction of ethnic civil conflict in the first place. There are good reasons to be apprehensive of a possible exclusivist chain reaction, because, as shown in Chapter 10, not only decisions to include – but also decisions to exclude – tend to diffuse across state borders. Thus, ethnic nationalism may be about to trigger a wider illiberal wave of exclusive practices than the one that appears to be already under way in Eastern Europe. The recommendation in this case would be to do whatever is possible to minimize the pernicious influence of ethnic nationalism by strengthening actors that oppose such a development and who speak out forcefully in favor of tolerance (Cederman, 2019).

Finally, this book lends strong support to the United Nation's new emphasis on prevention (see especially the findings testing Master Hypothesis 4). In line with the conclusions of the *Pathways for Peace* report, our analysis of consequences of political violence indicates that the best way of minimizing suffering is through preventive measures. Going well beyond direct death and physical destruction, such consequences involve devastating long-term damage to social networks, human capital and trust in institutions that reinforce each other in powerful ways through perpetuation of violence and out-migration. The recent developments in the Middle East show that such a negative equilibrium can be very difficult to overcome. Indeed, most of the countries in this region exhibit high levels of inequality and conflict together with disappointing economic growth and meddling by self-interested regional and external powers. It is unlikely that this region will see lasting progress toward peace without external pressure on the region's states, giving them incentives to opt for more inclusive policies and institutions, in particular by adopting both governmental and territorial power sharing. If enacted before violence breaks out, however, such measures could contribute to keeping the peace in less violent regions of the world.

Obviously, some conflicts are so intractable that no amount of power sharing will be able to curb ongoing violence and reduce flaming hatred. In such cases, partition may offer a viable alternative to shared power. Yet, as existing research has shown, the conditions under which such drastic solutions promise to be effective may be vanishingly rare (see, e.g., Sambanis and Schulhofer-Wohl, 2009). Since this book has not tried to grapple with this issue systematically, we have to leave it for future research. For the time being, however, we conclude that in most cases, both governmental and territorial power-sharing practices, preferably in combination, offer effective means to reduce the risk of conflict. This is a recommendation without any guarantee in specific cases, but as this book shows, the historical record leaves us with plenty of evidence to conclude that shared power does secure peace.

Bibliography

Acemoglu, Daron and James A. Robinson. 2006. *Economic Origins of Democracy and Dictatorship.* Cambridge: Cambridge University Press.

Acemoglu, Daron, Simon Johnson and James A. Robinson. 2001. "The Colonial Origins of Comparative Development: An Empirical Investigation." *American Economic Review* 91(5): 1369–1401.

Acharya, Amitav. 2004. "Whose Norms Matter? Norm Localization and Institutional Change in Asian Regionalism." *International Organization* 58(3): 239–275.

Adebajo, Adekeye. 2002. *Liberia's Civil War: Nigeria, ECOMOG, and Regional Security in West Africa.* Boulder, CO: Lynne Rienner.

Adeney, Katherine. 2008. "Constitutional Design and the Political Salience of 'Community' Identity in Afghanistan: Prospects for the Emergence of Ethnic Conflicts in the Post-Taliban Era." *Asia Survey* 48(4): 535–557.

Almond, Gabriel A. 1956. "Comparative Political Systems." *The Journal of Politics* 18(3): 391–409.

Anderson, Liam D. 2013. *Federal Solutions to Ethnic Problems: Accommodating Diversity.* Oxon: Routledge.

Andeweg, Rudy B. 2000. "Consociational Democracy." *Annual Review of Political Science* 3(1): 509–536.

Ankomah, Baffour and Stuart Price. 2005. "'How Britain Undermined Democracy in Africa': An Exclusive Account of Nigeria's First Elections." *New African* (440): 8–13.

Arieff, Alexis. 2009. "Still Standing: Neighbourhood Wars and Political Stability in Guinea." *Journal of Modern African Studies* 47(3): 331–348.

Asal, Victor, Mitchell Brown and Angela Dalton. 2012. "Why Split? Organizational Splits among Ethnopolitical Organizations in the Middle East." *Journal of Conflict Resolution* 56(1): 94–117.

Asante, Richard and Emmanuel Gyimah-Boadi. 2004. *Ethnic Structure, Inequality and Governance of the Public Sector in Ghana.* Geneva: UNRISD.

Auer, Raphael A. 2013. "Geography, Institutions, and the Making of Comparative Development." *Journal of Economic Growth* 18(2): 179–215.

Austin, Dennis. 1985. "The Ghana Armed Forces and Ghanaian Society." *Third World Quarterly* 7(1): 90–101.

Azarya, Victor. 2003. "Ethnicity and Conflict Management in Post-Colonial Africa." *Nationalism and Ethnic Politics* 9(3): 1–24.

Bah, Abu Bakarr. 2005. *Breakdowns and Reconstitution: Democracy, the Nation-state, and Ethnicity in Nigeria.* Lanham, MD: Lexington Books.

Bakke, Kristin M. 2015. *Decentralization and Intrastate Struggles: Chechnya, Punjab, and Québec.* Cambridge: Cambridge University Press.

Bakke, Kristin M. and Erik Wibbels. 2006. "Diversity, Disparity, and Civil Conflict in Federal States." *World Politics* 59: 1–50.

Bar-Tal, Daniel. 2013. *Intractable Conflicts: Socio-Psychological Foundations and Dynamics.* Cambridge: Cambridge University Press.

Barak, Oren. 2012. "Representation and Stability in Postwar Lebanon." *Representation* 48(3): 321–333.

Barry, Brian. 1975a. "The Consociational Model and Its Dangers." *European Journal of Political Research* 3: 393–412.

"Review Article: Political Accommodation and Consociational Democracy." *British Journal of Political Science* 5: 477–505.

Basta, Karlo. 2020. "Performing Canadian State Nationalism through Federal Symmetry." *Nationalism and Ethnic Politics* 26(1): 66–84.

Bauer, Otto. 1907. *Die Nationalitätenfrage und die Sozialdemokratie.* Vienna: Verlag der Wiener Volksbuchhandlung Ignaz Brand.

Beardsley, Kyle. 2011a. "Peacekeeping and the Contagion of Armed Conflict." *Journal of Politics* 73(4): 1051–1064.

The Mediation Dilemma. Ithaca, NY: Cornell.

Beardsley, Kyle, David E. Cunningham and Peter White. July 2017. "Resolving Civil Wars Before They Start: The UN Security Council and Conflict Prevention." *British Journal of Political Science* 47(3): 675–697. http://dx.doi.org/10.1017/S0007123415000307.

Beck, Nathaniel, Jonathan N. Katz and Richard Tucker. 1998. "Taking Time Seriously: Time-Series–Cross-Section Analysis with a Binary Dependent Variable." *American Journal of Political Science* 42(4): 1260–1288.

Bednar, Jenna. 2008. *The Robust Federation.* New York: Cambridge University Press.

2011. "The Political Science of Federalism." *Annual Review of Law and Social Science* 7: 269–288.

Beissinger, Mark R. 2007. "Structure and Example in Modular Political Phenomena: The Diffusion of Bulldozer/Rose/Orange/Tulip Revolutions." *Perspectives on Politics* 5(2): 259–276.

Bell, Sam R., Tavishi Bhasin, K. Chad Clay and Amanda Murdie. 2014. "Taking the Fight to Them: Neighborhood Human Rights Organizations and Domestic Protest." *British Journal of Political Science* 44(4): 853–875.

Belmont, Katharine, Scott Mainwaring and Andrew Reynolds. 2002. Introduction: Institutional Design, Conflict Management, and Democracy in Divided Societies. In *The Architecture of Democracy: Institutional Design, Conflict Management, and Democracy in the Late Twentieth Century,* ed. Andrew Reynolds. Oxford: Oxford University Press, pp. 1–11.

Beramendi, Pablo. 2007. Federalism. In *Oxford Handbook of Comparative Politics,* ed. Carles Boix and Susan C. Stokes. Oxford: Oxford University Press, pp. 752–782.

Beramendi, Pablo and Sandra León. 2015. Federalism. In *Routledge Handbook of Comparative Political Institutions*, ed. Jennifer Gandhi and Rubén Ruiz-Rufino. London and New York: Routledge, pp. 209–225.

Berchtold, André and Adrian Raftery. 2002. "The Mixture Transition Distribution Model for High-Order Markov Chains and Non-Gaussian Time Series." *Statistical Science* 17(3): 328–356.

Bergstrand, Jeffrey H. 1985. "The Gravity Equation in International Trade: Some Microeconomic Foundations and Empirical Evidence." *Review of Economics and Statistics* 67(3): 474–481.

Bermeo, Nancy. 2002. "A New Look at Federalism: The Import of Institutions." *Journal of Democracy* 13(2): 96–110.

Bernhard, Michael, Christopher Reenock and Timothy Nordstrom. 2004. "The Legacy of Western Overseas Colonialism on Democratic Survival." *International Studies Quarterly* 48(1): 225–250.

Bertrand, Jacques. 2000. "Peace and Conflict in the Southern Philippines: Why the 1996 Peace Agreement is Fragile." *Pacific Affairs* 73(1): 37–54.

Betz, Timm, Scott J. Cook and Florian M. Hollenbach. 2018. "On the Use and Abuse of Spatial Instruments." *Political Analysis* 26(4): 474–479.

Bhaumik, Subir. 2007. "Insurgencies in India's Northeast: Conflict, Co-option and Change." Report. East-West Center, Washington DC.

Bhavnani, Ravi and Dan Miodownik. 2009. "Ethnic Polarization, Ethnic Salience, and Civil War." *Journal of Conflict Resolution* 53(1): 30–49.

Binningsbø, Helga Malmin. 2013. "Power Sharing, Peace and Democracy: Any Obvious Relationships?" *International Area Studies Review* 16(1): 89–112.

Forthcoming. Perspectives on Powersharing. In *Fragile Bargains: Civil Conflict and Power-sharing in Africa*, ed. Scott Gates and Kaare Strøm. New York: Cambridge University Press.

Birnir, Jóhanna K., Jonathan Wilkenfeld, James D. Fearon, David D. Laitin, Ted Robert Gurr, Dawn Brancati, Stephen M. Saideman, Amy Pate and Agatha S. Hultquist. 2015. "Socially relevant ethnic groups, ethnic structure, and AMAR." *Journal of Peace Research* 52(1): 116–119.

Blanton, Robert, T. David Mason and Brian Athow. 2001. "Colonial Style and Post-Colonial Ethnic Conflict in Africa." *Journal of Peace Research* 38(4): 473–491.

Blattman, Christopher and Edward Miguel. 2010. "Civil War." *Journal of Economic Literature* 48(1): 3–57.

Bochsler, Daniel and Edina Szöcsik. 2013. "Building Inter-Ethnic Bridges or Promoting Ethno-Territorial Demarcation Lines? Hungarian Minority Parties in Competition." *Nationalities Papers* 41(5): 84–108.

Bodson, Thibaud and Neophytos G. Loizides. 2017. Consociationalism in the Brussels Capital Region: Dis-Proportional Representation and the Accommodation of National Minorities. In *Power-Sharing: Empirical and Normative Challenges*, ed. Allison McCulloch and Brendan O'Leary. London: Routledge, pp. 87–102.

Bogaards, Matthijs. 1998. "The Favourable Factors for Consociational Democracy: A Review." *European Journal of Political Research* 33: 475–496.

2014. *Democracy and Social Peace in Divided Societies: Exploring Consociational Parties.* New York: Palgrave Macmillan.

2019. "Formal and Informal Consociational Institutions: A Comparison of the National Pact and the Taif Agreement in Lebanon." *Nationalism and Ethnic Politics* 25(1): 27–42.

Boix, Carles. 2003. *Democracy and Redistribution.* Cambridge: Cambridge University Press.

Boix, Carles and Milan W. Svolik. 2013. "The Foundations of Limited Authoritarian Government: Institutions, Commitment, and Power-Sharing in Dictatorships." *The Journal of Politics* 75(2): 300–316.

Bonikowski, Bart. 2017. "Ethno-Nationalist Populism and the Mobilization of Collective Resentment." *British Journal of Sociology* 68(S1): S181–S213.

Boone, Catherine. 1998. "State Building in the African Countryside: Structure and Politics at the Grassroots." *The Journal of Development Studies* 34(4): 1–31.

Bormann, Nils-Christian. 2014. The Causes and Consequences of Ethnic Power-Sharing, ETH Zürich [Dr. Sc. Dissertation].

Bormann, Nils-Christian, Lars-Erik Cederman, Scott Gates, Benjamin A. T. Graham, Simon Hug, Kaare Strøm and Julian Wucherpfennig. 2019. "Power-sharing: Institutions, Behavior, and Peace." *American Journal of Political Science* 63(1): 84–100.

Boyes, William J, Dennis L Hoffman and Stuart A Low. 1989. "An Econometric Analysis of the Bank Credit Scoring Problem." *Journal of Econometrics* 40(1): 3–14.

Brambor, Thomas, William Roberts Clark and Matt Golder. 2006. "Understanding Interaction Models: Improving Empirical Analyses." *Political Analysis* 14(1): 63–82.

Brancati, Dawn. 2006. "Decentralization: Fueling the Fire or Dampening the Flames of Ethnic Conflict and Secessionism." *International Organization* 60(3): 651–685.

Braumoeller, Bear F. 2004. "Hypothesis Testing and Multiplicative Interaction Terms." *International Organization* 58(4): 807–820.

2013. "Is War Disappearing?". Paper presented at the Annual Meeting of the American Political Science Association, Chicago, IL.

Brubaker, Rogers. 1996. *Nationalism Reframed: Nationhood and the National Question in the New Europe.* Cambridge: Cambridge University Press.

Brubaker, Rogers and David D. Laitin. 1998. "Ethnic and Nationalist Violence." *Annual Review of Sociology* 24: 423–452.

Brusis, Martin. 2003. "The European Union and Interethnic Power-sharing Arrangements in Accession Countries." *Journal of Ethnopolitics and Minority Issues in Europe* (1): 1–19.

Buchanan, Allen. 2004. *Justice, Legitimacy, and Self-Determination: Moral Foundations for International Law.* Oxford: Oxford University Press.

Buhaug, Halvard, Lars-Erik Cederman and Jan Ketil Rød. 2008. "Disaggregating Ethno-Nationalist Civil Wars: A Dyadic Test of Exclusion Theory." *International Organization* 62(3): 531–551.

Bunce, Valarie. 1999. *Subversive Institutions: The Design and the Destruction of Socialism and the State*. Cambridge: Cambridge University Press.

2003. "Cooperation, Compromise, or Conflict: Three Models of Center-Regional Bargaining in Ethnofederal States." Paper presented at the annual meeting of the American Political Science Association Philadelphia Mariott Hotel, Philadelphia, PA (August 27–September 5, 2003).

2004. Federalism, Nationalism, and Secession: The Communist and Post-communist Experience. In *Federalism and Territorial Cleavages*, ed. Ugo M. Amoretti and Nancy Bermeo. Baltimore: The Johns Hopkins University Press, pp. 417–440.

Bustikova, Lenka. 2014. "Revenge of the Radical Right." *Comparative Political Studies* 47(12): 1738–1765.

Butenschøn, Nils A., Øyvind Stiansen and Kåre Vollan. 2015. *Power-Sharing in Conflict-Ridden Societies: Challenges for Building Peace and Democratic Stability*. Aldershot: Ashgate.

Buzan, Barry. 1991. *People, States, and Fear: An Agenda for International Security Studies in the Post-Cold War Era*. Boulder, CO: Lynne Rienner.

Callahan, Mary P. 2003. *Making Enemies: War and State Building in Burma*. Ithaca and London: Cornell University Press.

Calori, Roland, Michael Lubatkin, Philippe Very and John F. Veiga. 1997. "Modelling the Origins of Nationally-Bound Adminstrative Heritages: A Historical Institutional Analysis of French and British Firms." *Organizational Science* 8(6): 681–696.

Cammett, Melani and Edmund Malesky. 2012. "Power Sharing in Postconflict Societies: Implications for Peace and Governance." *Journal of Conflict Resolution* 56: 982–1016.

Carment, David, Martin Fischer, Joe Landry and Sean Winchester. 2016. Conflict Prevention: A Policy in Search of a Theory or a Theory in Search of a Policy? In *Routledge Handbook of Ethnic Conflict*, ed. Karl Cordell and Stefan Wolff. 2nd ed. London: Routledge.

Carrubba, Clifford J., Amy Yuen and Christopher Zorn. 2007. "In Defense of Comparative Statics: Specifying Empirical Tests of Models of Strategic Interaction." *Political Analysis* 15(4): 465–482.

Carter, David B. 2010. "The Strategy of Territorial Conflict." *American Journal of Political Science* 54(4): 969–987.

Carter, David B. and Curtis S. Signorino. 2010. "Back to the Future: Modeling Time Dependence in Binary Data." *Political Analysis* 18(3): 271–292.

Cederman, Lars-Erik. 2013. *Nationalism and Ethnicity*. 2nd ed. London: Sage.

2019. "Blood for Soil: The Fatal Temptations of Ethnic Politics." *Foreign Affairs* 98: 61–68.

Cederman, Lars-Erik and Luc Girardin. 2007. "Beyond Fractionalization: Mapping Ethnicity onto Nationalist Insurgencies." *American Political Science Review* 101(1): 173–185.

Cederman, Lars-Erik and Kristian Skrede Gleditsch. 2009. "Introduction to Special Issue on 'Disaggregating Civil War'." *Journal of Conflict Resolution* 53(4): 487–495.

Cederman, Lars-Erik, Kristian Skrede Gleditsch and Halvard Buhaug. 2013. *Inequality, Grievances and Civil War.* New York: Cambridge University Press.

Cederman, Lars-Erik, Kristian Skrede Gleditsch, Idean Salehyan and Julian Wucherpfennig. 2013. "Transborder Ethnic Kin and Civil War." *International Organization* 67: 389–410.

Cederman, Lars-Erik, Kristian Skrede Gleditsch and Julian Wucherpfennig. 2017. "Predicting the Decline of Ethnic Conflict: Was Gurr Right and For the Right Reasons?" *Journal of Peace Research* 54(2): 262–274.

2018. "The Diffusion of Inclusion: An Open-Polity Model of Ethnic Power Sharing." *Comparative Political Studies* 51(10): 1279–1313.

Cederman, Lars-Erik, Simon Hug and Lutz F. Krebs. 2010. "Democratization and Civil War: Empirical evidence." *Journal of Peace Research* 47(4): 377–394.

Cederman, Lars-Erik, Simon Hug, Andreas Schädel and Julian Wucherpfennig. 2015. "Territorial Autonomy in the Shadow of Future Conflict: Too Little, Too Late?" *American Politcal Science Review* 109(2): 354–370.

Cederman, Lars-Erik and Manuel Vogt. 2017. "Dynamics and Logics of Civil War." *Journal of Conflict Resolution* 61(9): 1992–2016.

Cederman, Lars-Erik, Nils B. Weidmann and Kristian Skrede Gleditsch. 2011. "Horizontal Inequalities and Ethno-Nationalist Civil War: A Global Comparison." *American Political Science Review* 105(3): 478–495.

Cederman, Lars-Erik, Nils B. Weidmann and Nils-Christian Bormann. 2015. "Triangulating Horizontal Inequality: Toward Improved Conflict Analysis." *Journal of Peace Research* 52(6): 806–821.

Cederman, Lars-Erik, Andreas Wimmer and Brian Min. 2010. "Why Do Ethnic Groups Rebel? New Data and Analysis." *World Politics* 62(1): 87–119.

Cetinyan, Rupen. 2002. "Ethnic Bargaining in the Shadow." *International Organization* 56(3): 645–677.

Cetrà, Daniel and Wilfried Swenden. 2020. "State nationalism and territorial accommodation in Spain and India." *Regional & Federal Studies* 31(1): 1–23.

Chapman, Thomas and Philip G. Roeder. 2007. "Partition as a Solution to Wars of Nationalism: The Importance of Institutions." *American Political Science Review* 101(4): 677–691.

Cheeseman, Nic. 2011. "The Internal Dynamics of Power-Sharing in Africa." *Democratization* 18(2): 336–365.

Chenoweth, Erica and Orion A. Lewis. 2013. "Unpacking Nonviolent Campaigns: Introducing the NAVCO 2.0 Dataset." *Journal of Peace Research* 50(3): 415–423.

Christin, Thomas and Simon Hug. 2012. "Federalism, the Geographic Location of Groups, and Conflict." *Conflict Management and Peace Science* 29(1): 93–121.

Coggins, Bridget. 2011. "Friends in High Places: International Politics and the Emergence of States from Secessionism." *International Organization* 65(03): 433–467.

Cohen, Frank S. 1997. "Proportional versus Majoritarian Ethnic Conflict Management in Democracies." *Comparative Political Studies* 30(5): 607–630.

Cohen, William B. 1971. The French Colonial Service in French West Africa. In *France and Britain in Africa*, ed. Prosser Gifford and WM. Roger Louis. New Haven and London: Yale University Press, pp. 777–784.

Collier, Paul and Anke Hoeffler. 2004. "Greed and Grievance in Civil Wars." *Oxford Economic Papers* 56: 663–695.

The Political Economy of Secession. In *Negotiating Self-Determination*, ed. Hurst Hannum and Eileen Babbitt. Lanham, MD: Lexington Books, pp. 37–59.

Collier, Paul, Lani Elliott, Havard Hegre, Anke Hoeffler, Marta Reynal-Querol and Nicholas Sambanis. 2003. *Breaking the Conflict Trap. Civil War and Development Policy*. New York: World Bank and Oxford University Press.

Connor, Walker. 1994. *Ethnonationalism: The Quest for Understanding*. Princeton, NJ: Princeton University Press.

Cornell, Svante E. 2002. "Autonomy as a Source of Conflict: Caucasian Conflicts in Theoretical Perspective." *World Politics* 54(2): 245–276.

Crowder, Michael. 1964. "Indirect Rule – French and British Style." *Africa* 34(3): 197–205.

1968. *West Africa under Colonial Rule*. Hutchinson, London.

Cunningham, David E., Kristian Skrede Gleditsch and Idean Salehyan. 2009. "It Takes Two: A Dyadic Analysis of Civil War Duration and Outcome." *Journal of Conflict Resolution* 53(4): 570–597.

Cunningham, Kathleen Gallagher. 2011. "Divide and Conquer or Divide and Concede: How Do States Respond to Internally Divided Separatists?" *American Political Science Review* 105: 275–297.

2014. *Inside the Politics of Self-Determination*. Oxford: Oxford University Press.

Cunningham, Kathleen Gallagher, Kristin M. Bakke and Lee Seymour. 2011. "Shirts Today, Skins Tomorrow: The Effects of Fragmentation on Conflict Processes in Self-Determination Disputes." *Journal of Conflict Resolution* 56(1): 67–93.

Curtis, Devon. 2006. The South African Approach to Peacebuilding in the Great Lakes Region of Africa. In *Constitutionalism and Democratic Transitions: Lessons from South Africa*, ed. Veronica Federico and Carlo Fusaro. Florence: Firenze University Press, pp. 153–176.

Dahl, Robert A. 1971. *Polyarchy: Participation and Opposition*. New Haven, CT: Yale University Press.

Davenport, Christian. 2007. "State Repression and Political Order." *Annual Review of Political Science* 10: 1–23.

de Sousa, José and Julie Lochard. 2012. "Trade and Colonial Status." *Journal of African Economies* 21(3): 409–439.

Deiwiks, Christa, Lars-Erik Cederman and Kristian Skrede Gleditsch. 2012. "Inequality and Conflict in Federations." *Journal of Peace Research* 49(2): 289–304.

Diamond, Larry. 1994a. *Class, Ethnicity and Democracy in Nigeria*. Syracuse: Syracuse University Press.

1994b. "Toward Democratic Consolidation." *Journal of Democracy* 5: 4–17.

Diehl, Paul F. and Daniel Druckman. 2012. "Peace Operation Success: The Evaluation Framework." *Journal of International Peacekeeping* 16: 209–225.

Diermeier, Daniel and Keith Krehbiel. 2003. "Institutionalism as a Methodology." *Journal of Theoretical Politics* 15(2): 123–144.

Dobbin, Frank, Beth A. Simmons and Geoffrey Garrett. 2006. "The Global Diffusion of Public Policies: Social Construction, Coercion, Competition, or Learning?" *Annual Review of Sociology* 33: 449–472.

Dower, Paul Castañeda and Shlomo Weber. 2015. Fiscal Federalism and Conflict Prevention. In *Handbook of Multilevel Finance*, ed. Ehtisham Ahmad and Giorgio Brosio. Cheltenham: Edward Elgar, pp. 585–616.

Doyle, Michael W. and Nicholas Sambanis. 2000. "International Peacebuilding: A Theoretical and Quantitative Analysis." *American Political Science Review* 94(4): 779–801.

  2006. *Making War and Building Peace*. Princeton, NJ: Princeton University Press.

Du Toit, Pierre. 1989. "Bargaining over Bargaining: Inducing the Self-Negating Prediction in Deeply Divided Societies – The Case of South Africa." *Journal of Conflict Resolution* 33(2): 210–230.

Dunn, D. Elwood. 2010. "Liberia: In Countries at the Crossroads.". *www.freedomhouse.org/report/countries-crossroads/2010/liberia*

Elbadawi, Ibrahim and Nicholas Sambanis. 2002. "How Much War Will We See? Explaining the Prevalence of Civil War." *Journal of Conflict Resolution* 463(3): 307–334.

Elkins, Zachary and John Sides. 2007. "Can Institutions Build Unity in Multi-ethnic States?" *American Political Science Review* 101(4): 693–708.

Englebert, Pierre. 2000. "Pre-Colonial Institutions, Post-Colonial States, and Economic Development in Tropical Africa." *Political Research Quarterly* 53(1): 7–36.

Englebert, Pierre, Stacy Tarango and Matthew Carter. 2002. "Dismemberment and Suffocation A Contribution to the Debate on African Boundaries." *Comparative Political Studies* 35(10): 1093–1118.

Ero, Comfort. 1995. "ECOWAS and the Subregional Peacekeeping in Liberia." *Journal of Humanitarian Assistance* 66. https://sites.tufts.edu/jha/archives/66.

Falch, Ashild, Ida Rudolfsen and Megan Becker. Forthcoming. Power-Sharing to Build Peace? A Review of Power-sharing as a Peacebuilding Strategy in Burundi. In *Fragile Bargains: Civil Conflict and Power-sharing in Africa*, ed. Scott Gates and Kaare Strøm. New York: Cambridge University Press.

Fazal, Tanisha M. 2014. "Dead Wrong? Battle Deaths, Military Medicine, and Exaggerated Reports of War's Demise." *International Security* 39(1): 95–125.

Fearon, James D. 1995. "Rationalist Explanations for War." *International Organization* 49: 379–414.

  1998. Commitment Problems and the Spread of Ethnic Conflict. In *The International Spread of Ethnic Conflict*, ed. David A. Lake and Donald Rothchild. Princeton, NJ: Princeton University Press.

  2004. "Separatist Wars, Partition, and World Order." *Security Studies* 13(4): 394–415.

2010. "Governance and Civil War Onset." World Bank, World Development Report 2011, Washington, DC.

Fearon, James D. and David D. Laitin. 2003. "Ethnicity, Insurgency, and Civil War." *American Political Science Review* 97(1): 1–17.

2004. "Neotrusteeship and the Problem of Weak States." *International Security* 28(4): 5–43.

Fearon, James D., Kimuli Kasara and David D. Laitin. 2007. "Ethnic Minority Rule and Civil War Onset." *American Political Science Review* 101(1): 187–193.

Filippov, Mikhail, Peter Ordeshook and Olga Shvetsova. 2004. *Designing Federalism: A Theory of Self-Sustainable Federal Institutions*. Cambridge: Cambridge University Press.

Finnemore, Martha and Kathryn Sikkink. 1998. "International Norm Dynamics and Political Change." *International Organization* 52(4): 887–917.

Forsberg, Erika. 2013. "Do Ethnic Dominoes Fall? Evaluating Domino Effects of Granting Territorial Concessions to Separatist Groups." *International Studies Quarterly* 57(2): 329–340.

Fortna, Page V. and Lisa Morje Howard. 2008. "Pitfalls and Prospects in the Peacekeeping Literature." *Annual Review of Political Science* 11: 283–901.

Francois, Patrick, Ilia Rainer and Francesco Trebbi. 2015. "How Is Power Shared in Africa?" *Econometrica* 83(2): 465–503.

Gagnon, V. P. Jr. 2004. *The Myth of Ethnic War: Serbia and Croatia in the 1990s*. Ithaca, NY: Cornell University Press.

Gandhi, Jennifer. 2008. *Political Institutions under Dictatorship*. Cambridge: Cambridge University Press.

Gates, Robert M. 1993. "No Time to Disarm." *Wall Street Journal*, 23 August, A10.

Gates, Scott, Benjamin A.T. Graham, Yonatan Lupu, Håvard Strand and Kaare Strøm. 2016. "Powersharing, Protection, and Peace." *Journal of Politics* 78(2): 512–526.

Gates, Scott and Kaare Strøm. Forthcoming-*a*. The Appeals and Perils of Power-Sharing. In *Fragile Bargains: Civil Conflict and Power-sharing in Africa*, ed. Scott Gates and Kaare Strøm. New York: Cambridge University Press.

Gates, Scott and Kaare Strøm. Forthcoming-*b*. The Diversity and Fragility of Power-Sharing Agreements in Africa. In *Fragile Bargains: Civil Conflict and Power-sharing in Africa*, ed. Scott Gates and Kaare Strøm. New York: Cambridge University Press.

Geertz, Clifford. 1963. The Integrative Revolution: Primordial Sentiments and Civil Politics in the New States. In *Old Societies and New States: The Quest for Modernity in Asia and Africa*, ed. Clifford Geertz. New York: Free Press.

Gellner, Ernest. 1983. *Nations and Nationalism*. Ithaca, NY: Cornell University Press.

Gelman, Andrew and Donald B Rubin. 1992. "Inference from Iterative Simulation Using Multiple Sequences." *Statistical Science* 7(4): 457–472.

Gelman, Andrew and Jennifer Hill. 2007. *Data Analysis Using Regression and Multilevel/Hierarchical Models*. New York: Cambridge University Press.

Gerdes, Felix. 2011. "Liberia's Post-War Elite: A New Era of Inclusive Ownership or Old Wine in New Bottles?". Arbeitspapier 1/2011, University of Hamburg.

Gerring, John, Daniel Ziblatt, Johan van Gorp and Julián Arévalo. 2011. "An Institutional Theory of Direct and Indirect Rule." *World Politics* 63(3): 377–433.

Ghai, Yash P. 2000. Ethnicity and Autonomy: A Framework for Analysis. In *Autonomy and Ethnicity: Negotiating Competing Claims in Multi-Ethnic States*, ed. Yash P. Ghai. Cambridge: Cambridge University Press, pp. 1–26.

Girvin, Brian. 2020. "From Civic Pluralism to Ethnoreligious Majoritarianism: Majority Nationalism in India." *Nationalism and Ethnic Politics* 26(1): 27–45.

Glassmyer, Katherine and Nicholas Sambanis. 2008. "Rebel-Military Integration and Civil War Termination." *Journal of Peace Research* 45(3): 365–384.

Gleditsch, Kristian Skrede. 2002. "Expanded Trade and GDP Data, 1946–99." *Journal of Conflict Resolution* 46(5): 712–724.

Gleditsch, Kristian Skrede and Andrea Ruggeri. 2010. "Political Opportunity Structures, Democracy, and Civil War." *Journal of Peace Research* 47(3): 299–310.

Gleditsch, Kristian Skrede, Idean Salehyan and Ken Schultz. 2008. "Fighting at Home, Fighting Abroad - How Civil Wars Lead to International Disputes." *Journal of Conflict Resolution* 52(4): 479–506.

Gleditsch, Kristian Skrede and Michael D. Ward. 2006. "The Diffusion of Democracy and the International Context of Democratization." *International Organization* 60(4): 911–933.

Gleditsch, Kristian Skrede and Steve Pickering. 2014. "Wars Are Becoming Less Frequent: A Response to Harrison and Wolf." *Economic History Review* 67(1): 214–230.

Gleditsch, Nils Petter. 2008. "The Liberal Moment Fifteen Years On." *International Studies Quarterly* 52(4): 691–712.

Gleditsch, Nils Petter, Peter Wallensteen, Mikael Eriksson, Margareta Sollenberg and Håvard Strand. 2002. "Armed Conflict 1946–2001: A New Dataset." *Journal of Peace Research* 39(5): 615–637.

Gloppen, Siri. Forthcoming. Power-Sharing in a Dominant Party State: Fifteen years of Democracy in South Africa. In *Fragile Bargains: Civil Conflict and Power-sharing in Africa*, ed. Scott Gates and Kaare Strøm. New York: Cambridge University Press.

Goemans, H.E. (Henk), Kristian Skrede Gleditsch and Giacomo Chiozza. 2009. "Introducing Archigos: A Data Set of Political Leaders." *Journal of Peace Research* 46(2): 269–283.

Goldstein, Joshua S. 2002. "The Worldwide Lull in War." *Christian Science Monitor*, 14 May, p. 9.

2011. *Winning the War on War: The Decline of Armed Conflict Worldwide*. New York: Penguin.

Goodwin, Jeff. 1997. "State-Centered Approaches to Social Revolutions: Strength and Limitations of a Theoretical Tradition." In *Theorizing Revolutions*, ed. John Foran. London: Routledge, pp. 9–35.

Gourevitch, Peter Alexis. 1979. "The Reemergence of 'Peripheral Nationalisms':
Some Comparative Speculations on the Spacial Distribution of Political
Leadership and Economic Growth." *Comparative Studies in Society and
History* 21(3): 303–322.

Graham, Benjamin A.T., Michael K. Miller and Kaare W. Strøm. 2017. "Safe-
guarding Democracy: Powersharing and Democratic Survival." *American
Political Science Review* 111(4): 686–704.

Green, Elliott. 2011. "Decentralization and Political Opposition in Contemporary Africa: Evidence from Sudan and Ethiopia." *Democratization* 18(5):
1087–1105.

Griffiths, Ryan D. 2015. "Between Dissolution and Blood: How Administrative
Lines and Categories Shape Secessionist Outcomes." *International Organization* 69(3): 731–751.

2016. *Age of Secession*. Cambridge: Cambridge University Press.

Grigoryan, Arman. 2012. "Ethnofederalism, Separatism, and Conflict: What We
Have Learned From the Soviet and Yugoslav Experiences." *International
Political Science Review* 33(5): 520–538.

2015. "Concessions or Coercion? How Governments Respond to Restive
Ethnic Minorities." *International Security* 39(4): 170–207.

Grzymala-Busse, Anna. 2010. "The Best Laid Plans: The Impact of Informal
Rules on Formal Institutions in Transitional Regimes." *Studies in Comparative International Development* 45(3): 311–333.

Guha, Ramachandra. 2008. *India After Gandhi: The History of the World's Largest
Democracy*. London: Pan Macmillan.

Gurr, Ted Robert. 1993. *Minorities at Risk: A Global View of Ethnopolitical
Conflicts*. Washington, DC: United States Institute of Peace Press.

1994. "Peoples Against States: Ethnopolitical Conflict and the Changing
World System: 1994 Presidential Address." *International Studies Quarterly*
38(3): 347–377.

2000*a*. "Ethnic Warfare on the Wane." *Foreign Affairs* 79(3): 52–65.

2000*b*. *Peoples Versus States: Minorities at Risk in the New Century*. Washington,
DC: United States Institute of Peace Press.

Gurr, Ted Robert and Will H. Moore. 1997. "Ethopolitical Rebellion: A Cross-
Sectional Analysis of the 1980s with Risk Assessment for the 1990s."
American Journal of Political Science 41(4): 1079–1103.

Hale, Henry E. 2008. *The Foundations of Ethnic Politics: Separatism of States and
Nations in Eurasia and the World*. New York: Cambridge University Press.

Hall, Peter A. and Rosemary C. R. Taylor. 1996. "Political Science and the
Three New Institutionalisms." *Political Studies* 44: 936–957.

Hanmer, Michael J. and K. Ozan Kalkan. 2013. "Behind the Curve: Clarifying
the Best Approach to Calculating Predicted Probabilities and Marginal
Effects from Limited Dependent Variable Models." *American Journal of
Political Science* 57(1): 263–277.

Hariri, Jacob Gerner. 2012. "The Autocratic Legacy of Early Statehood."
American Political Science Review 106(03): 471–494.

Harrison, Mark and Nikolaus Wolf. 2012. "The Frequency of Wars." *Economic
History Review* 65: 1055–1076.

Hartzell, Caroline. 2019. Economic Power Sharing: Potentially Potent ... but Likely Limited. In *Power Sharing and Power Relations After Civil War*, ed. Caroline A. Hartzell and Andreas Mehler. Boulder, CO: Lynne Rienner pp. 125–146.

Hartzell, Caroline A. and Andreas Mehler, eds. 2019. *Power Sharing and Power Relations After Civil War*. Boulder, CO: Lynne Rienner.

Hartzell, Caroline A. and Matthew Hoddie. 2003. "Institutionalizing Peace: Power Sharing and Post-civil Conflict Management." *American Journal of Political Science* 47(2): 318–332.

2007. *Crafting Peace: Power-Sharing Institutions and the Negotiated Settlement of Civil Wars*. University Park: Pennsylvania State University Press.

2015. "The Art of the Possible: Power Sharing and Post-Civil War Democracy." *World Politics* 67(1): 37–71.

Hartzell, Caroline, Matthew Hoddie and Donald Rothchild. 2001. "Stabilizing the Peace After Civil War: An Investigation of Some Key Variables." *International Organization* 55(1): 183–208.

Hechter, Michael. 1975. *Internal Colonialism: The Celtic Fringe in British National Development*. Berkeley: University of California Press.

2000. *Containing Nationalism*. Oxford: Oxford University Press.

2004. Containing Ethnonationalist Violence. In *Facing Ethnic Conlicts: Toward a New Realism*, ed. Andreas Wimmer, Richard J. Goldstone, Donald L. Horowitz, Ulrike Joras and Conrad Schetter. Lanham, MD: Rowman and Littlefield 283–300.

Hegre, Håvard, Lisa Hultman and Hvard Mokleiv Nygård. 2019. "Evaluating the Conflict-Reducing Effect of UN Peacekeeping Operations." *Journal of Politics* 81: 215–232.

Hegre, Håvard and Nicholas Sambanis. 2006. "Sensitivity Analysis of Empirical Results on Civil War Onset." *Journal of Conflict Resolution* 50: 508–535.

Helmke, Gretschen and Steven Levitsky. 2004. "Informal Institutions and Comparative Politics: A Research Agenda." *Perspectives on Politics* 2(4): 725–740.

Henisz, Witold J. 2000. "The Institutional Environment for Economic Growth." *Economics & Politics* 12(1): 1–31.

Hensel, Paul R. 2009. "ICOW Colonial History Data Set, version 0.4." *Online:* www.icow.org/colhist.html *(15/08/2012)* .

Herbst, Jeffrey. 1989. "The Creation and Maintenance of National Boundaries in Africa." *International Organization* 43(04): 673–692.

2000. *States and Power in Africa: Comparative Lessons in Authority and Control*. Princeton, NJ: Princeton University Press.

Heston, Alan, Robert Summers and Bettina Aten. 2011. "Penn World Table Version 7.0." Center for International Comparisons of Production, Income and Prices at the University of Pennsylvania.

Hirschman, Albert O. 1964. "The Paternity of an Index." *American Economic Review* 54(5): 761–762.

Hoddie, Matthew and Caroline Hartzell. 2003. "Civil War Settlements and the Implementation of Military Power-Sharing Arrangements." *Journal of Peace Research* 40(3): 303–320.

Hoddie, Matthew and Caroline Hartzell. 2005. Power Sharing in Peace Settlements: Initiating the Transition from Civil War. In *Sustainable Peace: Power and Democracy After Civil Wars*, ed. Philip G. Roeder and Donald Rothchild. Ithaca, NY: Cornell University Press, pp. 83–106.

Horowitz, Donald L. 1985. *Ethnic Groups in Conflict*. Berkeley: University of California Press.

2002. Constitutional Design: Proposals versus Processes. In *The Architecture of Democracy: Constitutional Design, Conflict Management, and Democracy*, ed. Andrew Reynolds. Oxford: Oxford University Press.

2013. *Constitutional Change and Democracy in Indonesia*. New York: Cambridge University Press.

2014. "Ethnic Power Sharing: Three Big Problems." *Journal of Democracy* 25(2): 5–20.

Hug, Simon. 2013. "The Use and Misuse of the 'Minorities at Risk' Project." *Annual Review of Political Science* 16: 191–208.

Huntington, Samuel P. 1991. *The Third Wave: Democratization in the Late Twentieth Century*. Norman: Oklahoma University Press.

1993. "The Clash of Civilizations?" *Foreign Affairs* 72(3): 22–49.

Hunziker, Philipp. 2014. "Civil Conflict in Petroleum Producing Regions." Dissertation ETH Zurich.

Ikejiaku, Brian-Vincent. 2009. "'Crime', Poverty, Political Corruption and Conflict in Apartheid and Post Apartheid South Africa: The Implications on Economic Development." *African Journal of Political Science and International Relations* 3: 451–59.

Ikporukpo, C.O. 1996. "Federalism, Political Power, and the Economic Power Game: Conflict over Access to Petroleum Resources in Nigeria." *Environment and Planning C: Government and Policy* 14(2): 159–177.

Imai, Kosuke, Luke Keele and Dustin Tingley. 2010. "A General Approach to Causal Mediation Analysis." *Psychological Methods* 15(4): 309–334.

Imai, Kosuke, Luke Keele, Dustin Tingley and Teppei Yamamoto. 2011. "Unpacking the Black Box: Learning about Causal Mechanisms from Experimental and Observational Studies." *American Political Science Review* 105(4): 765–789.

International Crisis Group. 2007. Nigeria: Ending Unrest in the Niger Delta. Technical report.

Jaggers, Keith and Ted Robert Gurr. 1995. "Tracking Democracy's 'Third Wave' with the Polity III data." *Journal of Peace Research* 32(4): 469–82.

Jarstad, Anna K. 2008. Power Sharing: Former Enemies in Joint Government. In *From War to Democracy: Dilemmas of Peacebuilding*, ed. Anna K. Jarstad and Timothy D. Sisk. Cambridge: Cambridge University Press.

Jarstad, Anna K. and Desirée Nilsson. 2008. "From Words to Deeds: The implementation of Power-Sharing Pacts in Peace Accords." *Conflict Management and Peace Science* 25: 208–223.

Jarstad, Anna K. and Timothy D. Sisk. 2008. *From War to Democracy: Dilemmas of Peacebuilding*. Cambridge: Cambridge University Press.

Jenkins, J. Craig and Augustine J. Kposowa. 1992. "The Political Origins of African Military Coups: Ethnic Composition, Military Centrality, and the Struggle over the Post-Colonial State." *International Studies Quarterly* 36(3): 271–292.

Jenne, Erin. 2006. National Self-Determination. A deadly mobilizing device. In *Negotiating Self-Determination*, ed. Hurst Hannum and Eileen F. Babbitt. Lanham, MD Lexington Books, pp. 7–36.

Jenne, Erin K., Stephen M. Saideman and Will Lowe. 2007. "Separatism as a Bargaining Posture: A Panel Data Analysis of Minority Demand." *Journal of Peace Research* 44(5): 537–556.

Johnson, Carter. 2008. "Partitioning to Peace: Sovereignty, Demography and Ethnic Civil Wars." *International Security* 32(4): 140–170.

Kalyvas, Stathis N. 2006. *The Logic of Violence in Civil War*. Cambridge: Cambridge University Press.

Kaplan, Robert D. 1994. "The Coming Anarchy." *Atlantic Monthly* 273(2): 44–76.

Kaufmann, Chaim. 1996. "Possible and Impossible Solutions to Ethnic Conflict." *International Security* 20(4): 136–175.

Kelley, Judith G. 2004. *Ethnic Politics in Europe: The Power of Norms and Incentives*. Princeton, NJ: University of Princeton Press.

Kenny, Paul D. 2015. "The Origins of Patronage Politics: State Building, Centrifugalism, and Decolonization." *British Journal of Political Science* 45: 141–171.

King, Elisabeth and Cyrus Samii. 2020. *Diversity, Violence, and Recognition: How Recognizing Ethnic Identity Promotes Peace*. Oxford: Oxford University Press.

King, Gary, James Honaker, Anne Joseph and Kenneth Scheve. 2001. "Analyzing Incomplete Political Science Data: An Alternative Algorithm for Multiple Imputation." *American Political Science Review* 95(MAR, 1): 49–69.

Kopstein, Jeffrey S. and David A. Reilly. 2000. "Geographic Diffusion of the Transformation of the Postcommunist World." *World Politics* 53(1): 1–37.

Kreutz, Joakim. 2015. "Human rights, Geostrategy, and EU Foreign Policy, 1989-2008." *International Organization* 69(1): 195–217.

Kuran, Timur. 1991. "Now Out of Never: The Element of Surprise in the East European Revolution of 1989." *World Politics* 44: 7–48.

1998. Ethnic Dissimilation and Its International Diffusion. In *The International Spread of Ethnic Conflict*, ed. David A. Lake and Donald Rothchild. Princeton, NJ: Princeton University Press.

Kymlicka, Will. 1998. Is Federalism a Viable Alternative to Secession? In *Theories of Secession*, ed. Percy Lehning. London: Routledge, pp. 111–150.

Lacina, Bethany. 2009. "The Problem of Political Stability in Northeast India: Local Ethnic Autocracy and the Rule of Law." *Asian Survey* 49(6): 998–1020.

2014. "How Governments Shape the Risk of Civil Violence: India's Federal Reorganization, 1950–1956." *American Journal of Political Science* 58(3): 720–738.

2015. "Periphery Versus Periphery: The Stakes of Separatist War." *Journal of Politics* 77(3): 692–706.

2017. *Rival Claims: Ethnic Violence and Territorial Autonomy under Indian Federalism*. Ann Arbor: University of Michigan Press.

Laitin, David D. 1987. "South Africa: Violence, Myths, and Democratic Reform." *World Politics* 39: 259–279.

Lake, David A. and Donald Rothchild. 2005. Territorial Decentralization and Civil War Settlements. In *Sustainable Peace: Power and Democracy After Civil Wars*, ed. Philip G. Roeder and Donald Rothchild. Ithaca, NY: Cornell University Press, pp. 109–132.

Lange, Matthew. 2004. "British Colonial Legacies and Political Development." *World Development* 32(6): 905–922.

2009. *Lineages of Despotism and Development.* Chicago and London: The University of Chicago Press.

Lange, Matthew, James Mahoney and Matthias vom Hau. 2006. "Colonialism and Development: A Comparative Analysis of Spanish and British Colonies." *American Journal of Sociology* 111(5): 1412–62.

Lange, Matthew and Matthew Dawson. 2009. "Dividing and Ruling the World? A Statistical Test of the Effects of Colonialism on Postcolonial Violence." *Social Forces* 88(2): 785–818.

Langer, Armin and Frances Stewart. 2013. "Horizontal Inequalities and Violent Conflict: Conceptual and Empirical Linkages." Working Paper No. 14, Center for Research on Peace and Development, Leuven.

Lauermann, John. 2009. "Amazigh Nationalism in the Maghreb." *The Geographical Bulletin* 50: 37–55.

Le Vine, Victor T. 2004. *Politics in Francophone Africa.* Boulder: Lynne Rienner.

Leemann, Lucas. 2014. "Strategy and Sample Selection: A Strategic Selection Estimator." *Political Analysis* 22(3): 374–397.

Lehmbruch, Gerhard. 1967. *Proporzdemokratie: Politisches System und politische Kultur in der Schweiz und in Österreich.* Tübingen: Mohr.

1974. A Non-Competitive Pattern of Conflict Management in Liberal Democracies: The Case of Switzerland, Austria and Lebanon. In *Consociational Democracy: Political Accommodation in Segmented Societies*, ed. K McRae. Toronto: McClelland & Stewart, pp. 90–97.

Leifer, Michael. 1992. "Power-Sharing and Peacemaking in Cambodia?" *SAIS Review* 12(1): 139–153.

Lemarchand, René. 2006. "Consociationalism and Power Sharing in Africa: Rwanda, Burundi, and the Democratic Republic of the Congo." *African Affairs* 106: 1–20.

2007. "Consociationalism and Power Sharing in Africa: Rwanda, Burundi, and the Democratic Republic of the Congo." *African Affairs* 106(402): 1–20.

LeVan, Carl. 2011. "Power Sharing and Inclusive Politics in Africa's Uncertain Democracies." *Governance: An International Journal of Policy, Administration, and Institutions* 24: 31–53.

Levy, Jack S. and William R. Thompson. 2013. "The Decline of War? Multiple Trajectories and Diverging Trends." *Review of International Studies* 15: 411–416.

Lewis, David, John Heathershaw and Nick Megoran. 2018. "Illiberal Peace? Authoritarian Modes of Conflict Management." *Cooperation and Conflict* 53(4): 486–506.

Lewis, Martin Deming. 1962. "One Hundred Million Frenchmen: The "Assim-ilation" Theory in French Colonial Policy." *Comparative Studies in Society and History* 4(2): 129–153.

Lijphart, Arend. 1968. "Typologies of Democratic Systems." *Comparative Political Studies* 1(1): 3–44.

1969. "Consociational Democracy." *World Politics* Xxi(2): 207–225.

1975. *The Politics of Accommodation: Pluralism and Democracy in the Netherlands.* Berkeley: University of California Press.

1977. *Democracy in Plural Societies.* New Haven, CT: Yale University Press.

1984. *Democracies: Patterns of Majoritarian and Concensus Government in Twenty-One Countries.* New Haven, CT: Yale University Press.

1985*a*. "Non-Majoritarian Democracy: A Comparison of Federal and Conso-ciational Theories." *Publius: The Journal of Federalism* 15(2): 3–15.

1985*b*. *Power-Sharing in South Africa.* Berkeley: University of California Press.

1996. "The Puzzle of Indian Democracy: A Consociational Interpretation." *American Political Science Review* 90(2): 258–268.

1999. *Patterns of Democracy: Government Forms and Performance in Thirty-Six Countries.* New Haven, CT: Yale University Press.

2002. The Wave of Power-Sharing Democracy. In *The Architecture of Democracy: Constitutional Design, Conflict Management, and Democracy,* ed. Andrew Reynolds. Oxford: Oxford University Press.

Lindberg, Staffan I. 2006. *Democracy and Elections in Africa.* Baltimore, MD: Johns Hopkins University Press.

Lindemann, Stefan. 2011. "Just Another Change of Guard? Broad-Based Politics and Civil War in Museveni's Uganda." *African Affairs* 110: 387–416.

Linder, Wolf and André Bächtiger. 2005. "What Drives Democratisation in Asia and Africa?" *European Journal of Political Research* 44: 861–880.

Lipset, Seymour Martin. 1960. *Political Man: The Social Bases of Politics.* New York: Doubleday.

Luckham, Robin. 1996. "Crafting Democratic Control over the Military: A Comparative Analysis of South Korea, Chile and Ghana." *Democratization* 3(3): 215–45.

Lugard, Lord Frederick J.D. 1922. *The Dual Mandate in British Tropical Africa.* London: Frank Caess.

Lunn, David, Chris Jackson, Nicky Best, Andrew Thomas and David Spiegel-halter. 2012. *The BUGS book: A Practical Introduction to Bayesian Analysis.* CRC Press.

Lustick, Ian. 1979. "Stability in Deeply Divided Societies: Consociationalism versus Control." *World Politics* 31(3): 325–344.

1997. "Lijphart, Lakatos, and Consociationalism: Almond and Lijphart: Competing Research Programs in an Early-Lakatosian Mode." *World Politics* 50(1): 88–117.

Lustick, Ian S., D. Miodownik and R.J. Eidelson. 2004. "Secessionism in Mul-ticultural States: Does Sharing Power Prevent or Encourage It?" *American Political Science Review* 98(2): 209–229.

Luttwak, Edward N. 1999. "Give War a Chance." *Foreign Affairs* 78(4): 36–44.

Mack, Andrew. 2002. "Civil War: Academic Research and the Policy Community." *Journal of Peace Research* 39(5): 515–525.

Maddala, Gangadharrao Soundalyarao. 1983. *Limited Dependent and Qualitative Variables*. Cambridge: Cambridge University Press.

Magaloni, Beatriz. 2008. "Credible Power-Sharing and the Longevity of Authoritarian Rule." *Comparative Political Studies* 41(4-5): 715–741.

Mahoney, James. 2010. *Colonialism and Post-Colonial Development: Spanish America in Comparative Perspective*. Cambridge: Cambridge University Press.

Mamdani, Mahmood. 1996. *Citizen and Subject*. New York: Cambridge University Press.

Mansfield, Edward D. and Jack Snyder. 2005. *Electing to Fight: Why Emerging Democracies Go to War*. Cambridge, MA: MIT Press.

March, James G. and Johan P. Olsen. 1984. "The New Institutionalism: Organizational Factors in Political Life." 78(3): 734–749.

Marinov, Nikolay and Hein Goemans. 2014. "Coups and Democracy." *British Journal of Political Science* 44(4): 799–825.

Marshall, Monty G., Ted Robert Gurr, Christian Davenport and Keith Jaggers. 2002. "Polity IV, 1800–1999: A Reply to Munck and Verkuilen." *Comparative Political Studies* 35(1): 40–45.

Marshall, Monty G., Ted Robert Gurr and Keith Jaggers. 2017. *Polity IV Project: Dataset Users' Manual*. Center for Systemic Peace: www.systemicpeace.org/polity/polity4.htm.

Martin, Andrew D., Kevin M. Quinn and Jong Hee Park. 2011. "MCMCpack: Markov Chain Monte Carlo in R." *Journal of Statistical Software* 42(9): 1–21.

Martin, Philipp. 2013. "Coming Together: Power-Sharing and the Durability of Negotiated Peace Settlements." *Civil Wars* 15(3): 332–358.

Masunungure, Eldred V. Forthcoming. Zimbabwe's Power Sharing Agreement. In *Fragile Bargains: Civil Conflict and Power-sharing in Africa*, ed. Scott Gates and Kaare Strøm. New York: Cambridge University Press.

Mattes, Michaela and Burcu Savun. 2009. "Fostering Peace After Civil War: Commitment Problems and Agreement Design." *International Studies Quarterly* 53: 737–759.

Maves, Jessica and Alex Braithwaite. 2013. "Autocratic Institutions and Civil Conflict Contagion." *The Journal of Politics* 75(02): 478–490.

McAlexander, Richard J. 2020. "A Reanalysis of the Relationship between Indirect Rule, Ethnic Inclusion and Decolonization." *Journal of Politics* 82: 1612–1615.

McCrudden, Chrisopher and Brendan O'Leary. 2013. *Courts and Consociations: Human Rights versus Power-Sharing*. Oxford: Oxford University Press.

McCrudden, Christopher, John McGarry, Brendan O'Leary and Alex Schwart. 2016. "Why Northern Ireland's Institutions Need Stability." *Government and Opposition* 51(1): 30–58.

McCulloch, Allison and Joanne McEnvoy. 2018. "The International Mediation of Power-Sharing Settlements." *Cooperation and Conflict* 53(4): 467–485.

McEvoy, Joanne. 2014. *Power-Sharing Executives: Governing in Bosnia, Macedonia, and Northern Ireland*. Philadelphia: University of Pennsylvania Press.

McGarry, John. 2017. Centripetalism, Consociationalism and Cyprus: The 'Adoptability' Question. In *Power-Sharing: Empirical and Normative Challenges*, ed. Allison McCulloch and John McGarry. London: Routledge.

McGarry, John and Brendan O'Leary. 1993. Introduction: The Macro-political Regulation of Ethnic Conflict. In *The Politics of Ethnic Conflict Regulation: Case Studies of Protracted Ethnic Conflicts*, ed. John McGarry and Brendan O'Leary. London: Routledge, pp. 1–40.

2004. Introduction: Consociational Theory and Northern Ireland. In *The Northern Ireland Conflict: Consociational Engagements*. Oxford: Oxford University Press, pp. 1–61.

2005. Federation as a Method of Ethnic Conflict Regulation. In *From Power Sharing to Democracy*, ed. Sid Noel. Montreal: McGill-Queen's University Press, pp. 263–296.

2009. "Must Pluri-national Federations Fail?" *Ethnopolitics* 8(5–25).

2010. Territorial Approaches to Ethnic Conflict Settlement. In *Routledge Handbook of Ethnic Conflict*, ed. Karl Cordell and Stefan Wolff. London: Routledge, pp. 240–255.

McKelvey, Richard D. and Thomas R. Palfrey. 1995. "Quantal Response Equilibria for Normal Form Games." *Games and Economic Behavior* 10(1): 6–38.

1998. "Quantal Response Equilibria for Extensive Form Games." *Experimental Economics* 1(1): 9–41.

McMahon, Patrice C. 2004/2005. "Rebuilding Bosnia: A Model to Emulate or to Avoid?" *Political Science Quarterly* 119(4): 569–593.

Mearsheimer, John J. 1990*a*. "Back to the Future: Instability in Europe After the Cold War." *International Security* 15(4): 5–56.

1990*b*. "Why We Will Soon Miss the Cold War." *The Atlantic Monthly* 266(2): 35–50.

Mehler, Andreas. 2009. "Peace and Power Sharing in Africa: A Not So Obvious Relationship." *African Affairs* 108(432): 453–473.

2013. "Consociationalism for Weaklings, Autocracy for Muscle Men? Determinants of Constitutional Reform in Divided Societies." *Civil Wars* 1: 21–43.

2016. Adapted Instead of Imported: Peacebuildling by Power-Sharing. In *Peacebuilding in Crisis: Rethinking Paradigms and Practices of Transnational Cooperation*, ed. Tobias Debiel, Thomas Held and Ulrich Schneckener. Abingdon: Routledge, pp.91–109.

Melander, Erik. 2000. "Anarchy Within: The Security Dilemma between Ethnic Groups in Emerging Anarchy." Monograph, Department of Peace and Conflict Studies, Uppsala University.

Meyer, John W., John Boli, George M. Thomas and Francisco O. Ramirez. 1997. "World Society and the Nation-State." *American Journal of Sociology* 103(1): 144–181.

Miguel, Edward, Shanker Satyanath and Ernest J. Sergenti. 2004. "Economic Shocks and Civil Conflict: An Instrumental Variables Approach." *Journal of Political Economy* 112(4): 725–753.

Miles, William F. 1994. *Hausaland Divided: Colonialism and Independence in Nigeria and Niger*. Ithaca and London: Cornell University Press.

Mill, John Stuart. 1962 [1961]. *Considerations of Representative Government*. Vol. Hentry Regnery Chicago.

Morelli, Massimo and Dominic Rohner. 2015. "Resource Concentration and Civil Wars." *Journal of Development Economics* 117: 32–47.

Mueller, John. 1994. "The Catastrophe Quota: Trouble After the Cold War." *Journal of Conflict Resolution* 38(3): 355–375.

Mukherjee, Bumba. 2006. "Does Third-Party Enforcement or Domestic Institutions Promote Enduring Peace After Civil Wars? Policy Lessons from an Empirical Test." *Foreign Policy Analysis* 2(4): 405–430.

Muller, Edward N. 1999. *Capitalism, Democracy, and Ralph's Pretty Good Grocery*. Princeton, NJ: Princeton University Press.

Mylonas, Harris. 2012. *The Politics of Nation-Building: Making Co-Nations, Refugees, and Minorities*. New York: Cambridge University Press.

Negash, Tekeste. 1997. *Eritrea and Ethiopia: The Federal Experience*. New Brunswick: Transaction Publishers.

Nilsson, Desirée. 2008. "Partial Peace: Rebel Groups Inside and Outside of Civil War Settlements." *Journal of Peace Research* 45(4): 479–495.

Nordlinger, Eric A. 1972. *Conflict Regulation in Divided Societies*. Cambridge, MA: Center for International Affairs, Harvard.

Norris, Pippa. 2008. *Driving Democracy: Do Power Sharing Institutions Work?* New York: Cambridge University Press.

O'Leary, Brendan. 2001. "An Iron Law of Nationalism and Federation?: A (Neo-Diceyian) Theory of the Necessity of a Federal Staatsvolk, and of Consociational Rescue." *Nations & Nationalism* 7(3): 273–296.

  2012. "The Federalization of Iraq and the Break-up of Sudan." *Government and Opposition* 47(4): 481–516.

O'Loughlin, John, Michael D . Ward, Corey L. Lofdahl, Jordin S. Cohen, David S. Brown, David Reilly, Kristian Skrede Gleditsch and Michael Shin. 1998. "The Diffusion of Democracy, 1946–1994." *Annals of the Association of American Geographers* 88(4): 545–574.

Olzak, Susan. 2006. *The Global Dynamics of Racial and Ethnic Mobilization*. Stanford, CA: Stanford University press.

Oster, Emily. 2016. "Unobservable Selection and Coefficient Stability: Theory and Evidence." *Journal of Business & Economic Statistics* 0(ja): 0–0.

Ottmann, Martin and Johannes Vüllers. 2015. "The Power-Sharing Event Dataset (PSED): A New Dataset on the Occurrence of Power Sharing in Post-Conflict Countries." *Conflict Management and Peace Science* 32(3): 327–350.

Paris, Roland. 2004. *At War's End: Building Peace After Civil Conflict*. New York: Cambridge University Press.

Park, Jong Hee. 2010. "Structural Change in US presidents' Use of Force." *American Journal of Political Science* 54(3): 766–782.

Pepinsky, Thomas. 2014. "The Institutional Turn in Comparative Authoritarianism." *British Journal of Political Science* 44(3): 631–653.

Petersen, Roger D. 2002. *Understanding Ethnic Violence: Fear, Hatred, and Resentment in Twentieth Century Eastern Europe.* Cambridge: Cambridge University Press.

2011. *Western Intervention in the Balkans: The Strategic Use of Emotion in Conflict.* Cambridge: Cambridge University Press.

Pevehouse, Jon. 2005. *Democracy from Above: Regional Organizations and Democratization.* Cambridge: Cambridge University Press.

Pieterse, Jan. 1982. "Rawlings and the 1979 Revolt in Ghana." *Race and Class* 23(4): 251–273.

Pinker, Steven. 2011. *The Better Angels of Our Nature: Why Violence Has Declined.* New York: Viking.

Pinker, Steven and Andrew Mack. 2014. "The World Is Not Falling Apart: Never Mind The Headlines. We've Never Lived in Such Peaceful Times." Slate, www.slate.com/articles/news_and_politics/foreigners/ 2014/12/the_world_is_not_falling_apart_the_trend_lines_ reveal_an_increasingly_peaceful.html.

Plummer, Martyn. 2010. "JAGS Version 2.1.0 user manual." International Agency for Research on Cancer Infection and Cancer Epidemiology (ICE) group.

Posen, Barry R. 1993. "The Security Dilemma and Ethnic Conflict." *Survival* 35(1): 27–47.

Posner, Daniel N. 2005. *Institutions and Ethnic Politics in Africa.* New York: Cambridge University Press.

Pospieszna, Paulina and Gerald Schneider. 2013. "The Illusion of 'Peace Through Power-Sharing'." *Civil Wars* 15: 44–70.

Powers, Kathy and Gary Goertz. 2011. "The Economic-Institutional Construction of Regions: Conceptualisation and Operationalisation." *Review of International Studies* 37(5): 2387–2415.

Prunier, Gérard. 1995. *The Rwanda Crisis: History of a Genocide.* New York: Columbia University Press.

2009. *Africa's World War: Congo, the Rwandan Genocide, and the Making of a Continental Catastrophe.* Oxford: Oxford University Press.

Przeworski, Adam. 2004. "Institutions Matter?" *Government and Opposition* 39(4): 527–540.

Przeworski, Adam and Jennifer Gandhi. 2006. "Cooperation, Cooptation, and Rebellion under Dictatorship." *Economics and Politics* 18(1): 1–26.

Przeworski, Adam, Michael E. Alvarez, José Antonio Cheibub and Fernando Limongi. 2000. *Democracy and Development: Political Institutions and Well-Being in the World, 1950–1990.* Cambridge: Cambridge University Press.

Quinn, Jason Michael and Madhav Joshi. 2016. Global Trends in the Implementation of Intrastate Peace Agreements. In *Peace and Conflict 2016*, ed. David A. Backer, Ravinder Bhavnani and Paul K. Huth. New York: Routledge, pp. 93–104.

Rabushka, Alvin and Kenneth A. Shepsle. 1972. *Politics in Plural Societies: A Theory of Democratic Instability.* Columbus: C.E. Merrill.

Rachman, Gideon. 2014. "The Strange Revival of Nationalism." *Financial Times*, September 23.

Rasch, Elisabet Dueholm. 2012. "Transformations in Citizenship: Local Resistance against Mining Projects in Huehuetenango (Guatemala)." *Journal of Developing Societies* 28(2): 159–184.

Regan, Patrick M. and Daniel Norton. 2005. "Greed, Grievance, and Mobilization in Civil Wars." *Journal of Conflict Resolution* 49(3): 319–336.

Regan, Patrick and Peter Wallensteen. 2013. "Federal Institutions, Declarations of Independence and Civil War." *Civil Wars* 15(3): 261–280.

Reilly, Benjamin. 2016. Centripetalism. In *The Routledge Handbook of Ethnic Conflict*, ed. Karl Cordell and Stefan Wolff. London: Routledge, pp. 288–299.

Renner, Karl. 1918. *Das Selbstbestimmungsrecht der Nationen in bosonderer Anwendung auf Österreich*. Leipzig and Vienna: Deuticke.

Reno, William. 1995. *Corruption and State Politics in Sierra Leone*. New York: Cambridge University Press.

Richens, Peter. 2009. "The Economic Legacies of the "Thin White Line": Indirect Rule and the Comparative Development of Sub-Saharan Africa." *African Economic History* pp. 33–102.

Riker, William H. 1964. *Federalism: Origin, Operation, Significance*. Boston: Little, Brown.

1980. "Implications from the Disequilibrium of Majority Rule for the Study of Institutions." *American Political Science Review* 74(2): 432–446.

Rivers, Douglas and Quang H. Vuong. 1988. "Limited Information Estimators and Exogeneity Tests for Simultaneous Probit Models." *Journal of Econometrics* 39(3): 347–366.

Rodden, Jonathan A. 2006. Federalism. In *The Oxford Handbook of Political Economy*, ed. Barry R. Weingast and Donald A. Wittman. Oxford: Oxford University Press pp. 357–372.

Rodrik, Dani. 2012. "Why We Learn Nothing from Regressing Economic Growth on Policies." *Seuol Journal of Economics* 25(2): 137.151.

Roeder, Philip G. 1991. "Soviet Federalism and Ethnic Mobilization." *World Politics* 43(2): 196–232.

2005. Power Dividing as an Alternative to Ethnic Power Sharing. In *Sustainable Peace: Power and Democracy After Civil Wars*, ed. Philip G. Roeder and Donald Rothchild. Ithaca, NY: Cornell Unversity Press, pp. 51–82.

2007. *Where Nation-States Come From*. Princeton, NJ: Princeton University Press.

2009. "Ethnofederalism and the Mismanagement of Conflicting Nationalisms." *Regional and Federal Studies* 19(2): 203–219.

2018. *National Secession: Persuasion and Violence in Independence Campaigns*. Ithaca, NY: Cornell University Press.

Roeder, Philip G. and Donald Rothchild, eds. 2005. *Sustainable Peace: Power and Democracy After Civil Wars*. Ithaca, NY: Cornell University Press.

Roessler, Philip. 2011. "The Enemy Within: Personal Rule, Coups and Civil War in Africa." *World Politics* 63(2): 300–346.

2016. *Ethnic Politics and State Power in Africa: The Logic of the Coup-Cvil War Trap*. Cambridge: Cambridge University Press.

Roessler, Philip and David Ohls. 2018. "Self-Enforcing Power Sharing in Weak States." *International Organization* 72(2): 423.454.

Roque, Paula Christina. 2010. "Angola's Façade Democracy." *Journal of Democracy* 20(4): 137–150.

Rothchild, Donald. 2008. *Africa's Power Sharing Institutions as a Response to Insecurity.* London: Routledge.

Rothchild, Donald and Michael W. Foley. 1988. African States and the Politics of Inclusive Coalitions. In *The Precarious Balance: State and Society in Africa*, ed. Donald Rothchild and Naomi Chazan. Boulder, CO: Westview Press, pp. 234–238.

Rothchild, Donald and Philip G. Roeder. 2005*a*. Dilemmas of State-Building in Divided Societies. In *Sustainable Peace: Power and Democracy After Civil Wars*, ed. Philip G. Roeder and Donald Rothchild. Ithaca, NY: Cornell University Press pp. 1–25.

2005*b*. Power Sharing as an Impediment to Peace and Democracy. In *Sustainable Peace: Power and Democracy After Civil Wars*, ed. Philip G. Roeder and Donald Rothchild. Ithaca, NY: Cornell Unversity Press.

Rothchild, Joseph. 1981. *Ethnopolitics.* New York: Columbia University Press.

Ruggeri, Andrea, Theodora-Ismene Gizelis and Han Dorussen. 2013. "Managing Mistrust: An Analysis of Cooperation with UN Peacekeeping in Africa." *Journal of Conflict Resolution* 57(3): 387–409.

Russett, Bruce M. 1967. *International Regions and the International System: A Study in Political Ecology.* Chicago: Rand McNally.

Rustad, Siri Aas. Forthcoming. Between War and Peace: 50 Years of Power-Sharing in Nigeria. In *Fragile Bargains: Civil Conflict and Power-sharing in Africa*, ed. Scott Gates and Kaare Strøm. New York: Cambridge University Press.

Rydgren, Jens. 2007. "The Power of the Past: A Contribution to a Cognitive Sociology of Ethnic Conflict." *Sociological Theory* 25(3): 225–244.

Saideman, Stephen M., David J. Lanoue, Michael Campenni and Samuel Stanton. 2002. "Democratization, Political Institutions, and Ethnic Conflict: A Pooled Time-Series Analysis." *Comparative Political Studies* 35(1): 103–129.

Salehyan, Idean. 2009. *Rebels Without Borders: State Boundaries, Transnational Opposition, and Civil Conflict.* Ithaca, NY: Cornell University Press.

Sambanis, Nicholas and Annalisa Zinn. 2006. "From Protest to Violence: Conflict Escalation in Self-Determination Movements." Unpublished paper, Yale University.

Sambanis, Nicholas and Branko Milanovic. 2014. "Explaining Regional Autonomy Differences in Decentralized Countries." *Comparative Political Studies* 47(13): 1830 – 1855.

Sambanis, Nicholas and Jonah Schulhofer-Wohl. 2009. "What's in a Line? Is Partition a Solution to Civil War?" *International Security* 34(2): 82–118.

Sambanis, Nicholas, Micha Germann and Andreas Schädel. 2018. "SDM: A New Data Set on Self Determination Movements with an Application to the Reputational Theory of Conflict." *Journal of Conflict* 62: 656–686.

Samii, Cyrus. 2013. "Who Wants to Forgive and Forget? Transitional Justice Preferences in Postwar Burundi." *Journal of Peace Research* 50(2): 219–233.

Savun, Burco and Daniel C. Tirone. 2011. "Foreign Aid, Democratization, and Civil Conflict: How Does Democracy Aid Affect Civil Conflict." *American Journal of Political Science* 52(2): 233–246.

Schädel, Andreas. 2016. "Signaling Weakness or Building Capacity: A Reassessment of the Reputation Argument in Separatist Conflicts." Dissertation ETH Zurich.

Schelling, Thomas C. 1971. "Dynamic Models of Segregation." *Journal of Mathematical Sociology* 1(2): 143–186.

Schneckener, Ulrich. 2002. "Making Power-Sharing Work. Successes and Failures in Ethnic Conflict Regulation." *Journal of Peace Research* 38(3).

Schneider, Gerald and Nina Wiesenhomeier. 2008. "Rules that Matter: Political Institutions and the Diversity-Conflict Nexus." *Journal of Peace Research* 45(2): 183–203.

Sesay, Max A. 1996. "Civil War and Collective Intervention in Liberia." *Review of African Political Economy* 23(67): 35–52.

Shepsle, Kenneth A. 1979. "Institutional Arrangements and Equilibrium in Multidimensional Voting Models." *American Journal of Political Science* 23: 27–59.

Signorino, Curtis S. 1999. "Strategic Interaction and the Statistical Analysis of International Conflict." *American Political Science Review* 93: 279–298.

2002. "Strategy and Selection in International Relations." *International Interactions* 28(1): 93–115.

Signorino, Curtis S. and Kuzey Yilmaz. 2003. "Strategic Misspecification in Regression Models." *American Journal of Political Science* 47(3): 551–566.

Simmons, Beth A., Frank Dobbin and Geoffrey Garrett. 2006. "Introduction: The International Diffusion of Liberalism." *International Organization* 60: 781–810.

Simmons, Beth A. and Zachary Elkins. 2004. "The Globalization of Liberalization: Policy Diffusion in the International Political Economy." *American Political Science Review* 98(1): 171–189.

Simon, Herbert A. 1955. "A Behavioral Model of Rational Choice." *The Quarterly Journal of Economics* 69(1): 99.

Singh, Gurharpal. 1993. Ethnic Conflict in India: A Case-Study of Punjab. In *The Politics of Ethnic Conflict Regulation: Case Studies of Protracted Ethnic Conflicts*, ed. John McGarry and Brendan O'Leary. Baltimore: Routledge Chapter 4, pp. 84–105.

Siroky, David S. 2011. Explaining Secession. In *Research Companion on Secession*. Aldershot: Ashgate, pp. 45–79.

Smith, Alastair. 1999. "Testing Theories of Strategic Choice: The Example of Crisis Escalation." *American Journal of Political Science* 43(4): 1254–1283.

Snyder, Jack. 2000. *From Voting to Violence: Democratization and Nationalist Conflict*. New York: Norton.

Sobotka, Eva. 2016. Multilateral Frameworks for Conflict Resolution. In *The Routledge Handbook of Ethnic Conflict*, ed. Karl Cordell and Stefan Wolff. London: Routledge, pp. 191–205.

Sondheimer, Rachel Milstein and Donald P. Green. 2010. "Using Experiments to Estimate the Effects of Education on Voter Turnout." *American Journal of Political Science* 54(1): 174–189.

Sorens, Jason. 2012. *Secessionism: Identity, Interest, and Strategy.* Montreal: McGill-Queen's University Press.

Sovey, Allison J. and Donald P. Green. 2011. "Instrumental Variables Estimation in Political Science: A Reader's Guide." *American Journal of Political Science* 55(1): 188–200.

Spears, Ian S. 2000. "Understanding Inclusive Peace Agreements in Africa: The Problems of Sharing Power." *Third World Quarterly* 21(1): 105–118.

2002. "Africa: The Limits of Power-Sharing." *Journal of Democracy* 13(3): 123–136.

2013. "Africa's Informal Power-Sharing and the Prospects for Peace." *Civil Wars* 15(1): 37–53.

Spruyt, Hendrik. 1994. *The Sovereign State and its Competitors: An Analysis of Systems Change.* Princeton, NJ: Princeton University Press.

Stamnes, Eli. 2004. "Critical Security Studies and the United Nations Preventive Deployment in Macedonia." *International Peacekeeping* 11(1): 161–181.

Starr, Harvey. 1991. "Democratic Dominoes: Diffusion Approaches to the Spread of Democracy in the International System." *Journal of Conflict Resolution* 35(2): 356–381.

Stedman, Stephen John. 1997. "Spoiler Problems in Peace Processes." *International Security* 22(2): 5–53.

Steiner, Jürg. 1974. *Amicable Agreement versus Majority Rule: Conflict Resolution in Switzerland.* Chapel Hill: University of North Carolina Press.

Stepan, Alfred. 2013. A Revised Theory of Federacy and A Case Study of Civil War Termination in Aceh Indonesia. In *Power Sharing in Deeply Divided Places*, ed. Joanne McEvoy and Brendan O'Leary. Philadelphia: University of Pennsylvania Press, pp. 231–252.

Stewart, Frances, ed. 2008. *Horizontal Inequalities and Conflict.* New York: Palgrave Macmillan.

Strang, David. 1994. British and French Political Institutions and the Patterning of Decolonization. In *The Comparative Political Economy of the Welfare State*, ed. Thomas Janoski and Alexander M. Hicks. Cambridge: Cambridge University Press, pp. 278–295.

Strøm, Kaare, Scott Gates, Benjamin A.T. Graham and Håvard Strand. 2017. "Inclusion, Dispersion, and Constraint: Powersharing in the World's States, 1975-2010." *British Journal of Political Science* 47(1): 165–185.

Strøm, Kaare W., Scott Gates, Benjamin A.T. Graham and Havard Strand. 2015. "Replication Data for: Inclusion, Dispersion, and Constraint: Powersharing in the World's States, 1975–2010." Harvard Dataverse. *https://doi.org/10.7910/DVN/29421*

Suberu, Rotimi T. 2004. Nigeria: Dilemmas of Federalism. In *Federalism and Territorial Cleavages*, ed. Ugo M. Amoretti and Nancy Bermeo. Baltimore, MD: The Johns Hopkins University Press, pp. 327–354.

Svolik, Milan W. 2009. "Power Sharing and Leadership Dynamics in Authoritarian Regimes." *American Journal of Political Science* 53(2): 477–494.

2012. *The Politics of Authoritarian Rule*. New York: Cambridge University Press.

Taylor, Rupert, ed. 2011. *Consociational Theory: McGarry and O'Leary and the Northern Ireland Conflict*. London: Routledge.

Thayer, Bradley A. 2013. "Humans, Not Angels: Reasons to Doubt the Decline of War Thesis." *Review of International Studies* 15: 405–411.

Thompson, Curtis N. 1995. "Society, Political Stability and Minority Groups in Burma." *Geographical Review* 85: 269–285.

Tiebout, Charles M. 1957. "A Pure Theory of Local Expenditures." *Journal of Political Economy* 64: 416–424.

Tilly, Charles. 1978. *From Mobilization to Revolution*. New York: McGraw-Hill.

Tir, Jaroslav. 2005. "Keeping the Peace After Secession: Territorial Conflicts Between Rump and Secessionist States." *Journal of Conflict Resolution* 49(5): 713–741.

Toft, Monica Duffy. 2002. "Indivisible territory, geographic concentration, and ethnic war." *Security Studies* 12(2): 82–119.

Tull, Denis M. and Andreas Mehler. 2005*a*. "The Hidden Costs of Power-Sharing: Reproducing Insurgent Violence in Africa." *African Affairs* 104(416): 375–398.

2005*b*. "The Hidden Costs of Power Sharing: Reproducing Insurgent Violence in Africa." *African affairs* 104(416): 375–398.

United Nations and World Bank. 2018. Pathways for Peace: Inclusive Approaches to Preventing Violent Conflict. Report World Bank Washington, DC: *https://openknowledge.worldbank.org/handle/10986/28337*.

van de Walle, Nicolas. 2009. "The Institutional Origins of Inequality in Sub-Saharan Africa." *Annual Review of Political Science* 12: 307–327.

van Schendelen, Marinus Petrus Christophorus Maria. 1984. "The Views of Arend Lijphart and Collected Criticisms." *Acta Politica* 19: 19–55.

Vandeginste, Stef. 2009. "Power-Sharing, Conflict and Transition in Burundi: Twenty Years of Trial and Error." *Africa Spectrum* 44(3): 63–86.

2013. "The African Union, Constitutionalism and Power Sharing." *Journal of African Law* 57(1): 1–28.

Vinson, Laura Thaut. 2017. *Religion, Violence, and Local Power-Sharing in Nigeria*. Cambridge: Cambridge University Press.

Vogt, Manuel, Nils-Christian Bormann, Seraina Rüegger, Lars-Erik Cederman, Philipp Hunziker and Luc Girardin. 2015. "Integrating Data on Ethnicity, Geography, and Conflict: The Ethnic Power Relations Dataset Family." *Journal of Conflict Resolution* 59(7): 1327–1342.

Vreeland, James Raymond. 2008. "The Effect of Political Regime on Civil War." *Journal of Conflict Resolution* 52(3): 401–425.

Wallensteen, Peter and Margareta Sollenberg. 1995. "After the Cold War: Emerging Patterns of Armed Conflict 1989–1994." *Journal of Peace Research* 32(3): 345–360.

1996. "The End of International War? Armed Conflict 1989–95." *Journal of Peace Research* 33(3): 353–370.

Walter, Barbara F. 1997. "The Critical Barrier to Civil War Settlement." *International Organization* 51(3): 335–364.

   2002. *Committing to Peace: The Successful Settlement of Civil Wars*. Princeton, NJ: Princeton University Press.

Walter, Barbara F. 2004. "Does Conflict Beget Conflict? Explaining Recurring Civil War." *Journal of Peace Research* 41(3): 371–388.

   2006*a*. "Building Reputation: Why Governments Fights Some Separatists but Not Others." *American Journal of Political Science* 50: 313–330.

   2006*b*. "Information, Uncertainty, and the Decision to Secede." *International Organization* 60: 105–135.

   2009. *Reputation and Civil War: Why Separatist Conflicts Are So Violent*. Cambridge: Cambridge University Press.

Walton, Matthew J. 2008. "Ethnicity, Conflict, and History in Burma: The Myths of Panglong." *Asian Survey* 48(6): 889–910.

Walzer, Michael. 1992. "The New Tribalism: Notes on a Difficult Problem." *Dissent* 39: 164–171.

Wantchekon, Leonard. 2000. "Credible Power-Sharing Agreements: Theory with Evidence from South Africa and Lebanon." *Constitutional Political Economy* 11(4): 339–352.

Weber, Max. 1946. *From Max Weber: Essays in Sociology*. New York: Oxford University Press.

   1978. *Economy and Society: An Outline of Interpretative Sociology*. Berkeley: University of California Press.

Weidmann, Nils B. 2009. "Geography as Motivation and Opportunity." *Journal of Conflict Resolution* 53(4): 526–543.

Weidmann, Nils B., Doreen Kuse and Kristian Skrede Gleditsch. 2010. "The Geography of the International System: The Cshapes Dataset." *International Interactions* 36(1): 86–106.

Weiner, Myron. 1971. "The Macedonian Syndrome: An Historical Model of International Relations and Political Development." *World Politics* 23(4): 665–683.

Weingast, Barry. 2005. The performance and Stability of Federalism: An Institutional Analysis. In *Handbook of New Institutional Economics*, ed. Claude Ménard and Mary M. Shirley. Dordrecht: Springer pp. 69–90.

Weller, Marc. 2005. Self-Governance in Interim Settlements: The Case of Sudan. In *Autonomy, Self-Governance and Conflict Resolution: Innovative Approaches to Institutional Design in Divided Societies*, ed. Marc Weller and Stefan Wolff. London: Routledge, Chapter 7, pp. 158–179.

Wennmann, Archim and Jana Krause. 2009. "Resource Wealth, Autonomy, and Peace in Aceh." CCDP Working Paper. Graduate Institute of International Studies, Geneva.

Wilde, Joachim. 2000. "Identification of Multiple Equation Probit Models with Endogenous Dummy Regressors." *Economics Letters* 69(3): 309–312.

Wilkinson, Steven I. 2000. "India, Consociational Theory, and Ethnic Violence." *Asian Survey* 40(5): 767–791.

2005. Conditionality, Consociationalism, and the European Union. In *From Power Sharing to Democracy: Post-Conflict Institutions in Ethnically Divided Societies*, ed. Sid Noel. Montreal: McGill-Queen's University Press pp. 239–262.

2015. *Army and Nation: The Military and Indian Democracy since Independence.* Cambridge, MA: Harvard University Press.

Wilson, Ernest J., III and Ted Robert Gurr. 1999. "Fewer Nations Are Making War." *Los Angeles Times*, August 22, 1999.

Wimmer, Andreas. 1997. "Who Owns the State? Understanding Ethnic Conflict in Post-Colonial Societies." *Nations and Nationalism* 3(4): 631–665.

Witt, Antonia. 2013. "Convergence on Whose Terms? Reacting to Coups d'Etat in Guinea and Madagascar." *African Security* 6(3–4): 257–275.

Wolff, Stefan. 2011. Consociationalism: Power Sharing and Self-Governance. In *Conflict Management in Divided Societies: Theories and Practice*, ed. Stefan Wolff and Christalla Yakinthou. London: Routledge, pp. 23–56.

2013. "Conflict Management in Divided Societies: The Many Uses of Territorial Self-Governance." *International Journal of Minority and Group Rights* 20: 27–50.

Wolff, Stefan and Karl Cordell. 2010. Power Sharing. In *Routledge Handbook of Ethnic Conflict*, ed. Karl Cordell and Stefan Wolff. London: Routledge pp. 191–205.

Wood, Elisabeth Jean. 2000. *Forging Democracy from Below: Insurgent Transitions in South Africa and El Salvador.* New York: Cambridge University Press.

2008. "The Social Processes of Civil War: The Wartime Transformation of Social Networks." *Annual Review of Political Science* 11: 539–561.

Wooldridge, Jeffrey M. 2010. *Econometric Analysis of Cross Section and Panel Data.* 2nd ed. Cambridge, MA: The MIT Press.

Wright, Theodore P. Jr. 1991. "Center-Periphery Relations and Ethnic Conflict in Pakistan: Sindhis, Muhajirs, and Punjabis." *Comparative Politics* 23(3): 299–312.

Wucherpfennig, Julian. 2021. Executive Power Sharing in the Face of Civil War. International Studies Quarterly. 65(4): 1027–1039.

Wucherpfennig, Julian and Lars-Erik Cederman. Forthcoming. "Pre-Colonial and Colonial Origins of Inclusive Peace." *Journal of Politics*.

Wucherpfennig, Julian, Nils Metternich, Lars-Erik Cederman and Kristian S. Gleditsch. 2012. "Ethnicity, the State, and the Duration of Civil Wars." *World Politics* 64: 79–115.

Wucherpfennig, Julian, Nils W. Weidmann, Luc Girardin, Lars-Erik Cederman and Andreas Wimmer. 2011. "Politically Relevant Ethnic Groups across Space and Time: Introducing the GeoEPR Dataset." *Conflict Management and Peace Science* 28(5): 423–437.

Wucherpfennig, Julian, Philipp Hunziker and Lars-Erik Cederman. 2016. "Who Inherits the State? Colonial Rule and Postcolonial Conflict." *American Journal of Political Science* 60(4): 882–898.

Young, Crawford. 1994. *The African Colonial State in Comparative Perspective.* New Haven, CT: Yale University Press.

    2004. "The End of the Post-Colonial State in Africa? Reflections on Changing African Political Dynamics." *African Affairs* 103(410): 23–49.

Young, John. 2006. *Peasant Revolution in Ethiopia: The Tigray People's Liberation Front, 1975–1991.* New York: Cambridge University Press.

Zukerman Daly, Sarah. 2014. "The Dark Side of Power-Sharing: Middle Managers and Civil War Recurrence." *Comparative Politics* 46(3): 333–353.

Index

Milton Keynes UK
Ingram Content Group UK Ltd.
UKHW052104040823
426060UK00036B/1173